IN AMERICA

SECOND EDITION

To the memory of my mother, Irene, and my father, Nat, who sacrificed some of their modest income, gave me all their love, and provided me with a blue-collar, working-class perspective that has been invaluable to me as a person and as a field researcher.

—C.R.H.

IN AMERICA

SECOND EDITION

C. RONALD HUFF

EDITOR

SAGE Publications
International Educational and Professional Publisher
Thousand Oaks London New Delhi

3441 3463

For information address:

 SAGE Publications, Inc.
2455 Teller Road
Thousand Oaks, California 91320
E-mail: order@sagepub.com

SAGE Publications Ltd.
6 Bonhill Street
London EC2A 4PU
United Kingdom

SAGE Publications India Pvt. Ltd.
M-32 Market
Greater Kailash I
New Delhi 110 048 India

Printed in the United States of America

Library of Congress Cataloging-in-Publication Data

Main entry under title:

Gangs in America / editor, C. Ronald Huff. — 2nd ed.
     p.   cm.
    Includes bibliographical references and index.
    ISBN 0-7619-0202-3 (cloth : acid-free paper). — ISBN
0-7619-0203-1 (pbk. : acid-free paper)
     1. Gangs—United States. I. Huff, C. Ronald.
  HV6439.U5G36 1996
  364.1'06'0973—dc20   96-9988

This book is printed on acid-free paper.

96 97 98 99 10 9 8 7 6 5 4 3 2 1

Production Editor: Vicki Baker
Designer/Typesetter: Christina M. Hill

Contents

Foreword
Diversity and Change in U.S. Gangs

JAMES F. SHORT, JR.

I began my chapter in the first edition of this volume with the observation that for the most part, current issues, including gang issues, represented "new urgencies to old issues" (Short, 1990b, p. 223). This remains the case with respect to many issues in criminology, but some of the most important gang issues appear to be new (see Fagan, this volume). Recent research has added much to our knowledge of gangs, their numbers, behaviors, and their relations with one another and their communities. Theoretical advance has come more slowly, in part perhaps because empirical work has been heavily descriptive. Most of the chapters in this book follow this emphasis on the empirical, though a few authors attempt to place their findings within particular theoretical frames. Although one might wish for theoretical breakthroughs, the chapters that follow nevertheless have special significance for the state of knowledge concerning gangs, for the future of both empirical and theoretical approaches, and for appropriate responses to problems posed by gangs.

Let us stipulate that evidence bearing on gang issues is by no means clear or unequivocal. Measurement and understanding of human behavior, including the effects of delinquency control programs (whether directed to individuals, groups, or communities) is extraordinarily difficult. Given the complexities of human behavior and of explanatory forces and processes, precise determination of neither the causes of behavior nor the effects of control programs is possible. This much is clear, however: No matter how successful efforts to punish, rehabilitate, or otherwise control delinquents may be, so long as the forces and processes that produce delinquent behavior exist, new delinquents will continue to be produced and new gangs will continue to emerge. Those forces, in fact, seem universal to modern, rapidly changing societies. It is therefore especially important that delinquency control programs—including gang control programs—be based on sound theoretical principles. Although the course of human history in this regard is not encouraging, the hope, if not yet the promise, is that we can do better. Chapters in Part 4 of this volume describe a variety of efforts to suppress, intervene with, or prevent gangs in several communities. Coupled with analyses of gangs in Parts 1 through 3, such efforts provide the basis for both theoretical development and practical application.

But I am getting ahead of my story. In his foreword to the first edition of this book, Albert K. Cohen stressed the importance of the fact that gangs are *collectivities*—"actors to which individual human beings or 'natural persons' are related as 'members' (Cohen, 1990, p. 9). It is, of course, the behavior of *gang actors* that most concerns law enforcement, schools and others in the public, as well as scholars. Cohen's point alerts us to the importance of distinguishing between individual and collective actions taken by gang members. Moreover, "membership in collectivities is part of the *identities* [italics added]" of members (Cohen, 1990, p. 11).

The importance of gang membership for the identities of gang members has been a matter of contention between those who study gangs. The discovery that members of the Chicago gangs we studied in the 1960s valued fellow gang members *less highly* than nongang boys and middle-class boys valued members of their own groups seems confirmed by more recent studies in Denver (cf. Esbensen & Huizinga, 1993; Gordon, Short, Cartwright, & Strodtbeck, 1963). When asked what role in the gang they would like to have or expect to have in the gang in the future, over 60% of the self-reported "gang members indicated that they would like to *not* be a member and expected *not* to be a member sometime in the future" (Esbensen & Huizinga, 1993, p. 570).

Yet, ethnographic research often finds gang members describing their homeboys, gangs, and cliques in terms customarily reserved for families and other loved ones. Many members say they join gangs for protection, and there is solid evidence to support such claims (see, e.g., Vigil & Yun, this volume; Chin, this volume). Yet, intragang conflict is endemic in most gangs, and gang membership clearly increases vulnerability to violence for many—perhaps most—gang members. Gangs present us with still other paradoxes: Many boys and girls join them for excitement, then spend most of their time waiting around for something to happen; and when something does happen it often gets them in trouble. Gangs are joined because they offer support for a sense of belonging, and members often speak of their gangs in family terms. Yet, for many, the gang proves to be an undependable form of human association in that most gangs lack stability of membership, cohesion, and continuity either with members' past or their future. Members join gangs for status, and in so doing are exposed to the status threats that all youngsters experience, but without the supportive roles that are provided by adults in more conventional institutional settings. How can we account for these seeming paradoxes?

Field observations on the shifting membership of many gangs and the relative ease with which adolescents can avoid gang membership (see Huff, this volume), and gang members may leave gangs (see Decker & Lauritsen, this volume), suggest that the importance of gang membership for the identities of individual members is quite variable. Gang members typically have weak ties among themselves, as well as to conventional institutions, such as schools, churches, local business and professional people, and traditional youth agencies. They are often rejected by more conventional peers and in conventional institutions (Fleisher, 1995). The gang may be, relatively or by default, the most important relationship in the lives of its members. Moreover, relationships with others outside the gang (e.g., with rival gangs, police, community adults, and institutions) may increase gang members' dependence on one another, increasing cohesiveness by their differences with others, including delinquent and criminal behavior. The gang *as a collectivity* thus may exert a great deal of influence on even marginal members, particularly on those who seek greater identification with and status within gangs.

This observation draws attention to the importance of *context* for behavior. Personal identity—including identity as a gang member—is heightened in the presence of other gang members. Gang identity, even when it is mistaken, may expose one to danger—of assault by rival gang members, of suspicion by police—in many social settings. Threats associated with gang membership and identity, however, are likely to be weaker in more conventional settings, providing those settings are hospitable and supportive of nongang (and nondeviant) identity. In the absence of such support, however, even conventional settings may reinforce gang identity. Weak ties to conventional institutions and peers increase the vulnerability of youth to "the code of the streets" (see Anderson, 1994).

The relevance of the gang for individual behavior (the focus of most criminal law) has been especially vexing for law enforcement, as well as for researchers, as Maxson and Klein discuss in Chapter 1. Entire gangs, as collectivities—even if gang rosters were reliable indicators of membership—are rarely involved in the commission of a crime. With a few notable exceptions, smaller groups of gang members (two or three, or only a few more) constitute the vast majority of offender groupings, as researchers from Shaw and McKay (1931) to the present (Reiss, 1986a; Warr, 1996) have found.

What, then, is the significance of the gang for behavior?

Gangs in America:
Diversity in Context and Behavior[1]

We know a little more about the impact of the gang on behavior than we did only a few years ago. Research on young people and on youth gangs has increased in the recent past, so much so that summarizing findings from that research has become extremely difficult. In support of the importance of peers for both delinquent and conventional behavior, longitudinal studies find that "avoidance of delinquent and drug using peers" is a "major protective factor for 'resilient youth'" who do not become delinquent despite their exposure to high-risk conditions (see Thornberry et al., no date; also Elliott et al., 1995). These authors were able to measure the behavior of young people when they are members of gangs and when they are not. Virtually all researchers found that gang members are not uniformly delinquent, and both in Denver and in Rochester, New York, longitudinal studies indicated that the frequency of delinquent behavior is higher during periods of gang membership than it is when these same adolescents are not members of gangs. Those who are members of gangs for consecutive years and longer periods are more delinquent than are both nongang members and "transient" members.

Several themes in recent gang research stand out: (a) the number of gangs in this country has increased rapidly in the recent past; (b) gang membership has become more diverse; (c) most gangs are neither very stable in membership or very cohesive, and gangs change, in these and in other respects; (d) the age spread of gang members has increased; (e) drug use and selling by gang members has increased and the impact of drugs on gangs and on communities has been profound; and (f) gang violence, always a problem, has become more widespread and more lethal. All but the third of these research themes is relatively new. The significance of membership stability (or instability) and cohesion (which varies greatly in response to both internal and external processes) remains an important, but insufficiently studied phenomenon (see especially Klein, 1995a).

Malcolm Klein (1995a) has documented the rapid spread of street gangs to perhaps as many as 1,100 cities in the United States (including 91 cities with less than 10,000 population; pp. 18, 90) compared to the relatively few large cities in which gangs were a problem only a few years ago (see also Curry, Ball, & Decker, this volume).

Diversity in gang membership comes as no surprise. Gangs probably have always been more diverse than they have been portrayed in either our limited studies or in the media. Increased scholarly attention to gangs, however, is documenting more diversity along more dimensions than earlier studies had suggested. Klein (1995a) warns that "consensus is not a feature of the current American police knowledge of gangs" (p. 102), and he notes a "bewildering" diversity of terms used to describe gangs, their size and structure, and so forth among police respondents to his surveys.

Other faces of gang diversity concern racial, ethnic, and gender composition—the latter the subject of much speculation and little research (but see Campbell, 1984/1990b; Chesney-Lind, Shelden, & Joe, this volume; Moore & Hagedorn, this volume). Klein (1995a) notes the decline of white gangs, except in smaller cities, with the result that gangs are now mainly Hispanic or African American (see also Sanders, 1994). The emergence of gangs from several Asian countries in several cities also has been noted (see, e.g., chapters in this volume by Chin; Chesney-Lind et al.; Fagan; Vigil & Yun; also Miller, 1982; Sanchez-Jankowski, 1991; Sanders, 1994; Spergel, 1995; Vigil & Yun, 1990). Among the newer Asian gangs, particularly in the chapter by Vigil and Yun (this volume), traces appear of intergenerational "old-" and "new-world" conflicts that are similar to those so vividly portrayed among immigrant families in the United States early in this century by W. I. Thomas, Robert E. Park, and H. A. Miller (1921).

The increase in the age spread of gang members has been noted in many studies (see, e.g., Hagedorn, 1988; Klein, 1995a; Sanchez-Jankowski, 1991). The mean ages of the African American gangs we studied in Chicago during the early 1960s, for example, was 17.2 years (standard deviation, 1.9); for white gang members the mean age was 18.2 years (standard deviation, 2.1) (Short & Strodtbeck, 1965/1974). In more recent studies, researchers find gang members' ages extending into the 40s. Among the 37 gangs studied by Martin Sanchez-Jankowski, age ranges of members varied widely. Latino gangs had members ranging in age from 12 to 42 years (mean age range from youngest to oldest members = 12.5 years). These figures for African American gangs were age 14 to 37 (mean = 12.3 years), and for white gangs, age 14 to 26 (mean = 7.6 years). Gangs classified as African American/Latino and Latino/African American also had broader age ranges than did white gangs.[2]

Ethnic differences in the age range of gang members highlight the major theoretical interpretation of their significance. William Julius Wilson has documented the decline of manufacturing jobs in large metropolitan inner cities, together with an increasingly segmented labor force in which whites have greater access to better-paying jobs, whereas minorities are consigned to low-wage (often part-time) work, welfare, and the illegal economy. The result, Wilson argues, is that a permanent underclass has been created in several U.S. cities (see Wilson, 1987, 1996; also Lynn & McGeary, 1990). Included in the underclass are many gang members who have been unable to move out of their gangs into conventional jobs (see especially Hagedorn, 1988). The underclass thesis is developed in several recent gang studies, including some in this volume (see, e.g., Fagan; Moore & Hagedorn; Short; Venkatesh). Klein (1995a) notes that police in many "newer gang cities" do not report gang membership in the upper age ranges, though "adolescent and young adult members are the norm in these cities, old enough to be seriously affected by high unemployment rates for inner-city minorities, but not so old as to be contributors, as yet, to the persistent and pervasive urban underclass" (p. 105).

Virtually all scholars stress the diversity of gang member behavior, with most indicating substantial involvement of gang members in drug use and selling, and in violent behavior. Most also report that street gangs are not involved *as gangs* in drug distribution, but disputes over drug selling often result in violent confrontations. Many gang members sell drugs, and many use them. Here again, however, much variation is observed, and we know little of the *salience of gang membership* for either behavior (but see Fagan, this volume; Huff, this volume). The latter point is especially important, inasmuch as the point is often made that although many gang members sell drugs, they often do so on their own and not as members of their gangs. They may do so under protective arrangements associated with gangs, however, and gang membership may be salient to drug selling in other ways, such as in recruitment of both drug sellers and users. Similarly, although there is little evidence that gangs evolve into adult criminal organizations (Fagan, this volume), gang membership may be salient to organized crime opportunities. The variety and complexity of relationships between gangs, drugs, entrepreneurial behavior, and violence defy simple description or explanation.

Violent behavior probably has always been an integral part of youth gang life, but a great deal of variety in this respect is evident in recent gang studies. As has been found in past studies, much of the violence of street gangs continues to be internally directed and related more to status than to instrumental concerns. The advent of drug selling by individual gang members, and in some cases the territorial control of drug selling by gangs, has led to increases in gang-related violence, however. Precisely how these developments relate to gang organization, recruitment, migration, and other behavior is not clear. Again, chapters in this book are relevant to these issues.

Several years ago, Joan Moore noted that the gangs she had studied over a period of many years are not the same as they were when she began studying them: "What anybody 'knows' about a gang in any given year—even a gang member's knowledge—may in certain specifics be out of date the very next year" (Moore, 1990, quoted in Klein, 1995a, p. 101). Change comes as no surprise, for change is such a ubiquitous feature of our times, and changes in particular gangs have been noted in many studies (Hagedorn, 1988; Huff, 1990; Klein, 1995a; Sanchez-Jankowski, 1991; Short & Moland, 1976).

Classification of gangs is a daunting task, and with inclusion of other youth collectivities, it is even more so. In addition to diversity and change, youth collectivities come in many forms, which sometimes merge and change in other ways: There are drug gangs, or "crews" (Williams, 1989); "wilding" groups (Cummings, 1993); milling crowds (Schwartz, 1987); smaller networks involved in delinquency (Reiss, 1986a; Sarnecki, 1986); "tagger crews" (Hutchison, 1993; Klein, 1995a); mods, rockers, and socker hooligans (Buford, 1991; Cohen, 1980; Taylor, 1971); skinheads and bikers (Klein, 1995a); prison gangs (Ralph et al., this volume); and so forth, seemingly ad infinitum. Little scholarly attention has been devoted to how these diverse and changing collective forms of youth organization and behavior relate to one another. The need for work in this area is highlighted by Mark Warr's recent analysis of group offending data from Martin Gold's 1967 survey of a national probability sample of 847 U.S. adolescents, aged 13-16 (see Warr, 1996).[3] The data confirm earlier findings that delinquent behavior is chiefly a group phenomenon, and that such groups tend to be small (Shaw & McKay, 1931). Moreover, although the delinquent groups in Gold's sample tended to be transitory, offenders commonly belonged to "multiple groups and thus have a larger network or pool of accomplices." According to Warr,

Groups appear to be more specialized than individuals, which suggests that offense specialization is the primary source of group differentiation. Most delinquent groups have an identifiable instigator, a person who tends to be older, more experienced, and emotionally close to other members. Males almost always follow other males, whereas females are much more likely to follow a member of the opposite sex. As a rule, offenders do not consistently assume the role of instigator or joiner over time, but instead switch from one role to the other depending on their relative position in the group in which they are participating at the time. The roles that offenders adopt are thus determined, not by some stable individual trait, but by the situational interaction of group and individual characteristics. (p. 11)

The gang status of these delinquent groups is unknown, but we see in the data many of the characteristics attributed to gangs. A viable typology of youth collectivities, including gangs, must include delinquent groups and networks such as these, as well as less transitory groups (gangs) and variations such as those noted, above. Regrettably, even the most recent gang studies provide little enlightenment concerning the group parameters noted by Warr.

ACCOUNTING FOR THE
INCREASE IN GANG PHENOMENA

My reference to gang phenomena in the section head, rather than simply the numbers of gangs, is deliberate. I suspect that much that passes as gang behavior, particularly in smaller cities, is, in fact, imitative behavior by small, and often transitory, groups of youngsters who have little idea of what gangs are all about. Such groups may, of course, become gangs, with prolonged association. The extent to which they become delinquent gangs depends on many contingencies, including internal group processes and reactions by others. Again, we need to know a great deal more about early group formation, and how such transformations take place.

In any case, the underclass thesis clearly cannot account entirely for the rapid increase in numbers of gangs throughout the United States. There is too much evidence of the spread of gangs in middle-class and suburban areas (see Atkinson, Walker, Schmidt, & Trump, this volume). As noted in my chapter in this volume, diffusion of both street gang culture and youth culture also are powerful influences that shape images of gangs and influence youthful appetites, fads, and fashions. The social and economic dislocations that have accompanied the expansion of gangs are also those that have accompanied the emergence of a permanent underclass, however (see Fagan, this volume; Klein, 1995a; Short, 1990a). Moreover, the vast majority of gangs in cities throughout the country arise among less-affluent youth in our inner cities. It is there that the problem is the most intractable, and it is among such youth that the diffusion of gang culture and pressures generated by media-hyped youth culture products exert the strongest influences toward gang formation and conflict. It is there, too, that—as my colleague, Laura Fishman, notes—appropriate arenas for respect and status have narrowed or disappeared (personal communication, October 1995, discussing her current research). It is among such youth, their families, and community institutions that lack the resources to provide opportunities for young people or to control their sometimes delinquent and violent behavior that solutions to gang problems are most needed.

Conclusion

Most youngsters do not become seriously involved in delinquent behavior. Those who do too often become society's criminals, wards of the criminal justice system, the specter of public fears, and a major drain on the public purse. Yet, despite the best intentions of reformers and the best efforts of scholars, the uncertainty of knowledge, the continuous need for socialization of the young, and social change ensure that there will always be youth problems and delinquents. Uncertainty is a problem in all fields of knowledge, even in the most advanced sciences and technologies. Although this may be small comfort to those who suffer as a result of these uncertainties and the many flaws in social systems, it should strengthen our resolve to understand these problems and address them with intelligence.

"Doing good" and "doing justice" are not always, and certainly not necessarily, incompatible. As Stan Cohen (1985) notes, "The ideology of doing good remains powerful. . . . It is the essence of a humanistic civilization to exert power and to do good at the same time" (p. 86). Critics of positivism and of doing good focus on their preemption and abuse by the powerful, especially in the form of state power. Yet, as many delinquency prevention projects demonstrate, the state has no monopoly on justice, nor is it necessary that control efforts directed at chronic delinquents and others in high-risk categories be the province solely of the criminal and juvenile justice systems. When criminal opportunity reduction and doing good are based on sound theoretical principles, delinquency prevention and rehabilitation programs can be both humane and successful.

A final note concerning both "doing good" and "knowing the score." Several years ago, I was invited to address a statewide conference on youth in Chicago. I was given conflicting reports on important aspects of youth gangs by several persons who had been on the scene for many years. All agreed that youth gangs were a serious problem. Beyond this there was very little agreement. Because my field research in the city had concluded nearly a decade before, I asked a number of questions. Was the gang problem more serious than it was previously—a decade, or two or three decades ago, for example? Was it different in character than in previous decades? What had happened to the "supergangs" that emerged in Chicago in the mid- to late 1960s? What had happened to the gang leaders who were imprisoned during the 1970s? and so on. I was given blank stares in response to many of my questions. In asking a specific question about a particularly well known supergang leader who had recently been released from prison, I discovered no one seemed to know what he was doing. Some thought he was organizing a new type of gang for political purposes. Some said he was organizing a church, but to what end they did not know. Others suggested he might be attempting take over Chicago's underworld. Some felt that all reports of his activities were false, or they discounted them in any case.

There is a lesson here, a very important lesson: *Familiarity with the territory is not enough.* Nor is knowing something about youth, or about youth work or the communities in which we live—even personal experience. None of these are enough. My Chicago informants were all knowledgeable people. Some had worked with young people for many years as professional social workers or volunteers. Some were researchers at well-known institutions. Some were even longtime associates of the Chicago Area Project, one of the most famous of all delinquency prevention programs, and one for which I have a special soft spot, intellectually and in my heart. The lesson is that *systematic and sustained research is necessary if we are to understand gangs or any aspect of human behavior.* A corollary is equally important. If they are to be successful, *efforts to prevent, intervene with, or suppress gangs also must be systematic, sustained, and based on local knowledge and on research that is systematic and up to date.*

There are no magic bullets for problems associated with gangs and other youth collectivities. To the extent that this analysis of forces in the larger society that influence gang behavior and of current trends in gang

behavior is correct, we can only hope to stem the tide of gang proliferation and contain the problem within reasonable limits. The research and
experience recounted in these pages offer both enlightenment and
hope—enlightenment as to some of the many varied patterns of gang
behavior, and hope in the experience and the modest claims of communities that have confronted these problems (see chapters in this volume
by Atkinson, Walker & Schmidt, Trump, and also the chapter by Huff).

Notes

1. Gangs are here defined as groups whose members meet together with some regular-
ity, over time, on the basis of group-defined criteria of membership and group-determined
organizational structure, usually (but not always: see Klein, 1995a) with some sense of
territoriality. Sanders (1994) adds a further criterion to distinguish between gangs and "ad
hoc groups based on a particular set of personalities"—that is, a gang "must transcend any
cohort and be treated as a phenomenon beyond the individuals that make it up at any one
time" (p. 19). He defines gangs by their violent behavior, however. Note that my definition
includes neither delinquent nor conventional behaviors, as these are what we wish to
explain. Nor does it include characteristic dress, names, or types of organization of gangs,
each of which varies in myriad ways that may help to understand gang behavior and that
may be important to gang identity and behavior for members and for others. Definitions
of gangs are a matter of some confusion and controversy, among scholars as well as others.
2. These figures are based upon Sanchez-Jankowski's (1991) Appendix, pp. 323-324.
3. The surveys grew out of Gold's study of Flint, Michigan (see Gold, 1970).

Acknowledgments

Since the first edition of *Gangs in America* was published in 1990, I have been most gratified by the favorable book reviews and personal comments of my peers. I attribute this positive reaction to the high quality of the chapters written by the contributing authors and to the timing of the book's publication as the issue of gangs began to take on greater salience in communities from the East Coast to Hawaii in the mid-to-late 1980s. As the second edition goes to press in 1996, the issue of gangs has assumed even greater prominence in both scholarly and public policy circles and it is beginning to be easier to list those communities that do *not* (or where officials publicly proclaim they do not) have a "gang problem" than those were the issue is acknowledged.

The literature on gangs has grown exponentially since that first edition in 1990. Scholarly journals have included many new and important research papers, and there have been a number of excellent books, including Malcolm Klein's (1995a) gem, *The American Street Gang*, which reflects decades of research on gangs, much of it contributed by the author himself. As a relative newcomer to gang research (I just completed my 10th year of field studies on gangs), I am indebted to scholars like Klein, Jim Short, Al Cohen, Walter Miller, and Irv Spergel who have dedicated decades of their professional and personal lives, systematically and persistently building our knowledge base on the subject of gangs and refuting many of the popular myths that have evolved over time and had such harmful impact on public policy.

In the development of this second edition, I have been greatly encouraged by my editor at Sage, Terry Hendrix, who is one of the most professional, competent, and personable editors I have had the pleasure of knowing. I also appreciate the assistance provided by Dale Grenfell, Senior Editorial Assistant at Sage, who always provides tender, loving care for my manuscripts until they become books. Terry Hendrix also carried out my request to elicit critiques of the first edition to determine what our colleagues would like us to consider including in the second edition.

I would like to express my appreciation to the following reviewers for their helpful comments concerning the first edition of this book: David A. Armstrong, Department of Social Sciences, McNeese State University; Al G. Mata, Jr., Department of Human Relations, the University of Oklahoma; Shirlee Owens, Department of Criminal Justice, Social Work, and Sociology, Northeast Louisiana University; Randall G. Shelden, Department of Criminal Justice, University of Nevada–Las Vegas; and Sheldon Zhang, Sociology Program, California State University–San Marcos. In editing this volume, I have attempted to be responsive to those suggestions, but I decided that the second edition would consist of all new material, rather than reprinting any chapters from the first edition, though that was certainly an option, given the high quality of those chapters. My intent was to bring together in this second edition scholars, community organizers, and practitioners to present a wide-ranging consideration of gangs and what might be done to respond to gangs. I am indebted to all my contributors for their willingness to assist me in this effort.

Finally, I'd like to express my appreciation to Georgia Meyer, Administrative Secretary for the Criminal Justice Research Center at Ohio State, for her diligent assistance throughout the preparation of this second edition. And once again, my family has been understanding and patient while I put in unusually long hours on this project. Fortunately for me, my wife is a hard-working, dedicated, and creative experiential science teacher who works long hours also and my daughters (Tamara, aka "Tammy," now 22; and Tiffany, now 20) are both students at Ohio State with part-time jobs, so they don't have as much time to miss "Dad" any more.

Introduction

C. RONALD HUFF

Like the first edition of *Gangs in America,* published 6 years ago, this volume is intended to bring together some of the best and most recent new scholarship on the subject of gangs. The second edition also includes a chapter reporting on the experiences of two communities (Aurora, Colorado; and Cleveland, Ohio) in organizing responses to the problems presented by gangs and gang-related crime. In assessing the scholarly and public policy issues associated with gangs in the mid-1990s, I made the editorial decision to focus this volume on four major subjects, which then became Parts 1 to 4 of this book. Part 1 addresses definitional and measurement issues; Part 2 assesses the behavioral, ecological, and socioeconomic dimensions of gangs; Part 3 focuses on the increasingly important factors of ethnicity and gender; and Part 4 presents both research and community experience concerning the reciprocal relationship between gangs and their communities.

Part 1 begins with Maxson and Klein's important update to their chapter in the first edition of this book. In the history of research and public policy discussions regarding gangs, no single issue has been as controversial as that of defining "gangs" and what constitutes "gang-related crime." More recently, an additional element of controversy has centered on the relationship between gangs and drugs and what role drug trafficking plays in gang-related violence. For this second edition, in addition to comparing the impact of employing "gang member" versus "gang motive" definitions of "gang-related" homicides, the authors introduce a new variable (drugs) to see what effects that might have, as well as to track what changes occurred over the time period (which has also been updated to include 1988 and 1989). They assess the impact of member-defined versus motive-defined gang cases versus nongang cases, with drug and non-drug involvement compared as well.

In Chapter 2, Curry, Ball, and Decker summarize the efforts made over a 20-year period to estimate the national prevalence of gangs, gang members, and gang-related crime. As the Uniform Crime Reports (UCR) system does not include a category for "gang-related crimes," such estimates are very important to scholars, policymakers, and practitioners alike. The authors present the results of a 1994 national survey of law enforcement agencies and discuss the multitude of methodological, conceptual, and political problems that have plagued our efforts to develop national prevalence data. They present both a "conservative" estimate and a more "reasonable" estimate, the latter reflecting an attempt to compensate for the underreporting that plagues the UCR.

Part 2 begins with Fagan's extensive analysis of the relationships among gangs, drugs, and neighborhood change. He places gangs in the context of the contemporary urban crisis; considers the various types of gangs, the nature of youth gang violence, and the role of drugs; and analyzes the linkage between gang formation and the socioeconomic makeup of communities, especially changes that are associated with the deindustrialization process. He skillfully assesses the complex interrelationships among the political economy of communities, the associated transformation of labor markets, the growth of the "drug economy," and the corresponding weakening of social controls in the community and the social and economic isolation of poor neighborhoods. He concludes with a look at the future, including the question of whether gangs might become institutionalized in our communities.

In Chapter 4, I present my own recent study focusing on the criminal behavior of gang versus nongang, at-risk youth in Cleveland, Ohio, and a longitudinal "tracking" study of gang leaders in Columbus, Ohio. This chapter is focused on three important questions:

1. What is the nature and extent of criminal behavior, including drug use and drug trafficking, committed by youth gangs collectively and by the individual members of those gangs?
2. Are there significant differences between the criminal behavior of youth gang members and comparably at-risk nongang youths (and their respective peers)?
3. What happens, over time, to the leaders of youth gangs?

The design of the Cleveland study permits comparisons of gang and nongang, at-risk youth who live in the same neighborhoods; attend the same schools; and are comparable with respect to age, gender, race, education completed, recent work experience, and family status. Data collected from confidential field interviews permit an assessment of the extent to which gang involvement contributes to criminal behavior, as well as some insight into the issue of gang resistance. The design of the Columbus study enables us to develop some appreciation for the magnitude of crime committed over time by 83 "key players" in the nation's 16th largest city—one with an emerging, rather than a chronic, gang problem.

The issues addressed in Chapter 4 include gang resistance; an equally important subject serves as the focus of Chapter 5 on leaving gangs. Decker and Lauritsen present the results of a recent field study of St. Louis gangs and ex-gang members. Their analysis includes a consideration of both *why* and *how* ex-gang members left their gangs. Their findings regarding gang *desistance*, coupled with the findings presented in Chapter 4 concerning gang *resistance*, have important implications for programs such as Drug Abuse Resistance Education (DARE), Gang Resistance Education and Training (GREAT), and other prevention and intervention initiatives used to dissuade youth from joining gangs and to encourage those already in gangs to sever their ties before they suffer what are often life-shattering or even fatal consequences. These data may be useful in attempting to counteract two of the prevalent myths concerning gangs—that one must join if approached and that one can never leave the gang.

The national surge in gang-related crime and the corresponding increase in arrests and convictions of gang members has also meant that states are increasingly faced with the problems posed by gangs in prisons. In Chapter 6, Ralph, Hunter, Marquart, Cuvelier, and Merianos discuss important aspects of this problem, including the role of inmate gangs, their relationship to prison violence, and the rise of Texas prison gangs in the 1980s as a case in point. The authors present extensive data concerning comparisons between gang and nongang prisoners and discuss the problems associated with attempts to control prison gangs and their associated violence.

The past decade has brought ever-increasing diversity to the gang phenomenon in the United States. In cities such as Los Angeles, where the roots of some gangs extend more than a century into the past, there are also newly developing gangs dominated by Central American immigrants. Throughout the United States, there are many examples of gangs that are racially and ethnically integrated and have both male and female members. One of the hottest topics among researchers and policymakers alike is the debate over female gangs and whether they are becoming more autonomous and more violent. Part 3 is focused on the increasingly important factors of ethnicity, race, and gender.

In Chapter 7, Vigil and Yun draw upon social control theory, multiple marginality, social ecology, opportunity theory, and strain theories to analyze how the weakening of social control can lead to deviant behavior. They illustrate these dynamics by presenting brief ethnographies of four gang youths from distinctly different cultural backgrounds—Vietnamese, Chicano, African American, and immigrant Latino. They skillfully demonstrate how the attachment processes of all four of these youths were affected by macrohistorical events and their families destabilized by socioeconomic factors. These ethnographies serve to illustrate some of the factors that fuel street gangs and impact social norms, leading to increased deviant behavior and crime.

Another aspect of gang diversity, Chinese gangs, is the subject of the nation's leading scholar on Chinese gangs, Ko-lin Chin, in Chapter 8. Based on data collected from personal interviews with 62 Chinese gang members, the author examines the participation rate, frequency, typology, causes, and restraining mechanisms of Chinese gang violence. Chin categorizes gang aggression in Chinatown into intergang violence, intragang violence, and violence directed at nongang victims, with the most prevalent type being intergang violence, and the least prevalent, force used against nongang victims. He demonstrates that the main causes or triggering events of intergang warfare are turf fights, staring, and provocative attitudes; intragang conflict tends to revolve around money, women, and power. He also discusses the often-claimed relationship between gang violence and drug use, drug trafficking, and organized crime. Finally, he presents a fascinating discussion of *kong so*, a practice employed by gang leaders and their affiliated adult organizations to negotiate and to prevent the escalation of gang conflicts.

Another important aspect of gang diversity is gender, a subject addressed in Chapters 9 and 10. In Chapter 9, Chesney-Lind, Shelden, and Joe address the widely made assertion that girls are becoming more like their male counterparts with respect to gang activities and violence. They first explore the role of the media in shaping our perceptions of "girl gangs" and female gang violence and then compare that socially constructed reality with official data, self-reports, and qualitative studies. Drawing extensively on personal interview data, the authors provide insight into the lives of these young women, their marginalized and chaotic neighborhoods, and the social role of the gang. The authors argue that some "explanations" of female involvement in gangs and associated crime are far too simplistic and that the choice of gang involvement is shaped significantly by an array of economic, educational, familial, and social conditions and constraints that enable the gang to facilitate members' survival in their world.

In Chapter 10, Moore and Hagedorn pose the question, "What happens to girls in the gang?" They also explore the related issues of how the adult careers of female gang members reflect their gang experience and whether the gang is a temporary career diversion or a major turning point for these young women. Their discussion builds on her interviews with samples of two long-standing Chicano gangs in poor Mexican and Mexican American communities in Los Angeles and with African American and Latino and Latina gang members in Milwaukee. Moore and Hagedorn offer very useful insight into the lives of these young women and the ways in which female gang members grow up in different ethnic communities and at different times. They conclude that although joining the gang does not mean "leaving the Brady Bunch for the Hell's Angels," it does have real impacts on their later lives. The authors explore the nuances of these impacts and how they vary across ethnic communities and at different times. They argue that the dismantling of our welfare system in the 1990s may turn out to be the most important influence on the future prospects of female gang members by reducing the support for women with children who have sought to avoid the illegal opportunities afforded by the drug economy.

Part 4 is focused on several important aspects of gangs and the community, beginning with Short's informative discussion of the nature of relationships between individual, group, and community careers in delinquency, in which he draws on his own exemplary research and other recent studies of street gangs. In this sweeping discussion, Short considers the histories of two Chicago gangs, the Vice Lords and the Nobles, the differences between their histories, and the factors that may account for those differences. He then analyzes the complex factors that have helped fuel the growth of street gangs in the United States, focusing especially on the development of the urban underclass, and considers what might be done to address the spread of gangs and gang-related crime. His discussion of the need for functional communities and the innovative efforts of the Beethoven Project in Chicago's Robert Taylor Homes housing project is especially illuminating and underscores the macrosocial and economic constraints, as well as the effects of the consumerist youth culture, that confront such programs and constantly undermine their efforts to improve the lives of these citizens.

Like the Beethoven project described by Short, Venkatesh's discussion in Chapter 12 centers on the Robert Taylor Homes housing project on Chicago's South Side, perhaps the world's largest public housing project and one with a long and notorious history of youth gang activity. Venkatesh, a doctoral candidate at the University of Chicago and student of William Julius Wilson's, conducted a remarkable and valuable 3-year participant observation study of the relations that formed among the community's youth gangs; the broader tenant population; and organizations such as the Chicago Housing Authority, local tenant management councils, and social service agencies. Prior to Venkatesh's study, little was known about how the residents and the organizations in "gang neighborhoods" adapt to the gangs and whether these relationships change over time. Venkatesh addresses these and other important questions and reveals the ambivalent accommodations that exist among the gangs, the residents, and local institutions. His results challenge some popular and intuitive assumptions regarding these relationships—assumptions that all too often misinform public policy and initiatives designed to prevent and control gang-related crime.

The volume concludes with Chapter 13, in which four community-based experts have the final word, discussing what their two communities (Aurora, Colorado; and Cleveland, Ohio) have done to address the surge in gangs and gang-related crime. Both the Aurora Gang Task Force and Cleveland's Task Force on Violent Crime (now known as the Partnership for a Safer Cleveland) are high-profile, successful, community-wide initiatives designed to promote a balanced approach with recognition of the importance of law enforcement suppression of gang crime to protect public safety while also emphasizing that in the longer term, prevention and intervention efforts are our best hope of reducing the problems posed by gangs. Atkinson summarizes the development and evolution of the gang problem and the community's response in Aurora (Colorado's third largest city, located adjacent to Denver); Walker and Schmidt provide an overview of Cleveland's experience. Finally, Trump addresses the important, but often ignored or underemphasized (partially due to denial) problems posed by gangs in schools and in suburban communities and discusses strategies for addressing these problems. As an ever-growing number of U.S. communities acknowledge the existence of gang-related crime and assign it a higher public policy priority, the experiences of these two particular communities will be instructive in designing community response to gangs and gang-related crime.

PART

I

Defining and Measuring
Gang Crime

Defining Gang Homicide

An Updated Look at
Member and Motive Approaches

CHERYL L. MAXSON
MALCOLM W. KLEIN

In our chapter for the first edition of *Gangs In America*, we presented Los Angeles homicide data from the years 1978 through 1982 to investigate the implications of two approaches to defining gang crime—the member versus motive definitions. In this chapter, we utilize homicide incidents from 1988 and 1989 to update our previous findings and to examine whether or not drug aspects introduce differences in the definitional analyses.

AUTHORS' NOTE: This research was supported by the Harry Frank Guggenheim Foundation and the Southern California Injury Prevention Center (under the auspices of the Public Health Service Centers for Disease Control Grant No. R49/CCR903622). We are grateful to officials in the Los Angeles Police Department and the Los Angeles Sheriff's Department for their cooperation. Many thanks also to the team of USC students who helped collect these data, under the supervision of the ever-vigilant Lea C. Cunningham. Points of view expressed herein are solely those of the authors.

The recent proliferation in U.S. cities of street gang activity increases the importance of investigating the relationships between gangs, violence, and drug distribution. In a recent study, we estimated a total of about 1,100 gang-involved cities and towns (Klein, 1995a)—cities of all shapes and sizes. Curry, Ball, and Decker (1995) report a national estimate of 735 jurisdictions with a population of at least 25,000 having gang crime problems. Our law enforcement respondents share a deep concern about the violence and drug activity reportedly associated with gangs in cities both large and small.[1] Furthermore, the implications of different law enforcement approaches to definitions of street gangs, gang membership, and gang-related crime extend to the vast array of cities; police officials are grappling with developing methods of counting, reporting, and understanding their gang problems.

But it is to Los Angeles, one of the "traditional" gang areas, often referred to as the gang "capital" of the United States, that we turned to address our research questions. The grim figure of 779 gang homicides occurring in the county of Los Angeles in 1994 provides corroboration for this appellation (W. McBride, Los Angeles Sheriff's Department, personal communication, August 21, 1995). We will, as before, refer to two definitional approaches, gang-member versus gang-motive homicides. The first are defined as homicides having a gang member as assailant or victim; the second are defined in terms of group loyalty (vs. individual interest) as the principal reason for the act. The primary research questions can be stated quite simply: Updating the implications of using member versus motive definitions of gang homicides,

- How many homicides appear to result from gang motives? Has the proportion of gang-motivated cases changed from 1978-1982 levels?

- What incident and participant characteristics distinguish member-defined gang cases from motive-defined gang cases? Are there different distinguishing characteristics when each group of cases is compared with nongang cases? Are there different patterns in each of these comparisons involving 1988-1989 homicides from those found in 1978-1982 homicides?

- How successful are these characteristics in classifying member-defined gang versus nongang cases and motive-defined gang versus nongang homicides? Are the classification rates similar to those found in earlier years?

Combining the drug and definition issues,

- What aspects of drug involvement distinguish member-defined gang cases from motive-defined gang cases, and each from their nongang counterparts?
- Is the classification of gang (member and motive) versus nongang cases improved by the consideration of aspects of drug involvement?

Following a brief discussion of the definitional issue and an overview of the study methods, we present the current Los Angeles data to address each of the research questions. We conclude with the implications of these findings for knowledge about gang violence in Los Angeles and elsewhere.

Definitional Approaches to "Gang Related" Crime

Law enforcement procedures for defining gang-related crime take on increased significance in the current context of the proliferation of cities with street gang problems. Despite the resurgence of ethnographic gang studies, these are limited in both the number of gangs and the cities investigated. Law enforcement is currently the best source available for comparisons of gang prevalence and violence. The definitional approaches adopted by these newer gang cities will have a distinct impact on perceptions of the scope and nature of gang violence in this country. There is a lack of consensus among law enforcement (Curry, Ball, & Fox, 1994; Curry et al., 1995; Spergel, 1988) and, for that matter, among researchers (Curry, 1991; Ehrensaft & Spergel, 1991), regarding the optimal definitional approach. There is even disagreement as to the presumed value of adopting common definitions (Decker & Kempf, 1991; Horowitz, 1990). Ball and Curry (1995) recently lodged the following criticism against their academic coworkers: "Unfortunately . . . few if any gang researchers and theorists have been sufficiently conscious of their own definitional stances, with the result that their definitions have carried too many latent connotations, treated correlates or consequences as properties or causes, or contributed to similar errors of logic" (p. 239). Yet, a recent symposium of street gang experts from state and local law enforcement agencies across the country issued a call for standardized definitions and provided a model based upon the consensus reached at this meeting (National Drug Intelligence Center [NDIC], 1995).

Among law enforcement agencies, there are two basic approaches to defining gang-related violence. Officials in Los Angeles and many other cities have adopted a rather broad definitional policy, designating an incident as gang related if either the suspect or victim is a gang member. This is the approach recommended by the NDIC gathering described above. Officials in Chicago and other cities apply the more stringent criterion of a direct link to gang function. In Chicago, there must be positive evidence that gang activity or gang membership was the motive for the encounter (Block, 1991). Examples of such motives are retaliation, territoriality, recruitment, and "representing" (graffiti, wearing gang colors, shouting gang slogans, etc.) (Bobrowski, 1988). We refer to these two approaches as "gang-member" and "gang-motive" definitions. (See Maxson & Klein, 1990, for a detailed description of these definitional approaches.) A recent national survey of prosecutors in 192 jurisdictions that have addressed gangs found that equal numbers in large jurisdictions adopted each approach (Institute for Law and Justice, 1994). More small jurisdictions (59%) use the narrower definition, that is, a crime committed by a gang member for the benefit of a gang.

For the current study, we posed questions regarding the implications of the two definitional approaches. The first is a prevalence question: What proportion of the homicides designated as gang involved by the member definition would also satisfy the motive requirement? This analysis has both operational and statistical significance. Gang homicides are often assigned to investigators with special gang expertise, which may produce more positive investigative outcomes (Maxson, Klein, & Gordon, 1990). The number of gang homicides reported would certainly differ. In 1994, law enforcement gang experts in the city of Los Angeles tallied 370 gang homicides, or a whopping 44% of all homicides occurring in the city in that year (Los Angeles Police Department, personal communication, August 23, 1995). On the other hand, the Chicago Police Department reported a 1994 figure of 293 gang homicides, a more moderate 32% of all homicides for that year (D. Hilbring, Chicago Police Department, personal communication, August 23, 1995).[2]

The second research question addresses the impact of the two definitional approaches on descriptions of the *nature* of gang homicide, particularly in comparison with nongang incidents. If the characteristics of the two types of gang cases are similar and the differences between gang and nongang incidents remain stable, then elements of gang violence can be compared from city to city, despite different operational approaches to defining gang-related crime. Legitimate, cross-city comparisons provide a foundation for building generalized knowledge about gangs.

That, in essence, was the conclusion we drew from the earlier analyses of two data sets made up of gang and nongang homicides that occurred in the city of Los Angeles and in county areas patrolled by the Los Angeles Sheriff's Department (LASD) (Maxson & Klein, 1990). The Los Angeles Police Department (LAPD) homicides were drawn from three station areas over the years 1979-1981; the LASD data spanned the years 1978-1982 and included all 19 station areas. The two data sets were analyzed separately, but the conclusions held for both jurisdictions: Applying the criterion of the presence of a gang motive reduced the number of gang homicides by about half, but for the most part, the qualitative differences between gang and nongang cases were constant, regardless of the definitional criteria used.

We noted some variation between the two jurisdictions, but these differences were minor in contrast with the overall stability of gang versus nongang distinctions. We confirmed the conclusions emerging from the bivariate analyses with discriminant analysis techniques, noting once again some differences, but an overall pattern of consistency between the two definitional approaches.

We wondered whether these conclusions would hold up in more recent homicides and whether drug aspects of homicides might introduce some differences in the definitional analyses that we were not able to examine in the earlier project. Thus, we were able to combine our interests in both the drug and definitional aspects of gang violence with analyses of current gang and nongang homicides while updating our prior findings.

Method

Our current study includes homicides from five station areas in South Central Los Angeles, selected due to high levels of gang and drug activity. Three of the five stations were within the jurisdiction of the

LAPD and two were county areas handled by the LASD. The data from the two departments are combined for all analyses reported in this chapter.

Gang and nongang homicides occurring in the five station areas during 1988 and 1989 were sampled using a random stratified approach to yield equal numbers of each type for collection. Officer-involved shootings and the few cases handled by specialized units other than the homicide division were deleted from the population. Lists of "gang-involved" cases were supplied by each jurisdiction's specialized gang unit. Both departments employ broad definitions of gang involvement including membership of participants on either side, behavioral indications during the incident, and other gang indicators that may emerge during the course of the investigation. In a previous study, we found the application of these criteria to homicide cases to be relatively stable over time in both jurisdictions (Klein, Gordon, & Maxson, 1986; Maxson, Gordon, & Klein, 1985). The sampling procedures resulted in 201 gang and 201 nongang homicides, reflecting about two thirds of the gang homicides and slightly less of the nongang homicides. Despite the inclusion of two station areas from the LASD jurisdiction, it should be noted that about three fourths of these cases are from the LAPD.

A team of data collectors extracted information from extensive homicide investigation files. On occasion, files could not be located, and in a few instances, access was denied by the detective in possession of the case material; these cases were replaced by randomly selected cases from the remaining population. Coded items included descriptors of the incident (e.g., setting, automobile involvement, weapons, related case charges, additional injuries, and gang motives), participants (e.g., numbers on each side, relationship, demographics of designated victims and suspects, and stated gang affiliations), and an extensive list of drug indicators (use and sales paraphernalia, drugs found in investigation, autopsy results, drug use or sales by participants, aspects of the location, and drug motives). Intercoder reliability was assessed by duplicate coding of 10% of the sample. Overall, reliabilities were quite high (over .90), but it should be noted that the data collection was closely supervised, with lots of involvement by senior staff in coding decisions.

Findings

ASSESSING THE IMPLICATIONS OF DIFFERENT DEFINITIONAL APPROACHES

We begin with the basic question of how many of the homicides labeled as gang involved by Los Angeles gang units, utilizing the broad member definition, would retain their gang status under the more stringent motive criterion. Then, moving beyond the issue of case numbers, we use the incident and participant characteristics to explore the differences between the two types of gang cases and the respective gang-nongang comparisons. Finally, discriminant analytic techniques permit an assessment of the overall impact of these variables in distinguishing gang from nongang homicides. We examine whether the motive approach produces a "purified" set of gang cases, more clearly distinct from nongang cases, with a wholly different character from homicides categorized using the member criterion.

Of the 201 homicides labeled by the gang units as gang-member involved, 120 (60%) also had statements of gang motives present in the case file investigation materials. Similar motive statements also appeared in 8 (4%) of the 201 nongang homicides.[3] Both figures are slightly higher than those found in the 1978-1982 homicides. In the earlier study, 52% of the member-defined gang homicides and 2% of the nongang homicides included statements of gang motives. This difference over time may reflect changes in the nature of gang activity, increased sensitivity of law enforcement investigators to gang issues, differences in the sampling strategies employed in the two studies, or some combination of these factors.

Clearly, a narrow definition such as Chicago's would reduce the reported Los Angeles rate significantly. The revised 1994 figure for Los Angeles city would be in the neighborhood of 222 gang-related homicides, as compared with the 370 incidents reported using the member definition.[4] Both figures are high and represent substantial human and social costs, but one could reasonably question whether 222 homicides would have provoked the intense law enforcement and press reactions to gang activity that we have observed over the last several years in Los

Angeles. Moreover, the new figure for Los Angeles is considerably lower than Chicago's total of 293. When the issue is *prevalence*, that is, the volume of gang activity, clearly comparisons between cities with different definitional styles would be quite inappropriate.

Putting aside the issue of comparative incident counts, we now turn to the question, "So what?" If reducing the pool of gang incidents to the presumably more "pure," motivated cases does not substantially alter the descriptions of gang violence, then comparisons regarding the *nature* of gang activity between cities with different definitional policies may be quite legitimate.

We approached this issue by utilizing a series of variables describing the incidents and participants and comparing gang with nongang cases. This required construction of a new data set made up of the 128 identified gang motive cases and a comparable group of 128 nongang cases, sampled randomly from a reconstituted population of the remaining homicides. This reconstitution was a complex procedure, but allowed those member-defined gang cases *not* meeting the motive criteria to fall within the nongang motive group. For the comparison member-defined data set, we sampled 128 gang and 128 nongang cases from the original 402 cases.[5] Table 1.1 shows the bivariate comparisons of gang-nongang differences in case characteristics, employing first the member definition and then the motive definition.

The construction of Table 1.1 permits several types of comparisons. Characteristics of the two types of gang cases are displayed in the first and fourth columns.[6] There is a striking similarity between the two sets of percentages and means. Motive-defined gang cases are slightly more likely to occur on the street and are slightly less likely to involve participants with a clear prior relationship than member-defined incidents. These differences are minimal and not substantially significant. In fact, comparing the incident and participant characteristics of the two types of gang cases suggests that we are not dealing with two distinct types at all. Descriptions of the nature of gang homicide categorized by either definitional approach are to all intents and purposes identical.

Does the similarity between the two types of gang cases extend to comparisons between the two groups of nongang homicides? Employing the motive definition results in the transfer of some member-defined gang cases[7] into the nongang population and may alter the aggregated character of the nongang comparison pool.

TABLE 1.1 Characteristics of Gang and Nongang Homicides Using Member and Motive Definitions

	Member Defined			Motive Defined		
	Gang (n = 128)[b]	Nongang (n = 128)[b]	p[a]	Gang (n = 128)[b]	Nongang (n = 128)[b]	p[a]
Late afternoon to evening occurrence	49%	32%	**	52%	34%	**
Automobile present	80%	44%	***	83%	54%	***
Street location	58%	35%	***	65%	32%	***
Fear/threat of retaliation	37%	20%	**	40%	19%	***
Associated charge: violent	41%	16%	***	38%	30%	NS
Associated charge: robbery	6%	6%	NS	2%	13%	***
Gun(s) present	95%	74%	***	98%	76%	***
Other victim injuries present	38%	12%	***	38%	20%	**
Clear prior relationship	24%	48%	***	18%	47%	***
Mean number victim participants	4.13	1.79	**	4.47	1.95	**
Mean number suspect participants	2.70	1.71	***	2.83	1.95	***
Proportion male victims	.88	.73	***	.92	.78	***
Proportion male suspects	.96	.85	**	.98	.89	***
Proportion black suspects	.86	.88	NS	.84	.82	NS
Mean age victims	24.2	33.1	***	22.7	31.8	***
Mean age suspects	20.5	29.6	***	19.7	26.5	***

NOTES: NS = not significant.
a. Significance levels were determined by chi-squares or t-tests (* $p < .05$; ** $p < .01$; *** $p < .001$).
b. Numbers of cases included in each analysis vary according to missing values.

A cursory review of the second and fifth columns of Table 1.1 suggests that the two groups of nongang cases show more differences than the two sets of gang cases. Presence of automobiles, associated charges, and other (than the homicide) victim injuries are higher in nongang cases using the gang motive approach than in nongang incidents under the member approach. This pattern suggests increased gang aspects of nongang cases when the gang-motive standard is applied. The direction of the slight differences in the participant characteristics (more participants, proportionally more males, more blacks, of younger ages) is consistent with this interpretation. Does this slight change in the nature of nongang homicides affect descriptions of the differences between gang and nongang incidents? The relevant comparisons are displayed by the two vertical halves of Table 1.1, with particular reference to the significance tests reported in the third and sixth columns.

The overall consistency between the two vertical halves of Table 1.1 is quite remarkable. With only a few exceptions, the same variables significantly differentiate gang from nongang homicides, and there are no reversals of direction. Consistent with the 1978-1982 incidents, the presence of associated charges seems to differentiate gang cases under one definitional approach but not the other, as exemplified by the lower proportion of nongang member-defined cases with additional violent offenses.

It appears that the motive approach is associated with a lower likelihood of gang designation when robbery is a feature of the case. This is hardly surprising and very consistent with conceptual distinctions between the member and motive definitions. Personal gain, rather than gang benefit, is more often viewed as the offender's primary motive. Perhaps more surprising is the marked similarity between the two definitional approaches in most of the incident and participant descriptors.

A more mixed picture emerges when we turn to more sophisticated, multivariate techniques to examine these distinctions further. Discriminant analysis organizes all the variables in such a way as to maximize their capacity to discriminate gang from nongang cases. The standardized coefficients reported in Table 1.2 show the relative contribution of each variable toward distinguishing gang from nongang incidents. The drug variables were not included in this analysis, and associated violent charges were dropped due to high correlations with other variables. The rank ordering of the size of the coefficients is provided in parentheses to facilitate the comparison between the two data sets. Eta^2 is a measure of the ability of the discriminant function to explain the variance between gang and nongang cases.

In both data sets, mean age of suspects emerges as by far the strongest discriminator between gang and nongang incidents. The value of eta squared and the classification results are similar, although slightly higher in the motive-defined analysis. The overall pattern is one of shared variables, but in a departure from the bivariate results, three variables did not achieve sufficient discriminatory power to enter the motive-defined function. Two of these variables, mean age of victims and automobile presence, ranked quite high in the member-defined function. Consistent with the bivariate analysis, robbery as an associated case

TABLE 1.2   Gang Versus Nongang Discriminant Analysis Results: Member- and Motive-Defined Comparisons

	Member Defined[a]	Motive Defined[a]
Mean age, suspects	−.555(1)	−.603(1)
Number suspect participants	.243(2)	.239(6)
Mean age, victims	−.224(3)	NS
Automobile present	.219(4)	NS
Clear prior relationship	−.207(5)	.266(3)
Other victim injuries present	.190(6)	.192(9)
Proportion male suspects	.184(7)	.253(4)
Proportion black suspects	.170(8)	.239(7)
Late afternoon to evening occurrence	.166(9)	.154(11)
Fear/threat of retaliation present	.162(10)	.243(5)
Number victim participants	.150(11)	.217(8)
Gun(s) present	.139(12)	.179(10)
Proportion male victims	.139(13)	NS
Associated charge: robbery	−.117(14)	−.444(2)
Street location	NS	.129(12)
Variance explained (eta^2)	.429	.461
Classification success (%)		
Gang	85.5	91.3
Nongang	71.4	75.0
Overall	80.6	83.4

NOTES: NS = not significant.
    a. Weights are standardized canonical discriminant function coefficients. Negative valence indicates inverse relationship with gang. Relative rankings are noted in parentheses. Member-defined analysis includes 113 gang cases and 98 nongang cases (45 cases dropped for missing values on at least one variable). Motive-defined analysis includes 115 gang cases and 108 nongang cases (33 cases dropped for missing values).

offense figured prominently in the motive function, but was the lowest-ranked variable in the member function. The rank-order correlation (rho) between the two columns of figures is a quite low .19. Further examination of the variable rankings in the discriminant analyses performed previously on the older LAPD and LASD homicide data sets shows equally low correlations.

Overall, data presented in Tables 1.1 and 1.2 do not suggest that drastic changes in the depiction of gang homicides or in the characterization of the differences between gang and nongang incidents occur when different operational approaches to gang crime definitions are applied by law enforcement. Descriptions of the *nongang* comparison group may be more vulnerable to definitional variations, but on the whole, we find a large measure of stability in the gang-nongang comparisons, at least at the bivariate level.

Multivariate analyses are less supportive of a stance that definitional policies make little difference in depictions of the character of gang violence. Despite similarities between the results of discriminant analyses of the two data sets, there are marked differences in the contributions that a few variables make to the discriminant functions. The import of robbery as an associated charge for the motive-derived function makes sense. It is possible that victim age and automobile presence failed to enter the motive function as a consequence of special features of robbery incidents, but there were too few such cases to examine this speculation. Expanding the analysis to include drug aspects of the incident may prove useful.

COMBINING THE DRUG AND DEFINITION ISSUES

The presence of robbery as an associated case offense affects whether or not a homicide would be handled as a gang crime in departments, depending on their different definitional policies. Drug involvement may well have a similar impact. Drug information was collected on quite specific items, most of which did not produce sufficiently high frequencies to support analyses of gang-nongang differences. This fact in itself throws some doubt on the purportedly close relationship between gangs, drugs, and violence. Alternatively, we computed variables that represent more general aspects of drug involvement and reflect the gang-drug issues in South Central Los Angeles. Most drug (excluding alcohol) mentions were coded to indicate the type of drug involved. From these, we computed a variable for any *mention of cocaine* in the case. The *presence of any type of sales or distributional aspect* of the case could derive from the nature of the incident location, sales involvement by participants on either side, or motives related to drug distribution. Finally, *mentions of any drug-related motive* for the homicide includes conflicts over drug use, although these are far less frequent than motives stemming from drug distribution (for example, conflicts over drug territory and dealer rip-offs). In Table 1.3, we present the data on the three drug dimensions in gang and nongang incidents reflecting the two definitional approaches.

TABLE 1.3 Drug Characteristics of Gang and Nongang Homicides Using Member and Motive Definitions

	MEMBER DEFINED			MOTIVE DEFINED		
	Gang $(n = 128)^b$	Nongang $(n = 128)^b$	p^a	Gang $(n = 128)^b$	Nongang $(n = 128)^b$	p^a
Cocaine involved	37%	47%	NS	29%	48%	**
Drug sales aspect	41%	28%	*	34%	37%	NS
Drug motive mentioned	20%	27%	NS	12%	28%	***

NOTES: NS = not significant.
a. Significance levels were determined by chi-squares or t-tests (* $p < .05$; ** $p < .01$; *** $p < .001$).
b. Numbers of cases included in each analysis varies according to missing values.

If drug sales are *not* intrinsically related to gang affairs, then one would expect the three drug dimensions to be less apparent in gang-motivated cases than in member-defined gang cases.[8] In comparing the first and fourth columns in Table 1.3, it appears that employing the gang motive definition reduces the proportion of gang cases with cocaine involvement, drug sales aspects, or drug motives (see Note 7). Two of these, cocaine involvement and the presence of drug motives, appear with similar frequency in nongang cases, regardless of whether they are classified nongang by virtue of having no gang members or no gang motive (see columns 2 and 5 in Table 1.3). But the third, the proportion of nongang cases with an aspect of drug sales, is higher when the gang motive criterion is employed.

Drug aspects of the incidents do distinguish gang from nongang cases, but these vary by definitional approach. For this analysis, we tested for gang versus nongang differences by comparing columns 1 and 2 (member approach) and then columns 4 and 5 (motive approach) in Table 1.3. The statistical tests for the significance of these respective differences are reported in the third and sixth columns. Drug sales involvement separates gang member cases from nongang incidents, but not from gang-motivated cases. Neither cocaine presence nor drug motives distinguish gang member cases from their nongang counterparts. On the other hand, both of these features differentiate motive-defined gang cases from nongang cases. These findings would be surprising to those who argue a close gang-drug-violence connection. Drug motives and cocaine involvement are less common in gang-motivated than in nongang homicides.

These bivariate results of the drug variables revealed interesting gang-nongang distinctions that varied between the two definitional styles. The "purification" of gang features resulting from the application of the motive approach reveals that drug aspects are important in distinguishing gang from nongang cases—cocaine and drug motives are more often featured in nongang cases.

Once again, we turned to discriminant analysis strategies to examine the relative impact of the drug variables. Unfortunately, the three drug dimensions have high intercorrelations that permitted the inclusion of only one drug variable in the multivariate analysis. A separate set of discriminant analyses were performed with the same set of incident and participant variables, plus mention of a drug motive.

As shown in Table 1.4, the drug motive variable entered both member and motive functions and ranked quite high (second) in the motive-defined data set. From the bivariate results, low ranking of drug motive in the member-defined function was not surprising. But the summary statistics (eta^2 and classification) were affected only minimally by the inclusion of drug motive, nor did it appear to influence the relative contributions of the other variables. The rank-order correlations between the two member-defined functions (i.e., with and without the drug motive variable) and between the two motive-defined functions both exceeded .95. Clearly, our quest to explain the differential contribution of variables to gang-nongang distinctions has not been aided by the inclusion of drug motive.

Conclusion

Overall, these analyses of 1988 and 1989 incidents confirm our prior conclusions about the implications of different law enforcement policies regarding the designation of gang homicides. Adopting the more narrow, motive criterion substantially reduces the number of gang homicides reported by jurisdictions confronting violent gang activity. Comparisons of rates between jurisdictions embracing different definitional approaches are clearly *not* valid unless motive information is available to restructure a member-defined population of incidents (or conversely,

TABLE 1.4 Gang Versus Nongang Discriminant Analysis Results: Member-and Motive-Defined Comparisons (drug motive included)

	Member Defined[a]	Motive Defined[a]
Mean age, suspects	−.532(1)	−.582(1)
Mean age, victims	−.241(2)	NS
Number suspect participants	.235(3)	.259(8)
Automobile present	.212(4)	NS
Clear prior relationship	−.200(5)	−.309(5)
Proportion male suspects	.198(6)	.310(4)
Other victim injuries present	.188(7)	.176(10)
Proportion black suspects	.184(8)	.277(7)
Fear/threat of retaliation present	.169(9)	.278(6)
Late afternoon to evening occurrence	.162(10)	.141(12)
Gun(s) present	.158(11)	.195(9)
Drug motive mentioned	**−.158(12)**	**−.397(2)**
Number victim participants	.146(13)	.175(11)
Proportion male victims	.129(14)	NS
Associated charge: robbery	NS	−.372(3)
Street location	NS	NS
Variance explained (eta^2)	.432	.495
Classification success (%)		
Gang	86.8	91.3
Nongang	74.5	75.9
Overall	81.3	83.9

NOTES NS = not significant.
   a. Weights are standardized canonical discriminant function coefficients. Negative valence indicates inverse relationship with gang. Relative rankings are noted in parentheses. Member-defined analysis includes 113 gang cases and 98 nongang cases (45 cases dropped for missing values on at least one variable). Motive-defined analysis includes 115 gang cases and 108 nongang cases (33 cases dropped for missing values).

if member information is available on nonmotive but gang member-involved cases).

Cross-city comparisons of bivariate descriptions of gang, as compared with nongang, homicide characteristics *are* appropriate, but within certain limitations. On the one hand, the use of firearms, participant demographics, and the number of and relationship between participants are among the many examples of case characteristics that appear to be unaffected by definitional styles. On the other hand, comparisons of drug involvement and additional violent offenses should be approached with extreme caution.

Other general statements can be derived from the data on drug aspects of homicide. The finding that drug motives and cocaine mentions appear more commonly in nongang cases but sales involvement is more frequent in gang incidents is interesting because most of the specific drug motives mentioned concerned sales rather than use. This suggests that although participants in gang homicides are more likely to have roles in the sales or distribution of drugs, this sales involvement may be less likely to figure as a "cause" of the homicide than in nongang cases. These findings do not support a strong connection between gang drug sales and violence. If anything, the sales-violence connection seems stronger in nongang cases. In any case, the term "drug related" is just as ambiguous as is the term "gang related." The "involved" versus "motivated" distinctions could be applied to an analysis of drug homicides just as we have used the member versus motive categories to investigate gang homicides.

Applying motive versus more general gang involvement criteria certainly results in different prevalence rates. Drug aspects emerge less frequently in cases designated as "gang" under the motive criterion. Given the ubiquitous association between gangs, drugs, and violence in the popular media, one wonders whether the connection would be made less readily if motive became the primary consideration for police (or media) reports of violence. Different definitional approaches to labeling gang and drug aspects of homicides could result in varying social constructions about the nature of gang and drug violence connections.

Because the use of discriminant analytic techniques is relatively limited in law enforcement circles, it remains for researchers to be somewhat troubled by the multivariate results. Frankly, we are stymied as to how to interpret the intricacies of the performance of certain variables and must fall back on the customary positions of caution and the call for more research of this type. In particular, it would be helpful if data from other cities could be investigated with similar analytic techniques.

Finally, there is the issue of which approach is better, more valid, or more useful. For local law enforcement, it is probably *most* important to apply definitional policies consistently, regardless of the type of definition used. Both approaches are vulnerable to the availability of information. Motives can be quite difficult to determine, even with the resources usually devoted to homicide investigation; motive information often is not available for other types of offenses. Reliable gang rosters are costly to develop and maintain, require a strong commitment to intelligence gathering, and place emphasis on systematic application of criteria for gang membership.

For research purposes, the broader member approach provides the data to examine incident-based characteristics of all homicides involving gang members. Data are also available on the subset of incidents closely tied to gang function or operations. Thus, there is more information accessible to researchers with the member definition. Finally, both definitional approaches present opportunities for valid comparisons between cities, a prerequisite for developing a comprehensive understanding of the nature of gang violence.

Notes

1. Space limitations do not permit an extended discussion here of street gang involvement in drug distribution. Perceptions of a tight or highly organized connection between gangs and drugs has been supported by some research (Mieczkowski, 1986; Padilla, 1992; Sanchez-Jankowski, 1991; Skolnick, 1988; Taylor, 1990a), but also severely challenged by many recent studies (Block & Block, 1994; Decker & Van Winkle, 1994; Esbensen & Huizinga, 1993; Fagan, 1989; Hagedorn, 1994a; Klein & Maxson, 1994; Klein, Maxson, & Cunningham, 1991; Maxson, 1995; Moore, 1990a; Waldorf & Lauderback, 1993). Interested readers should refer to the recent reviews of this literature by Klein (1995a) and Decker (1995).

2. The 1994 figure of 293 gang homicides in Chicago represents a marked increase over the 1993 figure of 129. Follow-up inquiries with the Chicago Police Department's Crime Analysis Unit confirmed the 1994 count. This unit has the official responsibility for designating gang homicides. Officials report that the command structure implemented a new definition in 1994 and encouraged the practice of inferring gang motive in ambiguous cases. The current Chicago definition of gang-related homicides is, "The offender must be a gang member and any of the following apply: 1) the offender is engaged in any activity which furthers the gang enterprise; or 2) the by-product of the offender's gang activity results in a death."

Crime Analysis Unit personnel report their perception that there has been a genuine increase in both turf and drug-motivated incidents but also acknowledge that the application of the new definition would produce higher gang homicide numbers than in prior years. This exemplifies the importance of examining shifts and definitional stances; Chicago perhaps should be removed from the group of cities that are thought to employ the "Chicago definition."

3. A brief review of the summary descriptions of these cases suggested two patterns. In most cases, there was speculation about various motives without confirmatory reports by witnesses or participants. In a few cases, the drug issues dominated the gang issues. Both patterns are also present in the gang incidents with gang motives, however, so it is not clear why these eight cases were not designated as "gang" by the units.

4. It should be noted that Los Angeles *city* figures, rather than county, are more appropriate for comparison with Chicago.

5. Data collectors recorded all statements of gang affiliation in the investigation files. It is interesting to note that 11% of the member-defined gang cases had no affiliation statements whereas 22% of the member-defined *nongang* cases had gang members possibly involved in the incident. Apparently, even the more inclusive definitional approach based upon gang status of the participants does not result in designating all cases with gang aspects as "gang crimes." The motive-defined nongang cases had only a slightly higher percentage (29%) of incidents with gang members involved.

6. Because the same cases can appear in both the member and motive categories, statistical tests would be inappropriate.

7. That is, those with gang members involved but without gang motives expressed as the cause of the incident.

8. Using a database maintained by the LAPD homicide unit, Meehan and O'Carroll (1992) found a much lower rate of narcotics involvement in gang-motivated homicides. "Gang motive" was entered by detectives in 345 of the 2,162 homicides occurring between January 1, 1986, and August 31, 1988. Only 18 of the 345 homicides also were coded positively by detectives as "narcotics involved." Meehan and O'Carroll examined investigation files on a subset (adolescent victims who died in South Central Los Angeles in a 20-month period) of the homicides in the LAPD database and report similar results. Although the number of gang-motive homicides we identified would be reduced by limitation to only those cases with clear *confirmation* of the gang motive (available in about 60% of the 128 homicides with gang motives mentioned in our data set), this would still not account for the much lower figure reported by Meehan and O'Carroll.

Estimating the National Scope of Gang Crime From Law Enforcement Data

G. DAVID CURRY
RICHARD A. BALL
SCOTT H. DECKER

Arriving at national estimates of the level of gang crime has been the cumulative product of a series of surveys extending over twenty years. With no Uniform Crime Report (UCR) data available on gang crimes, the results of these studies have been the only available national-level estimates of the scope of the problem. By viewing them as a cumulative process, their utility is greatly enhanced. The new information that is presented here is from a 1994 survey of law enforcement information on

AUTHORS' NOTE: This chapter was prepared under grants 93-IJ-CX-0040 and 94-IJ-CX-0066 from the National Institute of Justice. Points of view are those of the authors and do not necessarily represent the position of the U.S. Department of Justice. The authors are indebted to John McMullen, Mary Jo Ullom, Winnie Reed, Lorrie Hardy, Yolanda Gant, and Cathy McNeal for their assistance in the research from which this chapter is drawn.

gangs that is an extension of a 1992 national survey (Curry, Ball, & Fox, 1994). The methods used in both of these latter surveys are an extension of the methods used in the earlier surveys by Miller (1975, 1982), Needle and Stapleton (1983), and Spergel (Spergel & Curry, 1993). The utility of police statistics in understanding the scope of the nation's gang crime problems has been continually substantiated by the continuing work of Malcolm Klein, Cheryl Maxson, and their colleagues (Maxson, Gordon, & Klein, 1985; Maxson & Klein, 1990).

Over the 20 years that have produced these studies, the numbers produced by them have often served as a backdrop for research presentations and government reports but most frequently have been used as "scientific measures" of the magnitude of the national gang crime problem in media reports. In the media context, numbers of gangs and gang members are used alongside the temperature, barometric pressure, and a growing array of heat indices and chill indices. Such measures provide a kind of security that "experts" are keeping track of the problem. One of the goals of this chapter is replacing that false sense of security with an informed appreciation of how these numbers have come into being. Although we underscore the limitations of our understanding of the gang crime problem, we also want readers to become aware of how much our available awareness is limited to these numbers.

Foundations

Miller (1975, 1982) selected his study sites on the basis of population, the nature of local available information on gangs, and an effort to achieve "some order of regional representation." His first study included 12 cities; his second, 26 cities and two counties. Miller's studies differ from the 1992 and 1994 surveys in that Miller used multiple respondents at each site. His goal was to find a level of consensus on the presence of gang crime problems. Miller concluded that law-violating youth groups were present in all of the cities included in both of his studies. Of the 12 cities in Miller's 1975 survey, he identified 6 as having gang crime problems. In these cities, he estimated there to be 28,500 to 81,500 gang members involved in 760 to 2,700 gangs. In his expanded study, Miller identified 9 of the 26 cities as having gang problems. From his results,

Miller estimated that there were 97,940 gang members in 2,285 gangs in 286 U.S. cities.

In 1983, Jerome Needle and William Vaughan Stapleton published the results of their survey of 60 randomly selected cities with populations over 100,000. Although they produced no estimates of national or local statistics for gangs or gang members, their study was important to subsequent research because they conducted the first systematic analysis of official definitions of what constituted a gang, using five criteria derived from Miller's (1975, 1982) definition and an additional criterion for symbols worn or used by gangs and members. Presence of any one of the six criteria to identify gang problems constituted a local gang crime problem. In addition, whereas Miller used multiple respondents from within and outside law enforcement, Needle and Stapleton used only official respondents from police departments. Their use of law enforcement information presaged the studies on gangs using law enforcement data that would become central to understanding gangs, especially those of Maxson and Klein (Maxson et al., 1985; Maxson & Klein, 1990), Curry and Spergel (1988), and Block and Block (1992).

In 1988, as part of the Office of Juvenile Justice and Delinquency Prevention's (OJJDP) National Youth Gang Intervention and Suppression Research and Development Program, Spergel and Curry (1990, 1993) conducted a screening survey of sites in an attempt to identify "promising" responses to gang crime problems (Figure 2.1). Of 94 cities, 68 were identified, on the basis of contacts with law enforcement agencies, as having gang crime problems. From these cities, Spergel and his colleagues identified a population of sites and programs for further study as potentially promising sites. From survey data gathered from 35 law enforcement agencies within a larger respondent population, estimates of 120,636 gang members in 1,439 gangs were tabulated.

The 1992 survey of law enforcement agency antigang information resources was one of several National Institute of Justice (NIJ) efforts to produce national assessments of the gang crime problem (Figure 2.2). The survey encompassed officially identified respondents from law enforcement agencies in the 94 jurisdictions included in the 1988 OJJDP screening survey. The researchers (Curry et al., 1994) used a broad definition of *gang:* "For the purposes of this survey, to be counted as a gang, law enforcement officials had to identify the group as a 'gang' that was involved in criminal activity and included youth in its membership" (p. 2).

●   **Site with No Reported Problem**

☆   **Site Reporting Gang Problem**

Figure 2.1. Spergel's 1988 Survey Sites (N = 94)
NOTE: Data from Spergel and Curry (1993).

In 83 of these 94 cities, law enforcement agency representatives reported the presence of gang crime problems. The increase from 72.3% in
1988 to 88.3% in 1992 was statistically significant. Over the 5-year period,
the number of cities reporting gang crime problems had increased by
22.1%. Requesting only official statistics, the surveyors tabulated 3,274
gangs and 202,027 gang members in 68 sites. In addition to the cities
included in the 1988 OJJDP screening survey, the 1992 NIJ survey included 11 counties contacted in the OJJDP survey and 28 of the 79 largest U.S. cities not included in the earlier study (51 of the 79 largest U.S.
cities were included in the OJJDP screening survey). From the 79 largest U.S. cities, 43 smaller cities included in the OJJDP study, and 11
counties (133 total jurisdictions), the 1992 survey identified 121 jurisdictions with gang crime problems, 91% of the total. Reporting was not
consistent across sites; from 97 sites, 4,881 gangs and 249,324 gang
members were tabulated. From 59 sites, 46,359 gang-related crimes were

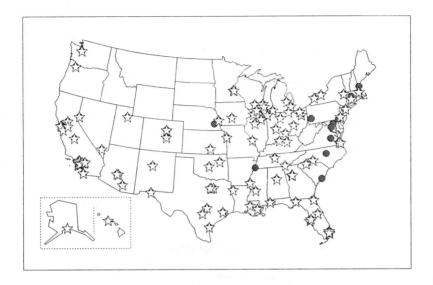

● **Site with No Reported Problem**

☆ **Site Reporting Gang Problem**

Figure 2.2. NIJ 1992 Survey Sites (*N* = 122)
NOTE: Data from Curry, Ball, and Fox (1994).

tabulated. This was the first tabulation of national gang statistics based only on official records. Still, even with this restriction, the national estimate of the number of gangs had increased from 1,439 gangs and 120,636 gang members in the 1988 OJJDP study to 4,881 gangs and 249,324 gang members in the 1992 study. This constituted a 239.2% increase in the national estimate of the number of criminally involved gangs and a 106.7% increase in the national estimate of the number of gang members.

Methodology of the 1994 Extended Survey

The 1994 extended national-level survey of law enforcement information on gang-related crime extended the 1992 NIJ survey in two ways:

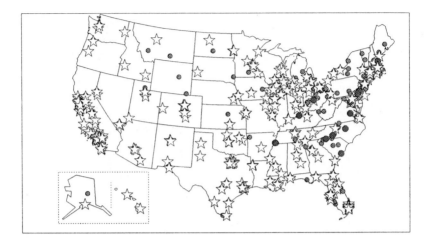

● **Site with No Reported Problem**

☆ **Site Reporting Gang Problem**

Figure 2.3. NIJ 1994 Survey Sites (*N* = 428)

Chronologically the study updated information on the 122 municipalities and 8 of the 11 counties included in the 1992 survey. The study was also extended geographically to include data on all U.S. cities ranging in population from 150,000 to 200,000 and to include a random sample of 284 of the 1,126 municipalities ranging in population from 25,000 to 200,000 (Figure 2.3).

As much as possible, the 1994 survey replicated procedures for gathering data used in the 1992 NIJ gang survey. Gang crime problems were defined in the same manner as in the 1992 NIJ survey where a gang

- Is identified by the police as a "gang"
- Participates in criminal activity
- Involves youth in its membership

The 1992 NIJ gang survey gathered information from the 79 largest U.S. cities and 43 smaller cities and 11 counties that were included in the

OJJDP national survey in 1988. To extend the 1992 survey systematically to encompass a broader geographic range of U.S. cities, the 1994 gang survey included all U.S. cities with populations over 150,000. All cities ($n = 76$) with more than 200,000 population were included in the 1992 survey, as were 17 cities with populations between 150,000 and 200,000. The additional 22 cities within that population range were contacted as new jurisdictions in the 1994 gang survey. A random sample of cities with populations between 25,000 and 150,000 was constructed. From 1,126 cities, 284 jurisdictions (25.2%) were selected. The 31 remaining smaller cities included in the 1992 study (17 were cities between 150,000 and 200,000 in population) were excluded from selection in this random sample.

As in the 1992 survey, a letter describing the nature of the survey was addressed to each law enforcement departmental administrator. For jurisdictions included in the 1992 survey, the letter repeated specific information that had been provided in response to the 1992 survey and identified the departmental representative who provided the 1992 data. Each letter was accompanied by a letter of support for the survey from an NIJ official. The senior law enforcement administrator, usually a chief of police or police commissioner, was asked to report whether or not a gang crime problem existed within the jurisdiction in 1994. If a problem was reported, the administrator was requested to identify a representative of the department to provide gang crime statistics and a representative who was most knowledgeable on antigang field operations. Sometimes, this was the same individual, but more often, separate departmental representatives were identified. Annual statistics on gang-related crime were then solicited from the departmental statistical representative.

In this chapter, we provide two sets of estimates of the national-level gang problem—one extremely conservative and the other reasonably larger. We characterize as conservative the technique employed in the analysis of the 1992 NIJ gang survey of following a methodology comparable to that used in the UCR for tabulating gang information. We characterize as reasonable an approach that generates statistical estimates to compensate for the underreporting in the previous method known to be associated with limits in information technology. A discussion of the sources of error affecting national-level estimates of gang crime problems follows and places both of our estimates within larger perspectives.

A Conservative Estimate of the
U.S. Gang Crime Problem

Neither the UCR nor the evolving National Incident Based Reporting System (NIBRS) includes information on gang-related crime. In the 1992 and 1994 NIJ gang surveys, an attempt was made to emulate data on gang-related crime if it was gathered in a manner comparable to UCR data. All available annual gang-related statistics were obtained from officially designated representatives of local law enforcement jurisdictions.

Interpreting the numbers on gang crime problems for the large U.S. cities under this approach is simple, straightforward, and conservative. There are 76 U.S. cities with populations over 200,000 (as recorded in the 1990 census). There are 39 U.S. cities with populations less than 200,000 and over 150,000. In the 1994 NIJ gang survey, we obtained available aggregate gang statistics from *all* 115 of these jurisdictions. Of the 76 cities with populations over 200,000, 68 report gang crime problems. (One of these jurisdictions, Washington, D.C., designates its problem as a "crew" problem and is discussed in more detail below.) Of these 68, 53 report the number of gangs; 46, the number of members; and 29, the number of incidents. The totals are 3,844 gangs; 196,587 gang members; and 26,731 gang crimes. Of the 39 cities with populations less than 200,000 and greater than 150,000, 34 report gang crime problems. Of these 34, 18 report the number of gangs; 18, the number of gang members; and 7, the number of gang crimes. The totals are 505 gangs, 10,698 gang members, and 10,382 gang crimes. Under the conservative approach, no adjustments or calculations are made in these numbers shown in Table 2.1.

There are 1,126 cities with populations between 25,000 and 150,000. For these cities, we have a random sample of 284 cities, or 25.2% of the population. This sample size provides estimates of the population parameters that fall within a 5% error range. Thus, our figures fall within standard ranges accepted in the social sciences. Of these cities, 56% report the presence of gang crime problems. Projecting from the sample to the entire population of 1,126 cities suggests that there are approximately 631 cities with populations between 25,000 and 150,000 that would report gang crime problems if asked. The 5% confidence interval produces an estimated range of 599 to 663 cities that would report gang crime problems for the designated population range.

TABLE 2.1 "Conservative" Estimate of National Gang Problem
From NIJ 1994 Extended Survey

Jurisdiction Size	Problem Reported (%)	Gangs 1993	Members 1993	Crimes 1993
Cities over 200,000[a]	89.5	3,844	196,587	26,731
Cities 150,000–200,000[a]	87.2	505	10,698	10,382
Cities 25,000–150,000[b]	56.0	2,193	25,620	8,497
1992 smaller cities[c]	87.1	165	10,636	1,284
Selected counties[d]	—	1,918	135,266	390,172
National total	57.0	8,625	378,807	437,066

NOTES: a. Tabulated from official reports.
    b. Estimated from 25.2% random sample.
    c. Tabulated from official reports from smaller cities included in Spergel and Curry (1993) and Curry, Ball, and Fox (1994).
    d. Tabulated from official reports from smaller cities included in Spergel and Curry (1993) and Curry, Ball, and Fox (1994). Members for Los Angeles County reduced 25% (Reiner, 1992).

If we assume that the reporting capacity of cities not surveyed is comparable to those surveyed (relatively low), it is possible to project what kinds of statistics would be obtained from contacting law enforcement agencies in all 1,126 cities. Applying the confidence intervals for our sample data produces conservative estimates of 2,193 (2,083 to 2,303) gangs, 25,620 (24,339 to 26,901) members, and 8,497 (8,072 to 8,922) gang crimes for cities ranging in population from 25,000 to 150,000.

In addition to data from all cities with populations over 200,000, all cities with populations between 150,000 and 200,000, and the sample of cities with populations between 25,000 and 150,000, we have data from 31 cities with populations under 150,000 that were identified as potential gang problem cities by Irving Spergel in the 1988 national gang survey (Spergel & Curry, 1993). In 1994, 87.1% of these cities reported the presence of a gang crime problem, substantially more than the 56% found in the random sample of cities of similar size. For this reason, we have treated these 31 cities as a distinct population with a greater likelihood of the reported presence of gang crime problems and higher levels of gangs, gang members, and gang-related crimes per city. Still, after having been included in at least three national-level studies of gang crime, we feel that the 165 gangs, 10,636 gang members, and 1,284 gang-related crimes for these cities must be included in any national estimate of gang crime problems. The same can be said for 8 of 11 counties included in the 1988 and 1992 national gang surveys that furnished data for the 1994 study, especially as one of these is Los Angeles County.

From these sources of data, shown in Table 2.1, it is possible to produce a conservative estimate for the scope of the U.S. gang crime problem as measured by local law enforcement records. Police departments in approximately 57% of all U.S. cities with populations over 25,000 report gang crime problems in 1994. The statistic is substantially higher (87.8%) for cities with populations over 150,000. Combining the estimates of 607 smaller cities with the known 102 larger jurisdictions reporting gang crime problems (68 over 200,000 population and 34 between 150,000 and 200,000 in population) and the 27 additional smaller cities with gang crime problems identified in the 1992 NIJ gang survey produces a national estimate of 760 jurisdictions with gang crime problems (5% confidence interval for smaller cities, 728 to 792 cities). This estimate compares favorably with Malcolm Klein's (1995c) estimate of "at least 800 gang cities" (p. 217), especially as Klein includes municipalities with populations under 25,000 in his computations.

Table 2.1 combines city data with data from eight counties (reducing the number of gang members reported for Los Angeles County by one fourth as suggested by Reiner, 1992), resulting in a conservative estimate of 8,625 gangs, 378,807 gang members, and 437,066 gang crimes for the U.S. in 1993 based on local law enforcement records. The degree to which the U.S. gang problem remains concentrated in larger cities is evident from Table 2.1.

A Reasonable Estimate of the U.S. Gang Crime Problem

The estimates of the 1992 NIJ national gang survey have been criticized for underestimating the magnitude of the U.S. gang crime problem. One way in which we know that the conservative estimates stated above are grossly underestimated results from jurisdictions with reported gang crime problems that do not produce annual tabulations of gang crime statistics. Under the conservative method of computing estimates used

TABLE 2.2 "Reasonable" Estimate of National Gang Problem
From NIJ 1994 Extended Survey

Jurisdiction Size	Gangs 1993	Members 1993	Crimes 1993
Cities over 200,000[a]	4,722	246,431	51,155
Cities 150,000–200,000[a]	788	19,478	46,616
Cities 25,000–150,000[b]	8,964	122,508	89,232
1992 smaller cities	251[a]	31,498[a]	3,156[c]
Selected counties[d]	1,918	135,266	390,172
National total	16,643	555,181	580,331

NOTES: a. 5% trimmed means substituted for jurisdictions with reported gang crime problems but not reporting annual statistics.
   b. Estimated from 25.2% random sample with 5% trimmed means substituted for jurisdictions with reported gang crime problems but not reporting annual statistics.
   c. Minimum number of incidents substituted for jurisdictions with reported gang crime problems but not reporting annual statistics; insufficient cases to compute trimmed means.
   d. Tabulated from official reports from smaller cities included in Spergel and Curry (1993) and Curry, Ball, and Fox (1994). Members for Los Angeles County reduced 25% (Reiner, 1992).

in the 1992 NIJ gang survey and above, jurisdictions that produce no annual statistics make no contribution to the national estimates of gangs, gang members, and gang-related crimes. Rather than count these jurisdictions as having zero gangs, zero gang members, or zero gang crimes, a more reasonable approach is to substitute some statistical estimate for the zero values used in the conservative approach. We have selected the 5% trimmed mean (Hoaglin, Mosteller, & Tukey, 1983) for each population level as a substitute for the zero values used above to produce the more "reasonable" estimates provided in Table 2.2. The trimmed mean is a robust measure in that it excludes the highest and lowest 5% of values from computations. For instance, in computing the 5% trimmed mean for gang members in cities over 200,000 population, Los Angeles and Chicago, with the highest numbers of tabulated gang members (61,362 and 35,000 respectively), and Virginia Beach and Tampa (25 and 67 respectively) were all excluded from the computations.

The capacity to report gang crime statistics was significantly related to city size, with 68.2% of cities over 200,000 population reporting the number of gang members, 52.9% of cities between 150,000 and 200,000 reporting this statistic, and only 4.4% of cities between 25,000 and 150,000 reporting it. The comparable range for numbers of gang crimes is 42.4% in the largest cities and 2.3% in the smallest cities. The revised estimates generate smaller increases where reporting was already most complete—22.8% for the number of gangs and 25.4% for the number of gang members in the largest cities. The greatest increases emerge where reporting capacity is lowest—a 950% increase in the number of gang-related crimes in the smallest cities. Using this method, there is a 46.6% increase in the estimate of gang members and a 32.8% increase in the estimate of gang-related crimes. The enhanced estimate of 555,181 gang members is comparable to Klein's (1995c, p. 217) estimate of half a million gang members; the number of gangs (16,643) is substantially larger than Klein's estimate of 10,000.

Sources of Error in
Law Enforcement Statistics

Although we have adjusted our national estimates to overcome one kind of known error—the absence of annual tabulations in many jurisdictions—other kinds of known error have to be acknowledged. At the simplest level, errors in antigang information can to some extent be traced to technological limitations. Jurisdictions with newly identified gang crime problems were often eager to report a computer system to record gang members and gang crimes. Although enhanced information technology can undoubtedly facilitate data collection and reporting, such technology is not in itself a complete answer to information needs. The 1992 NIJ national survey's analysis of information resources in a smaller subset of jurisdictions revealed that computer technology alone does not necessarily result in more accessible gang crime statistics. Still, of 109 law enforcement agencies recording gang crime information, 50% of agencies with computerized systems provided annual tabulations of gangs, gang members, and gang-related crimes, whereas only 20% of agencies with manual systems reported such complete statistics (Curry, 1995).

The major sources of error in conducting national assessments of gang crime problems are matters of policy, not technology. National-level policy making requires statistics that make it possible to assess the level of gang crime problems (Howell, 1994). Compiling aggregate statistical information on gang crime is not the major function for which local law enforcement data bases are designed. Invariably, law enforcement develops and maintains information resources on gang crime for the purpose of tracking and apprehending individual gang offenders. Hence, in asking law enforcement agencies to provide gang crime statistics for use by policy makers at the national level in responding to gang crime, we are asking local law enforcement representatives to provide us with a service that they may not routinely provide for local assessment and policy making. Although it has been argued that the most useful gang crime statistic for policy assessment is gang-related crimes, the most available statistics are numbers of gangs and gang members (Curry et al., 1994). To a large extent, the imbalance in the availability of statistics on gang-related crimes and gang members is a function of this difference in purpose.

Definitions remain a major source of error that cannot be easily controlled (Ball & Curry, 1995). Maxson and Klein (1990) demonstrated well the statistical implications of applying the Chicago and the Los Angeles definitions of a gang incident to Los Angeles gang homicide data. Imposing the Chicago definition on Los Angeles homicide data reduces the gang homicide statistic for Los Angeles by approximately half. Curry (1994), applying the Los Angeles definition to a broader range of offenses for a population of Chicago youths, found that the estimated number of gang-related crimes tripled. Analyses that apply more uniform definitions will continue to be a central requirement for developing reliable national-level estimates of gang-related crime problems.

Organizational changes also have an impact on the availability of gang information from year to year. In reporting to the 1992 NIJ national survey, the New York City Police Department included only crimes committed by Asian gangs. At that time, only Asian gangs were the object of concern for the gang crime unit. African American and Latin "drug organizations" were under the jurisdiction of the narcotics unit. By 1994, New York City officials developed a new system for identifying gang-related crimes and incidents that included African American and Latin gang crime. What was formerly identified as Asian gang crime is now statistically classified as part of "organized crime." In another city, the formation of a gang crime unit during our study nullified the approval previously granted by the police chief for reporting data to study staff.

In other cities, changes in personnel assignments interrupted gang statistical reporting practices. Such changes were sometimes at administrative levels and sometimes at operational levels. By gathering data at
two points in time (1992 and 1994), we have become aware that almost
as many cities lost the capacity to report annual gang crime statistics as
gained the capacity.

Perhaps the most uncontrollable source of error is the political nature
of jurisdictional responses to gang-related crimes (Huff, 1989). The number of the largest U.S. cities reporting gang crime problems in 1994 was
smaller than those reporting such problems in 1992. For all cities surveyed at the two points in time, the changes are interesting. In 1994, gang
crime problems were reported in five new cities where none were
reported in 1992. These were Baltimore; Raleigh; Pittsburgh; Lincoln,
Nebraska; and Springfield, Massachusetts. Baltimore had reported a
drug organization problem in 1992. Raleigh reported a "posse" problem
in 1992. Springfield had reported a problem to the OJJDP survey in 1988
but reported that the problem had disappeared by 1992. Cities that had
reported gang crime problems in 1992 that reported no problems in 1994
are Akron; Charlotte; Columbus, Ohio; Louisville; Philadelphia; and
Spartansburg, South Carolina.

Recommendations for enhanced information technology resources
and greater federal coordination of efforts to collect gang crime information date back to Miller's (1975, 1982) first national-level studies and
inspired the OJJDP's (1994) response, resulting in the creation of the
National Youth Gang Center (Institute for Intergovernmental Research,
1995) in Tallahassee, Florida. A recommendation of the 1992 NIJ national
survey (Curry et al., 1994) was that a field identifying incidents as "gang
related" be incorporated into the implementation of NIBRS by the FBI.
Until a long-term coordinated federal effort to collect gang crime information is in place, the national surveys of law enforcement agencies
reviewed in this chapter will remain the *only* source of estimates of the
changing nature of the U.S. gang crime problem.

Trends in National Survey Results

Until improved statistics on gang-related crime replace the national
survey approach, it is useful to take an overview of what trends emerge

TABLE 2.3   Measures of Magnitude of Gang Problem From National-Level
Surveys, 1976–1994

Survey	Gang Cities[a]	Gangs	Members	Crimes
Miller, 1975	6	1,730	55,000	N/P
Miller, 1982[b]	9	2,285	97,940	N/P
Needle & Stapleton, 1983	27	N/P	N/P	N/P
Spergel & Curry, 1988	68	1,439	120,636	N/P
Curry, Ball, & Fox, 1992	110	4,881	249,324	46,359
Curry, Ball, & Decker, 1994[c]	282	8,625	378,807	437,066

NOTES: Dates listed are for surveys not publications.
    N/P = Not provided.
    a. Specific cities identified are provided for comparability.
    b. Numbers of gangs and members are statistical estimates.
    c. Conservative numbers are provided for comparability.

from 20 years of such studies. Without question, assessments of the national magnitude of gang crime problems have followed upward trends. To some extent, Table 2.3 reflects the increase in survey breadth as well as increased perception of the national-level scope of gang crime problems. The increasing numbers of gang crime cities identified by name in the national surveys from 1975 to 1994 reflects an increased perception of the spread of the gang problem by those planning the surveys. But beyond this, we believe that the perceptions that led to larger numbers of cities being included in each subsequent survey reflects a greater perceived presence of gang crime problems over the 20-year period. Likewise, the increase from the six gang cities that were identified in Miller's 1975 survey to the 282 gang cities identified by the 1994 NIJ national survey constitutes a real expansion of the national gang crime problem as it is reported by local law enforcement. The estimate of a total of 760 gang crime jurisdictions nationwide produced from the 1994 national survey supports the conclusions of Spergel (1989, 1995) and Klein (1995c) that there has been a geographic spread of gang crime problems in the United States.

Of the other numbers used to measure changes in the national gang crime problem, we believe that the least important one is the number of gangs. We know that in cities with emerging gang crime problems, such as St. Louis, gangs are loosely organized, and continual changes in the number of gangs are indicative of the collective and contagious nature of gang behavior (Decker & Van Winkle, 1996); and even in cities with chronic gang crime problems, such as Chicago, once-powerful gangs can eventually become relatively unimportant parts of the gang crime problem (Toobin, 1994). The other two measures, number of members and number of gang-related crimes, however, merit more attention.

Number of members has a double importance. On one hand, it is a measure by law enforcement of the number of "at-risk" youth whose lives have been touched by gang crime problems. The number of gang members reflects individual youths who either are or *potentially* are offenders or victims in gang-related violence. With alleged national increases in violence by juveniles, these numbers are suggestive of the role that gang organization may play in those increases and the associated costs in young lives. On the other hand, these numbers reflect the criminalization of large numbers of poor, predominantly minority youths. Losing youths to prison is almost as much of a threat to their communities and families as losing them to gang violence. Regardless of how the finding is interpreted, the approximately half million youth officially identified as gang members by police is a sobering national statistic.

The final statistic, number of gang-related crimes, is the one that has been most neglected in law enforcement record keeping. The absence of estimates of gang crime from earlier surveys is predominantly a reflection of law enforcement policy rather than neglect by researchers. We believe that this statistic is the most important one for assessing the magnitude of gang crime problems at national and local levels. "Number of gangs" measures organizational changes that may have varying effects on the magnitude of gang crime, and "number of members" may in part reflect criminal justice labeling, but each counted gang-related crime reflects an actual violation of law that is associated with gang involvement. For violent and property crimes, each offense represents a victim or victims as well as an offender. As noted above, there must be careful control for variations in definition across jurisdiction and time in analyzing gang incident data, but we argue that the national conservative measure (and local measure from which it was aggregated) of 437,066 and the statistical estimate of 580,331 gang-related crimes for 1993 make excellent starting points for assessing the seriousness of the gang problem in years to come.

PART 2

Behavioral, Ecological, and Socioeconomic Dimensions

3

Gangs, Drugs, and Neighborhood Change

JEFFREY FAGAN

Gangs and the Urban Crisis

Youth gangs have been part of the urban landscape of North America for well over 200 years. In the late 18th century, gangs such as the Fly Boys, the Smith's Vly gang, and the Bowery Boys were well known in the streets of New York City.[1] As European immigration increased in the early 19th century, gangs such as the Kerryonians (from County Kerry in Ireland) and the Forty Thieves formed in the overcrowded slums of the Lower East Side. Gangs proliferated quickly in that time, with such colorful names as the Plug Uglies, the Roach Guards, the Hide-Binders (comprised mainly of butchers), the Old Slippers (a group of shoemakers' apprentices) and the Shirt Tails.

Illegal income also was a central feature of early gang life, including the illegal trade in alcohol. Many of these gangs were born in the corner groceries that were the business and social centers of the neighborhoods. These groceries also hid the groggeries that were important features of neighborhood life, and guarding them provided a steady income for the gangs. Although not involved in theft, robbery, or the "unsavory" professions of gambling or tavern keeping, these gangs warred regularly over territory with weapons including stones and early versions of the blackjack (Sante, 1991). They occasionally joined forces to defend their neighborhood, and nearly all were united in their opposition to the police.

Throughout the 19th century, gangs emerged in the large cities of the Northeast and in Chicago and other industrial centers of the Midwest. In the early 20th century, gangs also formed in the Mexican immigrant communities of California and the Southwest (Bogardus, 1943). Wherever neighborhoods in large cities were in transition, gangs emerged. The 1,300 street gangs identified by Thrasher (1927/1963) were located in the economically disadvantaged neighborhoods of industrial Chicago in the 1920s. Thrasher interpreted the rise of Chicago's gangs as symptoms of the deteriorating neighborhoods and shifting populations that accompanied the industrialization of the city, and the changing populations that lived in the interstitial areas between the central city and the industrial regions that ringed it.

Like their counterparts in New York and Philadelphia, the Chicago gangs were composed of children of European immigrants, mostly from Poland, Italy, and Ireland, as well as Germany, Russia, and Sweden. Thrasher identified fewer than 8% of the gangs as "Negro," and none were Hispanic. Although ethnic gangs of European descent persisted through the 1960s, gangs composed of African American and Puerto Rican adolescents emerged in the large cities in the years following World War II.

Until the 1970s, the term *gang* was synonymous with the large urban centers of New York, Chicago, Philadelphia, and Los Angeles. That is no longer the case today. Gangs now are present in large and small cities in nearly every state. By 1992, police departments in over 85% of the nation's 250 largest cities reported the presence of street gangs (Klein, 1995a). Gangs today reflect the ethnic and racial diversity of U.S. society. New gangs have formed in small cities in Texas, in the midsize cities of California, and in urban areas throughout the South and the Midwest. Fundamental changes in gangs have accompanied their emergence. Gang members today are likely to remain in the gang longer. Although limited in the past to adolescents, gangs today may range in age from preteen "wanna-bes" to young adults who may remain active beyond their 30th birthday (Klein, 1995a; Moore, 1991).

Traditionally, stealing and other petty economic crimes were the backbone of gang economic life.[2] For some contemporary gangs, however, entrepreneurial goals, especially involving drug selling, have replaced the cultural goals of ethnic solidarity and neighborhood defense that historically motivated gang participation and activities. A few gangs have loose but functional ties to adult organized crime groups (Chin, 1990, 1995a). A few others have become involved in drug selling and developed corporate structures that have replaced the organizations that in the past regulated gang life (see, e.g., Taylor, 1990a, 1990b; but see Moore, 1991).

Gangs no longer are the colorful, turf-oriented groups of adolescents from immigrant or poor neighborhoods. Whereas gangs in the past were likely to claim street corners as their turf, gangs today may invoke the concept of turf to stake claims to shopping malls, skating rinks, school corridors, or even cliques of women. Gangs use graffiti and "tagging" to mark turf and communicate news and messages to other gangs and gang members (Huff, 1989, 1994). The participation and roles of young women in gangs have also changed. Through the 1960s, women were involved in gangs either as auxiliaries or branches of male gangs, or as weapons carriers and decoys for male gang members (Campbell, 1990b). Today, female gangs have emerged that are independent of male gangs, and fighting is common among the new female gangs (Campbell, 1990b; Klein, 1995a). There also is some evidence of sexually integrated gangs, where females fight alongside males (Taylor, 1993).

Gang violence also has changed over the past quarter century. Violence always has been a staple of gang life; fights were common between gangs or between members of a gang. Fights often were rites of initiation or part of the gang's identity and style. But gang violence has become more lethal in the past decade. For nearly 20 years, starting in the mid-1970s, police records show that gang homicides have increased steadily in Chicago, Los Angeles, and the smaller cities surrounding these gang centers (Klein, 1995a). Although making precise estimates is complicated by the different ways that gangs are defined and data are collected, the increase in lethal violence may reflect the increasing number and firepower of weapons available to gang members. Yet, although gang violence has increased, and gang members continue to be heavily involved in violent acts and other crimes, violence also has increased among nongang youth in the same cities and neighborhoods. Many of these changes in gangs have been diffused into the popular culture through films, music, language and dress styles, and the news media.

Changes in gangs have occurred simultaneously with rapid changes in the social and economic structure of cities and suburbs (Bursik & Grasmick, 1993; Fagan, 1992a, 1992b; Hagedorn, 1988). The expansion of illegal markets and participation of gangs in them, the rise of gangs in small cities as well as large ones, the increasing lethality of gang violence, and the emergence of gangs in small cities are developments that have changed basic knowledge about gangs. What has been poorly understood, however, are the links between changes in gangs and changes in neighborhoods and communities. In this chapter, recent research is reviewed to describe and explain these links. In particular, I analyze the hierarchical influences of political economy, social structure, and neighborhood change as influences on contemporary gangs.

Gangs and Ganging

TYPES OF GANGS

Heterogeneity between and within gangs has been evident in gang research for over 75 years. Styles of gang membership and gang behaviors vary as do types of gangs. Beginning with Thrasher (1927/1963), gang research has distinguished between "entrepreneurial" gangs concerned with increasing their income through extortion and drug selling, and fighting gangs concerned primarily with increasing their status through violence. These types have been refined and elaborated in various studies.

Cloward and Ohlin (1960) studied gangs in New York City in the 1950s and argued that the type of gang that emerges depends on the balance of legal and illegal opportunities in the surrounding community. *Criminal subcultures* involve gang activity that produces income through illegal means in communities where the gang is well integrated with neighborhood residents. But *conflict subcultures* arise in neighborhoods where the gang is not well integrated with neighbors and where both legal and illegal income opportunities are scarce. Gangs in the conflict subculture are more likely to be violent and to use violence to attain status in the group and in the neighborhood. *Retreatist subcultures* involve gangs with members who, despite living in areas where adolescents are well integrated with neighborhood residents, have failed in both illegal and illegal activities. Other retreatist subcultures arise in socially disorganized areas when the gangs fail to achieve status through violence or illegal activities. Cloward and Ohlin contend that these gangs are burdened with the label of "double failure," and they often retreat into heavy drug use (p. 179).

Yet, gang research in other cities has not confirmed the typology offered by Cloward and Ohlin (1960). Short and Strodtbeck (1965/1974), studying Chicago gangs in the 1960s, failed to find either retreatist gangs or criminal subcultures. Hagedorn (1988) studied gangs in Milwaukee in the 1980s and found that they were nearly all "fighting," or conflict gangs. Taylor (1990a, 1990b), studying Detroit gangs in the 1980s, identified three types of gangs. *Scavenger gangs,* which are organizationally unstable and seem to have few goals, are involved in a variety of impulsive petty crimes. *Territorial gangs* seek control of neighborhood and "turf," both for defense from outsiders and for protection of their income-producing activities. They have a discernable leadership structure and share both economic and territorial interests. *Organized, or corporate, gangs* have elaborate and cohesive leadership structures. These gangs exist only to make money, and they mimic businesses in their rules and group dynamics. Instead of turf, they claim markets that may be quite spread out geographically.

In my (Fagan, 1989) research in Chicago, Los Angeles, and San Diego in the 1980s, I identified four types of gangs that were similar to those in Taylor's (1990a, 1990b) typology. Instead of scavenger gangs, I identified *party gangs,* mainly involved in drinking and drug use as well as drug sales, and *social gangs,* which used drugs and committed numerous petty crimes. I also found other gang types (*delinquent gangs, young organizations*) that resembled the territorial and corporate gangs described by Taylor. I noted consistent patterns of the four gang types across the three cities.

Gangs also may evolve over time from one type to another. Some gangs evolved from the break dancing and drill teams that were popular in African American communities in the early 1980s. More recently, conflict and fighting between "tagger" (graffiti) groups suggests their possible development into street gangs (Klein, 1995a). Some of Taylor's (1990a) scavenger gangs evolved into territorial gangs, and some territorial gangs evolved into corporate gangs. Padilla (1992) described the evolution of the "Diamonds," a pseudonym for a Chicago gang, from a street-corner group whose main interests were music and partying, to a fighting gang that also was entrepreneurial. Following the killing of one member by members of a neighborhood gang, the Diamonds consciously decided to use violence to protect their interests and themselves. Later on, some members began selling drugs to increase the gang's income, and the Diamonds developed a formal organizational structure to strengthen their economic and self-defense interests.

YOUTH GANG VIOLENCE

Although violence always has been intrinsic to gang life, data on gang homicides suggest that gang violence has increased. The broader societal problems of youth violence cannot be explained simply by the proliferation of gangs or the involvement of gangs in drug selling, however. The absence of comparable data across periods and locales, as well as the difficulties of classifying gang crimes as gang related, complicates efforts to determine whether the new gang cities have produced higher rates of gang violence. Nevertheless, data on gang homicides in Los Angeles and Chicago suggest real increases, however difficult it may be to measure them.

Not all gang violence is connected with selling drugs or other economic transactions, nor are drug selling and violence causally related within gangs. Moore (1978, 1991, 1992) and Chin (1990, 1995a) found no connection between gang violence and drug dealing among Chicano and Chinese gangs respectively. The African American Milwaukee gangs studied by Hagedorn (1988) and the white gangs in Boston studied by MacLeod (1987) were involved both in violence and (to some extent) in drug selling, but their violence was mostly unrelated to drug selling. Historically, gang violence was evident long before drug selling was a major income source for gangs and gang members.

Several factors may account for the apparent increase in lethal gang violence. First, as the upper age range of gang members expands, the participation of older gang members may contribute to violence. Violence rates increase throughout adolescence, and elevated rates of certain forms of violence—robbery, for example—continue into the early adult years before declining (Farrington, 1985). The involvement of older gang members at ages when they may be more likely to use violence may contribute to overall violence rates. Second, the higher rates of violence between and within gangs may reflect changing community contexts where gangs are active. In socially and economically isolated communities where the exits from gang life are truncated, social controls are weak and gangs may be poorly integrated into communities. Instrumental violence such as robberies by gang members provide a source of income, especially when formal or legal income sources may be unavailable. The social disorganization of the community may also weaken its ability to regulate gangs, removing the social restraints on gang violence.

Third, despite the absence of reliable data, there is broad agreement that the number and firepower of weapons available to gang members has increased. Gang members report that they steal guns from homes or other gun carriers, they buy guns from drug sellers who are trading up in firepower, or they buy them from a vast informal economy of guns (Sheley, Wright, & Smith, 1993). The presence of guns has contributed to changes in the lethality of violence; guns become a part of strategic decisions in settling disputes and challenges to "respect" and "honor" (Klein, 1995a). Guns are carried for self-defense or protection by many gang members, who perceive that others are armed and willing to use their weapons over the smallest interpersonal slight. Thus, some lethal violence is preemptive (Fagan & Wilkinson, in press-a, in press-b).

The need to present a self that is powerful and impenetrable has become an important but dangerous method of commanding respect, honor, or economic advantage (Anderson, 1994; Canada, 1995; Oliver, 1994). Skewed conceptions of power and masculinity have developed in these contexts, fueling a violent response to disputes. Violence and material wealth receive exaggerated attention as the influences of family, work, or school weaken in increasingly poor communities. The strategic importance of violence grows as the isolation of communities increases, cutting off both gang members' exits from gang life and the tempering influences of the broader society.

Nevertheless, violence often is very controlled and used only strategically between many gangs. The corporate gangs in Detroit use violence selectively to enforce organizational discipline or maintain selling territories (Taylor, 1990a). There is little expressive violence or use of violence to attain status in the gang. Chinese gangs are tightly controlled with strong leadership in a complex social order (Chin, 1995a; Chin & Fagan, 1994). Violence that is not sanctioned through the gang's leadership may lead to punishment or expulsion for jeopardizing the gang's extortion rackets or other business activities.

GANGS AND DRUGS

Drinking and Drug Use

Few phenomena have been stereotyped as easily as gangs, violence, and drug use, especially when they are taken in conjunction. Drug and alcohol use have always been a part of gang life, as has peddling of small quantities of whatever street drugs are popular at the time. Alcohol and marijuana have always been, and continue to be, the most widely used substances among both gang and nongang youth (Fagan, 1989, 1990; Sheley et al., 1993). Drinking and other drugs (primarily marijuana) consistently are mentioned as a common part of gang life throughout the gang literature. For instance, Short and Strodtbeck's (1965/1974) study of Chicago gangs showed that drinking was the second most common activity of gang members of all races, exceeded only by hanging out on the street corner. Although cocaine may be trafficked by many gang members, it is not often used in either its powder or smokable forms (Fagan, 1993).

Ethnographic studies of gang life also show the commonplace occurrence of drinking and its place in a broad pattern of substance use.[3] Dolan and Finney (1984) and Campbell (1990b) illustrated the commonplace role of drug use in gang life among both males and females. Stumphauzer, Veloz, and Aiken (1981) noted that use patterns varied within and between Los Angeles gangs and changed for individuals over time. MacLeod (1987) noted high rates of drinking among white gang members but only occasional beer use among the Brothers, a predominantly black (but somewhat integrated) gang. Sanchez-Jankowski (1991) found that all members of all gangs drank regularly, using gang proceeds for collective purchases. Although they used drugs in varying patterns, alcohol was mentioned consistently. But Sanchez-Jankowski also mentioned that the Irish gangs least often used illicit drugs, because access was controlled by nonwhites who they did not want to engage in business with.

Vigil (1988b) described a variety of meanings and roles of substances among Chicano gang members in East Los Angeles, from social "lubricant" during times of collective relaxation to facilitator for observance of ritual behaviors such as *locura* acts of aggression or violence. In these contexts, drug use provided a means of social status and acceptance as well as mutual reinforcement, and was a natural social process of gang life.[4] Vigil noted how gang members prepared for imminent fights with other gangs by drinking and smoking PCP-laced cigarettes. During social gatherings, the gang members used the same combinations to "kick back" and feel more relaxed among one another. Evidently, gang members had substantial knowledge about the effects of alcohol (and its reactivity to PCP), and they had developed processes to adjust their reactions to the mood and behaviors they wanted.

Feldman, Mandel, and Fields (1985) observed three distinct styles among Latino gangs in San Francisco that in part were determined by the role and meaning of substances in gang social processes. The "fighting" style included males in gangs who were antagonistic toward other gangs. They aggressively responded to any perceived move into their turf by other gangs or any outsider. Drinking and drug use were evident among these gangs but was only situationally related to their violence through territoriality. Violence occurred in many contexts unrelated to drug use or selling and was an important part of the social process of gang affiliation. The "entrepreneurial" style included youth who were concerned with attaining social status by means of money and the things money can buy. They very often were active in small-scale illegal sales of marijuana, pill amphetamines, and PCP. Although fighting and violence were part of this style, it was again situationally motivated by concerns over money or drugs. The last style was evident in gangs whose activities were social and recreational, with little or no evidence of fighting or violence but high rates of drinking and marijuana use.

Padilla (1992), studying a Puerto Rican gang in Chicago, described how alcohol and marijuana often accompanied the rituals of induction and expulsion of gang members. These ceremonies often were tearful and emotional, with strong references to ethnic solidarity. Padilla described how emotions intensified as the ceremony progressed, and drinking was a continuous process during the events.

My (Fagan, 1989) study of gangs in three cities showed diverse patterns of drug and alcohol use among gang members, and differences in the drug-violence relationships between gangs. Heavy drug and alcohol use, but with low levels of gang crime or violence, were reported by two types of gangs. These two types were differentiated only by their involvement in drug selling. Two other gang types used heavy drugs extensively and also were extensively involved in violence. Again, these two gang types also were differentiated by their involvement in drug selling.

Drinking or drug use also is disallowed in some youth gangs, regardless of the gang's involvement in drug selling, especially when it may interfere with drug "business." Chin (1990) found that intoxication was rejected entirely by Chinese gangs in New York City. They used violence to protect their business territories from encroachment by other gangs and to coerce their victims to participate in the gang's ventures. But "angry" violence was rare; violent transactions were limited to instrumental attacks on other gangs. Taylor (1990a) and Mieczkowski (1986) described organizations of adolescent drug sellers in Detroit that prohibited drug use among their members but tolerated drinking. Leaders in these groups were wary of threats to efficiency and security if street-level sellers were high and to the potential for co-optation of business goals if members became involved with consumption of the goods. The gangs were organized around income, and saw drug use (but not alcohol) as detracting from the selling skills and productivity of its members. Expulsion from the gang resulted from breaking this rule, but other violent reprisals also were possible. Gangs in both studies accepted recreational use of substances by members, primarily alcohol, marijuana, and cocaine in social situations not involved with dealing.

In Mieczkowski's (1986) study, the sellers particularly found danger in being high on any drug while on the job, and superiors in the gang enforced the prohibition against heroin use while working by denying runners their consignment and accordingly shutting off their source of income. Violence was occasionally used by superiors (crew bosses) to enforce discipline. Gang members looked down on their heroin-using customers, despite having tried it at some point in their lives, which in part explains the general ideology of disapproval of heroin use.

Buford (1991) depicted crowd violence between loosely knit bands of English football "supporters" as an inevitable consequence of the setting of football matches and the dynamics of crowds of youth. Expectancies of both intoxication and violence preceded the arrival of the "lads" at drinking locations surrounding the stadiums. The expectancies were played out in crowd behavior through rituals that were repeated before each match. Alcohol consumption before and during episodes of unrestrained crowd violence was an integral part of the group dynamic, but Buford does not attribute to alcohol either an excuse function or being a necessary ingredient for relaxation of social norms. In fact, he pointedly notes that the heaviest drinkers were incapacitated by inebriation and were ineffective rioters, whereas the crowd leaders were relatively light drinkers. In this context, alcohol was central but hardly necessary to the attainment of the expected behavior, and the setting itself provided the context and cues for violence.[5]

Drug Selling

Selling small amounts of drugs, especially marijuana, also has been a common feature of gang life for decades. But the cocaine and crack crises of the 1980s created opportunities for gang and nongang youth alike to participate in drug selling and increase their incomes. There is little evidence that gang members have become involved in drug selling more than nongang adolescents. Klein and his colleagues, based on police arrest reports following the appearance of crack in Los Angeles in 1985, found no evidence that gang members were arrested more often than non-gang members for crack sales or that drug-related homicides were more likely to involve gang members than non-gang members (Klein, Maxson, & Cunningham, 1991; Maxson & Klein, 1989).

Among gangs, involvement in the drug trade varies by locale and ethnicity. Chicano gangs in Los Angeles do not sell cocaine but sell small quantities of other drugs (Moore, 1991, 1992; Vigil, 1988a). The crack and cocaine trades in that city are dominated by African American youth, both gang members and nongang youth (Quicker et al., 1992). Crack sales only recently began in Chicago, more than 5 years after Los Angeles gangs began selling drugs. As in Los Angeles, both gang and nongang youth are involved. Crack sales in New York flourished beginning in 1986, but there was no discernable street gang structure that participated in drug selling (Fagan, 1993; Williams, 1989). Instead, loosely affiliated selling crews provided an organizational structure for drug sales (Johnson, Williams, Dei, & Sanabria, 1990). Chinese gangs have remained outside the cocaine and crack trades (Chin, 1990, 1995a), although their members (but not the gangs themselves) have been involved in transporting or guarding heroin shipments from Asia.

Not all gang members sell drugs even in gangs where drug selling is common. Drug-selling cliques within gangs are responsible for gang drug sales. These cliques are organized around gang members who have contacts with drug wholesalers or importers. Among the Diamonds, Padilla (1992) describes how drug selling is a high-status role reserved for gang members who have succeeded at the more basic economic tasks of stealing and robbery. Despite public images of gang members using drug profits for conspicuous consumption of luxury items, drug incomes in fact are quite modest for gang members who sell drugs. Drug incomes are shared within the gang, but the bulk of the profits remain with the clique or gang member who brought the drugs into the gang. The profits from drug selling, combined with the decline in economic exits from gang life, provides some incentive for older gang members to remain in the gang.

Despite the historically uneven relationship between gangs and drug use or selling (Fagan, 1989, 1993; Klein, 1995a; Spergel, 1989, 1995), recent studies contend that the lucrative and decentralized crack markets in inner cities have created a new generation of youth gangs (Skolnick, Correl, Navarro, & Rabb, 1988; Taylor, 1990b). Young drug sellers in these gangs have been portrayed as ruthless entrepreneurs, highly disciplined and coldly efficient in their business activities, and often using violence selectively and instrumentally in the service of profits. This vision of urban gangs suggests a sharp change from the gangs of past decades, and much of the change is attributed to the dynamics of the smokable cocaine market.

But empirical research suggests a different view (Fagan, 1989, 1993; Hagedorn, 1988; Klein et al., 1991; Moore, 1992; Padilla, 1992; Vigil, 1988a; Waldorf, 1992). Drug selling has always been a part of gang life, with diverse meanings tied to specific contexts and variable participation by gangs and gang members (Fagan, in press). For example, I (Fagan, 1989) found diverse patterns of drug selling within and across three cities with extensive, intergenerational gang traditions, and Klein et al. (1991) reported variability within and across Los Angeles gangs in crack selling.[6]

The variability in gang participation in drug use or selling within and across cities suggests that communities vary with respect to their drug markets and the violence that accompanies drug selling. Because gangs have emerged recently in many small cities and gangs in larger cities have expanded or intensified their involvement in drug selling, we also should expect *community change* to explain changes in gang behaviors (Bursik & Grasmick, 1993; Fagan, 1993; Klein, 1995a; Jackson, 1991; Reiss, 1986b; Shannon, 1986).

What changes have occurred in cities and communities that might explain variation and change in gang participation in drug selling? The social and economic restructuring of cities has reshaped neighborhoods and influenced the natural history of gangs, including the role of drugs within gangs. Two factors in particular have contributed to changes in gangs and the substitution of instrumental and monetary goals for the cultural or territorial affinities that unified gangs in earlier decades. First, cocaine markets changed dramatically in the 1980s, with sharp price reductions. Second, profound changes in the social and economic makeup of cities (Kasarda, 1989; Wacquant & Wilson, 1989) combined to disrupt social controls that in the past mediated gang behavior (Curry & Spergel, 1988). The interaction of these two trends provided ample opportunities for gangs to enter into the expanding cocaine economy of the 1980s. How these social and economic forces fostered gang involvement in drug selling are shown in the sections that follow.

MAKING MONEY

There is little reliable information on the economic lives of gang members. Recent studies have focused on gang members' involvement in drug selling, but for many gang members, drug selling is only part of a more complex dynamic of income and expenses (see, e.g., Padilla, 1992). Nevertheless, the importance of illegal work in the developmental sequences leading to gang initiation, gang "careers," and the exits from gang life are evident in ethnographic research on inner-city youth crime. Understanding the economic lives of gang members also requires a perspective beyond the rational economic perspective of costs, returns, and time allocation. It requires an understanding of the attractions of illegal work and its nonmonetary rewards, variables that often are unmeasured in quantitative studies on crime and work (Fagan, 1996;

Vicusi, 1986a, 1986b). Economists refer to these variables as tastes and preferences, and a detailed understanding of the motivations and rules of gang life are necessary to include them in a framework of the economic lives of gang members.

Very few studies of gang members provide systematic data on how gang members earn money. Milwaukee reported a wide range of drug incomes (Hagedorn, 1994a). Three in four of the 236 "founding members" of 14 male gangs (72%) had sold cocaine between 1987 and 1991. Of the 90 gang members interviewed, 73 were active drug sellers between 1987 and 1991. About one in four (28.7%) claimed they made no more money from drug selling than they could have made from legal work at the going rates for unskilled labor (about $6 per hour). One in five (20.7%) earned the equivalent of $7 to $12 per hour, and one in four (28.7%) reported drug incomes in the range of $13 to $25 per hour, or $2,000 to $4,000 per month. Few (3 of the 73 sellers) reported "crazy money" (more than $10,000 per month) at any time in their drug selling careers (202). Mean monthly drug sale income was $2,400, or about $15 per hour, compared to legal monthly incomes of $677.[7]

Recent ethnographic work illustrates how the abandonment of legal work has been accompanied by shifts in conceptions of work among young men and women in poor areas. Anderson (1990, 1994) describes how young males in inner-city Philadelphia regard the drug economy as a primary source of employment, and how their delinquent street networks are their primary sources of status and social control. Similar accounts were offered by Hagedorn (1988, 1994a, 1994b), Padilla (1992, 1993), Taylor (1990a, 1990b), and Moore (1991, 1992). Participants in the illegal economies in inner cities were engaged in a variety of income-producing crimes, including drug selling, fencing, auto theft, petty theft and fraud, commercial extortion, and residential and commercial burglary. In diverse ethnic communities in cities far apart, young men use the language of work ("getting paid," "going to work") to describe their crimes.[8] The confounding of the language of illegal and legal worlds of making money seems to signal a basic shift in the social definition of work. For the young men using this language, money from crime is a means to commodities that offer instrumental value as symbols of wealth and status.

Much of this illegal work is organized within ethnic enterprises combining shared economic and cultural interests. For gangs in these cities, there is less concern than in the past with neighborhood or the traditional "family" nature of gang life. Moore (1991) shows how gang members with limited exits from gang life remained longer in the gang, assuming leadership roles and manipulating the gang for their own economic advantage through perpetuation of gang culture and ideology. Chin and Fagan (1994) and Chin (1995a) describe the complex economic relationship between street gangs and adult social and economic institutions in three Chinatown neighborhoods in New York City. The adult groups, descendants of the *tongs* that were the shadow governments in Chinatowns a century ago, are involved in both legal, well-respected social and business activities *and* a variety of illegal businesses that employ street gangs. The gangs guard territories and act as surrogates in violently resolving conflicts and rivalries between the adult groups. Chin (1995a) concludes that the gangs prosper economically while functionally maintaining the cultural and economic hegemony of these ambiguous adult leadership groups. Moreover, the gangs are involved in a variety of income-producing activities, especially commercial extortion, that are shielded from legal pressures by cultural processes that tolerate and integrate their activities into the social fabric of everyday life in Chinatown (Chin & Fagan, 1994).

Padilla (1992, 1993) describes how the new pattern of exploitation of lower-level workers (street drug-sellers) in the gang was obscured by appeals by older gang members to gang ideology (honor, loyalty to the gang and the neighborhood, discipline, and ethnic solidarity) combined with the lure of income. Taylor (1990a), describing drug gangs in Detroit, and Padilla (1992) also talk about the use of money rather than violence as social control within African American and Latino drug-selling gangs—if a worker steps out of line, he simply is cut off from the business, a punishment far more salient than threats to physical safety. Drug-selling groups in these two studies superficially are ethnic enterprises, but function more substantively as economic units with management structures oriented toward the maintenance of profitability and efficiency. The institutionalization of these sources of illegal work, and their competitiveness with the low-status and low-income legal jobs left behind after deindustrialization, combine to maintain illegal work careers long after they would have been abandoned in earlier generations.

Patterns of illegal work vary in the gang literature. Some gang members abandon legal work after a period of employment, others drift in and out of legal work, and a few seem to choose from the outset exclusive careers in illegal work. There has been little research on how these changes come about, how often they occur, individual differences in shifts, or the decision processes that result in changes. Sanchez-Jankowski (1991), for example, claims to have found an "entrepreneurial spirit" as the "driving force in the work view and behavior of gang members" (p. 101) that pushes them to make rational decisions to engage in the profitable world of drug sales or auto theft.

Hagedorn (1994b) describes how gang members drift in and out of legal work over time, with decisions closely bundled and often reciprocal. Hagedorn claims that the drug labor market vigorously competes with the seemingly more "glamorous" opportunities in the illegal economy, despite the low wages, low status, dangerous and often part-time nature of the legal work. Hagedorn also describes how gang members at times double up between legal and illegal work, holding both types of "jobs" at the same time; at other times, they specialize in drug selling or other illegal work. The hazards and indignity of low-wage, low-status legal jobs cause others to discount the returns from legal work. For example, Bourgois (1989) claims that drug dealers who leave legal jobs to embrace the risks and rewards of drug selling are evidence of a "culture of resistance," preferring the "more dignified workplace" of drug selling than the low wages and "subtle humiliations" of secondary labor markets where racism dominates work conditions and social interactions (p. 641).

The changes in the structure of employment shaped not only job outcomes for young adults but also the outcomes of early legal problems. Sullivan (1989, 1991) tells how early involvement in crimes was normative in three ethnically diverse neighborhoods, but the outcomes of arrest varied by neighborhood. White families helped resolve disputes informally, using family support and job networks to soften the potential stigma of arrest. With high rates of joblessness, nonwhite families had few social buffers or job networks between them and the legal system. Not only did they lack access to job networks, but their families were of little help when their income-producing crimes (robberies) evoked official responses. Their disrupted job networks were unable to mitigate legal problems or ease the school-to-work transition, contributing to the continuity of criminality into early adulthood and adverse legal responses. In contrast, youth in predominantly white neighborhoods were able to make sometimes difficult but successful escapes from adolescent crime networks. Hagan (1993) links this to processes of "social embeddedness" that truncate future options and amplify the adverse effects of adolescent entanglements in the legal system.

Gangs and Drug Selling in the Wake of Deindustrialization

The link between gang formation and the social and economic makeup of communities is a consistent theme in the gang literature. Curry and Spergel (1988) showed how gang delinquency rates varied according to the social and economic well-being of particular neighborhoods, reflecting variation in the degree of structural inequality between neighborhoods. During the 1970s, when the decline in manufacturing jobs in large U.S. cities was steepest (Kasarda, 1988, 1989, 1992), gang formation occurred in communities that experienced the most extreme forms of economic disinvestment, labor market contraction, and social dislocation (Jackson, 1991). The location of gangs in low-income neighborhoods and among low-income populations reflects the consistent disadvantage politically of these neighborhoods and their residents compared to people in neighboring communities with greater wealth and access to resources (see Hagedorn, 1994b; McGahey, 1986; Taylor, Taub, & Peterson, 1986; Taylor & Covington, 1988).

These factors are part of the *political* economy of a community because they reflect dimensions of community life that are shaped by forces that lie beyond the control of communities: decisions by bankers and industrialists, technological changes, and the distribution of public resources through political power (Skogan, 1990). The social controls and social organizations that form in communities are the result of the interactions of individuals with the structural features of the community: housing choices constrained by decisions by banks and developers, jobs made available by the decisions of industrialists or banks supporting small businesses and shops, transportation choices that make jobs and other services accessible to neighborhood residents, and the quality and responsiveness of institutions such as police and schools. Accordingly, the social organization of neighborhoods is shaped by social and economic interactions of political decisions with residents' skills, family configurations, and cultural and lifestyle preferences.

Gang formation in neighborhoods reflects disadvantages in these choices: social organizations of adolescents that reflect constrained choices and weak social controls. Although some aspects of the social organization of communities are the result of "consumer" decisions, others are the result of closely guarded institutional practices (Skogan, 1990, p. 173). Job creation is especially critical, for the availability of stable employment at a wage level that can sustain families and small businesses that serve them are critical to maintaining social control within the community.

Gangs can be seen as an adaptive social organization of adolescents that form in response to disadvantages in the political economy of communities. Disinvestment or weak public resources act as constraints on social controls from schools and families. Weak labor market participation attenuates the social control function of older generations with primary roles for socialization and control of children. Accordingly, when social disinvestment destabilizes neighborhoods, the risks of gang formation grow. So too do the risks of drug activity: The constraints on social controls in communities make drug taking more salient, offer little resistance to the development of street-level drug markets, and are ineffective against the violence and disorder in the contexts of those markets. That these factors converge in inner cities offers a partial explanation of the confluence of the growth of gangs and their involvement in drug markets.

We do not know what neighborhood processes translate the effects of political economy into specific forms of social organization and neighborhood dynamics within communities. Social control involves the normative processes and ethics of social interaction that regulate everyday social life (Doyle & Luckenbill, 1991) as well as the mobilization of community that occurs in response to problem behaviors. To the extent that political economic decisions weaken informal and formal social controls and the formation of social capital (Coleman, 1988), these decisions launch processes that give rise to the formation of gangs, the formation of drug markets, and the confluence of the two problems.

In the following section, I analyze the effects of social and economic decisions on the regulatory processes within neighborhoods that seem to be implicated in the growth of drug markets and the formation of gangs. I review examples of the social processes that are launched when people in disadvantaged neighborhoods are exposed to criminogenic structural conditions, especially those factors that lead to gang activity and drug dealing.

THE TRANSFORMATION OF THE LABOR MARKET
AND THE GROWTH OF DRUG MARKETS

Two factors fundamentally changed the labor market for poor young men and women in urban areas since 1970: the replacement of unskilled and semiskilled blue-collar jobs with "pink-collar" jobs that required higher educational and skill levels, and the growth of the informal economy, especially the illicit economy around drugs (Kasarda, 1989; Wacquant & Wilson, 1989). The 1970s were a decade marked by surpluses of semiskilled and unskilled labor in inner cities, created by the relocation of manufacturing and other blue-collar jobs to "satellite cities" in surrounding suburbs. Kasarda (1989) shows that between 1970 and 1980, the number of blue-collar and clerical jobs declined by over 350,000 in New York City but increased by over 75,000 in the surrounding suburbs. Technical and managerial jobs in the city increased by over 250,000 during this time, and by over 400,000 in the suburbs. The net effect for inner city communities was dramatic increases in joblessness[9] among young minority men, especially African Americans, since 1970; higher rates of employment among women; and growing dependence on unregulated labor markets for employment and income (Kasarda, 1992).

Traditionally, African Americans have relied heavily on blue-collar jobs in manufacturing for economic sustenance and social mobility (Farley & Allen, 1987). Beginning in the 1970s, Puerto Ricans and other Latin American and East Asian immigrants "colonized" these jobs (Bourgois, 1995; Tienda, 1989), and African American employment in the manufacturing sector of New York declined (Sullivan, 1989). Thus, the economic restructuring of many U.S. cities resulted in large-scale exclusion of their nonwhite residents from constricting labor markets that also were transforming from manufacturing to services and shifting spatially from the inner city to the surrounding suburbs (Hochschild, 1989). Similar processes, compounded by language and other cultural barriers, created severe economic dislocations for Puerto Ricans, in turn creating conditions of severe impoverishment (Farley, 1987; Kasarda, 1992; Tienda, 1989) and growing dependence on the informal economy (Sassen-Koob, 1989).

Drug selling is an important part of the informal economy in urban areas in the United States (Hunt, 1990; Stepick, 1989) and other countries (Jimenez, 1989; Lanzetta, Castano, & Soto, 1989). Besides the motivation to reap profits, the decline of economic opportunities for labor force participation or licit informal income among inner-city residents strengthened incentives to sell drugs (Bourgois, 1995; Freeman, 1991; Johnson, Williams, Dei, & Sanabria, 1990; Moss & Tilly, 1991; Padilla, 1992; Taylor, 1990b).

Crack appeared in urban neighborhoods that had experienced profound social and economic declines since the 1970s (Fagan, 1992a; Johnson, Hamid, & Sanabria, 1990). For gang members and nongang youth alike, crack distribution became a major part of the informal economy where the unemployed could achieve economic returns well beyond the returns of low-wage jobs (see, e.g., Bourgois, 1995; Hamid, 1990; Williams, 1989). The introduction of this new and powerful cocaine product, and its popularity among a cohort of young adults with high base rates of drug use, created new demand that exceeded the capacity of established distribution systems (Fagan & Chin, 1990).

In turn, the expansion of the drug economy increased the opportunities for street-level drug selling through improved access to supplies, the availability of entry-level roles in drug distribution with a small capital investment, and the creation of "controlled" selling territories with a guaranteed income (Johnson, Hamid, & Sanabria, 1990; Williams, 1989). The potential for high profits from selling first cocaine and then crack attracted young people into drug dealing in social areas where legitimate economic activity had decreased. The informal drug economy offered economic opportunities that replaced formal opportunities lost as capital flowed out of inner-city neighborhoods in the decades preceding the expansion of crack and cocaine powder markets.

Before cocaine became widely available, drug distribution was centralized, with a smaller street-level heroin network of users responsible for retail sales (Curtis, 1992; Johnson et al., 1985). After its price declined and cocaine became widely available, the discontinuity in distribution systems across successive drug eras created new opportunities for drug selling and may have encouraged participation in it. The sudden change in cocaine marketing from a restricted and controlled market in the 1970s to a fully deregulated market for crack spawned intense competition for territory and market share (Fagan, 1992a; Williams, 1989). Law enforcement officials in New York City characterized the crack industry as "capitalism gone mad" ("Report from the field," 1989).

In an era of declining formal economic activity, when the traditional exits from gang life were attenuated by a shrinking manufacturing base, drug selling offered strong economic incentives to young men who were largely unskilled workers and either displaced by shifts in the labor markets in the preceding decade or excluded from it due to skill and spatial mismatches. Participation in this sector carried with it considerable risk of arrest and physical victimization, however (Fagan & Chin, 1990). Thus, the new drug markets also offered opportunities to young persons who already had developed careers in the illicit economies through drug selling or violence.

Accordingly, the drug markets may have simply provided "work" for a surplus labor pool of unskilled workers who lacked sufficient human capital for successful involvement in a shrinking formal (legal) labor market and were excluded from it (Freeman, 1991). Alternately, the declining returns from formal work may have increased the salience of the illicit economy of drug selling and attracted people from the formal labor markets. Evidently, the people who benefited most from the expansion of the drug economy had limited employment prospects in the formal economy prior to their involvement with crack or other drugs—they were either unemployed or earning low wages. Perhaps earlier involvement with both crime and drug use adversely affected their labor market entry and participation (Freeman, 1992). Or their skills and mastery of illicit economic activities positioned them to make the most of lucrative opportunities created by the expansion of drug markets (Fagan, 1992a).

THE DISRUPTION OF
INTERGENERATIONAL JOB NETWORKS

The decline of the manufacturing sector within urban centers fostered drug selling among gangs in indirect but important ways. First, it reduced legal economic opportunities that provided exits from gang life. In the past, manufacturing jobs provided entry positions on career ladders for African Americans and Latinos that provided stable if unspectacular earning potential (Farley & Allen, 1987), usually with the expectation of predictable annual increases and a cushion of health and other benefits. More recently, the public sector and jobs fueled by public spending (e.g., health care, social services) served similar functions for nonwhites entering the labor market. These jobs have become marginal as municipal and state fiscal crises worsen.

Second, the manufacturing decline depleted the informal social networks that provided access for each succeeding generation to enter the labor market. Within these networks, older workers (mostly males) provided information and personal contacts for young men to take advantage of job openings or union membership (see Anderson, 1990; Sullivan, 1989, for rich descriptions of how such networks operated). As employment was restructured and opportunities diminished, people with long-standing attachments to local employers both large and small began their exodus (Wilson, 1987, 1991). In turn, the job networks that facilitated each generation's entry into stable employment collapsed or were severely weakened. Both the economic opportunities themselves and the types of people who mediated adolescents' transition into young adulthood no longer were present or effective in the neighborhoods (Fagan, 1993).

Accordingly, economic change broke the intergenerational linkages that in the past helped each generation find its way to stable employment and immersion in conventional life roles. These relationships are critical elements in the social capital of a community (Coleman, 1988, 1990), an asset of the neighborhood that sustains both its economic viability and its social rules across generations. These linkages also are an important part of the informal social controls that mediate the interactions of individuals and the social contexts they live in. These processes play an important part not only in shaping the behavior of children and adolescents but also in mediating their access to economic opportunities and resources (Sampson, 1992).

In the past, the involvement of older residents provided young people with a range of models for adulthood and conveyed a vision of the future (Anderson, 1990). The departure of a generation of men who were the links to work also weakened the stabilizing influence of the remaining "old heads" both as teachers and mediators of adolescent behaviors (Anderson, 1990). Traditionally, old heads in a neighborhood would guide young men as they exited from gang life and entered stable life roles (Anderson, 1990; Moore, 1978; Vigil, 1988a). But the departure of old heads over a one- or two-decade span, or the decline in their influence as their own social situations worsened, created a void in the socialization of the neighborhoods' younger residents. The expectations of young people for the future changed from stable employment (in steady, if unspectacular jobs) to a bleak vision of chronic unemployment or low-wage earnings in low-status jobs where exploitation was common and hostility from Anglo employers was unchecked (see, e.g., Bourgois, 1989; Padilla, 1992).

In some inner-city communities, drug sellers replaced the old heads as the links to employment, role models for younger males and regulators of social and economic behaviors in poor urban neighborhoods (see, e.g., Anderson, 1990). In neighborhoods where gangs were active and influential participants in community life, their influence quickly expanded to fill this void. Gang influence as the dominant informal control and socialization force outweighed the influences of the schools, the licit economy, and legal institutions (see, e.g., Hagedorn, 1988, 1994a, 1994b).

Gang members in particular no longer could use the traditional exits from gang life to assume conventional jobs and instead looked to older gang members for stability of employment and income. Where gang careers in the past evolved through the natural stages of initiation, maintenance, and desistance, the exits from gang life to stable employment and conventional life roles no longer were salient. The pathways out of the gang either were closed off by the shrinking job market or became unattractive alternatives to street life where illicit incomes were available (though at the risk of physical danger or incarceration).

Without a diversity of job networks, the economic and social significance of the drug markets increase. The drug market appears to be an extreme form of labor market segmentation, with vast opportunities for entry in a diversity of roles. Participants in drug selling appear to be long-term participants with weak ties to legal work or newcomers whose weak skills excluded them from work (Fagan, 1992a). They are unskilled workers not well matched to either the service economy or technical jobs and lacking in the human capital necessary for success in the formal economy. They are matched both spatially and in terms of skills for the drug economy.

Although the restoration of intergenerational job networks appears to be essential to provide economically rational alternatives to participation in drug markets, the networks are ineffective without jobs to proffer. The relationships between residential patterns, social networks, and economic diversity are extremely complex and interdependent. And so long as successful residents leave their neighborhoods for better living circumstances, the daily patterns of social interaction that foster these networks of reciprocal social obligations will not develop. Accordingly, patterns of economic life, and the residential and social mobility within neighborhoods that result, are basic to sustaining the social capital that attenuates the allure of the drug economy.

THE INSTITUTIONALIZATION OF DRUG MARKETS

Changes in the economic and social organization of drug markets paralleled the changes in the formal labor market, and these reciprocal changes contributed to the growth of drug markets. The heroin markets from the 1970s were smaller than the crack market both in total volume of sales and the average purchase amount and quantity. Street-level drug selling in New York, for example, was a family-centered heroin and marijuana business until the 1980s, when new organizations developed to control distribution of cocaine (Curtis, 1992; Johnson, Hamid & Sanabria, 1990). The psychoactive effects of heroin and methods of administration limited the volume of sales and the number of users. But cocaine was different in every way—a stimulant rather than a depressant, ingested in a variety of ways (nasally, smoked, or injected), and with a shorter half-life for the high. Moreover, it was portrayed for many years as a "safe" drug that was not addictive, did not interfere with other social activities, and the use of which could be easily self-controlled.

Accordingly, as a generation of drug users with favorable definitions of drug use entered the peak years of drug use, both supply and demand for drugs changed in this era, especially cocaine powder (Kozel & Adams, 1985). This fueled a rapid expansion of the drug economy in inner cities (Fagan, 1990; Johnson, Hamid, & Sanabria, 1990). Cheap cocaine became available early in the 1980s, following widespread demand that grew sharply both in inner cities and nationwide. As licit job opportunities declined and informal economic activity grew, involvement in crime generally and drug selling in particular was a natural development in neighborhoods with weakened social controls. Both for gangs and nongang youth, the drug economy provided economic opportunity, although with risks of legal problems and physical danger. The market expanded faster than the ability of existing drug networks to meet demand, creating economic opportunities for both individuals and organizations (Johnson, Hamid, & Sanabria, 1990), but also organizational violence between groups competing for market share and profits (Fagan & Chin, 1990).

The gains from drug selling also far exceeded what could be expected from legitimate work in a shrinking and highly segmented labor market. To the extent that decisions to sell drugs were shaped by the choices available, drug selling was a reasonable if not attractive option for economically marginal inner-city youth. In the closed milieu of these neighborhoods, the tales of extraordinary incomes had great salience and were widely accepted, even if the likelihood of such riches was exaggerated (Bourgois, 1989; Fagan, 1992a, 1993, 1996; MacCoun & Reuter, 1992; Reuter, MacCoun, & Murphy, 1990). The focus of socialization and expectations shifted from disorganized groups of adult males to (what was perceived as) highly organized and increasingly wealthy young drug sellers.

As drug selling expanded into declining local labor markets, it became institutionalized within the local economies of the neighborhoods. Drug selling in storefronts, from behind the counters in bodegas, on street corners, in crack or "freak" houses, and through several types of "fronts" was a common and visible feature of the neighborhoods (Hamid, 1992). Young men and, increasingly, women had several employment options within drug markets: support roles (lookout, steerer), manufacturing (cut, package), or direct street sales (Johnson, Hamid, & Sanabria, 1990). Legendary tales, with some truth, circulated about how a few dollars' worth of cocaine could be turned into several thousand dollars within a short time. These quick riches had incalculable appeal for people in chronic or desperate poverty.

With few conventional social or economic processes to counter it, and in increasingly physically and socially isolated circumstances, drug selling was institutionalized economically and socially within the neighborhoods. Drug selling became a common form of labor market participation, and young men began to talk about drug selling as "going to work" and the money earned as "getting paid" (Padilla, 1992). Many other sellers kept one foot in both licit and illicit work, lending ambiguity to definitions of work and income (Fagan, 1992a; Reuter et al., 1990).

Secondary economies sprang up to service the drug industry (see Taylor, 1990a). As the size and stakes (relative to legitimate income) of the cocaine economy grew, newcomers entered the business and willingly used violence as a regulatory process (Fagan & Chin, 1990). So too were other cultural norms: Exaggerated wealth skewed perceptions of status and achievement. Expectations of time frames for attainment of wealth were truncated based on the skewed tales of instant wealth.

DRUG MARKETS AND THE
EROSION OF SOCIAL CONTROLS

Just as the economy transformed fundamentally, the social processes that followed transformed too in basic ways. The interdependence of economic and social norms was evident in the social institutionalization of drug selling. In earlier eras, social interactions were organized and reinforced by economic structures. With the advent of drug economies in neighborhoods isolated from other economic and social influences, work and social interactions were now organized around these criminal activities, enforced and regulated increasingly by violence.

Social controls in weakened neighborhoods were overwhelmed by the volatile drug markets or violent crimes such as robbery (Fagan, 1992a; Hamid, 1990). Informal social controls broke down when social networks of neighborhood residents in changing communities were disrupted through high residential mobility or economic disruptions (Sampson, 1987; Skogan, 1990). Violence associated with crack resulted from several parallel processes: competition between sellers and protection of territory (Goldstein, 1989; Goldstein, Brownstein, Ryan, & Belluci, 1989); regulation of employees in new selling organizations (Cooper, 1987; Johnson, Hamid, & Sanabria, 1990; Williams, 1989); the urge for drugs or money to buy it among habitual users (Hamid, 1990; Reinarman, Waldorf, & Murphy, 1989); its liquid value among poor and poorly paid persons (Hamid, 1990); and for a small group, its psychoactive effects (Reinarman et al., 1989; Washton & Gold, 1987).

Collective supervision of youth, a critical source of informal social control and socialization, suffered as intergenerational relationships were disrupted. In turn, as employment in general and male employment in particular declined, the socialization of young people fell disproportionately on women or to formal authorities such as schools and legal institutions. Socialization by older residents of the neighborhoods became a passive or nonexistent process as these traditional forms of informal social control—cohesion among neighbors, social sanctions, group norms—became weaker. Again, these dynamics fostered conditions that facilitated the formation of youth groups into loosely structured gangs.

THE REDISTRIBUTIVE FUNCTION
OF DRUG SELLING

Drug selling often plays an important part of the economic context of the region surrounding each neighborhood, and several studies describe a political economy of drug distribution. Increasingly, poor neighborhoods alone could not sustain the dollar amounts and quantities that compose the drug industry (Fagan, 1992a, 1993; Padilla, 1992; Sullivan, 1991; Taylor, 1990a), and buyers from other areas are important contributors to the local drug economy. Accordingly, drug selling serves an important redistributive function in bringing money into the poor neighborhoods and fosters the interdependence between isolated poor neighborhoods and the areas surrounding them.

Drug sellers are suppliers of important goods and services to residents of more affluent areas (Sullivan, 1991), and the vitality of a drug market in a neighborhood is bound up with the relationships within poor neighborhoods and between these neighborhoods and other parts of their cities. To the extent that selling is spatially concentrated in a few areas, the interdependence of those areas with the larger city will sustain a drug market regardless of efforts to improve the material circumstances of its residents.

CLASS AND CULTURAL CONFLICTS

One consequence of the structural transformation of urban neighborhoods has been the flight of middle-class residents to neighborhoods, towns, and villages surrounding the urban core (Wilson, 1987). Taking advantage of higher incomes, more stable and better-paying jobs, and the slow erosion of housing segregation in urban and suburban areas, middle-class residents of inner cities often moved out of their old neighborhoods. These former inner-city residents had themselves avoided poverty through ascension to professional, technical, and supervisory jobs in the public and private sector. They left behind the poorer residents in the inner cities, but their jobs often remained there. This was especially true for minorities with public sector jobs, but their only contact with their former inner-city neighbors or the children of those neighborhoods was in official capacities in institutional contexts. Often, these institutions were agencies of social control: welfare, schools, public health, and criminal justice. Class conflict was inevitable between those left behind and those returning as agents of social control.

An important consequence of the flight of the middle class from inner cities is the erosion of the political power that African Americans and other minorities had gained in the 1960s and 1970s (Skogan, 1990; Wilson, 1991). This loss of political power reversed gains made in earlier decades in the allocations of services and budgets. The exodus of middle-class residents of inner-city neighborhoods weakened the efforts of community organizers to fight plant closings, stave off job loss, and counter the trend toward the recentralization of social and health services (Fagan, 1992b).

These losses weigh heavily in poor communities and on adolescents living there. The repair of streets and removal of snow or garbage, the allocations of resources to schools or libraries, and the tenor of legal institutions all reflect the political power of the neighborhood. These important features of urban life also are essential to limiting the effects of community decline (Skogan, 1990), or what Wilson and Kelling (1982) referred to as the "broken windows" syndrome. These political dimensions also interact with social resources to strengthen social controls and increase the personal investments and commitments of the individuals who live there (Reiss, 1986b; Sampson & Groves, 1989).

ISOLATION AND INSULATION OF NEIGHBORHOODS

By 1980, poor urban families were more likely to have poor neighbors than a generation earlier (Wilson, 1987). Although increases in urban poverty per se contributed in part to this trend, residential segregation along racial and economic lines was the primary cause for the growing concentration of poor people in inner cities (Massey, 1990). Together with growing income inequality between African Americans and whites (Moss & Tilly, 1991) and the opening of housing and job opportunities to minorities outside the urban core, poor urban dwellers became increasingly isolated physically, economically, and culturally. Predictably, the concentration of poor people in poor areas has had negative effects on the ability of neighborhoods to shape the lives of their residents. When social norms and values develop in a homogeneously poor context, void of material and social inducements toward conventional norms, the ties of the residents to the social contract are attenuated and deviance is a logical and perhaps inevitable adaptation (Elliott et al., in press).

As the middle-class residents of the urban core left for the better housing and schools of the suburbs or the promise of greater racial tolerance in integrated neighborhoods, the insulation of the neighborhoods was reinforced by the depletion of the housing stock and the flight of basic commercial services. In gang cities including Detroit (Taylor, 1990a) and South Central Los Angeles (Quicker, 1992), thriving commercial districts transformed within a decade into areas dominated by liquor stores and fast-food outlets. In turn, the informal commercial activity that vitalized street life also was weakened. For example, the health food and craft shops in the Caribbean shopping districts in Brooklyn closed down (Hamid, 1990). These services, which often were locally owned, closed or moved elsewhere, removing jobs and the small amount of capital they created. These stores and the traffic they generated were stabilizing parts of both the commercial and the cultural life of the neighborhood. Their departure altered the normative patterns of interaction that constituted "street life," an important part of the social regulation of behaviors for young people.

Social and economic isolation not only may complicate efforts to escape poverty but can foster beliefs that poverty is inevitable and another life is beyond the reach of most inner-city residents. The concentration of poor people within poor neighborhoods, compounded by segregation (Massey & Eggers, 1990) narrows residents' visions of a better life in the near term and changes their expectations for the future.

In Detroit, for example, both racial and income segregation worsened following the devastating 1967 riots (Taylor, 1990a). The spatial patterns of development, especially transit, that had developed there beginning in the 1940s (when the worst U.S. race riots took place) provided a means by which workers could work in Detroit by day and escape each night to the surrounding suburbs. According to Taylor, freeway patterns in Detroit show how the isolation of the neighborhoods was planned and institutionalized: All roads provide entry and exit paths to the suburban ring but no facilitation of an internal traffic flow across city neighborhoods (see Skogan, 1990).

The concentration of poor people in poor neighborhoods, without expectations for improvement, has shaped their social interactions and economic relationships. Their physical and social isolation tends to block out influences from outside the neighborhood, and natural processes such as social comparisons and contagion can become skewed and distorted through a lens of poverty. The social norms that developed in this context are likely to be influenced by the informal and illicit economies, which will confer a disproportionate share of both economic wealth and, in turn, social status when legal work is not an option.

In these circumstances, the significance and social status attached to gang membership in several neighborhoods is obvious. The social isolation of poor neighborhoods skews social norms and ensures that contagion of norms and values will be amplified within a closed social system (Elliott et al., in press; Tienda, 1991). Thus, the social status of drug selling increases when drug income is the primary route to gaining both the material symbols of success and wealth and social standing in the neighborhood. For young men, the drug industry offers many of the benefits of self-determination and economic independence so cherished in the broader culture in Horatio Alger stories or an escape from the petty humiliations and harassment faced by nonwhites in the segmented labor markets for unskilled and manufacturing labor (Bourgois, 1995).

The Future: The Institutionalization of Gangs

Stability and change characterize street gangs in the United States in the post-World War II era. Stability is evident in the lasting importance of gangs in urban neighborhoods in cities throughout the country. Gangs continue to be developmentally important for adolescents even as the social meaning of adolescence itself changes. The basic "form" of street gangs has endured for decades, even as between-gang variability in gang structures and cohesion continues from era to era (Klein, 1995a; Short, this volume; Spergel, 1995). Ethnicity, fighting, status, getting high, and community are themes as important to gang members today as they were nearly half a century ago.

Change, too, is evident in gangs in the past decade, changes that reflect shifts in the social and economic structure of the United States since the 1960s. Drug selling has become a common part of the economic lives of some gang members. Gang violence has become more lethal, as has violence among adolescents generally. Gangs have emerged in small cities and suburbs, in many cases borrowing the names and reproducing the behaviors of big-city gangs (Klein, 1995a). With the arrival of new ethnic groups in large and small cities, gangs emerge as a natural organizational form for the marginalized among their adolescents (Vigil & Yun, 1990; Vigil, Yun, & Long, 1992). Economic goals now compete with neighborhood defense and ethnic solidarity as motivations for gang participation and conflict, in some cases changing the organizational logic and structure of gangs. Young men and women marginalized from adult social and economic roles now remain in gangs longer, often into their early and middle adult years when in the past they might have left gangs to enter stable careers and start families. In some cases, ties to adult crime groups have become more functional and efficient as prison populations have grown (Moore, 1991; Skolnick et al., 1988).

The structural changes in U.S. society that gave rise to these new forms of gangs and ganging will not easily be undone. If gangs have evolved in a way that responds to the new social, economic, and cultural realities of the late 20th century, then gangs may become a durable and lasting feature of adolescent and neighborhood life—that is, gangs may become institutionalized in U.S. suburbs and cities as a part of the social and cultural ecology of neighborhoods and a career choice for young adolescents that may compete with diminishing jobs and other social roles. What will a future look like when gangs are institutionalized in the social and cultural life of communities and compete with schools and other institutions as sources of opportunity and social control?

Gangs as Work. Illegal markets compete effectively with legal markets in many urban areas, raising the stakes on crime incomes as prospects for legal incomes decline. In the past, the economic returns from hustling and petty crime were a small and often unimportant part of gang life.

Today, the increasing importance of the economic dimension of gang life fits well with declining wages for unskilled workers and the changing structure of labor markets. Drug markets have had important impacts on the balance of legal and illegal work and on expectations of young people about the monetary returns from the drug business (see, e.g., Mayer, 1989). As Sullivan (1989) notes, crime will become perceptually interchangeable with legal work.

Just as gangs continue to provide status opportunities, they may also replace the unskilled labor market as a primary source of economic opportunity. As wages for unskilled work remain flat or fall, illegal work becomes more salient and attractive (Fagan, 1996). Thus, the economic opportunity structure of gangs is likely to compete with, or in some cases even replace, the unattractive and shrinking opportunity structure of the legal labor market.[10]

The politics of crime control, the political demand for punishment, and the expansion of the gang enforcement "industry" also will contribute to these trends (Klein, 1995a). Gangs will increasingly become the target of specialized enforcement efforts, fueling an already overheated correctional population. But recall that early incarceration experiences disadvantage adolescents, especially males, as they attempt to enter legal labor markets (Fagan & Freeman, in press; Hagan, 1993; Sampson & Laub, 1993). The weight of mandatory incarceration and longer sentencing policies has fallen disproportionately on nonwhite males in urban areas, especially those involved in drug offenses (Tonry, 1995). Accordingly, the transition to work will be increasingly difficult for young males with criminal histories, contributing to the social and economic attractions of illegal work and the weakening of social control that legal work often provides.

Gang Careers. Longer gang "careers" are one of the important changes in gangs over the past decade (Klein, 1995a). As young adults remain in gangs longer, their own crime and their influence on the crime rates of younger members is likely to increase. If rates of crime and violence increase among adolescents during periods of gang involvement (Thornberry et al., 1993), longer gang careers will mean longer involvement in violence and other crimes. Age grading also is likely to influence the crime rates of younger gang members, as older gang members create more circumstances where violence and other crimes occur.

Gang violence will continue to provide a primary source of status within gangs.[11] As the number of gang cities and gangs increase, clashes between rival gangs in new gang cities may be more likely as new gangs emerge and compete for status and territory. Gang members vying for status in emerging gangs may be sensitive to the challenges to "honor" and "respect" that require a violent response. This may provide motivation for the formation of still newer gangs, incentives for individuals to join them, and opportunities for conflicts to arise between newly formed gangs. Accordingly, one consequence of the growth in gangs and groups such as "tagbangers" (Klein, 1995a) may be an increase in the number of adolescents involved in gangs and an increase in their crime participation.

Like other adolescent violence, gang violence is likely to continue to be lethal. There are several pushes in this direction. For example, the presence and availability of large-caliber automatic weapons changes strategic thinking about violence, and this technology makes participation in lethal violence easier (Zimring & Hawkins, in press). The widespread possession of these weapons creates an "ecology of fear" among gang members, making violence a first and final tactic that preempts retaliation (Fagan & Wilkinson, in press-a, in press-b). As young people "come up" in this climate, their perceptions of danger from other gang members will continue to motivate lethal violence as a means of survival.

Young Women and Gangs. The roles of young women in gangs have changed in the past decade. Today, there is female membership in previously all-male gangs, as well as female gangs (Campbell, 1990b). Not much is known about female gangs, however, and predictions here are especially risky. Women in gangs face a dual fight: conflicts with males over gender roles and conflicts with other gangs (Taylor, 1993). Also, developmental contexts for young women have changed at the same times and in the same ways as have the contexts for males, and the generally weaker social controls provide a context for women to assume social roles that reflect "street life," including street gangs (Anderson, 1994). Hypermasculinity and conflicts between males and females also provide motivation for women to "show heart" to avoid exploitation by men (Taylor, 1993). The motivations for ganging among young women may be weaker and shorter in duration compared to their male counterparts, however. For example, the barriers to women entering the workforce are weaker than those facing men, easing their transition from adolescence to adult roles and reducing the influence of the gang in their everyday social and economic lives.

Whatever the future of female gangs, the trend toward young women to demand status and respect is likely to continue. Whether this results in the emergence of gangs and groups of women and whether these groups are less cohesive and more transient is too hard to say. Nevertheless, the "traditional" role of female auxiliaries is gone, replaced by women struggling for respect and autonomy against male dominance, both in gangs and outside them.[12]

THE INSTITUTIONALIZATION OF
GANGS IN COMMUNITIES

Gangs have been a recurrent criminological problem for centuries. Their importance has varied over different eras, emerging in times of social change to occupy a central role in political conversations about crime and delinquency. Because gangs usually have been transient features of cities and a predictable but finite developmental phase for youth from blue-collar and poor neighborhoods, gangs have not been institutionalized in most places. In a few cities, gangs have been institutionalized for generations. But in other cities, such as Philadelphia and New York, gangs have declined in importance in recent decades or even disappeared.

Gangs have emerged today in more cities than ever before, however, in response to profound social structural changes, fueled by processes of rapid and efficient cultural diffusion, and sustained by a gang enforcement apparatus that itself has diffused to legal institutions across the country. Initially fueled by changes in drug and other illegal markets, the economic function of gangs has become more prominent for gang members and now lives side by side with the traditional motivations of neighborhood and self-defense. Whether gangs will be institutionalized in the social organization of small and large cities, or whether they will continue to be a transient social phenomenon that comes and goes across generations, is as yet unknown.

The future of gangs is tied to the future of urban crises in social control, social structure, labor markets, and cultural processes in a rapidly changing political and economic context. Although gangs will continue to be a part of the urban (and, increasingly, the suburban) landscape, their institutionalization will depend on a series of interdependent tipping points: the threshold of gangs as dominant sources of socialization and social control, the threshold of social and economic marginalization of neighborhoods and communities, the cultural diffusion and reproduction of gangs and ganging, the levels of violence by and against adolescents, and the responses of legal institutions to recurring developmental crises of adolescents in a highly segmented social structure. Of course, gangs may fade as another transient social form, culturally rejected and replaced by some other, as yet unenvisioned, structure of adolescence. This seems unlikely, however. The future of gangs may be uncertain, but recurring social crises in the coming decades are likely to ensure that gangs will be an important part of the future.

Notes

1. See Sante (1991) for a detailed history of gangs in New York beginning in the 18th century.

2. Saint Francis of Assisi commented that nothing gave him greater pleasure than stealing in the company of his friends. English common law in the 13th century accorded especially harsh punishments to the roving bands of youth who moved across the countryside stealing from farmers and merchants. The House of Refuge, the first U.S. institution for delinquent boys, opened in New York City in 1824, largely in response to the unsupervised groups of youth who roamed the city stealing and drinking (Rothman, 1980).

3. Virtually every gang ethnography illustrates this point (see, e.g., Hagedorn, 1988; Campbell, 1990b; Stumphauzer, Veloz, & Aiken 1981; Vigil, 1988a; Padilla, 1992; Moore, 1978, 1991, 1992; Taylor, 1990a, 1993).

4. Vigil (1988a) notes that these patterns are confined to substances that enhance gang social processes—alcohol, marijuana, PCP, and crack cocaine. There is a sanction against heroin use among Chicano gangs. Heroin involvement is seen as a betrayal of the gang and the barrio: One cannot be loyal to his addiction and the addict ("tecato") culture while maintaining loyalty to the gang.

5. See Burns (1980) for a similar account involving youth in drinking locations in and around Boston.

6. Drug *use* among gang members also is highly variable, ranging from drug use tied to specific social contexts (Vigil, 1988a) to total abstinence (Chin, 1990; Taylor, 1990a). Gang members in my three-city study (Fagan, 1989) also varied in their use of alcohol, marijuana, and more serious drugs. The types of drugs used and the contexts that influence them are as variable for gang members as they are for nongang youth in cities across the country.

7. To better illustrate the higher expected returns from drug selling, Hagedorn (1994a, pp. 202-203, Table 2) reports, "The *maximum* amount of money earned monthly by any gang member from legal income was $2,400, the *mean* for gang drug sales."

8. See Sullivan (1989), Padilla (1992), Taylor, (1990a, 1990b), Waldorf (1992), and Williams (1989). For example, Felix Padilla (1992) describes how gang members in a Puerto Rican Chicago neighborhood regarded low-level drug sellers in their gang as "working stiffs" who were being exploited by other gang members.

9. Official employment statistics are quite limited in portraying trends in unemployment or labor market participation more generally. Jencks (1991) points out that youth unemployment appears to rise during periods when school attendance increases, because students technically are not in the labor force. Fagen (1992b) shows the increase in the residual pool of long-term unemployed and low educated males below 25 years of age since 1970 in the six study cities. Equally important is the exclusion of "discouraged workers" who drop out of the hunt for work, also participants in the informal economy. Income from crime and drug selling are excluded not only from formal employment but also from most estimates of the informal economy (Sassen-Koob, 1989).

10. One trend we are unlikely to see is the transition of street gangs into adult organized crime groups. For decades, very few gangs have evolved from adolescent street gangs into adult criminal organizations. Nevertheless, adult organizations have had a mediating role in the future of gangs in several studies, from Cloward and Ohlin (1960) to Chin (1995a). Will adult organizations continue to influence gangs and gang youth? There is only weak evidence of gangs generally forming into the types of adult criminal organizations that have been evident among Chinese and Italian street gangs. This is not likely to change. Adult criminal organizations in these two ethnic groups have historical origins in the social structure and culture of their native countries. Moreover, there is little evidence of street gangs developing into adult groups. Chin (1990, 1995a) portrays street gangs as a contract labor force for adult groups who use these economic relationships as a source of social control. "Talented" young gang members may be brought into the adult groups, much in the same way that some college athletes or minor league baseball players are brought into professional sports.

There are weak parallels for street gangs today. There is some interaction between Chicano street gangs in Southern California and prison gangs, but there remains a disjuncture between the adolescent and adult groups (Moore, 1992b). There is no evidence of adult organized crime groups among other ethnic groups, such as drug gangs, evolving from street gangs or incorporating these gangs into their organizations (Hagedorn, 1994a, 1994b; Klein, 1995a). The transition remains one of individuals, not of groups.

11. This is a consistent theme in gang research (see, e.g., Cohen, 1955; Sanchez-Jankowski, 1991).

12. See, for example, Chesney-Lind, 1993.

The Criminal Behavior of
Gang Members and
Nongang At-Risk Youth

C. RONALD HUFF

During the past decade, gang-related crime in the United States has clearly become a very important public policy issue. Earlier in this

AUTHOR'S NOTE: The author wishes to express his appreciation to the (Ohio) Office of Criminal Justice Services for its support of this study with funds appropriated under the federal Juvenile Justice and Delinquency Prevention Act. Although space limits the number of acknowledgments, the study benefited especially from the invaluable assistance of Jacqueline Schneider, who played a major role in the collection and analysis of the Columbus gang-tracking data; Kenneth Trump, field coordinator for the Cleveland sample; the Columbus Division of Police (especially Commander Kent Shafer); the Cuyahoga County Juvenile Court (especially William Kurtz, Court Administrator, and the staff of the Cuyahoga County Juvenile Detention Center); the Ohio Department of Youth Services (especially director Geno Natalucci-Persichetti); Lee Norton (database management and coding supervision); Luying Wei (computing and data analyses); Sandra Floyd, Milagros Merced, Brenda Peak, Rodney Thomas, and Stephanie Wolfe (field interviews); Eddie Carrera (transcription of field interviews); and Georgia Meyer (secretarial assistance and coordination).

volume, Curry, Ball, and Decker provided a "reasonable" estimate that the United States has more than 16,000 gangs with more than one-half million members who commit nearly 600,000 crimes per year. Such staggering numbers raise additional questions that need to be addressed. This chapter is based on a recent study that was designed to address three critical research questions:

- What is the nature and extent of criminal behavior, including drug use and drug trafficking, committed by youth gangs collectively and by the individual members of those gangs?
- Are there significant differences between the criminal behavior of (a) youth gangs and their members and (b) comparably at-risk but nongang youth?
- What happens, over time, to the leaders of youth gangs?

The issue of gang-related crime is one that has interested researchers since Thrasher's (1927/1963) landmark study of Chicago gangs. Comparatively little research, however, has been focused on comparing the criminality of gang members with that of nongang youth. Klein (1995a), referring to the crime and delinquency associated with male gangs of the 1950s and 1960s, recently noted: "Gang members were far more criminally active than nongang boys were, and more so than delinquent nongang boys as well. Some gangs, by the same token, were more criminal and some more violent than others" (p. 67).

According to Miller's (1982) baseline survey, gang members in the major "gang problem" cities of the United States accounted for about 11% of all arrests of male youth and 42% of arrests for serious and violent crimes. About 6% of all arrests of gang members involved drug offenses, and although nongang youth were more likely to be arrested for drug offenses, Miller noted that the involvement of gang members in the drug trade appeared to be increasing. Even more ominous, homicide arrests of juveniles increased by 40% in the 1970s and "gang killings" increased by more than 200% in that same decade.

More recently, studies in Denver, Colorado, and Rochester, New York, appear to demonstrate that youth are more likely to engage in delinquent behavior during periods when they are gang members than either prior to or after their involvement in gangs (Esbensen & Huizinga, 1993; Thornberry, Krohn, Lizotte, & Chard-Wierschem, 1993).

The Cleveland Gang-Nongang At-Risk Youth Study: Design and Methodology

To address the critical issues listed above, this research project was designed to provide a comparison of the criminal behavior of (a) currently or formerly active youth gang members with that of (b) youth who are comparably "at risk" of crime and delinquency but have not become active in gangs. By constructing samples that consisted of both active gang members and youth who were comparably at risk but had not joined gangs, it became possible to make direct comparisons of their behavior and, by inference, to make a reasonable assessment concerning the role that gangs play in the lives of these young people who were otherwise comparable.

In constructing the sample of Cleveland gang members, it was important not to rely on official police perceptions of gang members. Although a number of researchers have done this, such samples include considerable bias, from a scientific standpoint, because they include only those persons who have been arrested or have had contact with the police. Left out of such samples are those who have been able to avoid police involvement, and they may or may not be comparable to those with official police records or contact.

I do not suggest that the sample included in this study is perfectly representative of gang members, either, because without knowing the "universe" of all gang members, it is impossible to construct a perfectly representative sample. Sampling gang members is not the same thing as sampling the members of the PTA or the police department, for example, because both of the latter have known universes of membership. Instead, I relied in this study on a strategy of stratified reputational sampling. The sample for the Cleveland gang component of this study was based on knowledge gained from expert informants[1] concerning (a) existing gangs in Cleveland and (b) which persons are or have recently been active in those gangs. Sources of information included a large number of individuals who interact with gangs and gang members in Cleveland on a daily basis, including staff in neighborhood centers, social service workers, school personnel, and gang prevention experts.

The sample was stratified in the sense that it intentionally included members of the major gangs in Cleveland (see Table 4.1 for a list of those gangs) and took into account both geography and gender. This sample represents four major groupings (or "nations") of Cleveland gangs (Folks, Vice Lords, Crips, and "independent" gangs not claiming any affiliation with the above). It was reputational in the sense that it was based on the reputations of those referred to the project by key informants. The final sample for this study is believed to be quite representative of the distribution of youth among Cleveland gangs, because about 75% of all known gang members at the time of data collection claimed affiliation with Folks, Vice Lords, or Crips. A total of 50 interviews were completed, with the following breakdown:

1. Geography: 29 Eastside, 21 Westside
2. Gender: 42 males, 8 females
3. Gang "Nations": 27 Folks affiliated, 9 Vice Lords affiliated, 7 Crips affiliated, 7 independent

Of these 50 interviews, 34 were completed in the community (in neighborhood centers or other "neutral" sites), 13 were conducted in the Cuyahoga County Juvenile Detention Center, and 3 were conducted in correctional facilities operated by the state of Ohio. For those 34 interviews conducted in the community, scheduling was established so that the safety of all human subjects would be protected. For example, members of rival gangs were never scheduled for sequential interviews, so as to avoid their arriving at the same site at the same time. A total of 47 of these interviews qualified for inclusion in the final sample of gang-involved youth, and 40 of these (85.1%) represented the three major gang nations in Cleveland. Table 4.1 summarizes the distribution of the final sample of 47 interviews.

For comparison purposes, the "at-risk" sample of youth who were comparably at-risk of criminal behavior but not gang involved included 50 referrals who fit the following profile:

1. Geography: 29 Eastside, 21 Westside
2. Gender: 40 males, 10 females

A total of 49 of these 50 interviews qualified for inclusion in the final sample. All 49 of these interviews were conducted at community locations, generally in neighborhood centers.

TABLE 4.1 Distribution of Sample by Gang and Gang Affiliation

Gang/Affiliation	Number in Sample
Folks [Folks]	9
Black Gangster Disciples (BGD) [Folks]	1
Gangster Disciple Folks (GD Folks)[Folks]	2
Gangster Disciple Nation (GDN) [Folks]	3
Insane Gangster Disciples (IGD)[Folks]	1
Insane Gangster Nation (IGN)[Folks]	1
Maniac Latin Disciples (MLD)[Folks]	4
C-Town [Folks]	1
Killer Town [Folks]	1
Hell's Kitchen [Folks]	1
SUBTOTAL (Folks):	24
Vice Lords (VL) [Vice Lords]	3
Conservative Vice Lords (CVL) [Vice Lords]	4
Insane Vice Lords (IVL) [Vice Lords]	2
SUBTOTAL (Vice Lords):	9
Rolling Twenties Crips (RTC) [Crips]	6
Shot Gun Crips [Crips]	1
SUBTOTAL (Crips):	7
Eight Ball Posse [Independent]	1
Storming/Straight Off Superior (SOS) [Independent]	2
West 28th Posse [Independent]	1
Y Far Side [Independent]	1
Deuce/Baby 141st Street Posse [Independent]	1
Hot Sauce Hustlers [Independent]	1
SUBTOTAL (Independents):	7
TOTAL:	47

Figure 4.1 presents a graphic comparison of the geographic residences of the gang and the at-risk samples. This figure provides further evidence of the comparability of the samples, in the sense that these young people come from the same neighborhoods, attend the same schools, and generally face similar environmental circumstances.

All interviewees were paid for their time with movie coupons purchased from a local theater chain. Given the neighborhood "turf rivalries" that exist among gangs in different neighborhoods, it required some time to identify a theater chain whose outlets were located in all of the

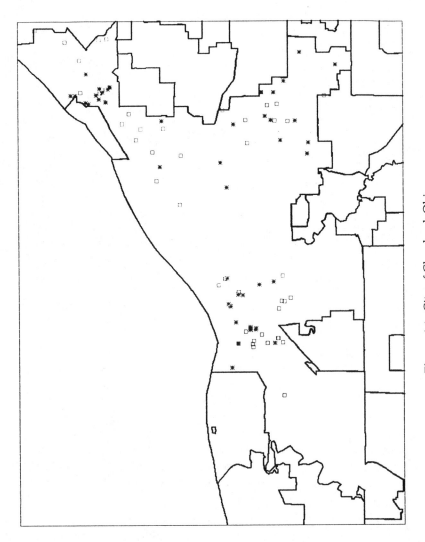

Figure 4.1. City of Cleveland, Ohio

NOTES: Boxes = Residences of gang members in sample
Asterisks = Residences of nongang at-risk youth in sample

80

different "gang areas" so that the interviewees could actually use their movie coupons without fear of being attacked for "intruding" into "enemy territory" to go to the movies. Otherwise, one could hardly call these movie coupons a "reward" for their cooperation. In addition to the movie coupons, those individuals who had been ordered to complete community service requirements were given the opportunity to request that the principal investigator contact the court in their behalf to ask that their cooperation in the interview be counted toward the community service requirement.

At the beginning of each interview, the interviewer read to each interviewee some basic information about the study and the relevant information concerning human subjects requirements. The interviewee then had the option of participating or refusing to participate in the study. Those who chose to participate were then interviewed, using either the "gang member" instrument or the "at-risk youth" instrument.

SUMMARY OF MAJOR FINDINGS

First, it is important to compare the two samples (gang members and nongang at-risk youth) to determine the degree to which the two samples are comparable with respect to potentially important variables and attributes. This comparison is presented in Table 4.2, which demonstrates that the two samples are quite comparable with respect to age, gender, race, educational attainment, work experience within the past year, and family status. The gang members were slightly older (15.9 years of age, compared to 15.0 for nongang at-risk youth), were somewhat more likely to be male (85.1% to 79.6%), were less likely to be African American (70.2% to 73.5%), had comparable grades of education (8.8 to 8.5); had similar levels of work experience in the past year (40.4% to 49.0%), and had comparable family status (40% to 55% had two parents while growing up). For these important attributes and variables, the differences between the two samples were statistically nonsignificant, indicating that the two samples were indeed comparable.

One of the key questions addressed in this study is the degree to which gang members and a comparable sample of nongang at-risk youth differ with respect to criminal behavior. Most of the data that bear on that question will be presented below, but Table 4.2 indicates that there are statistically significant differences between gang and nongang at-risk

TABLE 4.2 Comparison of Gang and Nongang Member Samples

	Gang (%)	Nongang (%)	p^a
Age	$\bar{x} = 15.9$	$\bar{x} = 15.0$	NS
Gender (% Male)	85.1	79.6	NS
Race (% African American)	70.2	73.5	NS
Education completed	$\bar{x} = 8.8$	$\bar{x} = 8.5$	NS
Work (past year)	40.4	49.0	NS
Two-parent family	40.4	55.1	NS
Number of arrests	$Mdn = 3.0$	$Mdn = 0$	***
Age at first arrest	$Mdn = 14.0$	$Mdn = 15.0^b$	***

NOTES: a. p = level of statistical significance (* $p = < .05$; ** $p < .01$; *** $p < .001$; NS = not significant) based on either dichotomous or scaled responses.
b. Median (Mdn) for those arrested ($n = 19$).

youth with respect to both age at first arrest and total number of arrests. The median age at first arrest for gang members was 14.0, whereas most nongang members had never been arrested. For the 19 nongang members who had been arrested, however, the median age was 15.0, one year older than their gang counterparts. Further, the median total number of arrests for gang members was 3.0, whereas the median for nongang respondents was 0. These data provide the first suggestion that gang involvement may be a very significant criminogenic factor.

Gang Versus Nongang Member Activities

Because the gang members in this study were primarily adolescents and adolescents have certain age-typical developmental characteristics and needs, we would expect to find that certain activities are commonly engaged in by both gang and nongang youth. A number of items on the interview schedule were designed to address this question and to determine what, if any, differences exist in the extent to which these two samples engage in various activities. Table 4.3 suggests that with the exception of sporting events (where nongang youth report a 30% higher level of participation), gang members are significantly more involved in such activities. Although varying proportions of nongang youth engage in these activities, gang members are significantly more likely to "party"; attend musical concerts; "hang out"; "cruise"; engage in fighting, drink-

TABLE 4.3 Comparison of Gang and Nongang Member Activities

Activity	Gang (%)	Nongang (%)	p^a
Dances, parties	89.4	66.0	**
Sports events	46.7	77.8	**
Concerts	61.7	40.0	*
"Hang out"	100.0	87.5	*
"Cruise"	86.4	54.5	**
Fighting	93.6	20.5	***
Drinking	87.0	31.8	***
Drug use	34.0	7.0	**
Drug sales	72.3	9.1	***
Put up graffiti	95.7	46.9	***
Cross out graffiti	89.1	46.9	***

NOTE: a. p = level of statistical significance (* p = < .05; ** p < .01; *** p < .001; NS = not significant).

ing, drug use, and drug sales; and put up and cross out graffiti. These data provide further corroboration that it is appropriate to view youth gangs and other youth groups along a continuum ranging from acceptable to unacceptable, and even criminal, behavior.

Gang Versus Nongang Member Criminal Behavior

A major purpose of this study was to address the degree to which the criminal behavior of gangs is comparable to or differs from the criminal behavior committed by nongang but at-risk youth living in ostensibly similar circumstances. To address this issue, a large number of interview questions were designed to determine the involvement of the respondents and their gangs (or peer groups, in the case of the nongang at-risk sample) in such criminal behavior. Table 4.4 presents the findings with respect to the individual gang and non-gang member respondents *as individuals*.

As expected, certain types of crime are engaged in frequently by many youth, whether or not they are gang involved. Other crimes are engaged in very infrequently by youth, and again this does not depend on gang membership. But for a large number of crimes, especially violent offenses and major property crimes, both criminological theory and field experience over the years suggest that gang members are likely to exhibit

TABLE 4.4 Comparison of Gang and Nongang Member Criminal Behavior

Crime	Gang (%)	Nongang (%)	p^a
Shoplifting	30.4	14.3	NS (.058)
Check forgery	2.1	0.0	NS
Credit card theft	6.4	0.0	NS
Auto theft	44.7	4.1	***
Theft (other)	51.1	14.3	***
Sell stolen goods	29.8	10.2	*
Assault rivals	72.3	16.3	***
Assault own members	30.4	10.2	*
Assault police	10.6	14.3	NS
Assault teachers	14.9	18.4	NS
Assault students	51.1	34.7	NS
Mug people	10.6	4.1	NS
Assault in streets	29.8	10.2	*
Bribe police	10.6	2.0	NS
Burglary (unoccupied)	8.5	0.0	*
Burglary (occupied)	2.1	2.0	NS
Guns in school	40.4	10.2	***
Knives in school	38.3	4.2	***
Concealed weapons	78.7	22.4	***
Drug use	27.7	4.1	**
Drug sales (school)	19.1	8.2	NS
Drug sales (other)	61.7	16.7	***
Drug theft	21.3	0.0	***
Arson	8.5	0.0	*
Kidnap	4.3	0.0	NS
Sexual assault	2.1	0.0	NS
Rape	2.1	0.0	NS
Robbery	17.0	2.0	*
Intimidate/assault victims or witnesses	34.0	0.0	***
Intimidate/assault shoppers	23.4	6.1	*
Drive-by shooting	40.4	2.0	***
Homicide	15.2	0.0	**

NOTE: a. p = level of statistical significance (* p = < .05; ** p < .01; *** p < .001; NS = not significant).

greater involvement in these illegal behaviors. Theoretically, adolescents' attempts to deal with the problems associated with "coming of age" (biological, social, and economic challenges) often result in their parent(s) or other significant adult caregivers being drawn into conflict with the independence-seeking youth. The strain that ensues can help push adolescents even more toward social groups outside their family in a search for gratification, acceptance, and reassurance. Both classic differential association theory (Sutherland, 1947) and more contemporary social control theory (Hirschi, 1969) suggest that when youth make a commitment to a primary social group (the gang) whose values and social reward system favor certain types of criminal behavior, the youth are more likely to engage in such criminal behavior.

As indicated in Table 4.4, individual respondents are comparably involved in shoplifting; check forgery; credit card theft; assaults on police, teachers, and students; muggings; bribery of police; burglary of an occupied dwelling; drug sales at school; kidnapping; sexual assault; and rape. With respect to check forgery, credit card theft, bribery, burglary of an occupied dwelling, kidnapping, sexual assault, and rape, the base expectancy rate of these offenses is generally low to very low for adolescents whether they are gang involved or not, so this finding is not surprising. Conversely, the conflict and physical violence that seem to be present in contemporary youth culture, including schools, means that significant numbers of nongang youth assault other students, teachers, and even police. Finally, as is the case with male prison subcultures, the male-dominated gang subculture tends to regard as "unmanly" (therefore, disvalued) behaviors such as sexual assault and rape, unless one includes the "consensual" sex (from the perspective of male gang members) that occurs during the initiation of some female gang members. Thus, it is perhaps not surprising that the incidence of such behavior is comparably low for both gang and nongang youth in the sample.

Table 4.5 provides even more compelling evidence of the highly criminogenic nature of gangs. This table compares the *collective* criminal behavior of gangs with the *collective* criminal behavior of nongang peer groups, based on respondents' reports of the behavior of their fellow gang or peer group members. Again, from the perspective of criminological and sociological theory, these two groups (gangs and peer groups) are primary social groups that have powerful influences on the behavior of adolescents. In fact, given the tension, conflict, and estrangement that often accompany the process of emancipation from the family, it can be argued that for most adolescents, the peer group or gang is the most powerful socializing influence in their lives.

A major purpose of this study, then, was to compare the criminal behavior of gangs with that of comparable peer groups, using as respondents individuals whose age, gender, race, residence, schools, and family status were comparable. This sampling strategy allows assessment of the

TABLE 4.5 Comparison of Gang and Nongang (Peer Group) Criminal Behavior

Crime	Gang (%)	Nongang (%)	p^a
Shoplifting	41.3	37.5	NS
Check forgery	11.1	6.1	NS
Credit card theft	17.4	8.2	NS
Auto theft	82.6	53.1	**
Theft (other)	69.6	38.8	**
Sell stolen goods	61.7	34.7	**
Assault rivals	97.9	43.5	***
Assault own members	51.1	20.4	**
Assault police	46.8	27.1	*
Assault teachers	51.1	51.0	NS
Assault students	61.7	67.3	NS
Mug people	46.8	16.3	**
Assault in streets	58.7	28.6	**
Bribe police	25.5	10.4	NS (.055)
Burglary (unoccupied)	31.9	12.5	*
Burglary (occupied)	17.0	14.3	NS
Guns in school	80.4	34.7	***
Knives in school	72.3	38.8	***
Concealed weapons	93.6	53.1	***
Drug use	53.2	28.6	*
Drug sales (school)	59.6	32.7	**
Drug sales (other)	91.3	60.4	***
Drug theft	61.7	21.3	***
Arson	21.3	14.6	NS
Kidnap	23.4	2.1	**
Sexual assault	2.1	6.3	NS
Rape	4.3	2.1	NS
Robbery	38.3	10.2	**
Intimidate/assault victims or witnesses	51.1	18.8	***
Intimidate/assault shoppers	42.6	10.4	***
Drive-by shooting	80.9	10.4	***
Homicide	68.1	17.0	***

NOTE: a. p = level of statistical significance (* p = < .05; ** p < .01; *** p < .001; NS = not significant).

marginal contribution of gangs to the criminal behavior of otherwise comparable young people. The data in Table 4.5 indicate that the differences between collective gang criminal behavior and collective peer group/criminal behavior follow the same general patterns seen for individual respondents in Table 4.4, except that the differences become even more pronounced when the behavior of all group members is included.

What we see in Table 4.5 is that with the exception of those offenses that have generally low base rates for adolescents (e.g., check forgery), those that are more common within "youth culture" (e.g., shoplifting and school-related fights), and those that are perceived as "unmanly" (e.g., sexual assault and rape), gangs are significantly more involved in criminal behavior, especially the most serious crimes of violence and major property crimes. Although the involvement of comparable nongang youth in such crimes is clearly more extensive than is desirable in our society, the rates for gang members range from 56% greater for auto thefts to 678% greater for drive-by shootings to 1,014% greater for kidnapping, with kidnapping being a much lower volume offense than either auto theft or drive-by shootings.

Another major purpose of this study was to examine the differences between gang members and nongang at-risk youth with respect to drug sales. One of the major debates in recent years has been whether gang members are more likely than other youth to sell drugs, whether gangs and drug trafficking are nearly "synonymous," and whether gangs "control" drug-trafficking markets. The complex interaction between socioeconomic factors and the increased involvement of gang members in the illegal economy is well documented by Fagan in this volume. The data in Tables 4.6 to 4.8 help address these questions.[2] For the Cleveland sample, the following findings are clear:

- Table 4.6 indicates that individual gang members are significantly more likely to be involved in the sales of crack cocaine, powder cocaine, and marijuana than are comparable nongang at-risk youth. The differences between these two samples for lower-volume drug sales such as PCP, LSD and mushrooms, heroin, and crystal methamphetamine are statistically nonsignificant. It should be noted, however, that since the completion of this study, LSD sales and use in the Cleveland area (and nationally) have shown significant increases and it is not known whether gangs are more involved in these sales than are nongang at-risk youth or other individuals.

- When gangs and comparable nongang peer groups are examined (see Table 4.7), the data indicate that gangs are significantly more involved in the sales of cocaine (both crack and powder), marijuana, PCP, LSD and mushrooms, and heroin. Gangs are also far more likely to be involved in the sales of crystal methamphetamine (though the difference is not statistically significant because of the low base rate and the fact that the significance level is based on the original scaled responses focusing on the frequency of sales).

TABLE 4.6 Comparison of Gang and Nongang Member Drug Sales (Type)

Drug	Gang (%)	Nongang (%)	p^a
Crack Cocaine	65.9	20.4	***
Powder cocaine	26.1	0.0	**
Marijuana	48.9	6.2	***
PCP	4.3	0.0	NS
LSD/mushrooms	2.1	0.0	NS
Heroin	4.3	0.0	NS
Crystal methamphetamine ("Ice")	4.3	0.0	NS

NOTE: a. p = level of statistical significance (* p = < .05; ** p < .01; *** p < .001; NS = not significant), calculated for scaled responses, which were then dichotomized for this table.

TABLE 4.7 Comparison of Gang and Nongang (Peer Group) Drug Sales

Drug	Gang (%)	Nongang (%)	p^a
Crack cocaine	93.6	69.3	*
Powder cocaine	67.4	34.7	**
Marijuana	80.8	50.0	**
PCP	29.8	6.0	*
LSD/mushrooms	25.5	8.1	*
Heroin	37.0	10.2	*
Crystal methamphetamine ("Ice")	23.4	6.3	NS

NOTE: a. p = level of statistical significance (* p = < .05; ** p < .01; *** p < .001; NS = not significant), calculated for scaled responses, which were then dichotomized for this table.

"Crystal meth" ("ice") is far less prevalent in the Cleveland area than for cities such as Honolulu or certain West Coast cities (Drug Use Forecasting, or DUF, data and arrest data have confirmed this for a number of years).

- As indicated in Table 4.8, the typical gang member in the sample sells drugs on a daily basis, whereas the typical nongang at-risk youth in the sample does not sell drugs. But those nongang at-risk youth who do sell drugs (n = 11), report that they also sell on a daily basis.

- Table 4.8 also reveals that gang members who sell drugs report that they make, on the average, nearly 50% more in earnings per week ($1,000 compared to $675) with far fewer customers (30 compared to 80 per week). Thus, the average earnings per transaction for gang members is $33.33, compared to $8.44 per transaction for nongang at-risk youth (note that these are gross, not net, earnings). This finding is not unexpected, because the data indicate that gang members are far more likely to be involved in selling

TABLE 4.8 Comparison of Gang and Nongang Member Drug Sales
(Dynamics)

	Gang (%)		Nongang (%)		p [a]
Frequency (Days/wk)	Mdn = Daily		Mdn = Daily[b]		***
Wages/wk	Mdn = $1,000		Mdn = $675[b]		*
Customers/wk	Mdn = 30		Mdn = 80[b]		**
Gross earnings/transaction	$33.33		$ 8.44		—
Money kept for own drug use	Mdn = 0		Mdn = 0		NS
Drug source (location)	Local:	31.9	Local:	50.0	**
	Out of state:	17.0	Out of state:	14.6	
	Other Ohio:	12.8	Other Ohio:	4.2	
Drug source	Foreign:	26.1	Group:	18.8	**
(type of organization)	Gang:	21.7	Gang:	18.8	
	Org. crime:	10.9	Foreign:	12.5	
	Group:	8.7	Individuals:	10.2	
Legitimate wage to stop selling drugs (per hour)	Mdn = $15.00		Mdn = $17.00		NS
Who controls drugs?	Gangs:	9.8	Gangs:	11.9	NS
	Others:	70.7	Others:	61.9	
	Gangs & others:	9.8	Gangs & others:	14.3	

NOTE: a. p = level of statistical significance (* p = < .05; ** p < .01; *** p < .001; NS = not significant) based on either dichotomous or scaled responses.
b. Based on subsample who do sell drugs (n = 11). Median for total nongang, sample = 0.

higher-profit drugs, whereas nongang at-risk youth are most likely to be involved in the sales of crack cocaine and marijuana, both of which are characterized by higher-volume, lower-profit (per sale) transactions.

■ Neither gang members nor their nongang counterparts report using much, if any, of their drug profits to purchase drugs for their own use (Table 4.8 shows that the median for both subsamples is 0).

■ Gangs and comparable nongang peers differ significantly in the perceived sources of their drug supplies (see Table 4.8). Although the most likely perceived source of drugs for both subsamples is local and comparable proportions of both groups get drugs from other Ohio cities, gangs are far more likely to go out of state for their drugs (17% compared to 4.2%) or to rely on combinations of local and out-of-state suppliers. Also, with respect to the perceived *organizations* that supply their drugs, more than one fourth (26.1%) of gang members report relying on foreign suppliers (the most frequently mentioned category), followed by gangs (21.7%), organized crime (10.9%), and loosely knit groups (8.7%). Nongang peers report that the most common suppliers of their drugs are gangs and loosely knit groups (18.8% each), followed by foreign suppliers (12.5%) and individuals (10.2%).

- Both gang and nongang youth believe that it would require a significant legitimate wage to induce their peers to stop selling drugs. As indicated in Table 4.8, the median response to this question ranged from $15 (for gang members) to $17 (nongang at-risk peers). It should be noted, however, that although these median figures are the most representative responses, this means that 50% of both subsamples believed that a lower wage would be an acceptable inducement to stop selling drugs. Some respondents' answers to this question suggest that there are individuals (perhaps up to one fourth of all gang members) who may be willing to stop selling drugs in return for legitimate wages that are not much higher than are currently being paid by fast-food restaurants. Gang members have often told me that they are unable to obtain a sufficient number of *hours* of work per week at legitimate wages to offset their *total* earnings from illegal drug sales. Although often accurate and most regrettable, this view may also serve to reinforce gang members' own convenient rationalization (neutralization) of their criminal behavior.

- Finally, neither gang members nor their nongang counterparts believe that gangs control drug trafficking (only about 10% of each group hold that view, with about 20% to 25% believing that gangs control drugs along with other organizations). Consistent with their responses concerning the sources of their drugs, both gang members and their nongang peers clearly believe that drug markets are controlled by organizations other than gangs. It is especially noteworthy that gang members, who are much more likely to be involved in drug sales and therefore more likely to have better knowledge of the dynamics of drug markets are also more likely to believe that other organizations (such as foreign groups and organized crime) control drug markets.

Another question of interest is the extent to which gang members and comparable nongang at-risk youth possess guns and what types of guns they possess. Table 4.9 provides sobering evidence that guns are quite prevalent among both gangs and comparable nongang peer groups. One third more of gang respondents (74.5% compared to 55.6%) indicated that most or nearly all of their fellow gang members own guns. The lethality of these weapons is even more sobering. Unlike gangs and youth groups of previous decades who fought with fists, clubs, "zip guns" made from broken radio antennas, and similar weapons, contem-

TABLE 4.9 Comparison of Gang and Nongang (Peer Group) Gun
Ownership (in Percentages)

	Gang	Nongang (Peer Group)	p^a
Own guns	Most/nearly all: 74.5	Most/nearly all: 55.6	*
Type of guns	> Small caliber: 89.4	> Small caliber: 52.2	***

NOTE: a. p = level of statistical significance (* p = < .05; ** p < .01; *** p < .001; NS = not significant).

TABLE 4.10 Progression From "Wanna-be" to First Arrest

First association with gang:	$\bar{x}$ = 12.9
Joined gang:	$\bar{x}$ = 13.4
First arrest:	Mdn = 14.0

porary gangs and other youth are all too likely to have access to powerful
and highly lethal weaponry. As Table 4.9 reveals, more than one half
(52.2%) of the nongang at-risk sample and nearly 9 out of 10 (89.4%) of
the gang respondents report that members of their gangs or groups
possess weapons that are more powerful than small-caliber handguns.
A close examination of the data document that most of these groups have
members with weapons more powerful and more lethal than the standard weapons issued to law enforcement officers (often a 9mm or
comparable handgun).

The data collected in this survey also permit examination of the
progression from "hanging out" with the gang (commonly known as the
gang "wanna-be," or associate, stage) to joining the gang to getting
arrested. Table 4.10 depicts this progression in statistical terms. Gang
member respondents reported that they first began associating with the
gang at about age 13. They joined, on the average, about 6 months later.
They were then arrested for the first time at about age 14, one year after
beginning to associate with the gang and about 6 months after joining.

But even those young people who are approached to join a gang do
not always do so. Given the widely held belief that one must accede to
"pressure" to join gangs, gang member respondents were asked if they
were aware of individuals who had refused to join gangs and, if so, what
consequences, if any, that action had for them. As Table 4.11 suggests,
nearly three fourths (71.7%) of gang members knew someone who had

TABLE 4.11   Gang Resistance and Consequences (in Percentages)

Know someone who refused to join	71.7
Refusal techniques	
Said no:	35.5
Changed routines/dress:	12.9
Consequences	
Nothing:	66.7
Physical harm:	12.1

refused to join gangs. How did they refuse? According to the respondents, the two most widely employed methods of refusal were simply declining (though this probably ought to be done respectfully, rather than disrespectfully), an option cited by 35.5% of the subsample, and changing one's routines, dress, activities, and so forth (12.9%) so as to avoid the gangs as much as possible. Perhaps surprising to some, respondents reported that in two thirds (66.7%) of the cases with which they were familiar, nothing happened to the youth who refused to join. On the other end of the continuum, only 12.1% reported that they were familiar with an instance in which the person who refused to join suffered some physical harm (usually minor). Given the data on the relationship between gang membership and criminal behavior, it is clear that young people are far better off, statistically, refusing to join a gang and taking their chances that some reprisals might occur (with better than 5:1 odds that nothing will happen, compared to the possibility of suffering any physical harm) than to join the gang and greatly increase their chances of arrest, incarceration, injury, or even death (more on this later). Moreover, the most common initiation requirement among Cleveland gangs is getting "beaten in" (enduring a physical beating), reported by 69.6% of the gang sample. Thus, in Cleveland at least, one who is faced with the choice of joining a gang or refusing to join has a much better chance of avoiding physical harm by respectfully refusing to join.

The Columbus Gang Leader Tracking Study

A second major component of this study was designed to determine what happens over time to youth who are highly committed to gangs.

Through our earlier involvement in a study of emerging Cleveland and Columbus gangs in 1986, my coworkers and I established good working relationships with the police departments of both cities. And although we decided to base the Cleveland portion of this study on new data for current gang and at-risk youth, we thought that we had a unique opportunity in Columbus to track the original Columbus gang leaders who were instrumentally involved back in 1986 and determine what involvement they have had in criminal behavior in the intervening years. Toward this end, we asked three gang experts from the Columbus Division of Police to independently list those individuals who were Columbus gang leaders in 1986. Each gang expert provided names and independently rated the degree to which each person named played a key role in his gang in 1986. The highest rating possible was an A. These ratings were then used to construct the final sample of Columbus gang leaders. This procedure yielded a total of 83 leaders (78 representing the five major Columbus gangs at that time and 5 representing other gangs that existed in the city in 1986). The arrest histories of these individuals were then documented with the assistance of the Columbus Division of Police and form the basis of the discussion below.

SUMMARY OF MAJOR FINDINGS

Table 4.12 presents data concerning the number and types of crimes committed by these 83 gang leaders, indicating that fully 37% of their total arrests ($n = 307$) were for crimes of violence, 29% ($n = 239$) for property crimes, 18% ($n = 154$) for drug offenses, 6% ($n = 54$) for weapons offenses, and 10% ($n = 80$) for other crimes. As reflected in Table 4.13, these 83 Crips, Dozen Cousins, East Columbus Assassins, Enforcers, and Freeze Crew members, along with five other gang leaders, accounted for a total of 834 arrests between 1980 and 1994, an average of more than 10 arrests per gang leader.

Table 4.14 and Figure 4.2 present a summary of the arrest histories represented for each individual gang over the tracking period. Although the tracking study included arrests as early as 1980, Figure 4.2 demonstrates that the overwhelming majority of arrests began at or near the time of gang involvement (these gangs emerged in the mid-1980s), providing additional evidence of the criminogenic nature of these gangs. The declining frequency of arrest depicted in this graphic raises the

TABLE 4.12 Types of Gang Leader Arrests by Category, 1980 to 1994

Type of Offense	Type of Charge
Drugs	Trafficking offenses
	Aggravated trafficking offenses
$n = 154$	Drug abuse
$\% = 18.0$	Permitting drug abuse
$\bar{x} = 1.85$	Counterfeiting controlled substances
Violence	Murder/Attempted murder
	Rape/Attempted rape
	Kidnapping
	Aggravated robbery/Robbery
	Aggravated menacing/Menacing
	Felonious assault
$n = 307$	Aggravated assault/Assault
$\% = 37.0$	Resisting arrest
$\bar{x} = 3.70$	Domestic violence
Property	Aggravated burglary/Burglary
	Criminal trespass
	Breaking and entering
	Unauthorized use of motor vehicles
$n = 239$	Receiving stolen property
$\% = 29.0$	Grand theft/Petit theft
$\bar{x} = 2.88$	Criminal damaging
Weapons	Carrying concealed weapon
$n = 54$	Discharge
$\% = 6.0$	Possession/Manufacturing/Sales
$\bar{x} = 0.65$	Under disability
Other	Disorderly conduct
	Escape
	Fleeing
	Inducing panic
$n = 80$	Falsification
$\% = 10.0$	Obstructing official business
$\bar{x} = 0.96$	Possession of criminal tools

question of why these arrests declined around 1990-1991. Was this due to maturation? Incarceration? Death? Or was this decline attributable, at least in part, to policy decisions?

We believe that each of the above explanations accounts for some of the variance apparent in these arrest rates, although incomplete records

TABLE 4.13 Gang Affiliation of Leaders and Number of Arrests, 1980–1994

Affiliation	N	Number of Charges	Mean	SD
Crips	27	235	8.70	7.4
Dozen Cousins	10	107	10.70	5.6
East Columbus Assassins	7	65	9.29	4.5
Enforcers	14	154	11.00	7.0
Freeze Crew	20	237	11.85	6.3
Other	5	36	7.20	3.9
Total	83	834	10.05	6.5

TABLE 4.14 Total Arrests, All Gangs by Affiliation, 1980–1994

Affiliation	Number of Charges	Mean
Crips	235	8.70
Dozen Cousins	107	10.70
East Columbus Assassins	65	9.29
Enforcers	154	11.00
Freeze Crew	237	11.85
Other	36	7.25
Total	834	10.05

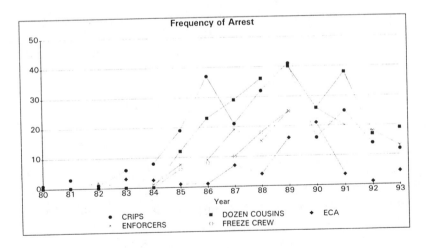

Figure 4.2. Total Arrests, All Gangs, 1980–1994

TABLE 4.15 Critical Events (Law Enforcement), 1986-1990

Period	Event
June 1986:	Juvenile Task Force formed (2 sergeants and 10 officers; focus: youth violence)
December 1988:	SCAT (Street Crime Attack Team) concept implemented (unit size increased from 10 to 16 officers; focus: street crime)
March 1990:	Two key personnel transferred from SCAT
April 1990:	Shift away from targeted, special unit gang/narcotics enforcement
April–July 1990:	Attrition occurs in special unit
August 1990:	Special unit officially disbanded

make it impossible to determine precisely how much of the variance is attributable to each factor. Certainly, some individuals may have "matured out" of gangs and crime, whereas others were incarcerated and were therefore not at risk of arrest in the community. But it also appears that public policy decisions played a major role in the decline of gang leader arrests around 1990. The principal investigator had the opportunity to observe decisions made by the Columbus Division of Police during the critical period between the mid-1980s, when gangs emerged, and 1990, when the data show arrests declining significantly. Table 4.15 summarizes key decisions made during that 4-year period, beginning with the creation of a juvenile crime task force in 1986; continuing with the expansion of that initiative to encompass an enlarged and more highly focused unit called the Street Crime Attack Team (SCAT) in 1988; and culminating in the gradual attrition and, finally, elimination of this targeted special unit in the summer of 1990. The focus of the Columbus Division of Police at that time shifted towards narcotics enforcement, and it was believed that the narcotics bureau could address both gangs and narcotics, as many gang members were becoming involved in drug trafficking.

I believed (and stated publicly) at the time that this policy decision was ill advised because (a) gangs and drugs are not synonymous and (b) it was unrealistic to expect that the narcotics bureau staff could pay sufficient attention to narcotics enforcement (at a time when crack cocaine had arrived in Columbus and was overwhelming enforcement efforts) and at the same time continue to collect timely intelligence information and carry out strategic enforcement efforts against gang

TABLE 4.16 Officially Verified Causes of Death, Columbus Gang Leaders

Sex	Race	Age	Cause
Male	Black	25	Gunshot
Male	Black	19	Multiple gunshot
Male	Black	17	Gunshot to neck
Male	Black	24	Gunshot to chest
Male	Black	19	Gunshot to chest
Male	Black	Unknown	Strangulation

crime. The events summarized in Table 4.15, when superimposed on the time series graphic depicting the arrest trends for the Columbus gang leaders in our sample (see Figure 4.2), suggest that arrests declined, at least in part, because of resource allocation decisions made by the Columbus Division of Police.[3]

In addition to maturation, incarceration, and resource allocation decisions made by the division, there is one additional factor that helps account for the declining arrests of our sample of gang leaders—death. As Table 4.16 reveals, at least six of our sample of gang leaders died during the period included in this study. Table 4.16 lists the officially verified causes of death for these six individuals. It is likely that this listing underestimates the mortality rate in the sample, because these data were obtained by using only local vital statistics. Given the mobility of offenders, it is quite likely that some additional offenders may have moved out of the state and died without our being able to document those deaths. Nonetheless, relying only on the six deaths reflected in Table 4.16 and not including any speculation about other deaths, we can say with certainty that a death rate of 7.2% in a cohort of adolescents and young adults is quite unusual. Insurance company mortality tables would not suggest that such a large proportion of young people would die violent deaths in such a short period at ages ranging from 17 to 25. This was not a random sample of young people, however, but a sample of gang leaders whose lifestyles exposed them to significantly more risk than would normally be expected, even for young African American males in general (a higher-risk group). This is an important finding, especially when many young people join gangs because they believe gangs will provide them with "protection." In reality, gang involvement

TABLE 4.17 Seriousness of Offense: Progression?

Gang		Peak Offense (Year)
Crips (*n* = 25; 219 Arrests)	Property:	1988
	Drugs:	1989
	Violent:	1989
Freeze Crew (*n* = 19; 227 Arrests)	Property:	1988
	Drugs:	1989
	Violent:	1989
Enforcers (*n* = 14; 154 Arrests)	Property:	1987
	Drugs:	1990
	Violent:	1989
Dozen Cousins (*n* = 9; 105 Arrests)	Property:	1987
	Drugs:	1989
	Violent:	1989

	Progression	
Property ⟶	Drugs:	+1.75 years
Property ⟶	Violent:	+1.50 years
Drugs ⟶	Violent:	−0.25 years

often increases the risks faced by young people—risks that include arrest, incarceration, injury, and even death.

Finally, the data in Table 4.17 address another important research question: Is there a progression in the seriousness of offense—from property crime to violent crime—or do the arrest histories of gang leaders suggest that their criminal involvement is just as likely to begin with violent crime? We also wanted to determine how drug-related arrests would fit into such a progression. Table 4.17 reports these data for the four major Columbus gangs best represented by our sample of gang leaders. With a database ranging from a low of 105 arrests for the 9 leaders of the Dozen Cousins to a high of 227 arrests for the 19 leaders of the Freeze Crew, it is possible to determine when the arrests for each gang peaked for each type of crime. Such peaks should reveal the progression of a gang, at least insofar as arrest can serve as a proxy for criminal behavior. Table 4.17 demonstrates that for the leaders of each of these four major Columbus gangs, arrests for property crimes peaked before arrests for either drug offenses or violent offenses.

These trends are summarized at the bottom of Table 4.17 in a simple "progression score" that captures the average time it took for gang leader

arrests to progress from property crime arrests to arrests for drug offenses and violent crimes. On the average, it took nearly 2 years (1.75)
from the time gang leaders' property crime arrests peaked to the time
when their arrests for drug offenses peaked. It took 1½ years for the
progression from property crimes to violent offenses to occur, on the
average. This also meant that peak arrests for violent offenses actually
preceded peak arrests for drug offenses by about 3 months, as reflected
in the final figure showing a negative sign (−0.25 years) for the drugs-
violent crime relationship. This finding may also reflect, in part, a close
connection between drug trafficking and the violence that is often associated with conflict over drug "turf."

Public Policy Implications

The findings presented in this chapter may have important implications
for public policy in confronting the challenges presented by the recent
proliferation of gangs and gang-related crime. I offer the following
recommendations, based on the data presented in this report:

- Those who join gangs tend to begin their association with gangs at about
  age 13, join about 6 months later, and get arrested about 6 months after they
  join the gang (age 14, on average). This underscores the vital importance of
  gang resistance education programs and other primary and secondary
  prevention initiatives directed at preteens. These initiatives are especially
  important for those young people who have significant exposure to multiple risk factors for delinquent and violent behavior (Hawkins, Lishner,
  Jenson, & Catalano, 1987). Such risk factors (all of which affect the samples
  used in this study) include economic deprivation (Farrington, 1991; National Research Council, 1993), neighborhood disorganization (National
  Research Council, 1993; Sampson, 1994), dysfunctional family structure or
  parenting (National Research Council, 1993), poor health and inadequate
  health care (National Research Council, 1993), school failure and inadequate
  schools (National Research Council, 1993), and the availability of weapons
  (Reiss & Roth, 1993), among others.
- The data also demonstrate that young people can refuse to join gangs
  without incurring a substantial risk of physical harm and that, statistically
  speaking, they are far better off to resist joining gangs than to expose
  themselves to the beating they are likely to take upon initiation and to the

increased risk of arrest, incarceration, injury, and death associated with gang membership. Such efforts will not deter all young people from associating with gangs, however. We must also address the brief window of intervention that opens in that year between first association with the gang (the "wanna-be" stage) and first arrest. It is imperative that we fund, develop, evaluate, improve, and sustain intervention programs that target this group of wanna-be gang associates and successfully divert them from the gang into meaningful and effective programs during that one year window of opportunity (see, e.g., Goldstein & Huff, 1993; Howell, Krisberg, Hawkins, & Wilson, 1995).

- A second window of opportunity for intervention occurs between gang members' first arrest for property crime and their subsequent progression into more serious drug-related and violent offenses. This window appears to last, on average, from 1½ to 2 years after the gang member's peak involvement in property crime. If we can successfully intervene (with, e.g., prosecutorial diversion programs targeting first-time, gang-involved property offenders), we stand to save a great deal of suffering by subsequent victims of property crime, drug trafficking, and violent crime and save substantial sums of money that will otherwise be required for further expansion of the juvenile and adult correctional systems. It is also worth noting that the funds to expand these correctional systems are increasingly likely to come from state higher education budgets, as is currently the case in California, where nearly all other state funds are obligated for other purposes. Ironically, underfunding education to build additional prison beds may only exacerbate the gang problem and the related (but far more extensive) problem of drug trafficking, because it will further restrict access to a legitimate means of improving one's position in life (education).

- Certain types of crimes are especially likely to involve gang members, and a sudden increase in those crimes may be viewed as a potential distant early warning signal that crime in the community may be increasingly gang related. Crimes that are especially worth monitoring closely and can realistically be monitored are auto theft and weapons in schools (see Table 4.4); and drive-by shootings (Table 4.4; Klein, 1995a, pp. 117-118), all of which are relatively high-volume offenses for gang members.

- Data from this study suggest that gang members are significantly more likely than comparable nongang peers to be involved in the sale of higher-profit drugs and to make nearly 50% more in earnings from drug sales per week with far fewer customers than their nongang peers. This underscores the need for prevention and early intervention programs that are designed to divert wanna-bes before they have an opportunity to get "hooked" on the illegal earnings that are possible through illegal activities such as drug sales.

- Although many gang members and nongang at-risk peers indicate that it would require a legitimate wage of around $15 per hour to induce a youth to stop selling drugs, a significant number of youth are likely to be amenable to far lower legitimate wages, especially if they can obtain a large number of hours of work per week and increase their total income. This is difficult, however, as many employers offer only part-time jobs, partly to avoid paying the fringe benefits associated with full-time employment. We must, as a nation, develop more effective policies and programs that address school-to-work transition, both by vocational education and training and by national employment and training priorities for youth. The United States will not be able to compete economically on a global scale if it does not have an educated, skilled workforce. That workforce will eventually consist entirely of today's youth and it will include increasing numbers of minorities. For example, about 45% of all net additions to the U.S. labor force in the 1990s will be nonwhite (Fullerton, 1987; Johnston, 1991).

- Gangs are likely to possess powerful and highly lethal weapons, despite the fact that many gang members are not yet old enough to drive a car legally. Efforts to reduce the number of illegal weapons possessed by youth and adults (such as the recent Kansas City experiment) should be emphasized and could have substantial impact in reducing gun-related crimes (see Cook & Moore, 1995, for a discussion of gun control strategies).

- Finally, gangs should be viewed not as *the* problem but rather as a symptom of more complex and pervasive problems in our society. Addressing these problems will require, first, that we begin to develop integrated, coordinated, and carefully developed *youth policy*. The fact is that our youth are our most valuable resource, yet we do not have carefully coordinated youth policy in our nation, our states, or our communities. The development of such policy, along with the establishment of *healthy communities* (see Hawkins & Catalano, 1992, for a discussion of a promising "Communities That Care" model) in which youth can develop into responsible and productive citizens, should be at the top of our public policy agenda. We must address these problems in the broader context of reconstructing our communities (Currie, 1993, pp. 280-332) and providing community-based interventions and services (National Research Council, 1993, pp. 193-234). Otherwise, the problems represented by gangs and drugs are likely to remain severe and Ohio and the nation are likely to decline in economic competitiveness because of our failure to cultivate an educated, skilled, and productive citizenry by ensuring that legitimate economic opportunities are more available and more compelling than those illegitimate opportunities that are available to our youth. The Achilles' heel of a free, democratic society is the inability to produce responsible and productive citizens. Gangs and the problems associated with gangs reflect this problem and underscore the importance of developing a coordinated public policy response that emphasizes the importance of healthy, functional communities.

Notes

1. The author is especially grateful for the assistance of Kenneth Trump, Michael Walker, and Linda Schmidt, as well as a number of staff members working in various neighborhood centers in Cleveland, in the identification and construction of the Cleveland gang and nongang at-risk youth subsamples utilized in this study.

2. Note that the levels of statistical significance reported in these tables are based on the original *scaled* responses (based on frequency of drug sales), which were then dichotomized to simplify the tables.

3. It is important to note that since these data have been presented to the chief and the top command staff, the Threat Group Coordinating Committee has been formed in the Division of Police to coordinate the division's efforts to address crimes committed by gangs and other threat groups, such as white supremacists and other hate groups. At the invitation of the Division of Police, I now serve as a regular member of the committee to ensure that our collective gang research knowledge is better utilized in the prevention and control of gang-related crime in Columbus.

Breaking the Bonds of Membership
Leaving the Gang

SCOTT H. DECKER
JANET L. LAURITSEN

Criminologists have long realized that adult membership in gangs is a rare phenomenon (e.g., Thrasher, 1927/1963). Similarly, recent surveys of high-risk youth have reminded us of the importance of studying gang membership through time as a transitory affiliation rather than as a fixed characteristic of an adolescent. For instance, Thornberry, Krohn, Lizotte, and Chard-Wierschem (1993) and Esbensen and Huizinga (1993), using longitudinal data from independent samples, found that the vast majority of youth who report being members of gangs indicate their membership is of short duration, typically one year or less. In addition, Rand (1987) reports that leaving the gang appears to produce reductions in criminal involvement. Nonetheless, analyses of the process of *leaving the gang* have been overlooked in favor of studies of becoming a gang member, despite the fact that such an understanding may be of significant practical importance. Criminologists have begun to focus attention on the process of desistance from crime, however (Sampson & Laub, 1993), in the hopes of understanding exits from crime. In this chapter, we discuss the importance of studying the process of leaving the gang and describe various dimensions of this phenomenon, using data from a recent field study of gang and ex-gang members in St. Louis. We conclude with a discussion of the complexity of resolving definitional issues and the need for additional information for theoretical and policy or programmatic purposes.

What Is Known About Leaving the Gang?

Klein noted in 1971 that there was no study of the progression of gang members to adulthood. Although Moore (1991) and Vigil (1988a) have begun to sketch out the details of such progression, it remains a topic about which too little is known. Sanchez-Jankowski (1991, p. 61) speculated that there are six ways gang members could exit their gang: (a) age out, (b) die, (c) go to prison, (d) get jobs, (e) join other organizations, or (f) leave as the gang subdivides. He observed no pattern in the way in which individual gang members left their gang, underscoring the diverse reasons that individual gang members provide when asked how they came to disassociate themselves from their gang.

Based on a series of prison interviews, Skolnick (1988) reported that the only way to leave the gang was to "fade out," by gradually withdrawing from the activities of the gang (p. 4). Despite this observation, he reported that the belief among prison gang members persisted that membership was permanent—that is, gang members had no way out of their gang other than death. A similar observation is reported by Fong, Vogel, and Buentello (1995). Based on data collected from the Texas prison system, Fong and his colleagues report that leaving prison gangs has far greater consequences than leaving street gangs, as the prison affords a closed system in which gang members cannot move, hide, or enmesh themselves in alternative associational networks. Despite this, Fong et al. report that substantial numbers of prison gang members leave their gang each year, generally without consequence. This suggests that leaving a prison gang may be more widespread than has generally been assumed and that beliefs about leaving the gang may not be synonymous with behaviors.

Vigil (1988) presents perhaps the most detailed discussion of the process of exiting the gang. In his analysis of Chicano gangs in Los Angeles, he found that there was a "succession quality" to leaving the gang—that is, most gang members leave the gang through a process not dissimilar to that which they use in entering the gang, a gradual series of steps and commitments. And like joining the gang, he reports, leaving was frequently accompanied by the ritual of being "beaten out." This process involves either running a line or being in a circle where the prospective members (or ex-members) must absorb the blows of their fellow gang members to prove their worth. Vigil found that leaving the gang was most often accompanied by increased ties to social institutions, often prison. He characterizes the process of leaving as more difficult than joining, however, in part because leaving the gang means rejecting one's friends and peers. Because the gang has provided a source of support and friendship, he argues that it often is not replaced until a suitable substitute has been found.

Hagedorn (1994a) has a long-standing research project with Milwaukee gang members. In 1987, he interviewed 47 members ("founders") of 19 Milwaukee gangs. In 1992, interviews were conducted with 101 founding members of 18 gangs, a sample that included 23 individuals previously interviewed as part of the 1987 study. Most of the members of the second sample were adults; indeed, the median age of that group was 26 years. Hagedorn identified a four-category typology of adult gang members, largely based on their relationship to drug sales and employment in the legitimate economy. Two of these categories are especially relevant for the current discussion, "Legits" and "Homeboys." Despite strong commitments to the goals of legitimate society, especially the labor market, few of the African American and Latino gang members from the original sample had become Legits, individuals who reported that they had left the gang, were not involved in drug sales, and were involved in jobs or school. These individuals represent a category of behavior, identification, and attachment that most easily could be classified as ex-gang members. The second category, Homeboys, was more difficult to classify with regard to status as active or ex-gang member. Homeboys were generally in their mid-20s, past the peak age of offending, and generally worked in the legitimate economy. The transition between the legitimate and the illegal economy was made quite frequently by these individuals. Despite commitments to conventional aspirations, Homeboys often found themselves unable to fulfill such aspirations. In the face of this dilemma, they moved between gang activity and other, more legitimate middle-age concerns. What remains uncertain in Hagedorn's descriptions of these two categories of active and ex-gang members is the specific mechanism that provides the impetus to leave or reduce ties to the gang.

Much of the gang literature suggests that gang members "age out" of the gang (Horowitz, 1983; Klein, 1971). Aging out may not be experienced uniformly by all gang members, however. Horowitz (1983) reports that "peripheral" or "fringe" members found it easier to leave the gang than did "core" members. It was more difficult for core members to leave the gang because of their increased involvement in gang activities and subsequent dependence on the gang for social support, and in some cases, instrumental benefits.

A variety of problems may emerge in trying to leave the gang; some of these stem from the gang itself, but many have their focus outside the gang. Despite announcing their decision to leave the gang, ex-gang members can continue to be seen as gang members by members of their own gang, rival gangs, the police, and the community. Gang identities often remain fixed well after the decision to leave the gang has been made and acted on, and a past gang identity complicates the already-difficult process of extricating oneself from the gang. For example, announcing the decision to leave the gang would not necessarily reduce the incentive for rival gang members to redress a previous act of violence committed against a member of their gang. Nor would such an announcement reduce the efforts of the police to make arrests for past criminal activities committed while a gang member. Past gang activity may also hinder an individual's ability to gain employment, making it more difficult for the labor market to exercise its power to produce conformity. Given the continued perception of individuals as gang members and the likelihood that the consequences of their activities as gang members will follow them when they leave the gang, many gang members may decide that in practical terms leaving the gang is not worth the effort. After all, what incentive is there to leave the gang when it is the source of their friends and when past criminal activities committed as gang members cause many groups to continue to treat them as if they remained in a gang? Stated differently, why sacrifice your friendships when you continue to be treated like a gang member anyway?

Current knowledge surrounding the process of leaving the gang is primarily descriptive. We found no research designed to systematically predict under what conditions members choose to leave the gang or what factors account for the length of time one remains a gang member. Gang members do report that they see themselves and others leaving for a variety of reasons and in numerous manners, however. These accounts can guide researchers' efforts in determining whether the decision to leave is driven by individual characteristics, experiences within the gang, microgroup processes in the gang, external ties such as investments in social institutions or attachments to prosocial persons, or some other set of unknown factors. We believe that to examine these factors, many definitional issues need to be addressed. These concerns became apparent in our investigation of this process among gang and ex-gang members in St. Louis.

The Data

To structure our discussion of the process of leaving the gang, we rely on data from a 3-year field study of gangs in St. Louis conducted between October 1990 and September 1993. The city of St. Louis has experienced the same types of economic and population losses that have plagued many other midwestern industrial cities. Gangs in St. Louis grew in number and membership during the mid-1980s (Decker & Van Winkle, 1996). For this project, the working definition of a "gang" included those age-graded peer groups that exhibited permanence, engaged in criminal activity, and had symbolic representations of membership. Contacts were made with active and ex-gang members by a street ethnographer who verified membership and observed gang activity in neighborhoods. The street ethnographer, an ex-offender himself, had built a reputation as "solid" on the street, both through his work with the community and previous research work. Using snowball sampling procedures (Biernacki & Waldorf, 1981; Wright, Decker, Redfern, & Smith, 1992), initial field contacts were made and the sample was built to include more subjects.

Individuals who admitted current or past membership and agreed to an interview became part of our sample. Current and past membership was also verified by information from previous subjects or observation and subjects were considered "ex-gang members" based on self-reports. Most subjects' status as an ex-gang member was also verified by the reports of other subjects. Three months had to pass since ex-members last belonged to their gang to qualify for our study.

Three features distinguish this work from most studies of gangs. First, no criminal justice contacts were used to gain access to the members of the sample. Using criminal justice channels (police, courts, probation, social service agencies) to contact gang members is likely to result in a different gang member than one found in the field. Second, the gang members themselves told their story. Although an interview instrument was used, ample opportunity was provided in open-ended questions for the subjects to elaborate on questions and add new insights. Third, this was a field study of gangs, not conducted in the offices of a social service or youth agency. All participants in the study were initially contacted in the neighborhoods where they live and act out their gang activities. This enabled project personnel to observe a number of gang activities, including violent encounters between gangs.

The data consist of interviews with 99 active gang members and 24 ex-gang members. The ex-members reported that they formerly had belonged to one of the six constellations of gangs from which our active gang members were recruited. We look at data from both sets of subjects to compare active members' perceptions of what leaving the gang would entail to the experiences of ex-members. Not unexpected, the ex-gang members were older (mean = 19 years of age) than the currently active gang members (mean = 17). Twenty-two of the of the ex-gang members were black males, two were black females. The sample of active gang members included 4 white males, 7 black females, and 88 black males. Half of the ex-gang members interviewed had left the gang for a period of less than a year at the time of the interview. Ex-gang members came from 17 different gangs. Eleven of the ex-gang members came from gangs with a "loose" organizational structure, lacking leadership and having few group goals and infrequent group associations. Five ex-members came from gangs with a high level of organization, and five came from gangs that were organized in moderate fashion.

Reasons for Leaving

Because little is known about the process of leaving the gang, we begin by examining the reasons ex-members offer for leaving the gang, as well as the way in which they left their gangs. When asked why they left their gangs, the majority (16 ex-gang members, or two thirds of this sub-sample) of our respondents offered a specific reason: They left because of the level of violence. Many of these individuals left because of violence they personally had experienced.

EX003[1] Well, after I got shot, I got shot in my leg. You know how your life just flash? I was walking to my father's house, he stay on the westside. I was walking and then I saw, see I don't like the color red, I hate the color red, and it was like a whole corner full of Bloods. It was like, what's up, Blood? I said no. They said, "What you claim?" And then we had a fight and I hit a few of them. It was like ten of them and then I ran and then all I heard was pow, I was still running. I had on some white jogging pants and I saw blood running down the back of my leg and I just ran over to my father's house. It [the bullet] didn't go in, it was like grazing me. It just scared me cause I ended up being shot at. I had a gun put to my head before but I never been shot at.

INT   Why did you quit being in the gang?

EX014   Because I was put in the hospital.

INT   You were hospitalized?

EX014   Yeah, for 4 days.

INT   What were you hospitalized for?

EX014   I got beat in the back of the head with a bat.

INT   By other gang members, some Bloods or something?

EX014   Hoover. [Crips].

INT   Why did you get out?

EX011   Because I got to realizing it wasn't my type of life. I didn't want to live that type of life. One time, I got seriously stabbed and I was in the hospital for like 3 months.

INT   Where did you get it?

EX011   Right in my back. Close to the kidney. I was in the hospital for like 3 months. After I got out of the hospital, I tried to cope with it a little more, but I just faded away from it.

In some cases, the threat of personal violence was sufficient to propel the individual to leave the gang.

INT   Why did you quit?

EX001   Because we might get shot. Somebody in our hood got shot last night and the day before that. They killing for no reason.

EX013   I didn't want to die. Just one day I got out.

In other cases, family members were the victims of violence, or violence was threatened against family members. For these individuals, this single event was enough to provoke the decision to leave the gang.

INT   Why did you leave?

EX018   My cousin got shot.

The majority of ex-members who cited violence as the reason they left their gangs underscored the vicarious nature of violence that had occurred against other members of their gangs.

EX016   Yeah, that really came to me because when one of my friends got killed and you look at his face, it was hard. It could have been me. His parents were at the point. . . . It was just hard on me because the reason why he got in was because of me. It was hard for me to go up to his parents. At that point, I was saying that it wasn't my fault. When I really woke up was when my friend died because we got in there together. He said I'm gonna get in if you get in.

INT   Can you tell me why did you decide to leave the gang?

EX002   Because all my friends were getting killed that I used to hang with and because the hood I'm staying in there's a lot of Bloods, which I didn't want to be.

INT   Why did you leave?

EX009   Because people was dying. It wasn't about nothing to me no more.

INT   Why did you leave?

EX012   My best friend, he got killed. We was in the eighth grade together [and] freshman year.

The remaining eight individuals offered diverse reasons why they left their gang. Three said that they had moved out of town, severing ties with the gangs in their former cities of residence. Two additional ex-members couldn't offer a reason why they left the gang. Three individuals cited maturational reform as the motivation behind leaving their gangs. In some cases, this involved caring for children; in others it was linked to obligations to family.

INT   Why did you quit?

EX021   Because I've got two children to live for.

Three individuals who indicated that violence had prompted them to leave also cited the role of family in leaving the gang.

INT   Why did you leave?

EX013   Because of my loved ones. I just couldn't keep neglecting them.

EX011   When I was in the gang I wasn't spending time with my daughter, I wasn't taking care of her, I wasn't doing, that's mainly why me and my baby's mother broke up because stuff I was getting in. She didn't want to be around me, the kind of person that I was then. Now, I have got me a job, I was getting locked up before.

In some of these cases, a single event (especially violence) was enough to encourage active gang members to leave their gangs; in others an accumulation of events and attachments preceded the decision. Clearly, the combination of maturational reform, aging, and proximity to violence was at work for a number of individuals. Just as Hagedorn (1994a) found that participation in gang activities declined with age, we observed that involvement in activities associated with postadolescent stages of the life course (job, family, concern about one's future) often corresponded to the reasons offered by ex-gang members for leaving their gangs.

Given that the majority of this sample of ex-gang members reported leaving their gangs because of violence, it is important now to describe *how* they left their gangs. Here, we seek to understand the specific route or method used to leave the gang. Once again, a single answer dominated the responses. Fifteen of the 24 ex-gang members (63%) told us that they simply quit their gangs and did not have to use a specific method to leave. This perhaps underscores an important structural feature of the gangs in this study; most of the ex-gang members were in gangs characterized by loose ties between members, few formal rules, and little structure. Gangs in St. Louis had few strong leaders. Rather, subgroups within the gang claimed stronger allegiances than did the larger gang (Decker & Van Winkle, 1996). It was in those subgroups that most illegal activities, especially drug sales, took place. Perhaps it was because friendship ties within the subgroup were so strong that the majority of these individuals experienced no retaliation for their decision to leave the gang.

EX001   I just quit. I stopped hanging out with them. There was about three of us that quit, we just stopped hanging out with them and everything.

INT   How did you leave? Did you have to announce something, did you get beat out?

EX008   Just stopped claiming.

INT   So when guys would ask you if you were claiming, you would say no, I'm out of that now?

EX008   Yeah.

INT   Did people respect that?

EX008   No.

INT   What did they do when you told them you weren't claiming any more?

EX008   Most of them started talking stuff. Once you in, you in it for life and all that stuff.

INT   How did you get out?

EX011   Some of them be funning saying they got to kill they mother but some of the stuff is true. How I really got out of it, I just got me a little job, stopped hanging out with them.

INT   How did you leave?
EX019   I just walked away.
INT   It was that easy? They didn't . . .
EX019   No, they didn't fuck with me.

A small number, however, told us they were threatened after they left the gang.

INT   How did you leave?
EX016   I just stopped socializing with them. I was threatened to get killed after I left but it really didn't faze me.

And a few ex-members report having to fight a member to formally leave the gang.

EX004   If you want to get out you get beat down.
INT   So you get out the same way you get in?
EX004   Right. There's more dudes on you. About six dudes on you.

INT   How did you leave the gang?
EX024   Moved out of there.
INT   You had to beat up on other members to get out?
EX024   Yeah.

A final group of five ex-members reported that they left their gangs by moving. One, who had moved to St. Louis from California, told us that one could never really leave the gang, but that moving out of state was the way he severed ties with his gang.

INT   When did you quit the gang?
EX006   I never did quit. You can never get out of the gang. Only way you can quit is to stop hanging around them or move to another state.
INT   How long [since] you moved from California?
EX006   Four years, really 3½.
INT   So [the] gang consider[s] you in the gang until you die, right?

EX006   You can get out of the gang if you really wanted to. But in California you have to kill somebody to get out of the gang. You got to kill your mother or somebody like that to get out of it. I can't get out of it. I ain't killing my mother.

These data from ex-gang members inform us of their self-described motives and recollections. Active gang members have their own perspective on leaving the gang, and we now turn to data from the 99 active gang members interviewed as part of this project. It has been argued that status as a gang member is typically perceived as a "master status," one that influences most behavior and is not shed easily (Sanchez-Jankowski, 1991). Active gang members have a stake in maintaining such a view of gang membership because the viability of the gang depends on the ability of active gang members to maintain the perception that leaving the gang is nearly impossible. Perhaps, in part, this explains the efforts of active gang members to foster the belief that drastic steps (e.g., killing one's mother) are the only means by which individuals can leave the gang. Such threats have an importance equal to that of the mythic intergang violence identified by Klein (1971) and others (Sanders, 1994; Short & Strodtbeck, 1965/1974) in maintaining gang solidarity.

Most active gang members strongly expressed the belief that one can never leave the gang. Despite this, a majority of the active gang members we interviewed knew individuals who had left their own gang. Indeed, 55 of the 81 active gang members who responded to this question (68%) told us they knew individuals who had left their gang. Interestingly, the reasons why these individuals left their gang closely paralleled those offered by the ex-gang members. In rank order, violence, maturational reform, and just stopping were the three categories identified most often by active gang members.

Almost half of the active gang members who knew an individual who left their gang identified violence as the primary reason. Being shot or beaten up was the reason offered most frequently.

INT   Why did they decide to leave, do you know?
036   Got shot in the head.

INT   Why did he get out of it?
048   Cause he was getting beat up too much.

INT	Why did they leave the gang?
083	They got beat up bad.

Other gang members left because they knew members of their own gang who had been the victims of violence.

INT	How did they decide to leave?
004	One of they friends got killed.

INT	Why did they leave?
035	Death in they family.
INT	You mean somebody was killed?
035	Somebody that was real close to them and they figured they had to leave.

Often, the victims were relatives of a gang member, making the violence more salient to them.

INT	Do you know why he decided to leave?
075	One person left because his brother got shot so he just went out.
INT	His brother didn't die, did he?
075	Yeah, he did.

Or in other cases, gang members grew weary of threats against their family.

INT	Do you know why he decided to leave?
087	Same reason I left from where I was at.
INT	Too much heat and static?
087	Yeah, cause it would get so far as they will harass your family, like shoot your house up or something.

The second-largest category of active gang members who knew a fellow gang member who had left the gang identified maturational reform as the primary reason for breaking the bonds of gang member-ship. Maturational reform most often involved family and job concerns.

INT	Do you know why he left?
093	This white boy Gary used to be with us, he use to be a Blood and stuff like that but he got this gal pregnant and he got his own house and he told us he didn't want to be in the gang any more.

INT	Do you know anybody who used to be in a gang but isn't any more?
021	My brother used to be in a gang but he don't claim no more.
INT	How come?
021	He was with the gang but he got serious with his girlfriend and got her pregnant and he said fuck that shit [the gang]. I'm just going to lay low with my gal, I ain't got time for that. He don't got time for that [gang] stuff.

037	My big brother [left the gang]. He was in the 38s. They say to get out of the 38s you got to kill your parents, kill one of your parents. My brother was making good grades, got him a scholarship and everything and he was like I'm leaving this alone. They tried to make him kill my mother. He was like, you must be crazy, and I was on his side.

Although violent experiences and maturational reform describe how the majority of individuals left their gang, a number of gang members told us they knew gang members who had simply stopped being in the gang. The process by which these individuals left their gang reinforces the view that gangs in St. Louis have limited control over their members and are loosely confederated subgroups.

INT	Are there people who used to be in your gang but aren't any more?
003	Well, we did have a few people who left but they had talked to us about it and said they didn't want to be in the gang any more. We said alright man that's cool. We a gang if you just want out you want out, you out of here.

INT	Do you know why they decided to leave?
011	Cause it don't prove anything cause everybody splitting up slowly cause it don't really prove nothing. If we need their help they will come back and help.

INT	Do you know anybody who used to be in a gang but isn't any more?
086	Yeah.
INT	Do you know why they decided to leave?
086	They just stopped. They not in it but they still a gang member.

These observations confirm the view that leaving the gang occurs through a variety of mechanisms. Whether data were drawn from ex-gang members or active gang members, similar findings were observed. According to these subjects, leaving the gang is not a process that requires taking exceptional steps and most ex-gang members report gradually severing the bonds between themselves and the gang. Indeed, in many instances active gang members saw the internal logic of such decisions made by their peers.

These data also illustrate some of the difficulties in determining precisely when gang membership ceases and what that means for future interactions and affiliations with active gang members. What some subjects describe as a rather simple experience in fact draws attention to important definitional issues. For example, the last two subjects (011 and 086) indicate that ex-gang members may still be viewed as being involved with the gang, either emotionally (086) or as individuals who can be counted on for involvement in certain gang activities (011).

Overall, most members of our ex-gang sample indicated they left the gang because of concerns over violence targeted directly at them or at members of their gang. Almost all gang members are either actively engaged in violence or under threat of violence on a regular basis, however. Indeed, many commentators (Klein, 1971; Sanchez-Jankowski, 1991; Short & Strodtbeck, 1965/1974; Vigil, 1988a; Yablonsky, 1973) identify violence as a defining feature of gang life. A large body of research indicates that gang violence (real or mythic) provides much of the solidarity that keeps gangs together (Klein, 1971; Moore, 1978; Short & Strodtbeck, 1965/1974; Thrasher, 1927/1963; Vigil, 1988a). Our findings suggest that violence may have contradictory consequences: The very activity that often keeps gangs together appears to have provided the impetus for the majority of this sample to leave the gang. This paradox is certainly worth theoretical development and detailed exploration.

Defining an Ex-Gang Member

As noted earlier, the comments of the active and ex-gang members raise complicated issues regarding status classification. Recall the methods that were used to leave the gang. Most ex-gang members told us that they just quit; they decided it was time to move on to other activities and they did so. In St. Louis, we found little evidence that leaving the gang requires group consent. If the gang itself does not confer this status, then certain issues of measurement arise. The lack of a specific ceremony or denoting act of renunciation of membership makes it more difficult to know who is a gang member and who has left the gang.

The answer to the question, "Is this person still a gang member?" is explicitly tied to the researcher's definition of what constitutes a "gang" and a "member." As many have argued, there is still considerable debate over this issue (see, e.g., Ball & Curry, 1995; Covey, Menard, & Franzese, 1992; Decker & Kempf, 1991). Most studies rely on self-report questions (e.g., "Are you a member of a street or youth gang?") and require that the group to which the youth belongs engage in some illegal activity (see, e.g., Esbensen & Huizinga, 1993). If we accept these two commonly used criteria, it seems reasonable to rely on self-reports for determining ex-gang member status. In other words, given that someone admitted past gang involvement, the answer to this question should be sufficient for most purposes.

A rather high level of ambiguity concerning ex-gang member status was found in interviews with gang and (self-reported) ex-gang members in St. Louis, however. Even though the ex-gang members all reported that they were no longer a "member of a gang," a considerable proportion claimed that they continued to participate in certain activities (criminal and noncriminal) with members of the gang, and others still had emotional ties to gang members. We found that two dimensions usually important in all friendship networks—activities and attachments—often continued to be reported by ex-gang members when they discussed their membership status. Using these two dimensions (activities and attachments), we display in Table 5.1 a typology for describing ex-members' relationships with their gangs.

Recall that all of ex-gang members in the St. Louis sample self-reported being ex-gang members. Persons who fall into category A in Table 5.1 are

TABLE 5.1 Relationship Between Emotional Ties of Ex-Gang Members and
Activities With Active Gang Members

		Emotional Ties (Attachments) With Members of Previous Gang Network	
		NO	YES
Engage in Activities With Members	NO	A	B
of Previous Gang Network	YES	C	D

the least ambiguously classified as ex-gang members. These individuals no longer have attachments to members of their former gangs and no longer engage in activities (criminal or noncriminal) with those members. The clearest example of such a category are those who have moved to new towns, leaving their gangs—activities and members—behind.

Alternatively, we also found self-proclaimed ex-gang members who said that although they no longer associated with members of their gangs, they still had friendship ties that were strong enough that they would "help out" their old associates if they were needed (category B in the table). These individuals claimed that they would assist members of their ex-gangs if there was "trouble." For theoretical proposes, it may be important to distinguish these ex-gang members from other ex-members, as these attachments may also influence individuals' criminal and noncriminal activities.

Category C in the table consists of those subjects who see themselves as ex-gang members primarily because they do not engage in criminal activity with members of their gangs (or use gang symbols), yet they still report these others as persons with whom they occasionally engage in *non*criminal activities. In the St. Louis data, these individuals are most likely to have left the gang through maturational reform. In these instances, the subject's self-definition of being a gang member is apparently determined by his or her own involvement in criminality. Although an argument could be made that these individuals are still active gang members (despite their own protests), to do so requires that the researcher change the working definition of membership to include only activity and attachments, and disregard self-reported status.

Finally, we also uncovered ex-gang members who reported engaging in activities such as playing basketball or going to dances with other gang members and who describe those attachments as important friendships (category D in the table). Identifying these individuals as equivalent to ex-gang members in category A is problematic because associational and emotional ties with active gang members remain. According to most theories of gang influence, active members should have the strongest influences over these ex-members' behavior.

Thus, we find that designating someone as an ex-gang member can be a controversial task because self-described ex-gang members report varying degrees of attachments and involvements with their prior gangs. Status assessments are also difficult because the process is often gradual. The objective of the analyses should determine the definition of ex-gang member status (Ball & Curry, 1995). For many purposes, this is likely to require more than a yes or no response to a self-report item. For example, gang facilitation hypotheses typically argue that attachments and activities are sources of gang influence on offending behavior. Without data on these dimensions, it may be difficult to assess how variations in these ties influence the decision to leave or how gangs might continue to influence ex-members' behaviors after they report having left.

Conclusions

Leaving the gang is a more complex and variable process than suggested in previous research. In some instances, it appears that persons make an explicit decision to leave; others simply drift away. The St. Louis data suggest that the way in which individuals "leave" the gang is likely to be a function of the characteristics of the group and the individual. Violent experiences motivated some gang members to leave. Unfortunately, with these data, we are unable to determine what factors distinguish those who will leave the gang following violent experiences from those who will stay.

We also found that the definitional complexities inherent in identifying a gang member (or gang activity) are equally present when trying to determine whether an individual has left the gang. Because the process of leaving the gang is typically a gradual one, identifying individuals as only active or ex-gang members could lead researchers and practitioners away from important subtleties during periods of change.

If we concede that little can be done to prevent individuals from joining a gang, then seeking means to induce individuals to leave their gang takes on greater significance. Perhaps, it is possible to shorten the duration of gang membership, to reduce certain types of violence and property crimes. One of the ironic findings noted above concerns the role of violence in deciding to leave the gang. A considerable volume of past gang research has underscored the role of violence in enhancing gang solidarity. Despite this, the majority of the ex-gang members in this sample said that violence had played a role in their decision to leave the gang. This suggests an important avenue for intervention. Although it is certainly not desirable to induce gang violence, gangs themselves seem particularly adept at accomplishing this task. Seizing opportunities when gang members have been victimized by violence or have witnessed a close friend's victimization may offer promising avenues for intervention.

Our findings suggest that the role of violence in enhancing cohesion may have an important time dimension. In the short term, violence may cause some gang members to reflect on the risks of their participation in the gang and to question the viability of their membership. The extent to which they are physically separated from the gang will likely play a large role in determining how salient violent victimization will be for their decision to leave the gang. Over the longer term, enhanced by interaction with other gang members, violence can serve to enhance cohesion (Klein, 1971; Short & Strodtbeck, 1965/1974). The trick, then, is to intervene immediately following acts of violence, when gang members are separated from their gang, or at least when they are in small groups that are apart from the gang. Such opportunities are not likely to exist in the offices of social service agencies. Rather, they are likely to be found in hospital emergency rooms, at the police station, or in family settings. Our results suggest that some of the most effective interventions may be those implemented immediately following violent victimization or witnessing the violent victimization of a close friend who is also a gang member. Such intervention is likely to be successful to the extent that it (a) occurs very shortly after the victimization, and (b) occurs separate from the influence of the gang. Follow-up services may be necessary, particularly to counteract the socializing power of the gang in "reconstructing" the violence in a fashion that serves to reintegrate the gang member into the collective.

Note

1. INT stands for interviewer; the 3-digit number stands for the number of the subject. Ex-gang members are denoted by EX before the subject number.

Exploring the Differences Between Gang and Nongang Prisoners

PAIGE RALPH
ROBERT J. HUNTER
JAMES W. MARQUART
STEVEN J. CUVELIER
DOROTHY MERIANOS

In the late 1960s and early 1970s, inmate criminal organizations began to be a significant factor in state prisons (Crouch & Marquart, 1989). This rise in prison gang activity is often associated with the structural changes that were occurring in many state systems, due in part to judicial intervention. The civil rights movement of the 1960s allowed inmates to become assertive to the point that they seemed almost militant in seeking redress from the courts (Jacobs, 1977). Judicial intervention, intended to make prisons safer and more humane, actually resulted in increased amounts of inmate violence and unrest. This organizational crisis, precipitated by the courts, resulted in a large number of inmates joining groups for self-protection and to achieve dominance and control of the prison economy (Jacobs, 1977). In some states, members of street gangs took advantage of this opportunity to extend their power into state prisons. In some cases, prison gangs established footholds in the free community (Crouch & Marquart, 1989).

Inmates have always grouped together, often on the basis of ethnicity, criminal history, neighborhood, or city affiliations (Irwin, 1970). Minority groups were among the first to form inmate gangs. For example, black Chicago street gangs, such as the Black Stone Rangers and the Devil's Disciples, became very powerful inmate groups in Illinois prisons in the mid-to-late 1960s (Jacobs, 1977). The Black Guerrilla Family, which espoused a revolutionary doctrine, was formed in California prisons in the 1960s. Hispanic prisoners formed gangs (e.g., the Mexican Mafia) to control prison rackets (Davidson, 1974).

A limited amount of systematic research exists on the nature of inmate gangs (Crouch & Marquart, 1989). Although the origin of the first inmate gang is often debated, most prison scholars generally agree that these organizations spread from the West Coast eastward (Crouch & Marquart, 1989). Camp and Camp (1987) found there was reported gang activity in 29 prison systems; 114 gangs were identified with over 12,000 inmate members. In 1985, the total U.S. prisoner population was 446,244 and gang members represented under 3% of the incarcerated population.

Inmates who are members of gangs actually make up a small proportion of the total prison population, but their impact on prison order is immense. Many problems are inherent in trying to control gang violence (e.g., identification of members, cell space for isolation of known members) and illicit activities within prisons (Cox, 1986). California prison officials estimate that prison gangs are responsible for well over half of the violence committed in their facilities. This is a significant percentage when considering the fact that gang members only make up 2.5% of the California inmate population (Cox, 1986). Between the years 1971 and 1979, prison gang members in California were responsible for over 200 homicides and thousands of nonfatal stabbings (Crouch & Marquart, 1989). In addition to this violence, gang members are also involved in many illicit activities both inside and outside prison (i.e., drug trafficking, extortion, prostitution, etc.).

Not all gang violence is committed by bona fide gang members. Associates of the gangs are not "made" members but present numerous problems for prison managers. For example, in California, associates only constitute 7% of the total inmate population, but due to their mobility and "anonymity" to prison staff they commit 70% of the gang criminal activity (Cox, 1986). This pattern of core versus fringe membership is reflective of juvenile gangs (Klein, 1968). No doubt, other prison systems are experiencing the same trends.

Despite the prevalence and seriousness of prisoner gang activity, few systematic analyses have documented this phenomenon. Compared to juvenile and adult street gangs, prison gang research has been isolated and has not yielded a strong theoretical and methodological tradition. We still lack basic information on gang member demographics or differences between gang members and nonmembers. Research has been conducted on prison gangs in several states: California (Porter, 1982), Illinois (Jacobs, 1977), Arizona (Crist, 1986), and New Mexico ("New Mexico Analyzes," 1990). Little research has been undertaken to examine the gang phenomenon in Texas prisons. This chapter is specifically concerned with discerning the differences between gang and nongang male inmates in Texas. First, we discuss the role of gangs in prisons, then we briefly describe the rise of Texas prisoner gangs. Data are presented from the Texas prison system that illustrate the differences between the two groups.

The Role of Inmate Gangs

Inmate gangs have their own code of behavior, which is dramatically different from the inmate code of the past. The traditional code exhorted inmates to "do your own time." Today, gang members and associates are compelled to "do gang time" and not subscribe to the code of the past. The goal of most inmate gangs is to obtain financial profit through illicit means. To do this, the gang members use violence and exploitation to prey upon fellow inmates. Gang members increase their rank (status) in the organization through violence and obedience to gang rules in all circumstances. The most often cited reasons for performing a "contract hit" (a planned killing) are either as part of initiation into the gang, to enhance one's reputation in the gang, or because it is the duty of a member.

Prison gangs, like delinquent street gangs, serve a number of functions: They provide something to do, promise protection, offer a way to "beat the man," and allow access to illicit goods and services (e.g., narcotics, "punks," clothes, and food). The gang provides a group in which men feel solidarity and brotherhood. This phenomenon has been described as a surrogate family both inside and outside the institution.

The main gang activities are selling protection, acquiring and distributing narcotics and sexual favors, and dealing in other contraband. Gangs increase their material resources and seize "market shares" in the lucrative prison rackets by adding "muscle," recruiting new members, and eliminating competition. Almost all gang-related crimes are attributable to furthering or protecting business interests (Beard, 1986).

Prison staff perceptions of the objectives of the gangs vary dramatically. Some prison officials (those who have little involvement in the gang intelligence work) often believe one of the primary goals of prison gangs is to undermine prison officials. To accomplish this, inmates file numerous frivolous legal writs and lawsuits, instigate food and work strikes, and cause major disturbances (Texas Department of Corrections [TDC], n.d.). Although gang members do engage in this behavior, it is more likely a leisure activity rather than an objective.

The Rise of Texas Prison Gangs

Until the mid-1970s, the Black Muslims were the only "organized" and potentially antistaff inmate group in Texas prisons. Throughout the 1960s, the Muslim movement gained members, but contrary to staff expectations and fears, these inmates were not particularly assaultive or disruptive (Price, 1975).

Texas, as compared to other states, was a relative latecomer to the gang phenomenon (Beard, 1986). The first gang-related homicide in Texas prisons, a Texas Syndicate murder, occurred in 1979. Gang violence then became an increasingly serious management problem and culminated in a wave of murder and unprecedented mayhem in the mid-1980s. In 1984 and 1985 alone, 52 inmate murders occurred, and well over three quarters involved gang members. Since that time, staff members have taken major steps to identify and isolate confirmed gang members in administrative segregation. Gang intelligence units have been formed in prison units to monitor gang activity and communication patterns—inside and outside the walls. These units were very successful in disrupting gang activities by acquiring their bylaws, organizational structures, and membership lists. For example, here is the captured constitution of the Texas Aryan Brotherhood:

Section 1: TITLE

The Texas Aryan Brothers is an independent organization of, by and for the Aryan Brothers of Texas. It is not affiliated with any other group or organization. Our Organization is a White Supremacy group; no pretense is or will be made to the contrary.

Section 2: SOLIDARITY

1. The Texas Aryan Brothers are solidarity (Brotherhood) among its members. Solidarity is our backbone; nothing is paramount to the Organization.
2. Each member is a mirror of his Brother. Your actions reflect on all Brothers, and breach of the Brotherhood is a serious matter which will be handled as such.
3. Those Brothers chosen for the Organization are life term members; death being the only termination of the membership.
4. Upon release from the TDC, a member will contact an incarcerated member to notify the Organization of his place of residence. The member notified will contact a member of the Steering committee who will take note of the place of residence.
5. Upon release from the TDC, a member will also contact a freeworld member and, after taking note of each other's place of residence, will always maintain regular contact with each other.
6. Newly released members will have a six month grace period after he is released from the TDC or halfway house. The grace period will be used to readjust to the freeworld. After the six month grace period the Brother will establish and maintain regular contact with incarcerated members by whatever means are possible. Incarcerated members for contact will be selected by the Steering Committee or by a Committee Member.
7. All incarcerated and freeworld members will give each other full support and will follow their designated chains of command regardless of their place of residence.

Characteristics of Prison Gang Members

In the early 1990s, 1,300 inmates in Texas units were officially identified as gang members. The main gangs are as follows: Texas Syndicate (Hispanic), Mexican Mafia (Hispanic), Aryan Brotherhood (white), Texas Mafia (white), the Mandingo Warriors (black), and the Self Defense Family (black) (Fong, 1987; Pelz, 1988). Of the 52 inmate murders in 1984-1985, most involved Texas Syndicate members.

Texas has a combination of imported and home-grown inmate gangs. The Texas Syndicate and the Mexican Mafia originated in California, and members, after their release from California prisons, migrated to Texas and eventually into the prison system. Prior to the *Ruiz v. Estelle* (1980) decision, building tenders (dominant prisoners or inmate guards) controlled the inmates, and known gang members were carefully monitored and not allowed the opportunity to organize, recruit, or expand their activities. Known gang members were not isolated but kept under control in the general prisoner population. Court intervention mandated the removal of the building tender system and in the authority vacuum that followed, the Texas Syndicate and Mexican Mafia became criminal organizations in the Texas prison system.

Since the mid-1980s, these inmate criminal organizations have successfully exported their operation to the streets of Texas's large urban areas, especially San Antonio. Included in the bylaws of the Texas Syndicate and Mexican Mafia is the requirement that gang members, when released from prison, get involved in the free-world activities of the gangs. The organization, goals, structure, power, and violence of the Hispanic prison gangs have therefore effectively been exported to and taken root in the free society.

The database for this chapter was obtained from the Texas Department of Criminal Justice—Institution Division. It contains extensive information on personal, psychological, educational, and criminal history and on institutional behavior. The original file contained all inmates imprisoned in Texas from 1980 to 1991. For this study, gang members are defined as inmates identified by Texas prison officials as belonging to disruptive groups. This study was restricted to male inmates, as female gangs do not seem to pose a problem in Texas institutions. A sample of nongang inmates discharged from 1980 to 1991 ($N = 13,218$) was com-

TABLE 6.1 Inmate Race

	Nongang (N = 13,204)	Gang (N = 1,744)
White	38.0%	20.2%
	(5,023)	(352)
Black	41.3%	7.4%
	(5,459)	(129)
Hispanic	20.4%	72.3%
	(2,696)	(1,261)
Other	0.2%	0.1%
	(26)	(2)

TABLE 6.2 Age at Entry to Prison

	Nongang	Gang
White	28.06 years	26.15 years
Black	27.86 years	25.64 years
Hispanic	27.96 years	26.38 years

pared to the population of gang members discharged during the same time period ($N = 1,744$).

The racial breakdown depicted in Table 6.1 of the gang versus nongang inmates was significant ($\chi^2 = 2172.03$, $p < .05$). Although African Americans made up 41.3% of the nongang group, they accounted for only 7.4% of the gang members. Similarly, white inmates were represented proportionately higher in the nongang group (38.0%) than among gang members (20.2%). The Hispanic inmates represented the majority of the gang population, making up 72.3% of the gang members. Hispanic inmates made up only 20.4% of the nongang sample, indicating their disproportionate involvement in gang activity.

Some differences in age were observed between gang and nongang inmates at the time they were received and discharged from prison (Table 6.2). Gang members were slightly younger when entering prison. Gang members were older at discharge (on average, 29.69 years) than nongang members (29.1 years). The younger age at reception and the slightly older

TABLE 6.3 Age at Discharge From Prison

	Nongang	Gang
White	29.17 years	29.83 years
Black	29.02 years	29.62 years
Hispanic	29.18 years	29.67 years

TABLE 6.4 Years of Education

	Nongang	Gang
White	7.18	6.49
Black	5.88	6.15
Hispanic	5.96	5.92
Other	7.13	10.50

age at discharge reflects the fact that gang members tended to have longer sentences than their nongang counterparts (Table 6.3).

There was little evidence of differences between education levels of the two groups (Table 6.4). It appears that white and Hispanic gang members were slightly less educated than their nongang counterparts. For African Americans, gang members had a slightly higher education level than nongang members.

OFFENSE CHARACTERISTICS

The first offense-related variable to be examined was the county of conviction for the inmates (Table 6.5). The majority of nongang inmates in Texas are convicted in Harris County (Houston is located in Harris County), but the majority of the gang inmates were convicted in Bexar County (the largest city in Bexar County is San Antonio.) Few gang inmates were convicted in Dallas County, but that county produced the second largest amount of nongang convictions.

Additional analysis, controlling for race or ethnicity and county of conviction, revealed an interesting pattern. We found no relationship between race and county of conviction for black prisoners, but a significant relationship emerged in separate analyses for whites and Hispanics.

TABLE 6.5   County of Conviction

	Nongang (N = 7,178)	Gang (N = 1,017)
Harris (Houston)	23.8% (3,146)	16.1% (281)
Dallas (Dallas)	16.1% (2,128)	7.6% (133)
Tarrant (Fort Worth)	6.3% (833)	3.4% (59)
Bexar (San Antonio)	4.7% (621)	22.5% (392)
Nueces (Corpus Christi)	1.3% (172)	4.6% (80)
El Paso (El Paso)	2.1% (278)	4.1% (72)

NOTE: Largest city in parenthesis.

The data showed that more white gang members emanated from Bexar County than any other Texas county. This latter finding was contrary to our expectations. We anticipated that white gang members would originate from Harris and Dallas counties. Additionally, and as expected, almost one third of the Hispanic gang members originated from Bexar County. There appears to be a strong relationship between membership patterns and county of conviction.

Table 6.6 illustrates an additional analysis of the relationship between gang membership and county of conviction. We calculated the relative odds (the proportion of gang members released to a given county of commitment divided by the proportion of gang members released in the entire state) of a gang member being released in a discharge cohort for a given year. (Prisoners choose their county of release.) These data show that some Texas areas are receiving a disproportionately large number of gang members (San Antonio, El Paso, and Corpus Christi). For example, for a given release, Bexar County in 1991 was almost three times more likely to receive a gang member than those released in the state overall. By contrast, Dallas County in 1991 received about half as many as would be expected. These odds ratios underscore the strong relationship between county of conviction and gang membership. The data also underscore the prison-street connection and the migration of gang members to certain urban areas. More research needs to be conducted on the

TABLE 6.6 Relative Odds of a Gang Member Being in a Discharge Cohort by County and Year

	Bexar	Dallas	El Paso	Harris	Nueces	Tarrant	Travis
1980	9.33	0.00	0.00	1.50	0.00	0.00	0.00
1981	10.75	0.00	0.00	2.00	0.00	0.00	0.00
1982	3.48	0.61	1.67	0.51	1.31	0.38	0.57
1983	3.96	0.26	0.00	0.87	0.00	0.00	1.96
1984	3.32	0.29	0.00	0.36	3.96	2.25	0.00
1985	3.13	0.58	0.00	0.37	2.75	0.98	0.56
1986	3.09	0.67	0.93	0.86	2.40	0.65	1.10
1987	2.99	0.50	0.96	0.74	3.32	0.68	0.96
1988	2.83	0.48	1.53	0.72	2.50	0.45	0.69
1989	2.87	0.61	2.16	0.71	2.50	0.44	0.72
1990	2.97	0.38	2.04	0.81	3.05	0.63	0.81
1991	2.99	0.52	1.09	0.68	2.96	0.61	0.99

prison as a breeding ground for proliferation of gangs in the wider society.

NUMBER OF PRIOR CRIMINAL OFFENSES

On average, gang members had more convictions (1.71) than non-gang members (1.55). Examining prior convictions showed that only 17.0% of the gang members were serving time for their first conviction, whereas almost half (46.1%) of the nongang group were first offenders (Table 6.7). The majority of the gang members were two-time offenders; 14.2% had three or more prior convictions.

A number of differences between the groups emerged when the prior criminal history of the inmates was examined. The average number of crime-related characteristics are found in Table 6.8. The gang members had higher averages for all of the listed indicators. They were more likely to have been in juvenile reformatories, have other prison incarcerations, and receive probation sentences. While in prison, they were in solitary confinement almost five times as often as non-gang members. The gang members' sentences were almost twice as long as those of non-gang members. Gang members were more likely to serve longer portions of their sentences as well: Gang members serve 34.38% of their sentence length, whereas nongang offenders only serve 27.26% of their time. Violent gang members (those convicted of violent current offenses) also

TABLE 6.7 Classification Based on Prior Convictions

	Nongang	Gang
First Offender	46.1%	17.0%
	(6,094)	(296)
Recidivist	47.5%	68.8%
	(6,279)	(1,200)
Habitual (3 or more)	6.4%	14.2%
	(846)	(268)

TABLE 6.8 Prior Criminal History

	Nongang	Gang
Prior Reformatories	.18	.47
Prior Institutions	.70	1.20
Prior Probations	.93	1.15
Prior Texas Prison	.58	1.05
Number of Times in Solitary	.51	2.53
Length of Sentence in Years	8.72	15.5

served a larger percentage of their prison time (39.95%) than do violent nongang inmates (34.95%).

When we examined the current offenses of the inmates, some differences did appear (Table 6.9). The largest proportion of both groups were incarcerated for burglary, but that was the only similarity. Gang members were more likely to have a violent current offense compared to non-gang members. This trend could explain why the gang members were more likely to stay in prison longer and thereby be discharged at an older age.

Thus far, this analysis of group differences between gang and non-gang members has been restricted to descriptive procedures. The application of discriminant analysis at this point offers the advantage of more clearly identifying and defining the boundaries between these two groups (Kachigan, 1986). It should be noted that discriminant analysis can be useful in other applications as both a prediction and classification model. Its application in this research, however, was restricted to measuring differences between gang members and non-gang members. We strongly caution that there is no advantage to using this particular discriminant model in the field as a predictive classification tool.

TABLE 6.9 Current Offense

	Nongang	Gang
Burglary	32.8%	36.6%
Drugs	16.2%	9.2%
Robbery	11.2%	17.4%
Larceny	10.9%	5.2%
Homicide	4.0%	12.2%
Assault	4.9%	7.7%

Searching for Differences Between Gang Members and Nonmembers

The following analysis was based on a clear dichotomy between gang and nongang members. There was, however, a notable difference in the sample sizes for the two groups. The previous analysis utilized a non-gang sample of 13,218 inmates compared to a group of 1,744 identified gang members. For the purpose of discriminant analysis, and to minimize the effects of the lopsided sample sizes, the nongang sample was reduced to more closely match the size of the gang group. A randomly selected subsample of 1,540 nongang members was used as a comparative group with the previously identified gang members (N = 1,744).

The analysis revealed clear differences between the two inmate groups. The previous descriptive data pointed to some diversity, but which differences provided the most influence, and were these differences strong enough to clearly differentiate the gang from nongang prisoners? The discriminant analysis identified four variables as predictive of membership criteria (Table 6.10). In and of themselves, these variables do not stand out as being particularly novel. These variables would also be identified by prison administrators as important indicants of gang membership. They are, by and large, singular variables that we would intuitively expect to have the most influence over gang membership. We are therefore, to some degree, confirming the obvious. The importance of this analysis, however, is the collective relationship of the influence of these variables. This paints a broader picture of group membership.

Of the four discriminant variables, the presence of prior adult correctional institution time offered the greater degree of influence on the

TABLE 6.10 Discriminant Model

Variable	Within-Group Correlations
Prior adult Incarceration	.67039
Length of current term imposed	.63967
Presence of serving time in a juvenile reformatory	.50947
Presence of any violent offense	.36448

membership criteria. Having served time in prison played a strong role in group membership. Length of sentence emerged as the second most influential factor. A history of serving time in a juvenile institution was the third most influential measure. A history of institutionalization as a juvenile would point to an offender with experience in the system, who has survival skills needed in a correctional institution. Last, a history of violent offenses adds to the discriminant model. Again, this comes as no surprise, and would verify the intuition of a seasoned prison manager.

When applied collectively to both the nongang and gang groups, the sum influence of the four criteria variables provided a high degree of accuracy in the dichotomous grouping—slightly over 70% of the gang members were correctly classified. The importance of these results is noteworthy. Intuitively, prison managers have felt that the "tougher" criminals became gang members. We can now say with a high degree of certainty that their observations have been correct. More important, we can say that not just one variable affects gang membership. A confluence of factors ultimately defines a gang member.

Conclusion

Inmate groups have been in existence in Texas prisons for many years. These groups never really posed problems for the custodial staff until the mid-1980s, when the groups turned violent over the struggle for power, members, resources, influence, and lucrative illegal markets. In 1973, the homicide rate in Texas prisons was 0.75 per 10,000 inmates; the national average was 7.44 per 10,000 (Crouch & Marquart, 1989). Between 1968 and 1978, the average number of inmate homicides per year was 1.7, but this was soon to change.

The first gang-related murder in Texas prisons occurred in 1979, and between 1979 and 1989, the average number of inmate homicides per year rose to 9.6. In 1984 and 1985, Texas prisons saw the largest number of murders in their history: 52 in 2 years. This dramatic increase was a result of a war between the two Hispanic gangs in TDC, the Texas Syndicate and the Mexican Mafia. Since that time, the gangs within the Texas prison system have been involved in the majority of homicides which have occurred.

Although prison gang members constitute a small percentage of the prisoner population, they contribute disproportionately to prison violence and vice. The majority of prison killings as well as a large proportion of assaults and other violent offenses are gang related. Inmate gangs are responsible for many illegal activities in prisons. The gangs often control drug trafficking, prostitution, contract killings, and protection rackets in institutions.

Although a number of methods of have been attempted to control gang activity, none have eliminated the problem. In most prison systems, officials try to monitor gang communications and stay abreast of illegal activities and membership patterns. Our data compared nongang prisoners and gang members within Texas prisons. Findings confirm the long-standing belief held by prison officials that gang members differ from their nongang counterparts. Members have a higher number of prior convictions, are more likely to have a juvenile history of incarceration, and their criminal history reflects a violent past. Data were also presented that explored the prison-street connection. Several Texas areas disproportionately receive paroled gang members, suggestive of an established prison-street connection. It would behoove gang scholars to conduct more work on this relationship.

A discriminant analysis explored areas where clear boundaries existed between these groups. This analysis revealed several differences between gang and non-gang members. This analysis confirmed that it would be premature to point to one or two influences as the leading facilitators of gang membership. Unfortunately, we still do not know enough about the complicated causal relationships that exist within the correctional environment and lead some inmates into gangs.

PART

3

Gang Diversity:
Perspectives on
Ethnicity and Gender

Southern California Gangs
Comparative Ethnicity and Social Control

JAMES DIEGO VIGIL
STEVE C. YUN

It has been estimated recently that there are now 8,000 gangs with over 400,000 members in the United States (Klein, 1995b). Since the early 1980s, gang violence, drug use and abuse, and criminal activities of all sorts have increased markedly, and the prison populations in many states have tripled during that period (Scheer, 1995). Gangs have become one of the most important urban youth issues (Boyle, 1995; Klein, 1995a). Of particular concern is the loss of social control over gangs and the (thus far) inadequate responses that society and law enforcement have instituted to curtail gang growth. Clearly, those who make the policy do not know how to address this problem. It is imperative that we examine more closely the factors that affect youth from various ethnic backgrounds who join gangs. There is a need to undertake cross-cultural, comparative work to begin to gain an understanding of the similarities and differences among gang youth in ethnic groups, using a framework that explains how and why disruption of social control creates and

139

perpetuates gangs. By isolating the key issues that collectively shape gang behavior and attitudes, we might better generate strategies and approaches to help alleviate and resolve the worst effects of gang life.

As anthropologists interested in a holistic, integrative assessment and interpretation of street gangs, we recognize the many strands and sources of gang delinquency stemming from ecological, economic, sociocultural, and psychological factors. We are also cognizant of the theories that incorporate these elements meaningfully (Covey, Menard, & Franzese, 1992; Vigil, 1988a). Most researchers are in accord that major macrohistorical and macrostructural forces are central to both the causation and persistence of street gangs. Although we subscribe to this orientation, we also acknowledge that long-term change will require a major overhaul of the current social system to eliminate or, minimally, effectively combat the gang problem. In the short term, however, we are addressing a middle-level range of research that has the possibilities of providing proximate and immediate attention to the involvement of both social environment and personal identity configurations. In particular, we examine cross-cultural examples of youth gang participants in the framework of social control theory, largely as set forth by Hirschi (1969).

To apply social control theory to the street gangs of southern California, however, modifications are required as certain elements of social control theory can be problematic (Wiatrowski, Griswold, & Roberts, 1981). We believe, along with Covey et al. (1992), that social control theory, "as integrated into ecological and other perspectives, appear[s] to be fundamental to understanding the formation and illegal behavior of juvenile gangs" (p. 173). As a result, our framework is also heavily influenced by an eclectic mix of other concepts and theories, including multiple marginality, social ecology, opportunity, and strain theories (cf. Cloward & Ohlin, 1960; Haviland, 1988; Shaw & McKay, 1942; Vigil, 1988a).

Hirschi (1969) argues that there is a natural, inherent trait that compels individuals to criminal behavior. The question then is not, "Why do people commit acts of delinquency?" Rather, it is, "Why do individuals *not* commit acts of delinquency?" In other words, "Why do individuals conform to the laws of society?" Hirschi argues that the answer to this question is found in socialization processes, which he defines as the bonds between an individual and different influences and levels of society (Edgerton, 1978; Hirschi, 1969). The weakening of these societal bonds, according to social control theory, thus allows the individual to act on his or her "natural motivation" to deviate. Social control theory further stipulates that the bond between the individual and society that facilitates conformity consists of four elements: attachment, commitment, involvement, and belief.

Attachment refers to the relationships an individual forms with significant others, primarily within the family. It begins with the parents as the child's introduction into the world includes expansion of social space (i.e., from the cradle to the bedroom to the home to the neighborhood) and is moderated by the parents.

Commitment is an expression of well-defined goals that begin in the family but are formally forged in the educational system. In complex societies, schools serve as the mechanism for youth to translate their aspirations into conventional, constructive goals. Conventional commitment is usually related to aspirations of a high-status job, but it can also be a reflection of the simple desire to just be "somebody." This desire can overlap with attachment in that the individual, because of strong attachment bonds, seeks the approval of significant others or wants to prove that he or she is motivated to pursue laudable goals.

Involvement focuses on how a youth spends his or her time and reflects the participation in conventional activities that lead to socially acceptable forms of success, such as spending time on homework. Ideally, appropriate and vigilant role models direct the youth toward activities that enhance his or her commitment to socially acceptable goals. Such activities should not only focus on school but could also involve doing chores at home, part-time jobs, volunteer service, or recreational sports. Exposure to such activities often requires strong attachment to significant others, primarily parents, to provide the youth with opportunities for such activities.

Belief is the acceptance of the moral validity of the central social value system. Belief is crucial in establishing social control, for individuals are obviously more likely to break the rules if they do not believe in the rules.

These four elements—attachment, commitment, involvement, and belief—are the basis of social control theory. In reviewing studies of the different ethnic gangs, our analysis points to a common theme—the weakening of these bonds "frees" the adolescent from social control and encourages deviant behavior. To further explore this point, we now turn to the stories of four gang youth from distinctly different cultural backgrounds. Using brief ethnographies, we examine the life of a gang member from each ethnic group and weave this microqualitative data into a broader macrocontext that reflects how society has lost control of sizeable segments of youth in these populations. The data employed here were gathered in 1989 and 1990.[1] During summer 1989, a questionnaire-guided survey of 150 incarcerated gang youth of different ethnicities was conducted by senior and graduate anthropology students under the direction of co-author Vigil. The case studies employed herein utilize data obtained in more intensive and extensive interviews with selected informants from four ethnic groups: Vietnamese, Chicano, African American, and immigrant Latino.

Huc: A Vietnamese Gang Member

Huc was born during the Vietnam War and raised outside Saigon in the aftermath of the war. Life then was marked by fear and hatred of the Communist government. The breakdown of social control in terms of the element of *attachment* occurred early in his life. His father was absent for most of his childhood, imprisoned in the government's "reeducation camps." When finally released, the father made plans to take his entire family to the United States, where he had heard there was freedom and streets literally paved with gold.

Huc and his family escaped from Vietnam in 1979 on a dilapidated ship, which capsized, drowning his mother (who was also pregnant at the time), all his siblings, and his aunt. Such losses were unfortunately a common story for the Vietnamese "boat people," for as many as one third of all Vietnamese refugees lost their lives in the sea during their attempt to escape (Grant, 1979). Huc and his father survived and later reached the United States, both still numbed by their loss and absolutely unprepared for their new life here. Like most other second-wave refugees, they were poor, had low educational backgrounds, and came from the countryside (Kelly, 1977; Nguyen & Henkin, 1982). In contrast, the first wave of Vietnamese refugees who escaped immediately after the fall of Saigon were relatively well educated and urbanized, and most important, were generally able to make it to the United States with their families intact (Liu, 1979; Marsh, 1980).

Although Huc and his father had a close relationship when Huc was a child, after their refugee experience his father became more distant, sullen and withdrawn. Huc was eager to learn English and meet new friends, but his father preferred to stay only in the Vietnamese business district and he was too embarrassed to learn English. As Huc became more Americanized, he began losing his fluency in Vietnamese. Eventually, he realized that he had little in common with his father any more. At the same time, he was ambivalent about his new identity as an "Americanized Vietnamese": "You don't know what you are really . . . the confusion about what you want to be, trying to convert yourself into American. You're stuck in between, you don't know where you supposed to belong. So alone . . . you don't know who you are."

Huc's relationship with his father was further strained when his father decided to remarry. Still haunted by nightmares of his mother's death, Huc resented his stepmother tremendously. Huc's father would beat him for being disrespectful to his stepmother, which only strengthened Huc's rebellious spirit. He saw less and less of his father and stepmother over time, however, as they both worked long hours in menial jobs. In terms of attachment, Huc's life was marred by tragedy and culture conflict, and his bond with his family was very attenuated.

Huc's *commitment* was also problematic. His initial experiences in school were disorienting and embarrassing. The federal government dispersed Southeast Asian refugees across the county in an effort to alleviate antirefugee sentiment, and so Huc and his father were first assigned to a sponsoring family on the East Coast. They quickly made plans, like thousands of other dispersed refugees, for a secondary migration to Southern California, home to Little Saigon, the largest concentration of Vietnamese outside of Vietnam. Over the course of a year, they moved from city to city until they reached Los Angeles. This constant movement also meant that Huc was moving from school to school, usually the only Vietnamese student in each of them. School was initially a demoralizing and confusing experience for Huc. He could not speak English at this time, and he found even asking the teacher to go to the bathroom a major event. On top of all this, because of his poor English, Huc was placed by his father in a class several grades below his age. This was a very common practice among Vietnamese refugees, who assumed that this strategy would help their children compensate for their poor English. Thus, Huc's classmates were often 3 to 4 years younger than him, which made them even more difficult to relate to as peers. In fact, despite the widespread media depiction of Asian students as "super whiz kids" and the "model minority," data reveal that many Vietnamese students are unable to make successful commitments to schooling; for example, in some high schools near Little Saigon, the dropout rate for Vietnamese students is three times higher than average (Vigil & Yun, in press).

In junior high school, Huc's *involvement* in school activities was hampered by the constant harassment he received from members of the Chicano gangs in his school. To protect himself, he began carrying a knife, and he spent most of his time in and out of school banding together with the other Vietnamese students to fight the Chicano gangs. As he spent more time fighting, he found he had less interest in participating in school activities. He was also enjoying the popularity that his fighting gave him; he became known as a good fighter and other Vietnamese students looked up to him. His core group of friends quickly became a cohesive unit: "This is the only family I know. You grow in the gangs. You might start out with 5 or 6 friends, then suddenly you have 20 friends. It's a happy family." To support his lifestyle with his "family," Huc began skipping school regularly and spent his time stealing cars and robbing homes of other Vietnamese refugees.

Huc's father never understood the extent of his gang activity. He was often too busy working to monitor him, and whenever he received a notice that Huc had been suspended from school for fighting, Huc had to translate the notice for him. (Not surprising, Huc would never translate the message absolutely correctly.) Moreover, Huc's father was completely unfamiliar with the educational system and other institutions in the United States, and he was not able to help Huc with his homework or provide him with direction. Eventually, Huc ran away from home and spent his nights instead with his new "family" in motels as they travelled from city to city on the West Coast.

Huc's *belief* in the American Dream and streets paved with gold quickly turned cynical. As he saw his father toiling in menial jobs for minimal pay, Huc wanted a shortcut to his American Dream. Gangs provided him with that shortcut and gave him a new value system. His new value system, in fact, is emblazoned on his thigh in the form of a tattoo that depicts four Ts, representing the Vietnamese words for love, prison, crime, and money.

Puppet: A Chicano Gang Member
From East Los Angeles

Puppet was born in East Los Angeles, and his *attachment* bonds were tenuous from the start. His parents were both members of older, well-established Chicano gangs, and they were also polydrug abusers. Puppet's father was incarcerated several times for drug dealing; the last time Puppet saw him was in court, handcuffed and being scolded by the judge. He has not seen his father since. His mother was eventually found unfit to care for her children because of her drug addiction, and from the time he was 8 years old, Puppet lived in the homes of various relatives. Although Puppet's story may represent an extreme case, aspects of his story are relatively common in the barrio, where macrohistorical forces and socioeconomic stresses have cultivated an environment that actually discourages the formation of attachment bonds within some marginalized families. Family breakdown, single-parent households, and the lack of positive male role models are unfortunately too prevalent in the barrios of Los Angeles (Moore, 1991; Vigil, 1988a, 1988b), by-products of the racist barriers that for so long prevented full integration of Mexican Americans into the mainstream. Such blatant obstacles worked to suppress the motivation for youth to exercise responsibility and discipline for work and family duties, as they found the paths to achievement blocked (Moore & Vigil, 1993; Vigil, 1993). This marginalization of the Mexican population created a process of *choloization* (taken from the term *cholo*, which is used to describe Indians in Latin America who are not acculturated to the Hispanic urban culture), which in tandem with the street socialization process generated the Chicano gang subculture.

Puppet was also shuttled from one family to another, which caused him, in his words, to repeatedly "trip out." Moving in this "musical chairs" fashion also meant that Puppet, too, went from school to school, which limited his ability to form a *commitment* to conventional goals. As the perpetual new kid in school, Puppet felt he had to fight to prove his worthiness to classmates. As a result of his fighting, he was often labeled a problem student by his teachers. Most of his schools were also in Anglo areas; Puppet's Spanglish (a slang combination of Spanish and English) did not go over well with his teachers and his academic performance was poor. His guardians did little to encourage him in school, as they were often too busy with their own children's problems; in fact, they regularly made him feel as a burden to family resources. "They always complained about everything, even when I had to buy shoes—they said that I wore out my shoes too fast."

In high school, Puppet went to live with his uncle's family in his old barrio. Although he was originally from the barrio, Puppet now got beat up repeatedly at school. He soon decided that he needed the protection of a group. As a result, he joined the gang in his barrio and his homeboys quickly became his new foster family. "I don't care how they looked to anyone else. My uncle didn't like that at all—he thought all *cholos* were just bums and punks. But my homeboys were good to me and that's the only thing that mattered." Puppet also repeats a common theme: He claims his gang was his family, and he often referred to his homeboys as *carnales* (translated approximately as "of the same flesh").

His *involvement* in the gang intensified during his high school years. He began to routinely ignore the commands and pleas of his uncle and spent more time away from home with his homeboys. His gang provided him with a way to cope with street pressures and realities, and it gave him new goals, values, and activities. For example, as a gang member, Puppet proudly exchanged the *firme* arm salute with his homeboys, and conversely, he and his homeboys would curse those who were not part of the gang with *levas,* or avoidance sanctions. He listened intently to the old war stories of the *veteranos.* To enhance his reputation in the gang, Puppet also generously shared his drugs with his homeboys and eagerly "defended" his neighborhood from rival gang members. He was arrested several times for assault, which only enhanced his reputation, and he saw several of his homeboys killed.

Despite the destructive violence around him, Puppet remained unfazed. His *belief* in the value of his gang and his homeboys remained firm. Life on the street was a game of Russian Roulette, and those who survived were *locos.* The art of *locura,* that is, acting crazy or playing with craziness, is highly valued, and those who can exhibit the *"locura* syndrome" attain high status in the gang. As Puppet says, "Everybody is going to get killed, and it depends on how you handle yourself. . . . You really didn't care what was happening. I just wanted to do crazy things."

Bean Dog: A Black Gang Member
From South Central Los Angeles

After World War II, there was a dramatic and significant increase in the African American population in Los Angeles, as blacks migrated from the south to California and elsewhere. Bean Dog's parents were part of this migration. Although they had extensive family in Texas, they moved to Los Angeles in search of better jobs. Subsequently, Bean Dog was born in Los Angeles. Before he was even born, then, he was separated from his larger, more rural, extended family, precluding *attachment* to that network.

Although Bean Dog's parents both had stable jobs, family life was often chaotic. Bean Dog's father often was not home because of his job and his mistresses. He would drink often, physically abusing Bean Dog when he was drunk. Bean Dog's mother, a deeply religious woman, took frequent vacations to get away from her husband, leaving the boys with their grandmother or neighbors. Despite Bean Dog's seemingly intact family, he experienced isolation and neglect, as did his friends who grew up in single-parent households that lacked a positive male role model. This frequent lack of positive male role models in the African American community has roots in macrohistorical forces—the legacy of slavery, the denial of civil rights, and the socioeconomic discrimination that still persists today—that created a large class of African American men who cannot find adequate employment and thus cannot carry the burden of raising a family (Fainstein, 1986; Leibow, 1967; Wilson, 1987).

Detached from his family, Bean Dog spent most of his childhood roaming the streets of his neighborhood in South Central Los Angeles, where the Crips and Bloods gangs dominated street life. The Crips and Bloods, in comparison to some of the older Chicano gangs, are relatively new, as they did not come into existence until the late 1960s and early 1970s. With the contraction of war on poverty programs and the explosive rise of the drug trade, African American gangs grew exponentially, in line with an increase in the already concentrated poverty in the ghetto. By the time Bean Dog reached the fifth grade, the street culture had already undermined his *commitment* to school. Bean Dog had initially been a good student, regularly attending church, participating in drum corps and Pop Warner football. But by the fifth grade, his teachers noted that he had a "defiant, impudent attitude . . . [and that he was] easily provoked by peers."

In looking back, Bean Dog is unapologetic about his attitude toward school. In contrast to the streets, school was boring, useless, and lacked relevance to real life. Most important, Bean Dog saw no one who actually benefited from school. There were no lawyers or doctors in his neighborhood, and he and others ridiculed those who did well in school as "whities." His derogatory use of the word whities is especially interesting because it connotes the feeling that academic success is an Anglo trait, and thus must be rejected by African Americans who have endured generations of systematic oppression. Educational researchers (Ogbu, 1978, 1987) identified such reactions as part of the development of a "resistance culture" that minorities use to defend themselves against a legacy of racist oppression. Overwhelmed by the lack of jobs and racial oppression, this resistance culture has been passed down from generation to generation, gradually creating a pessimistic outlook on the individual's ability to succeed in school and aspirations for a higher occupation. Although a resistance culture may be a natural psychological defense mechanism in response to a history of mistrust and rage toward Anglos, it also undermines the ability to succeed in school, and thus the attitude to commit oneself to conventional goals.

Bean Dog's resistance culture was only reinforced further when his mother, trying to redirect her son, pushed him to attend a suburban, predominantly Anglo, Catholic high school. He was ostracized at that school, especially because of his gang-style clothes, and Bean Dog ended up dropping out in the 10th grade. His mother also attempted to redirect him by sending him back to live with relatives in Texas, but not surprising, he soon became bored with rural Texas life and clamored to return home. In short, his mother made many attempts to change her son's behavior, but Bean Dog was already too involved in street life.

As for *involvement*, Bean Dog was already engaging in petty crime in junior high school, but he also did try to find conventional employment. He had several jobs, including working as a parking attendant and warehouse janitor. But these low-paying, menial jobs gave him little satisfaction. A large food-processing factory opened up in his neighborhood, and Bean Dog was actually excited about working there. Despite many meetings with community activists, however, the factory hired no one from the neighborhood, instead opting for Mexican immigrants who were willing to work for minimum wage. The only job Bean Dog truly enjoyed was working as a studio attendant for a major film studio. The work was interesting, and the pay was good ($10 per hour). His girlfriend at the time was especially impressed by his job, and their relationship became more serious. Bean Dog began to consider leaving the street life and settling down. The studio job, however, was only temporary and his girlfriend, who had been a stabilizing force in his life, left him after he was laid off and went back on the streets. Returning to his street friends, Bean Dog was reminded that a job had very little value according to street criteria.

Bean Dog's labor experiences are in line with the experience of the African American community in general. South Central Los Angeles lost 70,000 high-wage jobs between 1978-1982 alone (Soja, Morales, & Wolff, 1983), and during that same period of time over 200 manufacturing companies left Los Angeles (Johnson & Oliver, 1991). Those companies that remained in depressed areas like South Central Los Angeles tended to opt for cheaper labor, foreign immigrants and undocumented workers willing to work for minimum wages (Levy, 1987). As a result, some researchers estimate that as many as 50% of African American males in several South Central Los Angeles neighborhoods may be unemployed (Oliver, Johnson, & Farrell, 1993).

Instead of legitimate employment, Bean Dog found that the streets provided its own set of lucrative activities and values. With limited economic opportunities in the ghetto, African American gangs had turned from being conflict-oriented to focusing primarily on drug dealing, especially dealing crack cocaine (Taylor, 1990a). Bean Dog was first exposed to this after being laid off from his studio job. As he was relaxing at his friend's house, the older brother of his friend—an established gang member and drug dealer—walked in with a pile of cash. He asked Bean Dog to count his money for him and paid him generously for this simple task. "Ever since then I wanted to sell dope, " he said, because "I saw what it could do. I used to see all my older homeboys. They all had money, girls, whatever they wanted. I thought maybe I could be like that." In actuality, most drug dealers are not gang members and only one third of gang members in Los Angeles are involved in drug trafficking (Klein, Maxson, & Cunningham, 1988), but Bean Dog felt he needed the protection of a gang to engage in this lifestyle.

Bean Dog subsequently made the decision to become a formal member of the Crips. As part of his initiation into the gang, he had to participate in a drive-by shooting to prove his loyalty. His homeboys drove him to a house of a rival gang member and told him to shoot. The damage he caused is unknown; Bean Dog simply closed his eyes and started shooting, and then they drove away. This incident dramatically symbolizes Bean Dog's ultimate lack of *belief* in the conventional moral system. By this time, the value system of the gang had completely taken over.

David: A Salvadoran Gang Member
From Downtown Los Angeles

David was born in San Salvador, where he lived with a large extended family in a large home. His *attachment* bonds were noticeably lacking, however, as his father left the family soon after David was born. When David was 7, his mother decided to take him with her to the United States, where there were job opportunities, and more important, where they would not be touched by the civil war that was raging in El Salvador in the early 1980s. The civil war had become an increasingly dangerous part of their lives. Two of their cousins had been killed by government death squads, and David's mother feared that her son might soon be "recruited" into the war, that is, kidnapped and forced to fight. In all, over 40,000 civilians had been killed and as many as one million may have fled the country (Aguayo, 1986; Brown, 1985). As many as 300,000 of these refugees came to the United States (LeFeber, 1984), including David and his mother, who were able to reach the border by taking a bus through Mexico and then entered the United States illegally.

David was initially excited about coming to the United States. He remembered thinking that "Everyone in the United States had a big car, fancy house, and lots of money. I imagined that people in this country made money as easily as they breathed in the air." But when he arrived in Los Angeles, he and his mother lived in a tiny apartment in a small building that itself was incredibly overcrowded, with 10 to 15 people sometimes living in one apartment. His neighborhood, in the middle of Los Angeles, was teeming with other recent Salvadoran immigrants. Despite the presence of other Salvadorans, however, he felt incredibly homesick, as he was separated from his extended family and even from his mother. To support their new life in the United States, she cleaned houses 7 days a week, 10 to 14 hours a day. His mother also remarried, and David transferred all his anger and disappointment with his biological father to his stepfather. Consequently, David refused to obey his stepfather, and his mother was often absent.

David still respected his mother, however, and he tried his best in school because of his mother's belief in and *commitment* to the power of an education. School was a lonely experience for him, however, because of his initially poor language skills and the growing realization that he was poorer than his classmates. The most poignant incident occurred one day when it was raining. He lacked a raincoat, and his mother fashioned one for him out of a garbage bag. At first, David proudly walked to school in his new raincoat, which he thought made him look like a soldier. After walking into school, however, David was immediately the subject of everyone's laughter, including the teacher's. Since that incident, David still gets physically angry whenever he is the target of ridicule.

Later, in junior high, David was bused to a suburban school that was predominantly Anglo and Asian. Again, he felt alienated because of his poverty and his ethnicity, and he felt he was explicitly discriminated against by his teachers. Several teachers referred to him as being "one of those kids that won't make it," and one teacher in particular would make him stand up in front of the class and pick up all the trash. As he claims, "All the teachers never seemed to give us [Latino kids] a break."

The only pleasure David found in school was fighting, as it was the one way he could gain instant respect. Rather than getting *involved* in extracurricular activities or sports, David found that fighting gave him popularity: "I instantly had a bunch of friends. Girls that had only looked past me in the beginning began to speak to me. During this time, I got into a number of fights with a variety of kids, and every time, regardless of whether I won or lost, I seemed to get more respect."

Although his mother would have been able to redirect David had she known about his fighting, she was too busy working to monitor his school activities. David would even try to get her involved by giving her every notice of teacher conferences or PTA meetings, but his mother could never attend. Eventually, he stopped giving the notices to his mother and swallowed his disappointment, because he knew "if she didn't work, we didn't eat." David also began to lose respect for his mother. "When friends asked me what my mom did, I didn't want to talk about it. I mean, my mom cleaned other people's houses. I was ashamed of her job and of her bad English. I still loved her, but I was ashamed of her, too."

As his school performance declined, David spent more of his time out of his apartment and in the streets. He especially loved the freedom of the streets, because his apartment building was so overcrowded. In the streets, he was free to roam, supporting his forays by stealing change from parking attendants or by selling stolen bicycles. On the streets, however, David encountered more and more members of the Mara Salvatrucha, the primary Salvadorean gang in his neighborhood, who would challenge him by asking, "Where are you from?" Because he belonged to no gang, he was often beat up for his lack of allegiance to the Mara.

Later, a relative of his stepfather's, who had been one of the first members of the Mara, came to live with the family. As a relative of a well-established gang member, David was automatically accepted as a homeboy, and he was given the freedom (and even protection) to roam the streets as he wished. Access to the streets was particularly important for David, because the streets were, as he calls it, his "newspaper," his way of connecting to the events and people in his neighborhood. The gossip of the streets also gave David information about rival gangs and their supposed plans to raid his neighborhood, and David would feed this information back to his homeboys.

Soon David began to feel very close to his homeboys. Unlike with his Mexican friends, David could speak Spanish with his homeboys without worrying about his accent or his particular slang. He could go to soccer games and root for the Salvadorean team, especially when they played against a Mexican team. With his homeboys, David would go over to the Mexican fans at soccer games and rip a Mexican flag to shreds in front of them. He became very aggressive in defending the Mara, and he was often the first to ask strangers in the street, "Where are you from?" The Mara became David's family, and he says that he would have "proudly died to defend it."

David's *belief* in other institutions in the United States, however, turned cynical. At times, when he accompanied his mother to work, David saw the mansions his mother worked in, and he bitterly compared that to his own relatively squalid living conditions. Already suspicious of governmental authority because of his experience in El Salvador, David became extremely wary when he heard about the sudden disappearance of some of his neighbors, rumored to have been deported by the INS.

David also became extremely suspicious and critical of law enforcement, especially after seeing police beat his friends with a stick at a local movie theater, even though they had done nothing criminal and were already handcuffed. This fueled a resentment of police that led David to "dis" (disrespect) them at every opportunity. He and his friends, for example, would vandalize and throw stones at the small police substation in their neighborhood. The police would never retaliate. Instead, according to David, they "cowered inside that little station, never trying to come out into the neighborhood. They were a joke."

Analysis and Conclusion

As these examples illustrate, many gang members have failed to form conventional attachment bonds, the first and probably most important element of social control. Interestingly, the attachment processes of all four youths were initially undermined by macrohistorical forces. In the case of Huc and David, it was the trauma of war and its aftermath. For Bean Dog, it was the historic, post-World War II migration of African Americans from the South that separated him from his rural roots and extended family. For Puppet, his parents were consumed by the destructive street life environment, in which an earlier generation of gang members had been socialized due to marginalization of their own families.

Such macrohistorical trends and macrostructural consequences are an important backdrop that help explain the alteration of attachment processes, but there are additional, observable reasons for the lack of secure, strong ties within the family. An example of this is the early and continuous break between the parents and those youth who eventually join the gang, as seen dramatically in Puppet's case. Socioeconomic factors (such as poverty, economic dislocation, divorce and single-parent households, and racism) placed severe stresses on many household units, so that family life is regularly unstable and often involves the child being pushed into the streets. The youth rebels against the parents or primary caretakers and instead gravitates and adapts to the role models of the street subculture. Among the gang youth we interviewed, we repeatedly heard the refrain, "I wanted to be like my older homeboys."

Culture change is a particularly predominant disruption in the lives of ethnic street youth, whose experiences of culture shock and adaptation can lead to a phase of ethnic identity ambivalence and confusion. The inherent strain between generations, that is, between parents and children, is often exacerbated by culture conflict, thus adding another barrier to the formation of attachment between the youth and family. This is particularly true for David and Huc, who were both members of the "1.5 generation," in that they immigrated while they were still children. Caught between cultures, they encountered confusion and ambiguity in reconciling their transitional identity with the traditional cultural identity of their parents. Huc simply said outright, "You don't know who you are," and David, although verbally proud of his ethnicity, felt ashamed of his mother's poor English.

Early street experiences and pregang cohorting play a significant role in undermining a youth's commitment to conventional goals. This is exacerbated by inadequate and unsuccessful schooling experiences. Ethnic minorities have historically had negative, damaging experiences in the educational system. A growing body of research also shows that standard policies—such as tracking by ability group and the use of standardized tests as the ultimate measure of educational performance and ability—have worked against minority students (Orfield, 1988). Dropout rates for ethnic minorities, especially for Latinos and African Americans, are notoriously high. In some South Central Los Angeles high schools, the rates are up to 79% (California Basic Educational Data System, 1989). Out of school, the students "drop into" gangs and commit themselves to the gang's values and norms. Street socialization additionally alienates youth from what is learned in the schools, and societal discrimination and economic injustice further erode allegiance to conventional commitments. These developments reached a peak in Bean Dog's life by the time he was in the fifth grade, despite efforts by his mother to reclaim and redirect him.

Merton (1949) and Cloward and Ohlin (1960), in addressing the social and cultural strains of the lower-income, impoverished population, have underscored the importance in U.S. society of inequalities in access to desired goals and roles, for example, attaining a high-status job. Alienated youth whose education and occupational prospects preclude them from the "respectable status system" face severe problems in establishing for themselves a social identity (Cohen, 1955). Under these conditions, the disjunction between future goals and the avenues to achieve them serves as a catalyst for deviance, and in substitution, the gang directs the youth toward activities in which the youth can attain a "respectable status" in the streets. At least for male gang members, getting arrested or fighting a rival gang member elevates a youth's social status and enhances his street reputation. All four informants found that they could easily gain respect by fighting or acting "loco." In such cases, the youth and his relationship to the gang alters his definition of commitment and success to one that is deviant, unconventional, and not amenable to social control.

In terms of *involvement*, the ethnographic examples show how some minority youth receive very little direction from their parents toward conventional activities. In many cases, it is not due to parental psychopathology, but from the fact that the parents are too busy working and struggling to survive. Often, the parents, especially Vietnamese and Latino parents, may have limited knowledge as to the workings of U.S. lifeways, a foreign culture and system to them. Racism and language difficulties often play a significant role in hindering involvement in conventional activities, both through the problems they cause parents and by directly affecting the youth. Although David had the benefit of an English-as-a-Second-Language class, Huc initially struggled with English and felt embarrassed by being placed with younger classmates. Even minor requests (such as asking to go to the bathroom) became a major source of anxiety for him at school.

With breakdowns in terms of attachment, commitment, and involvement, youth have weakened ties to society's conventional values. In the vacuum created by these breakdowns, the gang is established and persists because it provides an alternative socialization process that meets (at least for a time) the needs of its creators. In essence, attachment, commitment, and involvement have shifted to the gang, and in the process, a new, deviant set of morals or beliefs has been created to compete with, and often dominate, the conventional belief system. Society's social control institutions (namely family, school, and the police) are thus caught in a double bind (Rodgers, 1969) when the youth lacks acceptance of the conventional moral system—for once youth stop believing in the law enforcement system, not only are they free of the law and its accompanying values, but they create their own defiant and often destructive set of values.

Note

1. The summer research project was funded by the Social Science Research Council and the University of Wisconsin.

8

Gang Violence in Chinatown

KO-LIN CHIN

According to law enforcement authorities and government officials, Chinese gangs are becoming a major crime problem in the United States (U.S. Department of Justice, 1985, 1988; U.S. Senate, 1992). Chinese gangs are reported to be involved in extortion, robbery, debt collection, and protection of Asian-owned vice businesses (President's Commission on Organized Crime, 1984). Besides, Chinese gang leaders are alleged to be active in systemic violence; heroin trafficking; and most recently, human smuggling (Kinkead, 1992; Lay & Dobson, 1993; Lubasch, 1992; Treaster, 1993). Some Chinese gangs are believed to be closely affiliated with members of community-based adult organizations known as tongs[1] (Meskil, 1989) or Hong Kong-based organized crime groups known as triad societies[2] (Grace & Guido, 1988).

In New York City, 10 Chinese gangs are often mentioned in police and media reports.[3] Gangs affiliated with community adult organizations are

AUTHOR'S NOTE: Support for this research was provided by Grant 89-IJ-CX-0021 (S1) from the National Institute of Justice. The opinions are those of the author and do not necessarily reflect the policies or views of the U.S. Department of Justice. This chapter is excerpted from *Chinatown Gangs: Extortion, Enterprise, and Ethnicity* by Ko-lin Chin. Copyright © 1996 by Oxford University Press, Inc. Reprinted by permission.

relatively well established and deeply entrenched in Chinatown, located in the lower east side of Manhattan. Gangs not associated with community organizations are relatively small and are most active in the newly established Chinese communities in Queens and Brooklyn. Both groups could be defined as "gangs," according to Klein's (1971) definition, but law enforcement practitioners are more inclined to define Chinese gangs as "organized gangs" rather than "youth gangs" because (a) Chinese gang leaders are alleged to be relatively old (late 20s and early 30s), (b) some Chinese gangs are considered to be the extension of adult organizations that control vice activities in the Chinese community, and (c) Chinese gang activities are believed to be mainly profit oriented (Posner, 1988). It is not certain how valid these assertions about Chinese gangs are and whether these assertions are sufficient to justify the definition of Chinese gangs as "organized gangs." Nevertheless, between 1985 and 1994, nine Chinese gangs in the United States were indicted by federal authorities as illegal enterprises under the Racketeering Influenced and Corrupt Organization (RICO) statute (Chin, Fagan, & Kelly, 1994).

Chinese gangs have a reputation for violence (Daly, 1983; Dannen, 1992). Since the mid-1970s, violence has often erupted in the Chinese communities in North America. In 1977, for instance, 5 people were killed and 11 were wounded when three assailants opened fire on customers inside a Chinese restaurant in San Francisco's Chinatown (Ludlow, 1987). In 1982, masked gunmen shot dead three young Chinese and seriously wounded seven others in a bar in New York City's Chinatown (Blumenthal, 1982). Similar incidents have occurred in Seattle (Emery, 1990), Boston (Butterfield, 1991), Vancouver (Dubro, 1992; Gould, 1988), and Toronto (Kessel & Hum, 1991; Lavigne, 1991; Moloney, 1991). Most of these incidents were reported to be related to Chinese gangs, and in some, innocent bystanders were wounded or killed.[4] Law enforcement authorities believe that the emergence of Vietnamese and Fujianese gangs, drastic shifts in political alliances among Chinese community organizations, rapid but destabilizing economic expansion in Chinese communities, and the involvement of Chinese gangs in heroin trafficking and in the smuggling of aliens have created an escalation in gang violence over the past several years (U.S. Senate, 1992).

Although there have been anecdotal reports in the media and de facto charges made in official indictments, there has been no reliable information on the frequency and seriousness of aggression involving Chinese gangs.[5] The patterns and causes of such aggression have yet to be empirically and systematically examined.

Lack of research has limited the development of theoretical explanations of gang violence in the Chinatowns of North America, although two hypothetical interpretations of Chinese gang violence emerged in the late 1970s. In the first, according to Thompson (1976), Chinese gang violence is a cover-up for racketeering activities such as gambling and prostitution; violence between Chinese gangs is thought to be condoned or encouraged by adult criminal groups to divert police attention from rampant organized crime activities in the community.

The second perspective, in many ways similar to the first in its orientation, was proposed by Takagi and Platt (1978). They hypothesize that violence in North American Chinatowns is not instigated by members of street gangs. Instead, members of adult organizations who control organized crime and the community's political economy plot violent activities in the Chinese community. Takagi and Platt conclude:

> We have tried to carefully distinguish two different kinds of crime in Chinatown: "organized" rackets and violence associated with those who control the political structure and legitimate business; and ordinary "street" crime. The violence so much in the news today has more to do with the former than the latter. There is no evidence to support the argument that violence is related to youth gangs. Organized violence appears to be related to the business of protection rackets and political intimidation of progressive organizations rather than to an "irrational" youth "subculture." (p. 22)

In this chapter, I examine the participation rate of gang members in gang violence in New York City's Chinatown; the frequency, typology, and causes of such violence; and the restraining mechanisms on such violence. I estimate the general level of aggressive behavior among members of Chinese gangs and explain how and why Chinese gang members direct their aggression toward members of rival gangs, members of their own gangs, and nongang victims. I also discuss the mechanisms used to check gang aggression in the Chinese community. Finally, I evaluate prior explanations of Chinese gang violence in light of my findings.

Method

SAMPLE

The targeted sample of this study consisted of 62 male subjects who were former or active members of New York City's Chinese gangs. Most participants ($n = 58$) were recruited by a former gang member.[6] Others were referred by a Chinatown journalist. The sampling goals for the study were to interview (a) at least one subject from each of the active Chinese gangs, (b) gang members from all ranks, and (c) a proportionately representative number of subjects from each active gang.

The sample achieved most of the goals. First, it included at least one respondent from each of the 10 Chinese gangs active in New York City. Second, it included ordinary (lowest-level) gang members, street leaders, and faction leaders.[7] I was unable, however, to interview the top gang leaders. Third, with the exception of one gang (the Fuk Ching gang), the sample included, proportionately, more members from the larger and more active Chinese gangs and provided a close approximation of the actual distribution of gang members in the neighborhood.

This part of my study has some limitations. First, the use of nonrandom sampling techniques may limit the generalizability of the study results to the Chinese gang population in New York City at large. Because of the lack of concrete, reliable information about the number of Chinese gang members in New York City, however, random sampling was simply not feasible. Second, the findings of this study may not be applicable to Chinese gangs in other cities or to non-Chinese Asian gangs. Compared to Chinese gangs in other urban centers such as San Francisco (Toy, 1992a, 1992b), Los Angeles (Dombrink & Song, 1992), Vancouver (Dubro, 1992), and Toronto (Lavigne, 1991), Chinese gangs in New York City are considered to be more stable, better organized, more entrenched in the Chinese community, and more involved in profit-generating criminal activities (Bresler, 1981; Chin, 1990; Kinkead, 1992). Also, Chinese gangs are uniquely different from the gangs formed exclusively by other young Asian immigrants such as the Vietnamese, Cambodians, Laotians, and Koreans (Badey, 1988; Knox, 1992; Vigil & Yun, 1990). Third, my inability to interview top gang leaders may have resulted in the underestimation of certain types of aggression, especially the premeditated violence associated with drug trafficking, human smuggling, and turf expansion (Daly, 1983; Meskil, 1989).

TABLE 8.1 Respondents' Personal and Group Characteristics ($N = 62$)

Personal	N	%	Group	N	%
Place of birth			Gang		
Hong Kong	15	24	Flying Dragons	14	23
Taiwan	3	5	Ghost Shadows	10	16
China	9	15	Tung On	4	6
Vietnam	5	8	Freemasons	5	8
United States	22	35	Canal Boys	14	23
Other	8	13	White Tigers	5	8
			Green Dragons	4	6
Ethnicity			Other	6	10
Cantonese	42	68			
Non-Cantonese	20	32	How do members get along?		
			Very well	24	39
Age			Well enough	27	44
16 and younger	7	11	Not so well	10	17
17	8	13			
18	19	31	How well organized is your gang?		
19	8	13	Very well	19	32
20	9	14	Somewhat	34	58
21 and older	11	18	Not at all	6	10
Education			Is there a division of labor in your gang?		
6th grade or less	1	2			
7th to 9th grade	7	11	Yes	46	81
10th to 12th grade	40	64	No	11	19
College	14	23			
Attending school or employed?			Are there rules in your gang?		
Yes	49	79	Yes	57	92
No	13	21	No	5	8
Ever arrested?			Does your gang have its own territory?		
Yes	32	52	Yes	60	98
No	30	48	No	1	2
Ever imprisoned?			Is your gang involved in legitimate business?		
Yes	9	15	Yes	49	76
No	53	85	No	12	24

Table 8.1 displays the characteristics of the gang subjects and their gangs. Most respondents were foreign born (primarily in Hong Kong and China) Cantonese[8] in their late teens from working-class families.[9] The majority of them had completed junior high school and were attend-

ing school or working. About half of them had an arrest record and nine had served time in prison. In gang characteristics, the first four gangs listed on Table 8.1 and the Fuk Ching gang are affiliated with an adult organization. All 10 gangs are independent from one another and they are not divisions of larger gangs. Most subjects suggested that their gangs were either very well organized or somewhat organized, with a division of labor among members. Almost all Chinese gangs have rules and territories. The majority of the subjects indicated that their gangs are involved in legitimate businesses.

DATA COLLECTION

Face-to-face interviews with gang members were conducted in the summer of 1992 by a female Chinese interviewer in an office located near Manhattan's Chinatown. The recruiter (the former gang member) arranged for two to three subjects who belonged to the same gang to be interviewed in the field office every day. While one subject was being interviewed in a separate room, the recruiter and the other subjects played cards in an adjacent room. A third room was served as the field office for the researcher who positioned himself in the office to monitor the interviews. At the end of the day, after all the subjects had been interviewed, the recruiter would escort the subjects out of the office building. Each subject was paid $50 for the interview.

A standardized questionnaire with both closed and opened-ended questions was used for the interviews. The questionnaire had both English and Chinese versions. Prior to the interview, subjects were asked to read and sign an informed consent letter and to choose the language with which they were most comfortable. The interviewer would use the language selected to conduct the interview.[10] Most interviews were conducted in English or Cantonese; a few were conducted in Mandarin. Information was collected about the subjects' socioeconomic status, the stages they went through in becoming a gang member, the structure of their gangs, and patterns of gang activities.

VALIDITY AND RELIABILITY

Efforts were made to ensure the validity and reliability of the data. The recruiter and the interviewer had known each other for more than 6 years, and the recruiter had complete trust in the interviewer, who was his high school counselor.[11] Most subjects were acquaintances of the recruiter and appeared to trust him. The interviews were conducted in a private office inside an office building located on "neutral turf." The subjects were relaxed and seemed to be candid in their answers to most of the questions. Most subjects appeared to be uneasy when asked about their involvement in burglaries, the number of members in their gangs, and the amount of money they earned from their criminal activities.[12]

At the end of each session, the interviewer was asked to evaluate the subject's honesty based on her subjective perceptions. The interviewer's ratings thus provided some assessment of the respondents' honesty in answering the questions. According to the interviewer's evaluations, most subjects were perceived as being either "very honest" or "honest" in answering the questions.

Findings

PARTICIPATION IN AND FREQUENCY
OF CRIMINAL ACTIVITIES

Respondents in this survey of gang members reported that they were fairly active in violent activities such as simple assault, shooting, and robbery. Almost all (96%) admitted they had assaulted someone in 1991, the year prior to the interviews.[13] Eighty-two percent revealed that they had committed one or more robberies, and 52% acknowledged that they had used a gun against someone in 1991 (see Table 8.2). Respondents appeared to have a higher participation rate in simple assault (beating), aggravated assault (shooting), and robbery than did the gang members in other ethnic communities studied by Fagan (1989). These findings are consistent with the findings of the Los Angeles County District Attorney (1992) that members of Asian gangs are relatively active in violent crimes.

Table 8.2 shows that most respondents were regularly (i.e., three or more times per year) involved in simple assault (93%) and robbery (70%). About two out of three subjects (67%) said that they were frequently (i.e., 12 or more times per year) involved in simple assaults; over half (54%) said that they frequently committed robberies, although only 5% said that they frequently opened fire on others. Again, in comparing these figures with Fagan's (1989) study, it seems that Chinese gang members are more regularly and frequently involved in assaults and robberies than are members of other ethnic gangs, though members of other ethnic

TABLE 8.2   Frequency and Participation Rates in Criminal Activities
(in Percentages, $N = 62$)

Self-reported criminal activities	At least once	Regular: Three or more times	Frequent: Twelve or more times
Individual acts: Prior year violence			
Assault	96	93	67
Robbery	82	70	54
Shooting	52	33	5
Victimization of businesses			
Theft of goods/services	97	93	87
Protection	90	88	78
Asking for lucky money	86	82	61
Selling items	68	53	22
Drug use			
Alcohol	94	91	73
Marijuana	52	37	21
Crack	10	3	0
Cocaine	10	3	2
Heroin	8	2	0
Individual acts: Ever involved			
Drug sale	17		

NOTE: Victimization of businesses in the forms of extortion may be classified into four types. In the first type of victimization, theft of goods or services, gang members may refuse to pay for goods or services, or may ask for heavy discounts. Protection denotes a regular demand for a fixed amount of money from a business to ensure that the business will not be disturbed by a gang or by other predators. Asking for lucky money means the sporadic and spontaneous demands for money from business owners by gang members. Finally, gang members sell commodities to business owners at prices higher than market value.

gangs may be more frequent participants in shootings or in chronic aggravated assault.

According to the data presented in Table 8.2, in 1991 participation in assault was second only to theft of goods and services, which was the most frequently reported criminal activity. Frequent involvement in simple assaults was less likely than frequent involvement in providing protection to illegal businesses, theft of goods and services, and alcohol use. The respondents were more likely to engage in violent crimes than to participate in other drug and nondrug crimes traditionally considered typical gang activities. Participation rates and frequency of involvement in two types of violent crime—robbery and shooting—were considerably higher than frequency of hard drug use. We may conclude that

TABLE 8.3   Frequency and Participation Rates in Criminal Activities by Gang
Peers (in percent, N = 62)

How many of your gang members were actively involved in the following activities in the past year?	At least a few	At least some	Most
Fighting	100	97	71
Extortion	100	95	68
Guarding gambling houses	97	83	62
Gambling	96	81	52
Drug use	81	54	12
Drug sale	72	47	8

NOTE: Extortion here denotes all four kinds of gang victimization of business owners mentioned in Table 8.2.

violent activities such as assault, robbery, and shooting were frequent activities among the Chinese gang members we interviewed.

The gang members we interviewed also indicated that their peers were involved in such activities. When asked about how many members of their gangs were involved in a list of crimes, most (71%) responded that fighting was the activity that most gang members were regularly involved in (see Table 8.3). Sixty-eight percent of the respondents indicated that most members of their gang were involved in extortion, and 62% believed that most members of their gang were providing protection to illegal gambling establishments. Thus, fighting appears to be the most prevalent activity among Chinese gangs, surpassing extortion and guarding gambling establishments, the two activities suspected by law enforcement authorities of being the main activities of Chinese gangs (U.S. Senate, 1992).

Table 8.3 also suggests that gang members are relatively inactive in hard drug use, although they do consume alcohol. Only about one in two gang subjects used marijuana at least once in 1991, and only one in five reported frequent marijuana use. Only 8% to 10% of the respondents reported having used crack, cocaine, or heroin at least once in 1991. About 2% to 3% admitted to regular use of hard drugs, but none admitted to frequent use of crack or heroin. In comparison, more than 70% of the Los Angeles gang members are reported to use drugs, usually about once a week (Los Angeles County District Attorney, 1992). Other researchers (Fagan, Piper, & Moore, 1986; Hagedorn, 1988) reported extensive drug use by Hispanic and African American gang members. The Chinese gang members in my sample appeared to be more interested in gambling than in drug use. Over half of the respondents reported that most of their fellow gang members were active in gambling (Table 8.3). Guarding gambling establishments is a major function of Chinese gangs, and many gang members may have learned to gamble while protecting gambling establishments.

Although law enforcement authorities and the media have attributed the dramatic increase in Southeast Asian heroin in the United States to Chinese gang involvement (Bryant, 1990; Kerr, 1987; U.S. Senate, 1992), only 17% of our subjects reported that they had ever participated in a drug sale. According to one report, about half of the Los Angeles gang population sells drugs in any given year (Los Angeles County District Attorney, 1992).

TYPOLOGY AND CAUSES OF GANG VIOLENCE

Gang violence is a term used to refer to violent activities involving gang members. Gang violence may be classified into three types depending on the gang affiliation of the victim: intergang violence, intragang violence, and violence directed at nongang victims. In the first, the aggressor and the victim belong to different or rival gangs. In the second, both the aggressor and the victim belong to the same gang. Interfactional and intrafactional disputes may also be included in this category. In the third type of gang violence, the victims are usually not affiliated with any gang.

INTERGANG VIOLENCE

Most respondents (92%) indicated that they had been involved in at least one confrontation with a different gang. The most frequently cited reason for intergroup clashes was "staring" (or "looking down") (see Table 8.4). These incidents were spontaneous responses to being stared at or being asked, "Where are you from?" or "Who is your *dai lo* [big brother or leader]?" Gang members interpreted this sort of behavior as disrespectful and challenging. A person who stares at another is considered arrogant and aggressive. Asking a gang member the identity of his leader is also construed as a serious challenge; it conveys an intention to

TABLE 8.4   Causes of Gang Violence (*N* = 62)

Reasons	Number of respondents who said these things were the reasons for the conflicts	
	Intergang	Intragang
Staring/Provocative attitudes	35	5
Turf warfare	28	1
Girls	6	13
Revenge	3	2
Money	3	15
Misunderstanding	1	6
Pride	1	1
No reason	1	0
Insubordination/Disciplinary	0	4
Power struggle	0	7
Verbal argument	0	4
Drunkenness	0	1
Jealousy	0	1
Drugs	0	1

NOTE: Respondents could provide more than one reason.

belittle or degrade the reputation or power of a gang. These incidents were most likely to take place in recreational centers and restaurants located in neutral areas. Two respondents described separate violent incidents sparked by staring, both of which ended tragically:

> We went to a party and saw that people there were very arrogant. There were a lot of different gangs, and they were staring at one another. I asked my friends whether we needed more men [for support]. They said no, so we began to dance. One guy was perhaps jealous because of whom I was dancing with. He asked me "Where are you from? Where is your *dai lo?*" I pointed at my *dai lo*. He said, "I want you to leave." I hit the guy. Everybody jumped in and shots were fired. My friend had a gun. I only had a knife. He fired shots. When we went back a few days later, we were arrested. A friend of mine killed one guy and wounded two.

> We fought with members of a gang in Queens. It happened in a pool hall. My brothers started the conflict. I didn't know why. I wasn't there. I think it was because members of the Queens gang were staring at us. That's why we got into an argument. I got a call from my gang. I went there, but everybody was gone. One of my brothers was killed.

More often, staring at members of a rival gang only resulted in fist-fights. A respondent described a typical violent incident caused by staring:

> I was involved in a fight with the Ghost Shadows. We were staring at one another. They asked, "Who are you staring at?" and pulled out a gun. They threw the first punch. We thought they had only two guys, but after the fight started, three or more of them were involved. We punched them back. After the fight, we were lying on the floor. They told us they were the Ghost Shadows and left.

The display of aggressive attitudes by gang members also triggers conflict. In some cases, trivial matters can set off an incident. Some respondents reported that they attacked other gang members simply because they disapproved of the other gang members' appearance: "We beat up a group of Fujianese at a night club because we didn't like the way they looked. They looked disgusting."

Turf is the second most often cited reason for intergang aggression. All the active gangs in Manhattan's Chinatown have their own turf, which normally includes the commercial areas surrounding the headquarters of the adult organization with which the gang is affiliated. The invasion of a gang's turf not only signifies a threat to its status and authority but also may, if successful, deprive that gang of real income. Moreover, the act is a challenge to the power and authority of the adult organization located in the area. Consequently, protecting turf is important not only for saving face and for financial reasons but also to fulfill a major responsibility delegated to the gang by the affiliated adult organization. Many observers and gang members themselves have indicated that it would be difficult for the gangs to exert control over their turf without the full support of the adult associations (U.S. Senate, 1992). To maintain the support of the adult organizations, Chinese gangs will do whatever it takes to protect their turf in Chinatown.

Violence is often sparked by turf wars that occur when one gang wishes to acquire part or all of the territory of another gang or when two different gangs confront each other over the same piece of unclaimed or disputed territory. Because most core areas in Manhattan's Chinatown have been occupied for decades by well-established gangs and adult organizations, planned turf-related intergang hostilities are more likely to occur in newly developed commercial blocks in virgin territory that has not been claimed by any gang or adult association. Turf wars in certain areas of the Chinese communities of Queens and Brooklyn are common because these areas are not well defined by turf territorial prerogatives and because the tongs do not control these areas. Without the backup of a stable and visible adult organization, a gang's claim to an area is susceptible to challenge and may lead to invasions by other gangs.

A subject from a gang located in Manhattan described how his gang intruded into a rival gang's turf in Flushing, Queens:

> We fought with a gang in Queens because our *dai lo* [leader] wanted to take over Flushing. We went to Flushing and called their [the rival gang's] *dai lo* and told him to leave Flushing or we would mess him up. Later, five to six members of that gang showed up in a restaurant in Flushing to collect protection money. We tried to talk to them first, but they wouldn't listen. We had 30 guys. They tried to pull out their guns, but we overpowered them before they could reach for their guns. It happened outside a restaurant. They were no match for us. They underestimated us. We just beat the crap out of them. Our *dai lo* told them, "Go home, and tell your *dai lo* this [turf] is ours." However, it [occupying the turf] didn't last too long because Flushing is too far away from Manhattan's Chinatown. It takes half an hour to get there. If someone [a "brother"] is in trouble, it's hard to send help.

In other turf-related incidents, the invading party may have had no intention of taking over a territory and may only have wanted to extort "lucky" money from business owners in that territory. Such acts were considered serious challenges by gang members.[14] A gang member described how his gang handled such a threat: "We shot at a bunch of XX gang members. They came over to our turf and tried to collect protection money from our store owners."

Some intergang violence was triggered by accidental trespassing into a rival gang's turf. In these instances, in which territorial violations were unintentional and innocent, the gang that controlled the area could not discern the intruders' intentions, so the normal reaction was to treat the event as if it were a deliberate show of disrespect for the gang's turf. A subject revealed how risky it could be for a Chinese gang member to wander into a rival gang's area:

A Chinese gang member walked into our turf and was wandering around. We beat him till he could not get up from the floor. Fifteen of us were beating him. My "brother" said he had seen the guy with the XX gang. If we see a suspicious guy in our turf armed with a gun, we will kill him right away.

Because gang turfs in Manhattan's Chinatown are close to one another or contiguous, it is often necessary for a gang member to walk through a rival gang's territory to reach his own. Violence has often erupted at the edges where gang boundaries meet. This phenomenon has also been observed with African American and Hispanic gangs in Los Angeles (Los Angeles County District Attorney, 1992) and San Diego (Sanders, 1994). Most turf-related intergang violence in Manhattan's Chinese community, however, appears to be spontaneous reactions to accidental encroachment rather than planned invasions.

The issue of money is linked closely with the turf issue. This becomes apparent in the struggles over territory. Because income expands when gangs receive protection money from more stores or restaurants, the primary goal of turf expansion is economic. A large turf, especially one situated on busy streets, is very lucrative. As one respondent maintained, turf is equivalent to money for Chinese gangs: "The reason for intergang fights was mainly to expand the gang's turf and to make more money. A larger turf means more income. It's all about money."[15]

Other violent episodes between gangs occur simply because gang members show up at recreational establishments frequented by their rivals:

We were hanging out in a pool hall in our turf. Some Green Dragons walked in. They stared at us. One of my friends was playing video games by himself. One of them came around and questioned my friend. Since that was our turf, we had things like guns and sticks there. We swung at them with pool sticks, hit them until we beat them up. We also shot a guy in the leg. We warned him that if he returned, it [the shooting] was going to be in the head.

Women, revenge, and money were also mentioned as underlying causes for hostilities between members of rival gangs. The fact that some women associate with members of different gangs creates animosity and jealousy among gang members. A respondent explained how a joyful occasion turned into an explosive confrontation because of arguments concerning women:

> Once, a friend of mine just graduated from college, and we decided to have a celebration. A couple of girls were invited to the restaurant, and they brought some Green Dragons with them because one of the girls' boyfriends was a Green Dragon. After we bumped into them, we chased after them. We threw rocks and garbage cans at their cars. Later that night, the two gangs decided to meet. We were prepared to fight, but we talked it out.

Another reason for intergang conflict is revenge. When a gang member has been assaulted or killed by another gang, revenge is sought, and this generates a recurring cycle of violent incidents. Three subjects described the vicious cycle of gang retaliations:

> Once, two to three kids were in "our" pool hall. We knew they didn't belong there. We took them down to the bathroom and mugged them. They said they were members of the XX gang and left. They came back 20 minutes later and shot at the pool hall's window. More than one gun was fired. One of my friends was shot, another guy in the pool hall died. We went after them, but you could rarely find them when you are angry at them. Later, we found a couple of them and robbed them. I wanted to do it by myself, so I told my friends to step back. I wanted them to have a fair chance. I beat them up until they were lying on the floor.

> On one occasion, we fought with the Green Dragons because they came over to "our" pool hall. We didn't like that. We fought, but we were caught unguarded. We used pool sticks and tried to get a gun. The owner of the place helped us. The Green Dragons left but came back again and beat up our *sai lo* [little brother or follower]. We went to their turf and shot them. We always have to watch over our shoulder. It's back and forth.

> Members of a rival gang came to Canal Street and beat up one of us. The next day, we went back and shot at them.

Drug sales are one of the major reasons for intergang violence among black and Hispanic gangs (Sanders, 1994), but none of my respondents mentioned drugs as the cause of conflicts among rival gangs. Because Chinese heroin importers are believed to be rarely involved in street sales and only a small number of the gang members in my survey admitted to having been lured into drug dealing, it seems unlikely that Chinese gang members fight for control of street-level drug markets.

The data also show that warfare between Chinese and non-Asian gangs is almost nonexistent. Chinese gang members may fight with members of the Vietnamese Born-to-Kill gang, but not with members of black or Hispanic gangs. Studies of other ethnic gangs confirm that intergang hostilities are basically intraethnic rather than interethnic (Hagedorn, 1988; Los Angeles County District Attorney, 1992; Sanchez-Jankowski, 1991; Sanders, 1994).

Moore (1978), Horowitz (1983), Vigil (1988a), and Sanders (1994) point out that machismo, honor, and respect are subcultural values related to aggression among Hispanic gangs. In this study, I find that these values or psychological dimensions of behavior also appear relevant to Chinese gang violence. Although only one subject mentioned pride as a reason for gang aggression, staring and provocative attitudes displayed by rivals—the major etiological factors for gang aggression mentioned by my respondents—could be equated with an affront to a gang's sense of pride and honor. In sum, my findings support the conclusion reached by Reiss and Roth (1993) on gang violence, that "gang conflict often occurs when a gang believes that its status or reputation, its turf, or its resources are threatened by another gang" (p. 142).

INTRAGANG VIOLENCE

Intragang violence is defined as violent behavior against members of the same gang. Intragang assaults among Chinese gangs appear to be not as frequent as clashes between members of different gangs. A substantially smaller number of subjects (28%) indicated that they had participated in intragang conflicts. Intragang aggression is less common among Chinese gangs than among other ethnic gangs (Reiss & Roth, 1993; Sanders, 1994). Unlike aggression between rival gangs, however, according to my survey, fights between members of the same gang are mainly over money, women, and power (see Table 8.4). Violence between members of the same gang is often spontaneous, and weapons are rarely used.

Money was the most often cited reason for intragang disputes, perhaps because gambling is reportedly widespread among gang members (Kinkead, 1992). Disputes over gambling debts often led to physical confrontations. One respondent described how he got involved in an altercation with a member of his gang: "We fought over money. Last month, we were gambling and a guy owed me money. We yelled and pushed but it didn't go too far."

In addition to gambling debts, disputes over the distribution of profits from illegal businesses are also a major cause of intragang tensions. There are rules about how extorted money should be distributed within a gang. After collecting money from victims, gang members often turn it over to their faction leader, who then distributes it among his followers. If ordinary members and street-level leaders are not satisfied with the way their faction leader handles money, intragang violence may ensue. During the late 1970s and early 1980s, disputes of this kind resulted in several vicious attacks among members of the Ghost Shadows and forced the gang to split into two factions (*U.S. v. Yin Poy Louie et al.*, 1985). One of my subjects explained how he became involved in an intragang struggle because of money:

> Once, a guy in our gang said something bad about our group. He expected us to guard the streets. I said, "If you want me to take over [the streets], I'll keep the money [collected from the stores]." I told him he had no rights [to ask for a share of the extortion money]. I told my brothers [10 of them] to jump this guy. It was a fistfight; no weapons were used.

Women were the second most frequently mentioned reason for intragang violence. Women are an essential part of Chinese gangs, although they are not allowed to be members. Many Asian females associate with Chinese gangs, and they are often seen in public places in the company of gang members. But qualitative data from the gang subjects reveal little about specifically why and how women associates provoke conflicts within gangs because the subjects rarely elaborated on this issue.

All the gangs in Chinatown have, at one time or another, experienced major internal clashes (Chin, 1990; Daly, 1983; Meskil, 1989). Many Chinese gangs are divided into rival factions, each of which is headed by its own leader. Although the primary leader may try to maintain peaceful coexistence among the different factions under his control, members of the different factions may nonetheless fight among themselves without his knowledge. In fact, some factional clashes within gangs are as brutal as some of the more bloody episodes of warfare between rival gangs (Chin, 1990). A subject explained why members of his faction would fight with members from another faction of the same gang: "The Y faction fights with the Z faction. They don't care that they all belong to the same gang. For our gang, each faction has its own territory, and members are not supposed to go to other factions' territory. You cannot walk on the wrong street."

Thus, the very notion of a street gang among the Chinese appears similar to other ethnic gangs. Although Chinese gangs appear to be relatively well integrated units, with clear lines of power and authority, they may be more accurately described as loose confederations of smaller cliques precariously held together by a shared interest in a turf that is affiliated with a tong. This is much like the African American and Hispanic gangs examined by Short and Strodtbeck (1965/1974), Klein (1971), Fagan (1989), and Sanders (1994).

Misunderstandings, bad attitudes, and verbal altercations were also mentioned by respondents as the causes of intragang conflicts. Ironically, members of different factions of a gang may attack one another simply because they do not know they belong to the same gang. Some gangs have three or more factions and there is little communication between ordinary members of these factions. It is not unusual for gang members not to recognize members of other factions. A subject explained how this can happen: "We were walking, they started coming at us. We exchanged words. We hit them. After we fought, the older guy [a member of the affiliated tong] was called and he came over, and then we found out that we belonged to the same gang."

Intragang violence, especially assaults within a particular faction, is also used for disciplinary purposes. Because a gang is an illegal organization, its means for disciplining its members are limited. The disciplinary action usually employed for breaking gang rules or for failing to fulfill gang-related duties is some type of physical punishment. The ultimate punishment may be execution. Two subjects explained why some members were attacked by their peers:

It [the attack] sometimes happens when the followers didn't collect money from the stores, or they mugged people on the streets, or they didn't listen to the *dai lo,* or they complained too much. In these cases, we will punch them a few times.

Small stuff. It's like he's supposed to go up to mug a guy and he didn't do it. He had to do it because he was the guy with the knife. He was scared, and he backed down. We had four more guys to help him, and the other guys did the mugging. We lost face, so later we beat him up.

Among some black and Puerto Rican gangs, drug use and drug dealing have been found to be responsible for escalation of violence (Padilla, 1992; Taylor, 1990a). The media and some law enforcement authorities have made allegations that Chinese gangs are increasingly involved in heroin trafficking, which, in their view, is also the major reason for violence among Chinese gangs. This study does not offer support for that contention. Drug use and drug dealing were not rampant among the gang subjects interviewed or the gang members they knew. Also, the hypothesis that the heroin trade is a catalyst for Chinese gang violence is not supported by my findings. Klein, Maxson, and Cunningham (1991) maintain that although crack dealing was alleged to be the cause of the recent escalation in gang violence among black and Hispanic gangs, an examination of official data in Los Angeles did not support such an allegation. A report prepared by the Los Angeles County District Attorney (1992) also concluded that, "Contrary to popular belief, most gang homicides are not random shootings nor are they disputes over drugs or some other crime. Gang homicides are the products of old-fashioned fights over turf, status, and revenge" (p. xx).

Generally, although gang members admitted to participating in violence with members of other gangs and with members of their own gang, I found that for the most part (a) violence between gang members is freelance and erupts rather spontaneously over personal matters, and (b) gang leaders strive to control and contain violence for purely pragmatic purposes.

VIOLENCE AGAINST NONGANG VICTIMS

In comparison with intergang and intragang aggression, violence against nongang victims by Chinese gang members is relatively rare. Of the 340 gang-related violent incidents reported in the New York newspapers between 1968 and 1992, only 10 incidents (3%) were reported to have involved extortion-related violence against business owners. Data from another survey conducted by the author also suggest that victims of Chinese gang extortion were unlikely to be attacked by gangs (Chin et al., 1994). Out of 603 subjects, only 2 reported being physically assaulted for resisting the gangs.

As was mentioned earlier, many gang respondents admitted that they were relatively active in committing robberies. Gang members not only mug people in the streets of Chinatown but also rob stores, gambling clubs, massage parlors, and residences. Victims of muggings are unlikely to be injured, but victims of other types of robbery may be assaulted or killed by heavily armed gang members. Although the media have reported several robbery cases in which the victims were brutally murdered, there is no statistical information available that would permit us to make a determination of the extent of physical assaults in commercial and home-invasion robberies committed by members of Chinese gangs.

One of the alleged major activities of Chinese gangs is debt collection for gambling dens and alien-smuggling rings (Chin, 1990). Gang members may use violence to coerce debtors who are behind in their payments or they may assault illegal aliens who default on their payments to smuggling rings in the United States. Recently, several illegal aliens were kidnapped and tortured by Chinese gang members because they failed to repay their smuggling debts (Kifner, 1991; Lorch, 1991; Strom, 1991).

Gang members may also employ violence to silence those who dare to testify against them in court. A Chinese merchant was shot and killed by gang members after he agreed to testify in a robbery charge against the Born-to-Kill gang (English, 1995; Steinberg, 1991). Likewise, a young Chinese woman and her boyfriend were abducted and executed by members of the Green Dragons gang after the young woman testified against the gang in a double-murder case (Dannen, 1992; *U.S. v. Chen I. Chung*, 1991). Two prominent Chinatown leaders were also believed to have been viciously attacked for their cooperation with law enforcement authorities (Gold, 1991; Hechtman, 1977). The likelihood of Chinatown residents being assaulted for testifying is rare, however, because few are willing to testify against Chinese gangs ("Police Chief Urges," 1992).

KONG SO: A RESTRAINING MECHANISM OF GANG VIOLENCE

Sanchez-Jankowski (1991) found that violence among Hispanic and African American gangs "is not unrestrained" (p. 139). Likewise, it appears that gang violence in the Chinese community is held in check. According to qualitative data from this study, faction leaders, perhaps under pressure from top leaders or tong members, instruct street-level or clique leaders to control ordinary members and prevent them from becoming involved in spontaneous violence. One of the most challenging jobs for a street-level leader is to prevent his followers from engaging in deadly confrontations with rival gang members. In instances of disputes or violent confrontations between gangs or within a gang, street-level leaders try to resolve problems through peaceful negotiation, a process known among Chinese gangs as *kong so*.

Many gang members (69%) indicated that when intergang conflicts occurred, faction or street-level leaders from the parties involved selected a place (normally a restaurant located in neutral territory) to sit down and talk, or negotiate. As in formal negotiations between nations, the representatives from each gang are expected to be of equal status. A street leader explained how negotiations are carried out between Chinese gangs:

[When there is an intergang dispute], I will have to do the negotiation. If they [the rival gang] feel like I am not qualified, they will ask me to send my *dai lo*. Sometimes, when they see that I look young, they will say that I am not qualified. I will then call my *dai lo*, and he will try to regain face for me. If the negotiator from the rival gang is of the same rank as myself, we will sit down and talk.

It appears that when intergang conflicts erupt between Chinese gangs, *kong so* is the norm rather than the exception. It is certainly expected to give the parties involved an opportunity to cool down and figure out a nonviolent way to save everyone's face. Money may be relayed to the party that was insulted or physically harmed. The party judged to be guilty may treat the "victims" to a lavish dinner, a popular method of settling dispute, known as *bai tai zi* (literally, setting a table). *Bai tai zi* is also a common practice among gang members in Hong Kong and Taiwan for redressing grievances and soothing ill feeling (Chi, 1985; Zhang, 1984).

It is not known how often negotiations between Chinese gangs prove to be successful in resolving conflicts. In some cases, fatal shoot-outs have occurred when negotiations broke down (James, 1991). A street leader who participated in this study speculated about how he would react should a negotiation prove unsuccessful: "I will talk to them [the rival gang] first. If the negotiation breaks down, I'll tell them to wait there. I'll then tell my kids to do the attack. I won't show any anger [during the negotiation]."

Another gang member described what led him to participate in a negotiation with a rival gang and what happened when talk failed to settle the conflict:

> A couple of days ago, the XX gang thought that one of our brothers wanted trouble. They speculated that our brother was trying to threaten them. Our brother denied, but they wanted him to apologize. Our brother refused. We went to a restaurant at Lafayette Street to meet with them. At the meeting, our brother refused to apologize. They asked if we wanted to start anything. We walked out and waited. When they came out, we beat them up.

Not only intergang clashes can be resolved through *kong so;* intragang confrontations may also be quelled through the same mechanism. Gang members (84%) said that their *dai lo* would intervene when a serious conflict between members developed. If the situation warranted, the *ah kung* (the tong member who acts as the middleman between the tong and the gang) would also step between the warring parties. One gang member explained how it works:

> If the conflict among us is serious, the *ah kung* will have to come out and resolve it. If not, the *dai los* will sit down and talk. If members of other gangs know that we are fighting among ourselves, they will laugh at us. Sometimes we will fight among ourselves, but not openly. We will shake hands and apologize, though we still fight behind the backs of the *dai los*.

The capacity for violence appears to be one of the key defining characteristics of street gang culture. Its employment, however, is shaped and determined by a cluster of constraints related to profit-generating goals. Violence between and within gangs is regulated through an agent or *ah kung* who attempts to channel aggressive behavior in ways that effectively maintain gang coherence. Gang coherence in turn supports the gang's involvement in extortion activities and in the provision of protection services to organized vice industries in the community.

Kong so is a regulatory mechanism designed to achieve several ends; it may mute violence or define its parameters so that the gangs retain their viability and do not self-destruct. Gang leaders have a vested interest in containing and controlling the violent behavior of the members of their gangs. By elaborating the thresholds of permissible and impermissible violence, gang leaders consolidate their authority and manipulate an asset to their own advantage. Violence is a key criminal resource that needs to be utilized and exploited efficiently if it is to be effective. Many gang leaders recognize that this resource should not be wasted.

The identification of *kong so* illuminates many aspects of Chinese gang organization. For instance, we may think of gang structure as both a consequence and an initiator of action. Street gang structure does not develop spontaneously or haphazardly. Rather, roles played by gang members are shaped by the criminal activity of the gangs. Moreover, because most of the gangs' criminal activities depend on the needs of the affiliated adult organizations, the power structure of the gangs reflects the needs of the tongs to communicate and effectively use the potential violence of the gangs for their purposes. Also, gang structure works as a control or constraint on the types of criminal activities gangs are likely to engage in. The development of gangs in turfs and the assignment of roles—criminal work roles—within the turf constricts their capacity for freelance crime and may even temper and tame their violence.

Leadership plays a pivotal role in the organization and discharging of collective violence. To harness a gang's energies for its projects—whether for turf defense, protection of adult criminal organization enterprises, or credible threats against extortion victims—gang leaders need to create and maintain asymmetrical information flows in which *dai lo*s possess greater knowledge and better networks of influence with faction leaders and others than do the members of the cliques.

Conclusion

Members of Chinese gangs appear to be quite active in committing violent crimes. Most of the gang members in this survey reported regular or frequent engagement in assault, shooting, and robbery. Gang violence in the Chinese community may be categorized into intergang violence, intragang violence, and aggression against nongang victims. Intergang violence appears to be the most common sort of violence, and violence against nongang victims is the rarest. The subjects indicated that provocations and turf warfare were the major reasons for intergang hostilities, and that disputes over money and women were important causes for intragang conflicts. Almost all gang-related violent incidents in Chinatown are intraethnic confrontations.

In studies of African American and Hispanic gangs, involvement in drug use and drug distribution has been found to be a major contributing factor to the escalation of gang assaults and murders (Padilla, 1992; Taylor, 1990a). My study suggests that Chinese gang members are, by comparison, less involved in drug use and drug selling. Only one subject reported drug selling as a reason for intragang violence. The use and distribution of drugs do not appear to be a vital factor in causing violence among the Chinese gang members we interviewed. This finding supports the conclusions of Fagan (1989), Sanchez-Jankowski (1991), Klein et al. (1991), and the Los Angeles County District Attorney (1992) that the use and selling of drugs is not necessarily related to the incidence of violence among street gangs.

Moore (1990a) and Sanchez-Jankowski (1991) have stressed the importance of differentiating between gang violence and individual violence in examining the nature of gang aggression. According to both Moore and Sanchez-Jankowski, most violent acts committed by gang members are not specifically motivated by group objectives. I also find that the aggressive behaviors of Chinese gang members are often not sanctioned or known by their leaders. Only a few violent incidents, mainly planned turf warfare, can be defined as collectively based violence, undertaken by the gang as a whole. In most incidents, gang leaders play an important role in the suppression of violence among young gang members because they wish to prevent escalation of minor conflicts into major showdowns. My findings suggest that most Chinese gang violence consists of individual or clique-based activities, either committed by younger members on their own or sanctioned only by their clique.

This study fails to confirm Thompson's (1976) view that gang violence in Chinatown was used as a mask for racketeering activities operated by adult organizations in the community. My data reveal that gang members are very active in providing protection to vice operations in Chinatown, but this activity was not reported to be a factor in promoting violence. My subjects also did not indicate that their aggression was sanctioned or instigated by operators of vice businesses.

This study also does not lend much support to Takagi and Platt's (1978) theory, discussed earlier, regarding gang violence. Careful examination of the data reveals that most of the violent incidents in Chinatown appear to be related to Chinese gangs. Tong members were involved either as instigators or victims in only a few incidents. Moreover, the "political intimidation of progressive organizations" (Takagi & Platt, 1978, p. 22) was not mentioned by my respondents as a factor contributing to gang violence. My data suggest that members of non-tong-affiliated gangs were involved in violent acts as frequently as members of tong-affiliated gangs.

Furthermore, information gathered from business owners and gang members suggests that Chinese merchants are rarely assaulted by gang members, which is contrary to the impression given by the media and the police. The merchants in this survey were rarely physically assaulted, even when they refused to comply with gang demands. Even verbal threats were rare when gang members approached business owners for money, goods, or services.

This study suggests that most violent activities in Chinatown are committed by gang members independent of tongs and other adult organizations, and that these violent incidents are not associated with protection rackets or related to political intimidation. These beliefs are inconsistent with those of earlier researchers (Takagi & Platt, 1978; Thompson, 1976); possibly the passage of time or the change of venue may have contributed to these differences.

In sum, drug use, drug trafficking, tong affiliation, protection rackets, and community politics appear to have little influence on gang violence in New York City's Chinatown. With the exception of planned attacks that are rare and that characterize turf-expansion violence, most Chinese gang assaults are spontaneous reactions to minor provocations, and they are often carried out on an individual basis. The findings in this study are in accord with Fagan's research (1989) and the reports of the Los Angeles County District Attorney (1992). Those studies showed that gang violence was seldom related to drug dealing and other organized crime activities but was usually fueled by traditional gang conflicts over turf, status, or revenge.

Notes

1. Tongs are fraternal associations that were originally formed by Chinese immigrants in the United States in the late 1850s as self-help groups (Lee, 1989; Liu, 1981; Ma, 1990). The word *tong* means "hall" or "gathering place" (Dillon, 1962). Because of their pervasive and consistent involvement in illegal gambling, prostitution, opium trafficking, and violence, the tongs are considered by U.S. law enforcement authorities to be criminal enterprises (Asbury, 1927; Gong & Grant, 1930). But the tongs, like the family and district associations, provide many needed services to immigrants who could not otherwise obtain help (U.S. Senate, 1992). Over the past 150 years, more than 30 tongs were formed in the United States, predominantly on the west and east coasts (U.S. Department of Justice, 1988). These associations became places for members to socialize, to seek help, and to gamble. Working-class Chinese who do not gamble join the associations because they want some place to turn to if they need help. Businesspersons join the associations mainly for protection. Most association members are law-abiding employed people who visit the associations only once in a while to meet friends and gamble; otherwise, they have little to do with the associations. But some members are closely identified with the associations— they are full-time employees of the associations, retired, or unemployed. Among them, quite a few are young, tough teenagers who have nowhere to go and nothing to look forward to. They become the strong-arm enforcers of the associations. Most tong organizations have a president, a vice president, a secretary, a treasurer, an auditor, and several elders and public relations administrators (Chin, 1990; U.S. Senate, 1992). Branches may be found in cities with large numbers of Chinese residents. Each branch has a ruling body resembling the headquarters organization staff and including a president, a secretary, a treasurer, an auditor, and several staff members (Chin, 1990). Since the 1960s, most tongs have abandoned the name tong and renamed the association because the word tong evokes unpleasant memories of the infamous tong wars (Glick, 1941; Glick & Hong, 1947; Lee, 1974; Minke, 1960/1974).

2. The English word *triad* refers to a triangle of heaven, earth, and humankind (Chesneaux, 1972). Triad societies are considered to be the largest, most dangerous, and best-organized crime groups in the world (Black, 1992; Booth, 1991; Chin, 1995b; Posner, 1988). These secret societies were formed in China three centuries ago by patriots fighting the oppressive and corrupt Qing Dynasty (1644–1911). When the Qing dynasty collapsed and the Republic of China was established in 1911, some triad societies became involved in criminal activities (Morgan, 1960). According to one source, there are currently 160,000 triad members in Hong Kong, belonging to more than 50 societies (Chang, 1991). In Hong Kong, triads appear to be in control of most illegitimate enterprises and some legitimate businesses as well (Fight Crime Committee, 1986). Triad activities are not limited to Hong Kong, however; law enforcement agencies in North America, Europe, and Southeast Asia report that triad activities are increasing in their jurisdictions (O'Callaghan, 1978; President's Commission on Organized Crime, 1984; U.S. Senate, 1992). In 1997, Hong Kong will be returned to China. The political uncertainty in Hong Kong has made law enforcement authorities in the United States, Canada, Australia, and other countries deeply concerned that triad groups might transfer their operations abroad (Grace & Guido, 1988; Kaplan, Goldberg, & Jue, 1986).

3. The 10 gangs are the Ghost Shadows, Flying Dragons, Tung On, Fuk Ching, Hung Ching, Canal Boys or the Born-to-Kill, White Tigers, Green Dragons, Taiwanese Brotherhood, and Golden Star.

4. The definition of a gang-related incident is controversial (Klein & Maxson, 1989). Journalists and police in the Chinese community appear to use the relatively loose definition adopted by the Los Angeles Police Department and the Los Angeles Sheriff's Department in defining gang-related incidents (Maxson & Klein, 1990)—that is, if a victim or an offender in a violent confrontation is a gang member, the incident is considered gang related.

5. Although violent episodes in North American Chinese communities that involve multiple victims or bystanders are often well publicized in English-language media, most gang warfare is only reported in Chinese-language media. Even so, Chinese-language media normally cover only incidents in which one or more victims are killed or seriously wounded. Thus, most minor gang clashes in these Chinese communities go unnoticed.

6. The recruiter was paid $50 per subject, both for his recruitment and for his protective role as bodyguard for members of the research team.

7. Subjects were asked to indicate what their positions were in the gangs, and their self-reported gang ranks were cross-validated by their roles in extortion and other gang activities.

8. Most overseas Chinese in New York City are Cantonese or Fujianese. Although both groups are southerners and considered adventurous by the northern Chinese, each group has its own customs and dialect. The Cantonese still dominate most North American Chinese communities because the majority of early Chinese immigrants were Cantonese. The Fujianese are now in a position to challenge the supremacy of the Cantonese in New York City's Chinatown, however. Most Fujianese came from Fuzhous City and its vicinity.

9. More than half of the subjects said their mothers worked in garment factories and only five indicated that their mothers were professionals. Likewise, the majority of the subjects' fathers were employed in restaurants, garment factories, or retail stores; only three had white-collar jobs.

10. When a subject indicated that he was more comfortable communicating in Chinese (either Mandarin or Cantonese), the Chinese questionnaire was used, and the interview was conducted in the dialect the subject was familiar with.

11. None of the subjects had any contact with the interviewer prior to the study. To prevent the subjects from viewing the interviewer as an authoritative figure, they were not informed that the interviewer was a school counselor.

12. It is not clear why the subjects were reluctant to talk about their involvement in burglary, but not other crimes, such as robbery and extortion. From informal discussions with the respondents and from examining the oaths and rules of Chinese gangs (Chin, 1990), it appears that burglary is considered a lowly act in the subculture of Chinese gangs, and as a result, gang members may be unwilling to be viewed as burglars. Respondents may have been reluctant to reveal the number of people in their gangs and the amount of money their gangs earned because they viewed such information as gang business and did not want to betray their organizations. Some, especially the ordinary members, appeared to have very little knowledge about these aspects of gang composition. As a result, these questions were excluded after the first few interviews.

13. If a respondent indicated that he had left the gang, the interviewer asked him to provide estimates for the year prior to his dissociation from the gang. Comparisons between active and former gang members in the sample show that there are no significant differences between the two groups in their involvement in violence and other criminal activities for a particular year, with the exception that active gang members were more involved in selling items to business owners than former gang members. As a result, active

gang status was not controlled for in the analysis of Chinese gang members' involvement in violence and other criminal activities.

14. Vietnamese members of the Born-to-Kill (BTK) gang were often accused of extorting money from store owners outside their turf and ignoring the gang rule of not stepping into other gangs' territories. Perhaps for this reason, the second-in-command of BTK was shot to death in BTK's turf by rival gang members. BTK members not only orchestrated a high-profile funeral for their deceased leader but also decided to have the motorcade pass through core areas of Chinatown not in their turf, in protest. When the mourners arrived at the cemetery in Linden, New Jersey, for the burial, three heavily armed men fired at them. Twenty-three young males and females were wounded (English, 1995). The authorities theorized that BTK's intentional encroachment on other gangs' territories in an unusual way angered their rivals and led to the shootings in the cemetery (Lorch, 1990).

15. Although this respondent linked these issues, I counted them as separate motives in my survey.

9

Girls, Delinquency, and Gang Membership

MEDA CHESNEY-LIND
RANDALL G. SHELDEN
KAREN A. JOE

The early 1990s have seen a curious resurgence of interest in female offenders engaged in nontraditional, masculine crimes—particularly girls' involvement in gangs. The purpose of this chapter is to critically assess whether girls are becoming more like their male counterparts in relation to gang activities and other forms of violent delinquency. We first describe the nature of this recent concern about girls in gangs, especially as it has been expressed in media accounts. We then examine the research evidence on young women's involvement in gang and criminal activities, focusing specifically on official data sources, self-report surveys, and qualitative studies. We conclude with a discussion of the distance between the media image of the "gang-banging" girl of the 1990s and the actual lives of girls involved in gang activity.

185

The Media Constructs Girl Gangs

In some ways, the fascination with a "new" violent female offender is not new. In the 1970s, a notion emerged that the women's movement had "caused" a surge in women's serious crimes, but this "liberation" discussion focused largely on the crimes of adult women (Chesney-Lind, 1986). The current discussion has settled on girl's commission of violent crimes, often in youth gangs. Indeed, there has been a veritable siege of these news stories with essentially the same theme—today, girls are in gangs, they are "meaner" than girls in earlier generations, and as a consequence, their behavior in these gangs does not fit the traditional stereotype of female delinquency.

On August 6, 1993, for example, in a feature spread on teen violence, *Newsweek* included a box entitled "Girls Will Be Girls," noting that "Some girls now carry guns. Others hide razor blades in their mouths" (Leslie, Biddle, Rosenberg, & Wayne, 1993, p. 44). Explaining this trend, the authors noted that "The plague of teen violence is an equal-opportunity scourge. Crime by girls is on the rise, or so various jurisdictions report" (p. 44). Exactly a year earlier, a short subject appeared on the CBS program *Street Stories*. "Girls in the Hood," a rebroadcast of a story first aired in January 1992, opened with this voice-over:

> Some of the politicians like to call this The Year of the Woman. The women you are about to meet probably aren't what they had in mind. These women are active, they're independent, and they're exercising power in a field dominated by men. In January Harold Dowe first took us to the streets of Los Angeles to meet two uncommon women who are members of street gangs ("Girls in the Hood," 1992).

These stories are only two examples of the many media accounts that have appeared since journalists launched the second wave of the "liberation" hypothesis. Where did this latest trend come from? Perhaps the start was a *Wall Street Journal* article, "You've Come a Long Way, Moll" published on January 25, 1990. This news piece noted that "between 1978-1988 the number of women arrested for violent crimes went up 41.5%, vs. 23.1% for men. The trend is even starker for teenagers" (Crittenden, 1990, p. A14). But the trend was accelerated by the identification of a new, specific version of this more general revisiting of the liberation hypothesis. The *New York Times*'s front-page story, "For Gold Earrings and Protection, More Girls Take the Road to Violence," opened in this way:

> For Aleysha J., the road to crime has been paved with huge gold earrings and name brand clothes. At Aleysha's high school in the Bronx, popularity comes from looking the part. Aleysha's mother has no money to buy her nice things so the diminutive 15 year old steals them, an act that she feels makes her equal parts bad girl and liberated woman. (Lee, 1991, p. A1)

This is followed by the assertion that "There are more and more girls like Aleysha in troubled neighborhoods in the New York metropolitan areas, people who work with children say. There are more girls in gangs, more girls in the drug trade, more girls carrying guns and knives, more girls in trouble." Whatever the original source, at this point a phenomenon known as pack journalism took over. The *Philadelphia Inquirer*, for example, ran a story subtitled "Troubled Girls, Troubling Violence" on February 23, 1992, that claimed,

> Girls are committing more violent crimes than ever before. Girls used to get in trouble like this mostly as accomplices of boys, but that's no longer true. They don't need the boys. And their attitudes toward their crimes are often as hard as the weapons they wield—as shown in this account based on documents and interviews with participants, parents, police and school officials. While boys still account for the vast majority of juvenile crime, girls are starting to catch up. (Santiago, 1992, p. A1)

This particular story featured a single incident in which an African American girl attacked another girl (who was described as middle class and appeared to be white in the photo that accompanied the story) in a subway. The *Washington Post* ran a similar story entitled, "Delinquent Girls Achieving a Violent Equality in D.C." on December 23, 1992 (Lewis, 1992), and the stories continue to appear. For example, about 2 years later (December, 12, 1994), the *San Francisco Examiner* printed a story with the headline "Ruthless Girlz" (Marinucci, Winokur, & Lewis, 1994).

In virtually all stories on this topic, the issue is framed in a similar fashion. Typically, a specific and egregious example of female violence is described. This is followed by a quick review of the Federal Bureau of

Investigation's (FBI) arrest statistics showing what appear to be large increases in the number of girls arrested for violent offenses, as well as quotes from the "experts," usually police officers, teachers, or other social service workers but occasionally criminologists, interpreting the events.

Following these print media stories, the number of articles and television shows focused specifically on girls in gangs jumped. Popular talk shows such as *Oprah* (November 1992), *Geraldo* (January 1993), and *Larry King Live* (March 1993) did programs on the subject, and more recently NBC's *Nightly News* broadcast a segment that opened with the same link between women's "equality" and girls' participation in gangs:

> Gone are the days when girls were strictly sidekicks for male gang members, around merely to provide sex and money and run guns and drugs. Now girls also do shooting . . . the new members, often as young as twelve, are the most violent. . . . Ironic as it is, just as women are becoming more powerful in business and government, the same thing is happening in gangs. ("Diana Koricke ," 1993)

For many feminist criminologists, this pattern is more than a little familiar, echoing the past. In 1971, a *New York Times* article entitled, "Crime Rate of Women Up Sharply Over Men's" noted that "Women are gaining rapidly in at least one traditional area of male supremacy—crime" (Roberts, 1971, p. 1).

A more expanded version, of what would come to be known as the "liberation hypothesis" appeared in Adler's (1975) *Sisters in Crime* in a chapter entitled "Minor Girls and Major Crimes":

> Girls are involved in more drinking, stealing, gang activity, and fighting—behavior in keeping with their adoption of male roles. We also find increases in the total number of female deviances. The departure from the safety of traditional female roles and the testing of uncertain alternative roles coincides with the turmoil of adolescence creating criminogenic risk factors which are bound to create this increase. These considerations help explain the fact that between 1969 and 1972 national arrests for major crimes show a jump for boys of 82 percent—for girls, 306 percent. (p. 95)

The female crime wave described by Adler (1975) and, to a lesser extent by Simon (1975) was definitively refuted by subsequent research (see Gora, 1982; Steffensmeier & Steffensmeier, 1980), but the popularity of this perspective, at least in the public mind, continues unabated. It remains to be seen whether in the 1990s something different might be going on, particularly with reference to girls' involvement in gangs and violence. Are these "new trends" supported by research findings? Or are we in the midst of what Cohen (1980) called another "moral panic." It is to these questions that we now turn.

Trends in Girls' Violence and Gang Membership: Quantitative Studies

Media portrayals of young women suggest that they, like their male counterparts, are increasingly involved in violence and gang activities. Several sources of information are available to look at these two issues.

GIRLS AND VIOLENT CRIMES

Let us turn first to the question of girls' violence. A review of girls' arrests for violent crime for the last decade (1984-1993) initially seems to support the notion that girls are engaged in more violent crime. Arrests of girls for murder were up 78%, robbery arrests were up 89.4%, and aggravated assault arrests were up 108.9%. Indeed, arrests of girls for all Part One Offenses[1] went up 36.4% (Federal Bureau of Investigation [FBI], 1994, p. 222).

These increases certainly sound substantial, but on closer inspection they become considerably less dramatic. First, the number of boys arrested for these offenses has increased during the last decade by 63.2%, so the rise in girls' arrests more or less parallels increases in the arrests of male youth. This pattern, then, reflects overall changes in youth behavior rather than dramatic changes and shifts in the character of girls' behavior.

Second, serious crimes of violence represent a very small proportion of all girls' delinquency, and that figure has remained essentially unchanged. Only 2.3% of girls' arrests in 1984 were for serious violent crimes. By 1993, this figure rose to 3.4% (14,788 arrests out of a total of

426,980 arrests). Moreover, girls' share of serious crimes of violence (i.e., the gender ratio for these offenses) has changed very little. In 1984, for example, arrests of girls accounted for 11.2% of all youth arrests for serious crimes of violence; in 1993, the comparable figure was 13.4% (FBI, 1978, p. 179, 1994, p. 222).

Finally, a detailed study of unpublished FBI data on the characteristics of girls' and boys' homicides between 1984 and 1993 found that girls accounted for "proportionately fewer homicides in 1993 (6%) than in 1984 (14%)" (Loper & Cornell, 1995, p. 7). Detailed comparisons drawn from these "supplemental homicide reports" also indicated that, in comparison to boy's homicides, girls who killed were more likely to use a knife than a gun and to murder someone as a result of conflict rather than in the commission of a crime. The authors' concluded that, "The stereotype of girls becoming gun-toting robbers was not supported. The dramatic increase in gun-related homicides . . . applies to boys but not girls" (Loper & Cornell, 1995, p. 16).

Self-report data trends in youthful involvement in violent offenses also fail to show the dramatic changes found in official statistics (specifically, a matched sample of "high-risk" youth (aged 13-17) surveyed in the 1977 National Youth Study and the more recent 1989 Denver Youth Survey). These data revealed significant *decreases* in girls' involvement in felony assaults, minor assault, and hard drugs, and no change in a wide range of other delinquent behaviors—including felony theft, minor theft, and index delinquency (D. Huizinga, personal communication, 1994).

Although many questions can be raised about the actual significance of differences between official and self-report data, careful analyses of these data cast doubt on the media construction of the hyperviolent girl. Still, these data are less helpful in providing us with an understanding of girls' involvement with gangs. The reason for this is simple: Changes in official crime statistics (and self-report data, for that matter) failed to signal the rise of youth gangs of either gender. As a consequence, it might be more useful to examine other sources of information on gangs and the role of gender in gang membership.

GIRL GANG MEMBERSHIP

Official estimates of the number of youth involved in gangs have increased dramatically over the past decade. Currently, more than 90%

TABLE 9.1 Gang-Related Crime by Type as a Percentage of Total Crime
Recorded by Gender

Offense Type	Male	Female
Homicide	2.3	4.5
Other violent	48.5	27.3
Property	14.7	42.6
Drug related	10.3	9.1
Vice	2.9	0.0
Other	21.2	16.5

NOTE: Data from Curry, Ball, and Fox (1994, p. 8).

of the nation's largest cities report youth gang problems, up from about half in 1983 (Curry, Box, Ball, & Stone, 1992). Police estimates now put the number of gangs at 4,881 and the number of gang members at 249,324 (Curry, Ball, & Fox, 1994). But what is the role of gender in gang membership? Let us look more closely at the characteristics of youth labeled by police as gang members.

Curry et al. (1994) conducted a review of the characteristics of youth identified by police as being involved in gangs. Girls account for a very small percentage of these youth (3.6%), though Curry and his associates note that some jurisdictions have "law enforcement policies that officially exclude female gang members" (p. 8). If only those jurisdictions that include girls and women are examined, the proportion climbs to 5.7%. Table 9.1 displays the offense profiles of male and female gang members in these police databases.

As can be seen, girls are three times more likely than boys to be involved in "property" offenses and about half as likely to be involved in violent offenses. Looking at these statistics differently, only girls' involvement in property offenses exceeded 1% of the total number of offenses tracked nationally. Although one can, with the data in Table 9.1, make much of the role of homicide in girl's offending, only 8 (0.7%) of the 1,072 gang-related homicides in this data set were attributed to girls.

If the jurisdictions that specifically count girls are examined, the numbers change slightly but still show dramatically less involvement of girls in gang-related offenses. In these jurisdictions, girls accounted for only 13.6% of the gang-related property offenses, 12.7% of the drug crimes, and only 3.3% of the crimes of violence. These data do show a higher proportion of girls' involvement in homicides (11.4%), but recall how small the numbers are in this category (Curry, Ball, & Fox, 1994, p. 8). Further, recall that detailed research on girls' homicides suggest that girls' homicides differ significantly from those committed by boys. Girls' homicides are more likely to grow out of an interpersonal dispute with the victim (79%) whereas boys' homicides are more likely to be crime related (57%) (e.g., perpetrated during the commission of another crime, such as robbery) (Loper & Cornell, 1995).

A more detailed look at differences between male and female gang members in police databases can be obtained from an analysis of files maintained by the Honolulu Police Department (HPD).[2] Examining the characteristics of a sample of youth ($N = 361$) labeled as gang members by the HPD in 1991 (see Chesney-Lind, Rockhill, Marker, & Reyes, 1994, for details of this research), the researchers looked at the total offense patterns of those labeled as gang members and compared a juvenile sub-sample of these individuals with nongang delinquents.

In the main, the Hawaii researchers found patterns consistent with the national data. For example, only 7% of the suspected gang members on Oahu were female and, surprisingly, the vast majority of these young women were adults (70%) (the median age for the young women in the sample was 24.5 and for the men, 21.5).

Virtually all the youth identified as gang members were drawn from low-income ethnic groups in the islands, but ethnic differences were also found between male and female gang members. The men were almost exclusively from immigrant groups (Samoan and Filipino); the women, by contrast, were more likely to be Native Hawaiian and Filipina.

Most important, women and girls labeled as gang members committed fewer of most offenses than men and they also committed less serious offenses. Indeed, the offense profile for the females in the gang sample bears a very close relationship to typical female delinquency. Over one third of the "most serious" arrests of girls (38.1%) were for property offenses (larceny theft). This offense category was followed by status offenses (19%) and drug offenses (9.5%). For males, the most serious offense was likely to be "other assaults" (27%), followed by larceny theft (14%). In essence, this profile indicated that although both the males and the females in this sample of suspected gang members were chronic but not serious offenders, this was particularly true of the girls.

In fact, the pattern of arrests found among these young women is comparable to general arrest trends of young women: The most common arrest category for girls in 1993 in the United States was larceny theft (FBI, 1994, p. 222), and the most common arrest category for these girls suspected of gang activity was larceny theft, followed by status offenses. Among boys suspected of gang activity, the pattern is somewhat more sobering, with "other assaults" (which probably means fighting with other boys) as the most serious arrest. In total, serious violent offenses (murder, sexual assault, robbery, and aggravated assault) accounted for 23% of the most serious offenses of boys suspected of gang membership but *none* of the girls' most serious offenses.

Finally, it is important to note that once police identified a youth as a gang member, the person apparently remained in the database regardless of patterns of desistence; for example, 22% of sample had not been arrested in 3 years and there was no gender difference in this pattern.

These patterns prompted a further exploration of the degree to which young women labeled by police as suspected gang members differed from young women who had been arrested for delinquency. A comparison group was created for those in the Oahu sample that were legally juveniles. Youth suspected of gang membership were matched on ethnicity, age, and gender with youth who were in the juvenile arrest database but had not been labeled as gang members. An analysis of offense patterns of this smaller group indicates no major differences between girls suspected of gang membership and their nongang counterparts. The modal most serious offense for gang girls was status offenses; for nongang girls it was other assaults.

This finding is not totally unexpected. Bowker and Klein (1983), in a examination of data on girls in gangs in Los Angeles in the 1960s, compared both the etiology of delinquent behavior of gang girls and their nongang counterparts and concluded,

> The overwhelming impact of racism, sexism, poverty and limited opportunity structures is likely to be so important in determining the gang membership and juvenile delinquency of women and girls in urban ghettos that personality variables, relations with parents and problems associated with heterosexual behavior play a relatively minor role in determining gang membership and juvenile delinquency. (pp. 750-751)

Similar studies, using comparison groups in Arizona (Zatz, 1985) with Hispanic gangs and in Las Vegas (Shelden, Snodgrass, & Snodgrass, 1993) with African American and Hispanic gangs, although not focusing on gender, found little to differentiate gang members from other "delinquent" or criminal youth.

These quantitative data do not provide support for the rise of a "new" violent female offender. Yet, we still have an inadequate understanding of the lives of girl gang members. There has been a small but growing number of excellent ethnographic studies of girls in gangs that suggest a much more complex picture wherein some girls solve their problems of gender, race, and class through gang membership. As we review these studies, it becomes clear that girls' experiences with gangs cannot simply be framed as "breaking into" a male world. Girls have long been in gangs, and their participation in these gangs—even their violence—is heavily influenced by their gender.

Girls, Femininities, and Gangs: Qualitative Studies

Curry et al.'s (1994) analysis of official police estimates indicated an extremely small proportion of girls involved in gang activity, but other estimates are higher. Miller (1975), in a nationwide study of gangs, found the existence of fully independent girl gangs to be quite rare, constituting less than 10% of all gangs, although about half of the male gangs in the New York area had female auxiliary groups. By contrast, in her important ethnographic work on gang activity in Los Angeles barrios, Moore (1991) estimated that fully one third of the youth involved in the gangs she studied were female (p. 8).

Given the range of estimates, one might wonder whether girls and their involvement with gang life resembles the involvement of girls in other youth subcultures, where they have been described as "present but invisible" (McRobbie & Garber, 1975). Certainly, Moore's (1991) higher estimate indicates that she and her associates saw girls that others had missed. Indeed Moore's work is noteworthy in her departure from the androcentric norm in gang research. The long-standing "gendered habits" of researchers has meant that girls' involvement with gangs has been neglected, sexualized, and oversimplified.[3] Thus, although there has been a growing number of studies investigating the connections between male gangs, violence, and other criminal activities, there has been no parallel development in research on female involvement in gang activity. As with all young women who find their way into the juvenile justice system, girls in gangs have been invisible.

This pattern of invisibility was undoubtedly set by Thrasher (1927/ 1963), who in his still-influential field observations of juvenile gangs in Chicago spent only about one page out of 600 discussing the five or six female gangs he found.[4] More recent discussions of gang delinquency actually represent a sad revisiting of the sexism that characterized the initial efforts to understand visible lower-class, male delinquency in Chicago over half a century earlier. Sanchez-Jankowski (1991), in *Islands in the Street*, implicitly conceptualizes gangs as a distinctly male phenomenon, and females are discussed in the context of "property" and "sex." Based on his fieldwork, he concluded,

> In every gang I studied, women were considered a form of property. Interestingly, the women I observed and interviewed told me they felt completely comfortable with certain aspects of this relationship and simply resigned themselves to accepting those aspects they dislike. The one aspect they felt most comfortable with was being treated like servants, charged with the duty of providing men with whatever they wanted. (p. 146)

Taylor's (1993) work *Girls, Gangs, Women and Drugs* marks a complete reversal in themes, with girls made the central focus, but from a male centered perspective. Taylor, like Thrasher and Sanchez-Jankowski, reflects a general tendency to minimize and distort the motivations and roles of female gang members as the result of the gender bias on the part of male gang researchers who describe the female experience from the male gang member's viewpoint or their own stance (Campbell, 1990a). Typically, male gang researchers have characterized female members as maladjusted tomboys or sexual chattels, in either case no more than appendages to male members of the gang.

Let us look more closely at Taylor's (1993) study, which provides a veneer of academic support for the media definition of the girl gang member as a junior version of the liberated female crook of the 1970s. It is not clear how many girls and women he interviewed for his book, but in the introduction he sets the tone for his work: "We have found that females are just as capable as males of being ruthless in so far as their life opportunities are presented. This study indicates that females have moved beyond the status quo of gender repression" (p. 8). He then stresses the similarities between boys' and girls' involvement in gangs, despite the fact that when the girls and women he interviews speak, it becomes clear that such a view is oversimplified. Listen, for example, to Pat responding to a question about "problems facing girls in gangs":

> If you got a all girls crew, um, they think you're "soft" and in the streets if you soft, it's all over. Fellas think girls is soft, like Rob, he think he got it better in his shit 'cause he's a fella, a man. It's wild, but fellas really hate seeing girls getting off. Now, some fellas respect the power of girls, but most just want us in the sack. (p. 118)

Other studies of female gang delinquency stress the image of girls as having auxiliary roles to boys' gangs (Brown, 1977; Flowers, 1987; Miller, 1975, 1980; Rice, 1963). Miller (1980) conducted an in-depth analysis of a Boston gang known as the Molls. This gang consisted of a core membership of 11 girls aged 13 to 16. They were white and Catholic (mostly Irish). These girls seemed to fit the stereotype of inner-city working-class girls; they spent most of their time "hanging out" on street corners looking and talking tough. They were known in the neighborhood as bad girls. Their illegal activities included truancy, theft, drinking, property damage, sex offenses, and assault, in order of frequency. Truancy was by far their most common offense, occurring about three times as often as the next most common offense, which was theft (predominantly shoplifting).

These girls were closely associated with a male gang in the area known as the Hoods. The girls aspired "to become recognized as *their* girls," an aspiration they furthered by approving, supporting, and abetting the criminal activities of the Hoods (Miller, 1980, pp. 243-244). In fact, to be accepted by the Hoods, the girls had no choice but to go along with their criminal activities. Contrary to popular belief, "the Molls did not flaunt their sexual exploits in order to win esteem" and they believed that the way to get the boys to like them was to imitate their behavior as much as possible, rather than be sexually accessible to them (p. 244).

Rice (1963) reported somewhat similar findings in his study of a New York gang, the Persian Queens. This girl gang was completely controlled by males and was oriented toward male activities. There was little they could do to achieve power or prestige in the gang world. Unlike the pattern Miller (1980) found, however, Rice reports that if the Persian Queens fought, the males would not like them; on the other hand, if they played a more feminine role, they were disregarded by the males, except for sexual gratification.

Similar findings have been reported in Philadelphia (Brown, 1977) and in New York City (Campbell, 1984). In general, although there have been some changes and some indications that girls are becoming more independent and aggressive, these studies portray girls who are part of gangs as either the girlfriends of the male members or "little sisters" subgroups of the male gang (see Bowker, 1978, p. 184; Hanson, 1964). Further, researchers suggest that the role for girls in gangs is "to conceal and carry weapons for the boys, to provide sexual favors, and sometimes to fight against girls who were connected with enemy boys' gangs" (Mann, 1984, p. 45).

Some firsthand accounts of girl gangs, although not completely challenging this image, are focused more directly on the race and class issues confronting these girls. Quicker (1983), studying Chicana gang members in East Los Angeles, found evidence that these girls, although still somewhat dependent on their male counterparts, were becoming more independent. These girls identified themselves as "homegirls" and their male counterparts as "homeboys," a common reference to relationships in the barrio. In an obvious reference to strain theory, Quicker notes that there are few economic opportunities in the barrio to meet the needs of the family unit. As a result, families are disintegrating and do not have the capability of providing access to culturally emphasized success goals for young people about to enter adulthood. Not surprising, almost all their activities occur within the context of gang life, where they learn how to get along in the world and are insulated within the harsh environment of the barrio (Quicker, 1983).

Moore's (1991) ethnography of two Chicano gangs in East Los Angeles, initiated during the same period as Quicker's (1983) study, brought the work forward to the present day. Her interviews clearly establish both the multifaceted nature of girls' experiences with gangs in the barrio and the variations in male gang members' perceptions of the girls in gangs. Importantly, her study establishes that there is no one type of gang girl, with some of the girls in gangs, even in the 1940s "not tightly bound to boys' cliques" and also "much less bound to particular barrios than boys. Other girls gangs did bear out the stereotype; but all the girls in gangs tended to come from "more troubled backgrounds than those of the boys" (p. 30). Significant problems with sexual victimization haunts girls but not boys. Moore also documents how the sexual double standard characterized male gang members' as well as neighborhood views of girls in gangs. Girl gang members were labeled "tramps" and symbolized as "no good," despite the girls' vigorous rejection of these labels. Further, some male gang members, even those who had relationships with girl gang members, felt that "square girls were their future" (p. 75).

Harris's (1988) study of the Cholas, a Latina gang in the San Fernando Valley, echoes this theme. Although the Cholas in many respects resemble male gangs, the gang did challenge the girls' traditional destiny in the barrio in two direct ways. First, the girls rejected the traditional image of the Latina woman as wife and mother, supporting instead a more "macho" homegirl role. Second, the gang supported the girls in their estrangement from organized religion, substituting instead a form of familialism that "provides a strong substitute for weak family and conventional school ties" (p. 172).

The same macho themes emerged in a study of the female "age sets" found in a large gang in Phoenix, Arizona (Moore, Vigil, & Levy, 1995). In these groups, fighting is used by the girls, as well as the boys, to achieve status and recognition. Even here, though, the violence is mediated by gender and culture. One girl recounts that she established her reputation by "protecting one of my girls. He [a male acquaintance] was slapping her around and he was hitting her and kicking her, and I went and jumped him and started hitting him" (p. 39). These researchers found that once respect was obtained, girls relied on their reputations and fought less often.

Girls in these sets also had to negotiate within a Mexican American culture which is "particularly conservative with regard to female sexuality" (Moore et al., 1995, p. 29). The persistence of the double standard in their neighborhoods and in their relations with the boys in the gang places the more assertive and sexually active girls in an anomalous position. Essentially, they must contend with a culture that venerates "pure girls" while also setting the groundwork for the sexual exploitation by gang boys of other girls. One respondent reported that the boys sometimes try to get girls high and "pull a train" (where a number of males have sex with one girl), something she clearly rejects for herself— even though she admits to having had sex with a boy she didn't like after the male gang members "got me drunk" (p. 32).

Fishman (1995) studied the Vice Queens, an African American female auxiliary gang to a boys' gang, the Vice Kings, that existed in Chicago during the early 1960s. Living in a mostly black community charac- terized by poverty, unemployment, deterioration, and a high crime rate, the gang of about 30 teenage girls was loosely knit and unlike the male gang lacked a rigidly hierarchical leadership structure. The gang pro- vided the girls with companionship and friends. Failing in school and unable to find work, the girls spent the bulk of their time hanging out on the streets with the Vice Kings, which usually included the consumption of alcohol, sexual activities, and occasional delinquency. Most of their delinquency was "traditionally female," such as prostitution, shoplift- ing, and running away, but some was more serious (e.g., auto theft). They also engaged in fights with other groups of girls, largely to protect their gang's reputation for toughness.

Growing up in rough neighborhoods provided the Vice Queens "with opportunities to learn such traditional male skills as fighting and taking care of themselves on the streets"; it was generally expected that the girls had to learn to defend themselves against "abusive men" and "attacks on their integrity" (Fishman, 1995, p. 87). Their relationship with the Vice Kings was primarily sexual, having sexual relations and bearing their children, but with no hope of marriage. Fishman perceptively points out that the Vice Queens were "socialized to be independent, assertive and to take risks with the expectations that these are characteristics that they will need to function effectively within the black low income commu- nity. . . . As a consequence, black girls demonstrate, out of necessity, a greater flexibility in roles" (p. 90). There has been little improvement in the economic situation of the African American community since the 1960s, and undoubtedly, today's young women face an even bleaker future than the Vice Queens. In this context, Fishman speculates that "black female gangs today have become more entrenched, more violent, and more oriented to 'male' crime" (p. 90). These changes, she adds, are unrelated to the women's movement, but are instead the "forced 'eman- cipation' which stems from the economic crisis within the black commu- nity" (p. 90).

Fishman's (1995) bleak speculation about the girls living in poverty-stricken neighborhoods in the 1960s has been largely confirmed by more contemporary research by Lauderback, Hansen, and Waldorf (1992) on an African American female gang in San Francisco. Disputing the traditional notions of female gang members in which they are portrayed as "maladjusted violent tomboys" or sex objects completely dependent upon the favor of male gang members" (p. 57), Lauderback et al. found an independent girl gang engaged in crack sales and organized "boosting" to support themselves and their young children. Looking past the gang's economic role in the members' lives, Lauderback and his associates noted that the gang fills a void in the lives of its members, as their own family ties were weak at best prior to their involvement in the group (p. 68). All under 25, abandoned by the fathers of their children, abused and controlled by other men, these young women wish they could be "doing something other than selling drugs and to leave the neighborhood," but "many felt that the circumstances which led them to sell drugs were not going to change" (p. 69).

Campbell's work (1984, 1990b) on Hispanic gangs in the New York area shows much the same pattern. The girls in Campbell's study joined gangs for reasons that are largely explained by their situation in a society that has little to offer young women of color (Campbell, 1990b, pp. 172-173). First, the possibility of a decent career outside of domestic servitude is practically nonexistent. Many of the young women come from female-headed families subsisting on welfare; most have dropped out of school and have no marketable skills. Their aspirations for the future were both gender typed and unrealistic, the girls expressing desires to be rock stars or professional models. Second, they find themselves in a highly gendered community where the men in their lives, although not traditional breadwinners, still make many decisions that circumscribe the possibilities open to young women. Third, the responsibility that a young Hispanic woman will have as a mother further restricts the options available to her. Campbell cites recent data revealing a very bleak future, as 94% will have children and 84% will have to raise their children without a husband. Most will be dependent on some form of welfare (p. 182). Fourth, these young women face a future of isolation as housewives in the projects. Finally, they share with their male counterparts a future of powerlessness as members of the urban underclass. In short, their lives reflect all the burdens of their triple handicaps of race, class, and gender.

For these girls, Campbell (1990b) observes, the gang represents "an idealized collective solution to the bleak future that awaits" them. The girls have a tendency to portray to themselves and the outside world a very idealized and romantic life (p. 173). They develop an exaggerated sense of belonging to the gang. Many were loners prior to joining the gang, having been only loosely connected to schoolmates and neighborhood peer groups. Even the gangs' closeness, as well as the excitement of gang life, is more fiction than reality. Their daily street talk is filled with exaggerated stories of parties, drugs, alcohol, and other varieties of "fun." But as Campbell notes,

> These events stand as a bulwark against the loneliness and drudgery of their future lives. They also belie the day to day reality of gang life. The lack of recreational opportunities, the long days unfilled by work or school and the absence of money mean that the hours and days are whiled away on street corners. "Doing nothing" means hang out on the stoop; the hours of "bullshit" punctuated by trips to the store to buy one can of beer at a time. When an expected windfall arrives, marijuana and rum are purchased in bulk and the partying begins. The next day, life returns to normal. (p. 176)

Joe and Chesney-Lind's (1995) interviews with youth gang members in Hawaii provide further evidence of the social role of the gang. Everyday life in marginalized and chaotic neighborhoods sets the stage for group solidarity in two distinct ways. First, the boredom, lack of resources, and high visibility of crime in neglected communities create the conditions for turning to others who are similarly situated, peer groups that offer a social outlet. At another level, the stress on families from living in marginalized areas combined with financial struggles creates heated tension, and in many cases, violence in the home. Joe and Chesney-Lind found, like Moore (1991), high levels of sexual and physical abuse; 62% of the girls they interviewed had sexually abused or assaulted. Three fourths of the girls and over half of the boys reported physical abuse.

The group, then, provides both the girls and the boys with a safe refuge and a surrogate family. The theme of marginality cuts across gender and ethnicity, but there were critical differences in how girls and boys—Samoans, Filipinos and Hawaiians—express and respond to the problems of everyday life. For example, let us look at the differences in boys' and girls' strategies for coping with these pressures—particularly the boredom of poverty. For boys, fighting and looking for fights is a major activity within the gang. If anything, the presence of girls around gang members depresses violence. As one 14-year-old Filipino put it, "If we not with the girls, we fighting. If we not fighting, we with the girls" (quoted in Joe & Chesney-Lind, 1995, p. 424). Many of the boys' activities involved drinking, cruising, and looking for trouble. Looking for trouble also meant being prepared for trouble. Although guns are somewhat available, most of the boys interviewed used bats or their hands to fight, largely but not exclusively because of cultural norms that suggest that fighting with guns is for the weak.

For girls, fighting and violence is a part of their life in the gang, but not something they necessarily seek out. Instead, protection, from neighborhood and family violence was a consistent and major theme in the girls' interviews. One girl simply stated that she belongs to the gang to provide "some protection from her father." Through the group she has learned ways to defend herself physically and emotionally: "He used to beat me up, but now I hit back and he doesn't beat me much now." As another 14-year-old Samoan put it, "You gotta be part of the gang or else you're the one who's gonna get beat up." Although this young woman said that members of her gang had to "have total attitude and can fight," she went on to say, "We want to be a friendly gang. I don't know why people are afraid of us. We're not that violent." Fights do come up in these girls' lives, "We only wen mob this girl 'cause she was getting wise, she was saying 'what, slut' so I wen crack her and all my friends wen jump in" (quoted in Joe & Chesney-Lind, 1995, pp. 425-426).

Gangs also produce opportunities for involvement in criminal activity, but these are affected by gender as well. Especially for boys from poor families, stealing and small-time drug dealing make up for a lack of money. These activities are not nearly so common among the female respondents. Instead, their problems with the law originate with more traditional forms of female delinquency, such as running away from home. Their families still attempt to hold them to a double standard that results in tensions and disputes with parents that have no parallel among the boys.

Girls' participation in gangs, which has been the subject of intense media interest, certainly needs to be placed within the context of the lives of girls, particularly young women of color on the economic and political margins. Girls' gang life is certainly not an expression of "liberation," but instead reflects the attempts of young women to cope with a bleak and harsh present as well as a dismal future. One 15-year-old Samoan captured this sense of despair when in response to our question about whether she was doing well in school she said "No, I wish I was, I need a future. [My life] is jammed up" (quoted in Joe & Chesney-Lind, 1995, p. 428).

None of these accounts confirm the stereotype of the hyperviolent, amoral female found in media accounts of girls in gangs. Certainly, the interviews confirm the fact that girls do commit a wider range of delinquent behavior than is stereotypically recognized, but these offenses appear to be part of a complex fabric of "hanging out," "partying," and the occasional fight in defending one's friends or territory. These ethnographies also underscore that although the streets may be dominated by young men, girls and young women do not necessarily avoid the streets as Connell (1987) suggests. The streets reflect the strained interplay between race, class, and gender.

LABELING GIRLS VIOLENT?

Historically, those activities that did not fit the official stereotype of "girls delinquency" have been ignored by those in authority (Fishman, 1995; Quicker, 1983; Shacklady-Smith, 1978). A close reading of ethnographies indicates that girls have long been involved in violent behavior as a part of gang life. During earlier periods, however, this occasional violence was ignored by law enforcement officers, who were far more concerned with girls' sexual behavior or morality.

Feminist criminologists have criticized traditional schools of criminology for assuming that male delinquency, even in its most violent forms, was somehow an understandable if not "normal" response to their situations. Girls who shared the same social and cultural milieu as delinquent boys but who were not violent were somehow abnormal or "overcontrolled" (Cain, 1989). Essentially, law-abiding behavior on the part of at least some boys and men is taken as a sign of character, but when women avoid crime and violence, it is an expression of weakness (Naffine, 1987). The other side of this equation is that if girls engage in even minor forms of violence, they are somehow more vicious than their male counterparts. In this fashion, the construction of an artificial, passive femininity lays the foundation for the demonization of young girls of color, as has been the case in the media treatment of girl gang members.

At best, media portrayals seem to suggest that girls engaged in what are defined as "male" activities such as violent crime or gang delinquency are seen as seeking "equality" with their male counterparts (see Daly & Chesney-Lind, 1988). Is that what is going on? Clearly, the research on girls and gangs indicates even this explanation is far too simplistic. Girls' involvement in gangs is obviously more than simple rebellion against traditional, white, middle-class notions of girlhood. Instead, their choice of gang membership is heavily shaped by the array of economic, educational, familial, and social conditions and constraints that exist in their families and neighborhoods. Careful inquiry into the lives of these girls documents the ways in which the gang facilitates their survival in their world. Additionally, focusing on the social role of the gang in girls' lives illuminates the ways in which girls' and boys' experiences of neighborhood, family, and violence converge and diverge.

Taken together, the ethnographic studies that have been done indicate the continued need to move beyond the traditional separations and gender-specific analyses of contemporary gangs. They also provide a strong challenge to public perceptions of gangs and youth violence dominated by racism and demonization.

Notes

1. Defined by the FBI as murder, forcible rape, robbery, burglary, aggravated assault, larceny theft, auto theft, and arson (added in 1979).

2. The Honolulu Police Department, City and County of Honolulu, is located on the island of Oahu where over three quarters of the state's population is located.

3. For exceptions, see Bowker and Klein (1983); Brown (1977); Campbell (1984, 1990a); Fishman (1995); Giordano, Cernkovich, and Puch (1978); Harris (1988); Moore (1991); Ostner (1986); Quicker (1983).

4. Thrasher (1927/1963) did mention, in passing, two factors he felt accounted for the lower number of girl gangs: "First, the social patterns for the behavior of girls, powerfully backed by the great weight of tradition and custom, are contrary to the gang and its activities; and secondly, girls, even in urban disorganized areas, are much more closely supervised and guarded than boys and are usually well incorporated into the family groups or some other social structure" (p. 228).

What Happens to Girls in the Gang?

JOAN W. MOORE
JOHN M. HAGEDORN

Anne Campbell (1984) laid the groundwork for the study of gang women in her classic *Girls in the Gang*. She argued convincingly that gang girls have rarely been studied as seriously as have gang boys. Instead, they have been stereotyped as promiscuous sex objects—segregated in "ladies' auxiliary" gangs—or as socially maladjusted tomboys, vainly trying to be "one of the boys." The stereotypes appeared in the social work literature and were also strongly embedded in much of the research literature.[1]

Both stereotypes—tomboy and slut—rest on the contrast between gang girls' behavior and that of "decent" girls. The implicit scenario is straight out of the 1950s—that adolescent girls who fail to conform to gender norms will jeopardize their futures. The premise is that marriage is the only serious career option for women and that improper behavior will alienate the kind of man who could be a good husband and provider. This is in sharp contrast with admonitions for boys. Even though gang membership also jeopardizes boys' futures, it's not because they are sexually promiscuous and fight but because they risk acquiring criminal records.

Most recent researchers on gang girls find that the stereotypes are greatly exaggerated. There is substantial variation both between gangs and within gangs in the ways in which girls behave, and girls are considerably more oriented to their gang girlfriends than the male-oriented early literature suggested. What, then, does happen to gang girls? How do their adult careers reflect the gang experience? Is the gang a temporary career diversion or a major turning point?

There is no single answer to these questions. One study showed that gang membership stigmatizes women on several levels and may seriously interfere with their later-life options—depending on how they come into and how they act in the gang, and on what kind of community they live in. Another study suggested that gang membership opens up opportunities for careers in drug dealing. Much of the answer depends on the time, the place, and the local culture of the community. And beyond this is the microculture of the particular gang and the initiative of the individual girl.

Time and Place: Variations in What Happens to Gang Girls

LEVELS OF LABELING IN LOS ANGELES

In an effort to understand the later lives of Los Angeles gang women, we analyzed interviews with random samples of 51 female and 106 male members of two long-standing Chicano gangs. All were adults when they were interviewed in 1986-1987. As teenagers, half had been active in the gangs in the 1950s and half in the 1970s.[2] The gangs were well established in very poor Mexican and Mexican American communities. Those communities, at that time, held very conservative values, particularly about how young women should behave. (See Moore, 1991, and cf. Campbell, 1990a, for Latina gang members in New York; and Horowitz, 1983, for Latinas in a Mexican community in Chicago).

Earlier we had found that gang members exhibited three major adult adaptations: (a) about 40% of the men and fewer of the women matured out of the gang into a "square" lifestyle; (b) more than a quarter of the men and fewer of the women became deeply involved with the life-style surrounding heroin—the climax drug in those communities at the time; and (c) the remainder followed an unstable, street-oriented life-style (Moore, 1991, pp. 125ff.). Although many gang girls did become "square" when they grew up, they were more likely than gang boys to fall into the third, street-oriented lifestyle—"just hanging out."

We were primarily interested in exploring the careers of women who had become at all involved with heroin. Forty-one percent of the gang women had used heroin at one time or another, as compared with 70% of the men. Whether or not they became addicted to the drug, any use of heroin represented extremely risky behavior for these women. We examined several points in their lives: their families of origin, their behavior in the gang, and their behavior in adulthood. It became evident that gang women who became involved with heroin had been largely confined to a street-oriented world throughout their lives. The gang was part and parcel of that life experience. (See Moore, 1994, for details.)

To begin with, girls who joined the gangs tended to come from different kinds of families than boys. Because it was more acceptable for boys to be "out on the streets," boys were more likely to come from conventional working-class families, whereas girls were more likely to come from "underclass" families and also from abusive families. Thus, if we take running away from home as some measure of problems in the family, we find that almost a third of the gang boys ran away from home—but fully three quarters of the girls ran away at least once. To put it succinctly, there was a self-selection process in gang recruitment that revolved around gender.

This selectivity was exaggerated for girls who wound up using heroin. Their families were even unhappier and more violent than those of other female gang members. Family members made sexual advances to a third of the girls who became heroin users and more than a quarter of those who did not, whereas such experiences were almost unknown among men. Girls were also more likely to have alcoholic or heroin-using parents.[3]

"Bad" families—including the children—were stigmatized in these communities, and respectable families would not allow their children to play with such children. In addition, street-oriented families may have been more likely than conventional families to be permissive with their daughters and to provide street-oriented opportunities and role models (Giordano, Cernkovich, & Pugh, 1978; Moore, 1990b). In effect, many of the girls may have been propelled by community and family dynamics to join a gang: this was a group that could sympathize with them, welcome them, and in some cases shelter them.

This initial selectivity is fateful, because membership in the heavily stigmatized gang further narrows a young woman's horizons and social opportunities, especially if she turns to heroin.[4] Traditional Mexican American gender norms tend to differentiate between "bad" and "good" girls, and *any* girl who joins a gang is defined as bad, no matter what her family is like. Labeling of boys in gangs is much less harsh.

Labeling happened even within the gang: Gang boys usually didn't consider themselves to be deviant just because they were in a gang, but many of them did consider the girls who joined a gang to be deviant. This was particularly true for the rowdier girls who fought, drank, or used drugs heavily. Not surprising, women who used heroin were more likely to have indulged in those behaviors. This meant that the more conventional boys wanted nothing to do with them and the girls were confined largely to the wilder boys in the gang—those who used heroin and often wound up in prison.

The experience in the gang was pivotal, channeling these girls' "deviant" careers ever more narrowly. The influence of the gang persisted into the heroin-using women's adult lives. Women heroin users were more likely to live with a male gang member at a very early age (16 or under), they were less likely to have been married formally, and they were less likely to work.

MILWAUKEE: ANOTHER TIME, OTHER ETHNIC GROUPS

In the early 1990s, we mounted a study of gangs in Milwaukee, Wisconsin, a large Rustbelt city that like many others in the East and Midwest began to experience serious gang problems in its inner-city neighborhoods as factory jobs faded from the scene.[5] We interviewed both African American and Latino (predominantly Puerto Rican) gang members—90 males and 64 females—when they were in their middle 20s. How did women's gang experiences relate to their later-life adaptations in Milwaukee? In many ways, they were very different from those of women in Los Angeles.

In contrast to the gangs in Los Angeles, which had long-standing, quasi-institutionalized traditions, the Milwaukee gangs were new. All of the men and women had been among the founding members of the gangs when they developed in the 1980s. The gangs adopted symbols and traditions from Chicago gangs (Hagedorn, 1988), which were very meaningful for the men, but for the women members—especially the African Americans— had little relevance. This meant that for the women— but not for the men—the gang was almost completely an adolescent experience. None of the African American women were involved in any way with the gang as adults, and fewer than 10% of the Latinas had any involvement. Almost all of the African American members, male and female, had moved out of the gang's old neighborhood, whereas a third of the Latinas still lived in the old neighborhood and the rest lived nearby.

The fact that the women had no gang ties in adulthood doesn't mean that gang membership had been a casual matter to these women when they were teenagers. Like the gang women studied in Los Angeles, female gang members in Milwaukee generally came from more troubled families than male gang members, and sexual abuse was far more prevalent. Thus, for many, the gang represented an alternative family.

Ethnic differences between Latina and African American gangs were important. Drug use differed dramatically, largely for historical reasons. Cocaine, the climax drug in these gangs, had been prevalent in the Latino neighborhood 5 to 10 years before it became popular in the African American neighborhoods, even though the neighborhoods were separated by only a mile. This meant that cocaine use was widespread among Latina gang members during their teens (with 89% using the drug), but nonexistent among the African Americans at the same age. In adulthood, though few were directly involved with the gang, a majority of the Latinas continued to use cocaine, and a third were reported to be heavy users. Cocaine use among African American women was much lower.

Drug dealing also differed. Many more of the Latinas (72% of the women and 81% of the men) than of the African Americans (31% of the women and 69% of the men) reportedly sold cocaine at some time in their lives. In at least one African American neighborhood two drug houses were run independently by women whose brothers or cousins were in the gang, and independent female-run drug houses were found elsewhere as well. At the time of the interview, however, none of the gang women was reported as supporting herself by selling drugs.

Several factors explain why Latinas were more active in the drug trade than African Americans. Of primary importance was the fact that the Latino drug markets were much more lucrative than the African American markets. Latino dealers served an affluent Anglo clientele from the adjacent downtown area, as well as a set of local customers, whereas most customers for African American dealers were also African American and many were from the local community (Hagedorn, 1994b). One Latina described the first male and the first female in her gang to sell drugs, and her account shows how the work was divided by gender:

> Bobby was the leader. Armida was a runner. She went places to go pick up large quantities. She'd go out of state for the dope and she'd bring it back. Yes, she was part of the group. She was a runner, a pick-up person.

At times, gang drug dealing led to severe sexual exploitation. One Latina explained that although the gang was a source of great support for her from a troubled family life, she was also ashamed of certain things. She nervously told the interviewer how she was offered to drug distributors to induce them to lower their wholesale price to a local gang dealer:

> He used me, to, you know . . . even thinking about it disgusts me, but it was, you know, I had to do it just to prove myself. . . . [It was] prostitution. . . . do extra favors, you know, starting the guys. You know, their drugs would be a lot cheaper [for the gang dealer].

Thus, comparing the Milwaukee women with the Los Angeles women suggests that ethnicity counts, but so do opportunities. For Latinas in both cities, gang membership tended to have a significant influence on their later lives, but for African American women in Milwaukee, the gang tended to be an episode. There is much less sense in Milwaukee that gang girls of any ethnicity were as heavily labeled in their community as were Chicana gang girls in Los Angeles. For Latinas in both cities, gangs tended more to be a family matter than they were for African Americans. In Milwaukee, Latinas tended to continue living in or near the gang neighborhood, cocaine tended to be more widely available, and there were better opportunities in drug marketing than there were for Latinas in Los Angeles or African Americans in Milwaukee.

Having Children: A Constant for Women

No matter what the cultural context, and no matter what the economic opportunity structure, there seems to be one constant in the later life of women in gangs. Most of them have children, and children have more effect on women's lives than on men's.

Gang men also have children, but for women the consequences are very much stronger. For women, but rarely for men, new responsibilities associated with child rearing may speed up the process of maturing out of the gang.

Part of this process has to do with reputation. Horowitz (1983) argues that a Chicana who has been labeled as "loose" has a chance to retrieve her reputation when she bears a child. If she becomes a "good mother," staying away from gang hangouts, her past is forgiven, but if she neglects her children and continues to hang out with her buddies, her bad reputation is simply confirmed. More important, perhaps, is that her relationship with her parents changes. Teenaged gang mothers usually find that they get more deeply involved with their parents, who may exert "ownership" rights over the children if they don't approve of their daughters' lifestyle (cf. Moore & Devitt, 1989).

But childbearing also generates internalized identity changes. For example, when we asked Mexican American gang members in Los Angeles what had been the major turning points in their lives, the differences between males and females were striking. In their teens, the most significant turning points for males usually had something to do with the gang, with drugs, and with being arrested and going to jail—all "tough-guy" stuff. For females, the significant turning points had to do with marriage and childbearing, with parents, and—a distant third— drugs.

Most of these women were primarily responsible for raising their children, often on their own, without the help of either stable husbands or their parents. Only a minority of the men, by contrast, raised their own children. (Differences between males and females are shown in Table 10.1.) Furthermore, because of the handicaps that gang girls in these communities faced in the marriage market, they were more likely to be encumbered with an alcoholic or heroin-using spouse. On the positive side, women with children have been able to secure income through the welfare system, and this source of income has helped keep many of them

TABLE 10.1   Who Raised Your Children? Gang Women and Gang Men in Los
             Angeles

	Female	Male
Respondent alone	50%	2%
Respondent with spouse	23	38
Respondent and other relative	12	2
"The children's mothers"	NA	50
Other relative	15	7
Total N (=100%)	(48)*	(86)*

NOTE: *These numbers include only those gang members with children. In the total sample of gang members, 94% of the women and 84% of the men had children.

from extensive involvement in drug selling. Drug dealing is a dangerous business with an ever-present hazard of prison. Women may be less willing to risk the violence or the chance of being separated from—or losing—their children through incarceration.

The Careers of Female Addicts

Gang members usually use a wide variety of drugs, in addition to alcohol. Heroin and cocaine are "climax" drugs—the "hard" drugs—which take a greater toll on their users. What are the lives of heroin- and cocaine-using gang women like?

The Los Angeles Chicana heroin addicts who were active a generation ago tended to take one of three routes (Moore, 1990b). More than a third (39%) became "street people," completely and degradingly immersed in the heroin lifestyle. As one woman put it,

> We were, like, in a separate group of people. We were using, ripping, running. People didn't let us go in their houses that knew us. . . . My family . . . I was considered like dead to them. . . . My friends . . . they didn't consider me like a human being any more.

More of the women—approximately half—were less intensely involved with the street lifestyle. They tended to alternate between dependence on a man—for their heroin supply and for protection, as well as for daily sustenance—or on their gang homeboys and homegirls. Some were able to conceal their addiction from their parents, and many were able to avoid involvement with the police; they were sheltered, at home.

A much smaller proportion of the women—perhaps 10%—fell into a third category. They grew up in families that were established in the drug trade. These women had much less stressful access to heroin, because they got it through family-member dealers, and they tended to be more restrained in their heroin use. They were less likely to become hog-wild addicts. Ironically, even though their families may have introduced them to this dangerous drug in the first place, their families had also given them a head start in coping with some of the most serious dangers of heroin.

The introduction of crack cocaine in the 1980s has often been portrayed in the media as leading to the ultimate in women's degradation. "Crack whores," trading sex for drugs, mothers deserting their children for cocaine—all of these are part of the new stereotype about women and drugs that echoes the old "slut" stereotype of the past. We found no support for this stereotype. Although male gang members in Milwaukee talked about the ease with which drug house workers could exchange cocaine for sex, nearly every female gang member we interviewed was indignant when we asked her whether she had "dope dated." Gang women in Milwaukee were not the primary customers of gang drug dealers and were not selling themselves for crack. Thus, they did not match the stereotype of the crack whore, nor were they regularly involved in prostitution.

Getting Into Dealing

Drug dealing is probably the most important illicit income-generating activity of male gang members. (Some also become sporadically involved in robberies or property crimes, but few rely on such work for a steady source of income in the way they rely on drug dealing.) Drug dealing, as a group enterprise, has been assumed to be particularly easy for gang members because the gang already provides established networks with proven mutual loyalty, willingness to use violence, and a degree of secrecy (Padilla, 1992; Steffensmeier, 1983).

Is that also true for gang women? After all, (unlike many conventional girls) they have the same kind of opportunities as gang boys to establish reputations in networks that would "qualify" them for more responsible roles. Many of them fight, stand up for the gang, and form intense loyalties to the gang as a whole. Some have argued that the intense sexism of the male underworld severely limits women's chances to rise above very narrow roles that emphasize their gender (Steffensmeier, 1983). Miller (1973) found that gang girls knew "their place," "actively" sought dependency on a male, and, moreover, that they "gloried in it" (p. 35). They were accomplices in their own dependency, and this accommodation may make the whole system of male domination work more smoothly.

It would thus seem that gang women's chances for a career in dealing drugs are limited by the intragang labeling of women and their reactions to it. Some data from Los Angeles corroborate this view. Even though almost half of a sample of Chicana heroin addicts "had the bag" (i.e., did some heroin dealing) at some time during their careers in the 1970s, most of those women were "employees," rather than entrepreneurs.[6] Only a small minority (perhaps 10%) were career dealers. But not every woman accepted a subordinate status—even then (Moore & Mata, 1981).[7]

Several authors argue that times have changed since the 1970s. Carl Taylor (1993), studying African American women in Detroit in the 1990s, asserted that "females have moved beyond the status quo of gender repression" (p. 118), and he went on to describe women's penetration into drug-dealing "corporate" gangs, some of which are independent of male domination altogether. Lauderback and his colleagues in San Francisco found that although in the late 1980s Latina gang members played a wide range of roles, very similar to those found in Los Angeles among Chicanas in the 1970s, at least one gang of African American women, resentful because they were not getting enough of the profits, had broken away from male-dominated selling activities altogether. Their gang was completely independent, operating out of several crack houses (Lauderback, Hanson, & Waldorf, 1992).

We have presented ample evidence from Milwaukee that gender repression has not disappeared, however. In all studies comparing male and female gangs, the level of women's dealing is reported as being lower than that of the men. The Milwaukee data show how much women's participation in drug dealing depends on opportunities (which were much greater for Latinas than for African American gang women), but also how much gender norms continue to shape most women's participation. Times may have changed, but gender exploitation persists. Cities may vary, and in each city, there are exceptional women who attain independent status as drug dealers of substance. But the norm is for a lower level of dealing, and for a general pattern of subordination to men.

Conclusion

In this chapter, we have focused on the variety of ways in which girls in gangs grow up in different ethnic communities and at different times. At the beginning, we asked whether the experience in the gang is a major turning point. What happens to girls in the gang does depend on time, place, ethnicity, the local culture, and economic opportunities. But girls who get into gangs are even more likely than gang boys to come from families in trouble, and this means that joining a gang does not necessarily result in their lives taking a sharp U-turn for the worse: They are not leaving the Brady Bunch for the Hell's Angels. Nonetheless, for most women, being in a gang does have a real impact on later life.

What about differences in time and place? What, in particular, has changed? Most of the changes occurred at the level of the broader society.

Changes Over Time and Place. First, and perhaps most important, the 1950s scenario that held out marriage and family as the ultimate ideals is much more difficult to obtain. Most gangs live in the nation's inner cities. The economies of these communities have been seriously damaged in the past generation. Even when a city has generally recovered from the crisis of deindustrialization, inner cities often continue to suffer critically high unemployment rates.

This means that most young males no longer have much of a future to look forward to, and it is much more difficult for women in most gang neighborhoods to look forward to marriage as a predictable aspect of their future. For example, Robin Jarrett (1994) cites one young African American woman in Chicago who sadly commented that marriage has become "a little white girl's dream." And in Milwaukee, a young Latina, marginal to a gang, in 1995 expressed the problem when she said she really wanted "a good husband." But then she added, "'Course if they are like the rest of these jerks right now, well I don't want one. I'll take care of myself and my kids" (Thomsen, 1996).

Second, there have been changes in gender ideologies corresponding to changes in opportunities for men and for women. Young women like the ones just quoted are now considerably more likely to see themselves as potentially independent, and young men's attitudes have also changed. In poorer neighborhoods, young males are likely to take on what Majors and Billson (1992) call the "cool pose," a facade of aloofness and control, which "counters the . . . damaged pride [and] shattered confidence . . . that come from living on the edge of society" (p. 8). The cool pose inhibits the formation of nurturant relationships with women and children. As those who listen to some rap music know, it can be very disparaging of women.

Third, the economy of many inner-city communities has become informalized, with a heavy illicit component. In Milwaukee's gang neighborhoods we found a drug-dealing business operating in virtually every other block of gang neighborhoods. The drug economy is much more important in the 1990s than it was in the 1970s, and immeasurably more important than in the 1950s.

There are also differences by place. Special traditions and patterns develop in particular communities. Los Angeles gangs will never be quite like those in Detroit or Milwaukee. The gang traditions are different and the cities are different in too many ways to be reduced to a few pat statements.

Differences by Ethnicity. In addition to changes over time, there are clearly differences between ethnic communities, largely having to do with the expected role of females. Women in Latino—especially Mexican American—communities are subject to more traditional expectations than those in African American communities, where for generations more women have been forced to assume independent roles, both economically and in the family. For example, when we asked Milwaukee gang women what they thought of the following statement: "The way men are today, I'd rather raise my kids by myself," we found sharp ethnic differences. Seventy-five percent of the African American but only 43% of the Latina gang members in Milwaukee agreed with that sentiment.

In a similar vein, 29% of the Latinas—but *none* of the African Americans—believed that "All a woman needs to straighten out her life is to find a good man." And two thirds of the African American women thought that women should have as much sexual freedom as men, whereas only 39% of the Latinas agreed.

Both in Los Angeles and in Milwaukee, we found that when women were asked to assess their gang experiences, they were more negative than the men, but there were interesting ethnic differences, as well. When we asked what they thought of the statement that "Gangs are not all bad," we found that 8% of the African Americans *dis*agreed—meaning that they thoroughly rejected the thought that there was any good in gangs. A much larger proportion of Latinas—57%—disagreed. This supports the notion that, at least in Milwaukee, the gang may well have more long-range effects on Latinas than on African American women.

Unfortunately, the future prospects for women at the bottom of the economic heap are not very promising. Gangs have been proliferating throughout the country, accurately reflecting a declining economy and a growing sense in many inner-city communities that there is no worthwhile future for most adolescents. More young women may now be involved in gangs than at any time in the past. Programs directed at gangs rarely consider the special needs of female members, and the media continue to be fascinated by these women's sexual experiences and to perpetuate the myth of the "new violence" of women's gangs. Ironically, the most important influence on gang women's future may be the dismantling of the nation's welfare system in the 1990s. This system has supported women with children who want to stay out of the drug marketing system and in addition has provided a significant amount of cash to their communities.[8] Its disappearance will deepen poverty and make the fate of gang women ever more problematic.

Notes

1. In the 1990s, the tomboy stereotype was embellished, at least in journalistic accounts, by the notion that female gangs had moved into a new and violent phase, emulating their male counterparts. Chesney-Lind (1993) saw this wave of coverage as exaggerating the evidence for increased violence and continuing the tradition of "demonizing" the young women. (See also Bowker and Klein, 1983, for an early refutation of the maladjustment approach.)

2. Research was supported by Grant #DA03114 from the National Institute on Drug Abuse, which bears no responsibility for opinions expressed in this chapter.

3. A quarter of the heroin-using women had an addicted father, and 14% an addicted mother, compared with 3% of the nonusing women's fathers and mothers. By contrast, only 7% of the heroin-using men had addicted fathers, and none had an addicted mother. No nonusing men had parents who were addicted to heroin.

4. Rosenbaum (1988) developed the concept of "a career of narrowing options" to understand the lives of women heroin addicts.

5. Research was supported by Grant #DA07128 from the National Institute on Drug Abuse, which bears no responsibility for opinions expressed in this chapter.

6. There were several routes to drug dealing. A third of the women had established good relationships with their connections, which led the latter to set them up as dealers. Another 16% had a stock of heroin on consignment. Almost 21% first got the bag through relatives, another 12% by dealing for a friends. Only 12% got the bag when their heroin-dealing husband went to prison. Another 9% got the bag by means that were too varied to be categorized. Other studies report that between 15% and 34% of women in gangs as far apart as New York, Los Angeles, and Detroit sold drugs (Fagan, 1990; Harris, 1988; Taylor, 1990a).

7. In Los Angeles, the gang was particularly important for women in making connections to obtain drugs for personal use. Thirty-two percent in the "Heroin" study (Moore & Mata, 1981) said that their connections were homies from the same gang, and an additional 28% connected through their boyfriends (who were often fellow gang members). A smaller fraction—11%—made their connections through relatives. Only 3% developed connections outside of these networks. As for dealers, most frequently (in a third of the cases) they obtained their stock of heroin through their connections. Another 16% first got it on consignment. Twenty-one percent first got their heroin from relatives, and 12% by selling for a friend. Only 12% got the bag when their dealer-husbands went to prison.

8. Almost a quarter of the income (21%) in Milwaukee's African American communities was provided by welfare.

PART

4

Gangs and the Community

Personal, Gang,
and Community Careers

JAMES F. SHORT, JR.

Recent research on communities and crime (Reiss & Tonry, 1986; Sampson, 1993; Sampson & Lauritsen, 1993) and on youth groups in their local settings demonstrates the continued importance of local communities and conditions in determining the behavior of young people (see, in addition to other chapters in this volume, Hagedorn, 1988; MacLeod, 1987; Schwartz, 1987; Sullivan, 1989). A more recent development concerns use of the concept of the criminal or delinquent "career" as an indication of the relationship of participation in delinquent activities, the frequency of offending, the seriousness of offenses committed, and the period (time) of active offending. This controversial proposal has been hotly debated (see, e.g., papers by Alfred Blumstein, Jacqueline Cohen, & David P. Farrington; Michael Gottfredson & Travis Hirschi; John Hagan & Alberto Palloni; Charles R. Tittle in the February 1988 issue of *Criminology*). A related notion—neglected in this debate concerning *individual careers*—is that youth gangs and communities also have careers in delinquency. Here, the primary causal forces are macrolevel, ranging

221

from the global to the neighborhood in scope (Sullivan, 1989), though microsocial processes also may alter the course of group and community as well as individual careers.

This chapter is focused on the nature of relationships among individual, group, and community careers in delinquency, with illustrations from the work of myself and my coworkers (e.g., Short & Strodtbeck, 1965/1974) and from more recent studies of street gangs.

Two Chicago Gangs:
The Vice Lords and the Nobles

The Vice Lords and the Nobles were located in quite different Chicago community areas. The Vice Lords' turf initially was in Lawndale, on the west side of the city, whereas that of the Nobles was in Douglas, in the traditional "Black Belt" on the south side. Henry McKay's analysis of delinquency rates demonstrated that between 1934 and 1961 (the latter at the midpoint of our most intense research activity with the Vice Lords and Nobles), Lawndale experienced the greatest *increase* in rates of delinquents of all 75 Chicago communities (Shaw & McKay, 1969). During this same period, delinquency rates in Douglas, though still high, experienced the greatest *decrease* of all Chicago communities.

The Nobles' and Vice Lords' communities also differed in other ways. For several decades, the great majority of Douglas residents had been African American. In contrast, Lawndale had only recently—and rapidly—undergone the classic ecological pattern of "invasion" followed by succession of an African American population. This change was accompanied by the now-familiar pattern of severe economic loss and institutional disruption.

The fact that most readers of this chapter will recognize the Vice Lords' name, whereas few will have heard of the Nobles, is a good indicator of the character of the two gangs. The Nobles were "a neighborhood play group that became a delinquent gang, integrated through conflict," in the classic manner described by Frederic Thrasher (1927/1963, p. 46). A dozen years after our initial contact with the gang, we asked a former member of the Nobles to reflect on the history of the gang. The Nobles, he said "originally was a baseball team for people who were much older than we were, people that were a generation before us" (Short & Moland,

1976, p. 166). A casual observer, he noted, would not be able to distinguish between members and nonmembers. But when boys from the Nobles' turf left the area "for a party or something and they would get into a humbug [gang fight,] they would send somebody around to . . . the hanging place for the whole area" for reinforcements. At the time of our study, the area was plagued with drugs (it was widely known as "Dopeville") and there was a good deal of interpersonal violence and other types of crime.

When we first became acquainted with the Nobles, 25 boys and 1 girl belonged to the gang. Three years later the Nobles numbered 45, and the group had become less cohesive. Older members had begun to drift away from gang life. The young woman had entered nurse's training. and many of the young men had turned their attention to jobs and families.

We sought information on former members of both gangs by means of interviews and informants. The Nobles gang no longer existed, and despite the efforts of key informants, we were able to obtain information on only 27 former Nobles, including 19 of the original 25 members. Of these, 4 (15% of those on whom information was available) were dead by the summer of 1971. At that time, of the 23 living and known Nobles, 19 were employed and none was incarcerated. Two of the three who were unemployed were involved in drug abuse, however.

The lack of information on so many Nobles is instructive. Extensive field observations over a 3-year period suggested that the gang never completely lost its play-group orientation despite heavy involvement in sometimes serious delinquent behavior. Most important, unlike the Vice Lords, the Nobles had no ongoing gang rivalries such as those that characterize many conflict gangs and tend to perpetuate gang identity as well as gang conflict. Importantly, they never became involved the "supergang" phenomenon in Chicago. As members aged, they left the gang, and most led conventional adult lives.

By several accounts, the Vice Lords began in 1958, 2 years before our initial contact with the gang (see Keiser, 1969). Our chief informant, its president and strongest leader, told us that the Lords began when several residents of a cottage in the Illinois State Training School for Boys (including himself) decided to pool their affiliations with separate gangs on Chicago's west side, choosing as their name the Vice Lords.[1] Their explicit purpose was to create the toughest gang in the city. In that resolve, the Vice Lords were notoriously successful. They were also aggressively expansive. At the time of our initial contact, 66 boys were identified as members of the Vice Lords. In less than 2 years, that number had risen to 311, constituting five Vice Lords branches. Unlike the Nobles, conflict between the Vice Lords and their rivals, the Imperial Chaplains, was continuous throughout our contact with the gangs (see Short & Strodtbeck, 1965/1974, for examples of conflict episodes between the Lords and the Imperials—labeled the Vice Kings and the Knights or Cherokees in that book).

This was only the beginning. The Vice Lords became one of the supergangs of the late 1960s, incorporating under the laws of the state of Illinois as a nonprofit organization and claiming some 8,000 members in 26 divisions (see Sherman, 1970). The "Vice Lord Nation" initiated a variety of economic and community service enterprises, none with notable success (see Short, 1976).

The instability marking the original Vice Lords (we focused only on our list of 66 members for the follow-up study) was overwhelming. Most had remained in Chicago, except when they were incarcerated outside the city. We lacked information on only 4 of the initial group. Of the remaining 62, 12 (19%) were dead, most as a result of criminal violence. Fewer than half (27, or 43.5%) were working. Among the unemployed, at least six and probably more were involved in a drug distribution network. Another 10 were in prison. Nearly all had served time in correctional institutions.

Many factors doubtless contributed to the observed differences between the Nobles and the Vice Lords: their communities, founding conditions, the presence or absence of traditional rivalries, and the supergang status of the Lords, as well as individual differences among gang members. The community context seems especially important, however. Chicago's supergangs emerged in communities characterized by recent and rapid population turnover. The most notorious of these, the Black P. Stone Nation, began in the community of Woodlawn, which like Lawndale had recently and rapidly undergone racial transition.[2] Others arose in communities of recently arrived immigrants from Puerto Rico and Mexico.

Communities that produced supergangs lacked stable populations and institutions, though instability may have less to do with ethnic invasion than with other destabilizing factors. In the 1960s, with the help of well-meaning but naive persons from outside the community (in some instances including funding from private foundations and the federal government), the supergangs emerged, ostensibly as multipurpose institutions including business and social service enterprises. For the most part, they were unsuccessful in both. Expectations held by gang members and by those who funded their efforts or tried to help in other ways were largely unfulfilled, and there was much bitterness in the aftermath. There was naivete on all sides—among those who wanted to help and among the gangs. The gangs did not possess the necessary skills for the enterprises undertaken, and there was little involvement of other community residents and institutions in the supergang projects. There was, in addition, considerable fraud in the administration of large grant funds. Projects were poorly monitored, and little technical assistance was provided. Official opposition, particularly by the police, undermined some seemingly well-intentioned programs (see Fry, 1973; Short, 1976).

Much has changed today, largely for the worse (see Klein, 1995a). Street gangs have emerged in many more communities than was the case only a few years ago. Some have become more sophisticated in crime than were their earlier counterparts, as jailed gang members returned to their communities disillusioned with mainstream social, economic, and political goals (see Hagedorn, 1988). Many of these young men have remained members of their gangs, rather than, as was the case with the Nobles, becoming conventional, "ordinary citizens." There are more, and more lethal, guns available ("zip guns" were the most common—if not the preferred—firearms among the gangs we studied in Chicago in the early 1960s). Drug abuse and trafficking have become more widespread, contributing to the devastation of community life (see Anderson, 1990). Importantly, the political and economic structure of many U.S. cities has changed.

Urban Poverty and the Underclass

William Julius Wilson (1987) has demonstrated the rapidity with which poverty has become urbanized in this country. Together with demographic and structural changes in the economy, the economic downturn of the 1970s resulted in the emergence of a ghetto underclass which, Wilson argues, has become permanent. "Urban minorities," Wilson argues, "have been particularly vulnerable to structural economic changes, such as the shift from goods-producing to service-producing industries, the increasing polarization of the labor market into low-wage and high-wage sectors, technological innovations, and the relocation of manufacturing industries out of the central cities" (p. 39). Unemployment rates among African Americans more than doubled between the end of World War II and the 1970s, remaining approximately twice those of whites in both good and bad economic years since the mid-1950s. The increase in numbers of the most crime-prone population (the young) in the country as a whole was especially pronounced in the inner cities and among the minority poor.

Although historical and continuing patterns of prejudice and discrimination against African Americans exacerbated all of these problems, African Americans were not the only affected minority (see Lieberson, 1980; Wilson, 1987). Between 1970 and 1984, African American and Hispanic families headed by women increased by 108% and 164%, respectively, compared with an increase of 63% for whites. Out-of-wedlock births to African American teenage mothers increased greatly, rising by 89% in 1983. The pattern was similar, but the numbers smaller (39%), among white teenagers. The result was that nearly half of all African American children under 18 years of age were in families with less than poverty-level income in 1983, and three fourths of these families were headed by females. These changes left in their wake a large population of the "truly disadvantaged" who were mired in poverty and ill equipped to participate in opportunities provided by civil rights advances or Great Society and affirmative action programs. Many of those who could do so moved out of the inner-city ghettos, thus removing from these communities their most economically successful and politically capable residents (see Anderson, 1990; Hagedorn, 1988). The effects on many minority communities have been devastating. The next generation of community-oriented delinquency prevention programs emerged even as problems of the ghetto underclass were becoming more apparent.

Recent Innovations

On the face of it, James Coleman and Thomas Hoffer's (1987) *Public and Private High Schools* would seem to have little to do with delinquency prevention. The book details research on the performance of students in public, Catholic, and other private high schools, comparing academic success, school dropout rates, continuation in college, and other matters. Summarizing their findings, students in Catholic private schools performed better on almost all counts than did public school students. Students in other private schools also fared better than those in public schools. Most important, disadvantaged students—minorities and the poor—in Catholic schools did particularly well compared with their counterparts in public and other private schools.

To explain these findings, Coleman and Hoffer (1987) draw on the notion of functional communities. In functional communities, institutions present a consistent pattern of norms and sanctions, reinforcing one another. Perhaps most important, *intergenerational* relationships, like other relationships between segments of the community, "arise out of the social structure itself" (p. 7). The downside of functional communities has often been documented—their tendency to stigmatize and exclude those who are "different," for example. Coleman and Hoffer stress more positive qualities in such communities, noting that they augment resources available to parents in their relationships with school authorities, in child supervision, and in monitoring their children's associations with adults as well as with peers. Feedback from friends and associates is an additional resource for parental monitoring of both schools and children.

The truly disadvantaged lack education, organizational skills, self-confidence, and "social capital"—the intangible but very real qualities consisting of "relations between persons." Coleman and Hoffer (1987) argue that social capital facilitates productive capacity just as physical and human capital do (see also Coleman, 1988). Indeed, without social capital, the relevance for children of human capital (e.g., education and technical skills possessed by their parents) may be diminished severely, as when parents employ their human capital exclusively at work or in other activities not related to their children's lives.

Functional communities provide opportunities for, but do not guarantee, the development of both human and social capital. The stigmatizing and self-serving qualities of social relationships in slum communities (hustling as a way of life, for example; see Valentine, 1978) make social capital development especially difficult and hamper the acquisition of human capital as well. Structural differences between families also pose barriers. It is more difficult to build social capital, for example, in single-parent families than in two-parent families, and more difficult still when the single parent is a teenager.

Coleman and Hoffer (1987) attribute the advantages achieved by students in Catholic schools to the embeddedness of youth and their parents in the religiously based functional communities of these schools. They argue that intergenerational functional communities are lacking in most contemporary urban communities as a result of structural changes in the family and media influences. To these must be added the structural economic changes noted above.

The challenges posed by these changes occur at many levels. Here, the focus is on promoting positive relationships between the generations as a basis for functional communities to create social capital. Is it possible to create and maintain functional communities in which social and human capital can be stimulated among the underclass? Recent innovations in community delinquency prevention and rehabilitation seem promising in this respect, but evaluation of their success is extremely difficult. Some of these programs are intended to create "functional extended families"; others focus on entire communities. The goal in each case is essentially the same, however: to create a community of values in which institutions and programs are mutually supportive. Ethnic and social class ties can be built on, rather than becoming barriers to the acquisition of human and social capital, for example. Individual needs for nurturance and boundaries regarding acceptable conduct, employment skills and opportunities, and access to the levers of community power all are of critical importance. Many of us recognize in these themes echoes of the Chicago Area Project and the Industrial Areas Foundation, associated long ago with the names of Clifford Shaw, Saul Alinsky, and others (for a perceptive analysis of these organizations, see Finestone, 1976).

"Crime prevention" programs tend to be focused narrowly on persuading community residents to protect themselves from crime by "target hardening" and other means of reducing opportunities for the commission of crime, ignoring the causes of crime. Lynn Curtis (1987) notes that many of these programs focus primarily on public relations and fear of crime rather than on crime reduction. He argues that grassroots initiatives that address the causes of crime as well as opportunities for crime demonstrate both greater success and greater cost-effectiveness.

A number of "natural experiments" have grown out of the concerns of local community residents and their attempts to create a sense of family or community, and to minister to special problems of youth. Unlike the supergangs, which often are viewed by local residents as a threat to personal property and safety, these projects have been supported by communities. They incorporate the gangs, rather than the reverse, so that the community and the gangs become more acceptable to one another (see Spergel, 1995; Curtis, 1987; Woodson, 1981). These programs emphasize local participation and control, and indigenous rather than professional leadership. Most rely to some extent on expertise from outside the community for consultation or training in skills relevant to program goals. They raise financial support from both public and private sources, but incentives are provided for continued funding through economic enterprise and local institutional support. Most are multipurpose, but job placement and recreational opportunities for youth are given high priority. Several have created job opportunities by initiating economic enterprises such as product manufacture and distribution and service businesses. Most reach out to young people who have been referred by juvenile courts or released from incarceration, as well as those who have not yet been caught up in the juvenile and criminal justice systems.

A few carefully designed community programs have been inspired by these natural experiments, some of them based on more abstract principles drawn from research and theory. Some of these have been the object also of extensive and intensive monitoring and evaluation (see Curtis, 1987).

A Note on Community-Based
Police Research and Innovation

Their frontline exposure to the social ills of the community provides unique opportunities for the police to identify emerging problems and to place choices before the community with respect to many problems, as well as to work aggressively with other agencies and the private sector in proposing solutions to identified problems. "Problem-oriented policing" is a proposal to do just that, by focusing on the nature of complaints, their location, and the relationship between reported incidents, noting the behaviors, people, and places that generate calls for police assistance. In the long run, Herman Goldstein (1990) suggests, the police role could change dramatically from dealing directly with crime problems to focusing primarily on supporting and strengthening community norms and helping citizens to solve their problems (see also Bureau of Justice Statistics, 1993). Rather than attempting to solve so many problems *for* the community, police would work *with* the community, especially in helping people to develop and promote a sense of community.

Were the police to emphasize skills in mediation and community organization, research methods, and interpretation, both police and community responses to delinquency would be affected profoundly. In many respects, police might become community advocates, for example, rather than community adversaries, as is so often the case in high-crime areas.

This vision of the police role is similar in important respects to the role of the Chicago Area Project community workers and that of community organizers and other consultants in the community-oriented programs noted above (i.e., as a resource for the community, aiding local residents and working with indigenous leaders to solve community problems with special focus on problems of young people). The goal, to return to the major point, is to promote human and social capital through the achievement of "functional communities," that is, communities in which family life, work, religion, education, law enforcement, and other institutional areas provide opportunities for young people and reflect and reinforce common values.

Communities and Individual Careers in Crime

Even in high-delinquency communities, most individuals do not engage in serious delinquent behavior, and most individual delinquent careers stop short of prolonged involvement in serious crime (see MacLeod, 1987, pp. 146ff.; Sullivan, 1989, pp. 62-63). It is difficult to generalize from such data, however, because contingencies affecting individual cases are so varied and complex. The point can be illustrated by comparing the lives of two young African American men who lived in the same westside Chicago community but whose careers differed greatly. One of these was the aforementioned "founder" and strongest leader of the Vice Lords. The other, when I knew him, was about to graduate from a prestigious university and was applying for admission to the best graduate schools in the United States.

There is much that we do not know about the early lives of these two young men (e.g., about the quality of their family experiences). I can report that they were physically similar: tall and muscular, each with a commanding appearance. Both spent a portion of their youth living in "Vice Lord territory" on Chicago's west side. The gang leader became embroiled with the law and a gang member at an early age, eventually being sent to the state training school for boys. Although much remains unclear, we know that this young man so impressed leaders of various youth programs that special efforts were made to work with him to prevent his continued participation in crime. For a time, these efforts seemed to be successful. He worked in a variety of ways with the YMCA program with which our gang research was associated (see Short & Strodtbeck, 1965/1974). Shortly thereafter, he was recruited to another program that offered him the opportunity to attend a small but prestigious eastern college, located in a largely rural setting. He did so and became for a short time a member of the football squad.

It would be hard to imagine a greater contrast than that between the social world of Chicago's westside gangland and that of the elite eastern college. By his own account, the college experience was dull for this young man. He did not do well in academic course work and soon became involved in selling drugs to other students. He left the college before completing his freshman year. When he returned to Chicago, he picked up where he had left off, peddling drugs and playing a prominent role in the Vice Lords.

Because this young man was knowledgeable about the Vice Lords, John Moland and I hired him to assist us in contacting members and former members of the gang, and in informing us concerning those who could not be contacted. He assured us that he wanted to return to college, this time in Chicago. He readily agreed to assist us in our research, and at first he performed well. It soon became apparent, however, that the small funds we were paying him could not compete with the income he derived from his thriving drug business. He began to lose interest in the research, and after a few months we found we could no longer depend on him.

The second young man, the university student, was a few years younger than the gang leader. The discovery that he was from Chicago and had grown up on the west side prompted me to ask that he tell his story as part of a course requirement. He reported that his uncle was a member of the Lords. I had known the uncle and several other Vice Lords members whom this young man professed to know. Other details of his story concerning the Vice Lords also were consistent with data from our research, lending credibility to his story.

Though "Jay" was "drafted" by several gangs, he never became an active member of a gang. As a young boy, he greatly admired members of the Vice Lords. He would sneak out on the front porch late at night to listen to his uncle and other members of the gang talk about their exploits; he noted, "without a doubt, that if my parents had decided not to move I would have become a Vice Lord" (personal communication, November 1975).

The fact that Jay was never an active gang member did not prevent him from extensive involvement in delinquent behavior. With his best friend, Jay stole car batteries and stripped auto parts. The practice was lucrative because a local fence purchased nearly everything they stole. These activities and his association with gang members drew Jay to the attention of the police, but his account fails to mention ever being arrested. As he grew older, much of the prestige that he had associated with the Vice Lords "faded away." The fact that Jay's family moved during his early years, first out of Vice Lord territory and then again later, helped to insulate him from the influence of gang members and from full participation in a delinquent subculture. Another important difference in the two careers arises from an apparent similarity. Like the Vice Lord leader, Jay was selected by a youth program for a scholarship to a prestigious university. His academic promise had been recognized earlier in life, however, and he was sent to an eastern prep school before his college scholarship. These clearly were important turning points in Jay's life (Sampson & Laub, 1993).

We know little of the "personalities" of these two young men, nor is it possible to determine with precision their basic intelligence. Those who knew them were impressed with their high intelligence and potential. But Jay was prevented from strong identification with a delinquent subculture, and he was removed completely from the social world of lower-class delinquents when he was a sophomore in high school. His academic success propelled him into still other opportunities. Both his human and social capital clearly were superior to that of the gang leader.

The gang leader was firmly embedded in the gang world; he was rewarded by his peers and by others as a result of his prominence in the gang. Intervention to remove him from this world occurred only after his established lifestyle made it virtually impossible for him to adjust to a social world so alien to his experience as that of the elite eastern university. To conclude, in Jay's words, "I suppose I was one of the lucky ones. *I was able to go away to school . . . and, unlike [the gang leader, whom he knew], I was . . . able to adjust to a totally different way of life* [italics added]" (personal communication, November 1975).

Timing clearly was critical in the lives of these young men, as it is inevitably for all events that may serve as turning points. So also, perhaps, was the fact that Jay was able to avoid entanglement in the juvenile justice system and the labeling experience. Yet, others have been able to survive such experiences without extensive careers in crime. Clifford Shaw's (1930) "Jack-Roller" managed to live an essentially law-abiding adult life after considerable involvement in crime as a child and in young adulthood and extensive and painful experience in both juvenile and criminal justice systems (see Snodgrass, 1982). Waln Brown's (1983) autobiographical account of a disturbed childhood, trauma, and delinquent behavior in a variety of institutional contexts documents his recovery and successful adult adjustment.

An Innovative Focus on Young Families and Children: The Beethoven Project

Wilson's (1987, 1996) policy agenda includes provision of child care services and subsidies to working-poor parents. Illustrative of an innovative and experimental child care program that also serves families is the Beethoven Project, operated by the Center for Successful Child Development in Chicago. The project also illustrates the problems faced by efforts to work in highly disorganized communities.

Known as the Beethoven Project because it serves the Beethoven Elementary School catchment area in Chicago, the project is centered in six units of Chicago's Robert Taylor Homes, allegedly the largest public housing project in the world. Stretched out along a 2-mile section of a major expressway (which effectively isolates the project from the rest of the city), Taylor Homes consists of 28 high-rise buildings housing approximately 20,000 people. Nearly all Taylor Homes residents are poor and African American. More than 90% of the households receive public assistance, and three quarters are headed by women.

Taylor Homes is plagued by every poverty-related problem: It is gang ridden, with high rates of drug abuse, crime, delinquency, unemployment and dependency, educational deficiencies that begin as early as the first grade, school dropouts, and health and nutrition problems. Initially, the Beethoven Project was focused on preparing mothers for parenthood and on the child's earliest experiences with his or her environment. The goal was "to prevent social, psychological, and physical dysfunction among . . . [a cohort of[children so that they will be fully prepared to enter kindergarten" (Center for Successful Child Development, n.d., p. 1). Like the family- and community-oriented projects discussed above, the Beethoven Project is multifaceted. A variety of health and social services aimed at both parents and children were provided, including a family drop-in center that was the project's physical base; a neurological, physiological, and psychological assessment and referral program for infants; parent-child relationship screening and parenting education; and home visitation and day care services. The initial targets of the project were the annual cohorts of children born between January 1, 1987, and January 1, 1992, in the designated housing units, and their mothers (who were identified prior to the births of their children). Others were to benefit, too, because many project personnel were residents of Taylor Homes, including home visitors trained specifically for this work. The project was designed to provide a "Head Start on Head Start" (Ounce of Prevention Fund, 1994).

In sum, the project was intended to remedy individual-level social, physiological, and psychological deficits that result from the operation of macrolevel forces affecting the lives of the target population. From the beginning, the approach was experimental, and it continues to be. There is a clear expectation that lessons will be learned that can be applied on a larger scale. Those lessons began early in the project when it was discovered that "families identified by the initial outreach visits had immediate needs to which the program had to respond in order to build relationships, and a high level of family mobility within the community made recruitment and retention of participants more difficult than expected" (Center for Successful Child Development, 1993, p. 2). Among these immediate needs, protection from the environment of Taylor

Homes, "by far the most unrelenting of obstacles to smooth program operation" (p. 11). The report quotes a participant in the program: "It have me scared to go out my door or carry my kids to the playground" (p. 11). Another mother says of her child, "He's scared and crying bad; stopped wanting to go to school 'cause of the shooting" (p. 10).

The project continues, but its goals have become more focused and more modest. Project leaders soon determined that the program had to become more flexible, "allowing families themselves to determine their level of need and involvement" (Center for Successful Child Development, 1993, p. 3). Although it was disappointing not to be able to serve entire cohorts, the new strategy was more realistic in attracting participants and building acceptance and trust—no mean feat in view of participants' experiences with "intrusive, judgmental social services" (p. 16; see also Hagedorn, 1995). Even the Chicago Housing Authority cannot keep track of occupancy in Taylor Homes. I spoke with a psychiatrist who had been associated with the project. "It's been a difficult community, " she said, "but they are still there. In that community, that's an accomplishment."

Indeed! As noted in the project report (Center for Successful Child Development),

> Center activities have frequently been interrupted by gang violence outside, and a home visitor suffered a bullet wound during a routine visit. It was necessary to move the entrance to the Infant-Toddler Center so that parents and children could avoid walking through a high drug-traffic area, and bullet-proof glass has been ordered for Center windows to reduce the risk of injury from nearby shootings. Moreover, of the first hundred families recruited, more than half have moved at least once either within Robert Taylor or out of the community entirely. (p. 14)

The Beethoven Project serves as an important object lesson. It is not surprising that the original goal of ministering to the very young and their immediate families, with little attention to the larger social milieu, proved to be impossible. Even had these goals been feasible, however, the project would almost certainly have failed to enable a cohort of infants and their parents to break out of the cycle of poverty, dependency, delinquency, and other social ills. The families that were (and are) the objects of this experiment constitute a small minority of families in

Robert Taylor Homes. Insufficient attention to the broader community context beyond those target families and to family maintenance beyond the kindergarten years clearly handicapped achievement of the initial goals. Moreover, focusing on kindergarten cohorts may have little impact on older children or on their elders unless changes also occur in job opportunities and in other institutional areas (see Hagedorn, 1988; Sullivan, 1989).

Despite these problems, successes are claimed. Parents and staff see "improvements in children's health care . . . and there seems to be a gradual movement from emergency care to preventive care" (Center for Successful Child Development, 1993, p. 15). Parents say "they better understand the individual and age-specific needs of their children" and note "improved social and interaction skills" (p. 15). It seems likely that parents and children alike "have made important strides in social competency" (p. 15) and self-respect. The hope and the basic point remain valid: Projects that are able to create and sustain functional families and communities have the *best chance* to promote conventional learning and achievement opportunities and bonds to conventional persons and lifestyles. With financial encouragement from the national Head Start program, the Beethoven Project is an evolving effort to reach young children and families at risk. Ongoing evaluation of the project promises to document project adjustments and achievements.

Conclusion: A Note on Cultural Diffusion

The underclass thesis clearly cannot account entirely for the rapid increase in numbers of gangs throughout the United States, though Malcolm Klein (1995a) regards it as its "foremost cause" and "likely best predictor of its continuation" (p. 194). In addition, he argues that *diffusion of street gang culture* plays a major role, quoting from David Dawley (1973), biographer of the Vice Lords and a gang activist during the 1960s:

Cultural symbols and associations run through our culture very fast through music and television. There are Crips in Portland that can't find Los Angeles on a street map and Vice Lords in Columbus or Cleveland who have never been to Chicago, and wouldn't let a Chicago Vice Lord come in and tell them what to do. But they share the symbols and the legends. (Klein, 1995a, p. 207)

Even strong antigang media messages may be interpreted quite differently by gang members and "wanna-bes." Klein's (1995a) conversation with "a gang cop in Texas" who blamed the movie *Boyz 'n the Hood* for perpetuating gang culture in his community, is illustrative. That movie had a particularly strong antigang message, but the officer explained that gang members focused on one special scene:

> In that scene, a gangbanging subhero follows up the automatic weapons shooting of several rivals by slowly and coolly approaching each on the ground and applying a single head shot to each. He then calmly returns to his car and drives off. "That's what the gang guys get off on," said the officer, "That was a righteous gang execution, and they really grab their jocks on that one; forget the rest of the movie." (p. 206)

More than gang culture has spread, however. *Youth culture* in varying degrees is shared by virtually all youth groups, including those that elude, or in any case, lack adult supervision. Peddled by media advertising and augmented by macroeconomic and social forces that cater to youthful fads, appetites, and dollars, youth culture is more powerful and widely diffused than ever before in history. These same macroeconomic and social forces fail to provide meaningful roles for young people, producing a powerful combination of forces that underlie both youth culture and gang culture.

More than 20 years ago, James Coleman noted a variety of developments during the 1960s which, taken together, produced youth culture on a large scale in the United States, perhaps for the first time. Large numbers of children born during the baby boom following World War II and the increasing affluence of many young people (a function of the general level of affluence in the country) created a youth market with great economic power. Education prior to entering the labor market was extended, creating an additional period in the lives of young people when they were not well integrated into adult society. Increasing numbers of women entered the workforce, further separating mothers from children, in the home and in the neighborhood. Increasingly, adults worked "in large organizations where youth are not present," adding to the separation of youth and adults. Mass media greatly expanded and catered increasingly to the youth market (see Coleman et al., 1974, pp. 114-119; also Coleman, 1961, 1971) Arguably, each of these developments is more pronounced today than when Coleman wrote about them. Certainly, their influence is more worldwide than ever.

Clearly, youth culture both adapts to and influences changes in the larger society. Gangs are more mobile now, and their territories may include a shopping mall rather than (or in addition to) a street or neighborhood, or an area drug market. The "youth-oriented" quality of troublesome youth in modern societies arises, in part, from the exclusion of young people from large areas of institutional life—that is, from the separation of young people and adults. Daniel Glaser (1971) noted many years ago that social separation produces cultural differentiation (p. 35). When social separation is categorical, for example, based on categories such as age, gender, race, ethnicity, or social class, the stage is set for subcultural formation, as often occurs among gangs and other youth collectivities.

The seductions of media-advertised products among less-affluent youth and the thefts and assaults that often are associated with their acquisition are well documented. Elijah Anderson (1994) describes the "zero-sum quality" that pervades the "code of the streets," as young African American males in the ghetto search for respect—respect that often is associated with items of clothing such as shoes and jackets (see also Anderson, 1990). Mercer Sullivan (1989) identifies "a set of mutually valorizing cultural symbols" for the groups he studied, noting that the *meaning of crime* is constructed in a "bounded milieu of inter-action out of materials supplied from two sources: the local area in which they spend their time almost totally unsupervised and undirected by adults, and the consumerist youth culture promoted in the mass media." Lacking legitimate employment that would permit their participation in youth culture, crime often becomes the source of necessary funds. Sullivan continues,

> The first consumption priority for most of them most of the time is clothing. Next comes recreation, including the purchase of drugs and alcohol as well as more innocent teenage consumption activities such as participating in sports and going to movies and dances. The point of their participation in crime is not to lift themselves and/or their families out of the ghetto but to

share in the youth culture that is advertised in the mass media and sub-
sidized for middle-class teenagers who attend school by their parents.
(pp. 248-249)

If the spread of gangs cannot be accounted for solely by the underclass
phenomenon, it is nevertheless the case that the vast majority of gangs
in cities throughout the country arise among less-affluent youth. It is
among such youth that the diffusion of gang culture and pressures
generated by media-hyped youth cultural products exerts the strongest
influences toward gang formation and conflict. And it is among such
youth, their families, and community institutions that lack the resources
to provide opportunities for young people or to control their sometimes
delinquent and violent behavior that creative solutions to gang problems
are most needed. It is hard to escape the conclusion, voiced by William
Julius Wilson, that, "Youth gangs can best be addressed by addressing
the larger problems in a more comprehensive way, thus helping the
ghetto underclass and significantly reducing youth gangs, whose membership is comprised largely of the inner city minority underclass"
(quoted in Klein, 1995a, p. 205).

Wilson's emphasis is on macrolevel economic and political forces,
forces that are captured in the title of his most recent book, *When Work
Disappears: The World of the New Urban Poor* (1996). If this analysis is
correct, among the larger problems that must be confronted is the consumerist youth culture that drives the search for status and respect
among young people (see Anderson, 1994).

Notes

1. Their name retained at least symbolic significance to the Vice Lords during the period
of our fieldwork. One of the Vice Lord leaders once showed me a collection of newspaper
articles and cartoons that he had compiled. Each of the items featured the Vice Lords,
usually stressing their involvement in criminal activities. The articles were bound together
with a cover featuring crossed pool cues in the center. Other symbols around the edges
included dice, cards, a stack of money, a smoking gun, and a dagger dripping with blood.
More recently, Martin Sanchez-Jankowski (1991) documents the attractiveness of media
coverage for the gangs he studied. Media portrayals of gangs enhance the reputations of
gangs and make them more attractive to prospective members. Sanchez-Jankowski argues
that gangs and media mutually exploit one another.

2. The YMCA Detached Worker program had a brief contact with the gang that became the Black P. Stone Nation when the director of the program received a telephone call from a boy who identified himself as a member of the Blackstone Rangers. The purpose of the call, the boy explained, was to solicit a detached worker for the gang. When the director inquired as to why the gang wanted to have a detached worker assigned to them, there was a pause, after which the boy replied, "Man, you ain't nothin' without a detached worker!"

The Gang in the Community

SUDHIR ALLADI VENKATESH

The mid-1980s witnessed a resurgence of both popular and academic interest in U.S. youth gangs. Although the greatest attention was given to *urban* youth gang activity, specifically in minority poor neighborhoods, studies have demonstrated that the growth and consolidation of youth gangs has also occurred in suburban and rural communities, many with predominantly white and nonpoor populations (Bursik & Grasmik, 1993; Muehlbauer & Dodder, 1983).[1] And in some cases, gangs of different geographic, class, and racial or ethnic status have joined ranks under a common "family" or "nation" umbrella (Spergel, 1995). Some of the most interesting studies on youth gangs have been written by ethnographers who observed gangs at an intimate distance and for extended periods of time. Their methodological commitment allowed them to gain the trust and confidence of their informants and obtain access to less visible aspects of gang members' lives. The fruits of these labors have

AUTHOR'S NOTE: I would like to thank the Johann Jacobs Foundation and the Chapin Hall Center for Children for their generous support and Katchen Locke for her comments and criticism.

resulted in greater knowledge of numerous aspects of the lives of youth gang members, including not only their participation in illicit activities (Padilla, 1992) but also their attitudes, beliefs, and values; their life histories; and their use of symbols and other forms of aesthetic expression (Vigil, 1988a). Such detailed research has nicely complemented the growth of quantitative and large-scale comparative studies of youth gangs.

One significant part of the social life of youth gangs is still not well documented, either in quantitative or qualitative research. This concerns the relationship of the youth gang to the neighborhood or community. With some notable exceptions (Horowitz, 1983; Sanchez-Jankowski, 1991; Spergel, 1995; Sullivan, 1989), we do not have a good understanding of the everyday experiences of individuals and organizations in communities living amid youth gang activity.[2] How do organizations such as law enforcement, neighborhood block clubs, schools, social service providers, and so forth come to terms with the violence, drug dealing, and high levels of criminal involvement that can accompany youth gang activity? Is there, in fact, a sharp divide between youth gangs and other residents, that is, an "enemy within" dichotomy? Or is there greater sympathy or tolerance by individuals for youth gangs than is commonly perceived?

Moreover, how does a youth gang's status in the community and its interactions with local institutions shift over time as its members get older and as other changes take place in the broader society? Several ethnographies focused on low-income and minority areas of the metropolis have been attentive to historical shifts that alter the nature of youth gang activity; these researchers, commonly referred to as the "underclass" school (cf. Hagedorn, 1988; Moore, 1991; Vigil, 1988a), have argued that the recent "corporatization" of youth gang activity[3] is partially an outgrowth of broader social structural changes in the economy and in government policy. The consolidation of "socially isolated" (Wilson, 1987) neighborhoods characterized by high rates of joblessness, decreased governmental support for public services, and fewer middle- and upper-class households provides little buffer against violent crime, the proliferation of drug economies, and the rise of violent street gangs. Despite their sensitivity to external social forces that condition youth gang behavior, the "underclass" youth gang ethnographies have tended to focus on the *internal* organization of youth gangs; they have paid most attention to the experiences of the gangs' members and the nexus of gang and community has not been well elucidated.

In this chapter, I address this gap by examining the interactions of youth gangs and local institutions in an extremely poor community on Chicago's South Side. For 3 years, I conducted participant observation in the Robert Taylor Homes, a low-income public housing development with a notorious history of youth gang activity (Lemann, 1991). I describe the relations that have formed between the community's youth gangs; the broader tenant population; and organizations such as the Chicago Housing Authority (CHA, the "landlord"), local tenant management councils, and social service providers. I argue that the "enemy within" conception of youth gangs, in which youth gangs are understood as a predator on the larger community or a destructive element in a community's social fabric, is inappropriate. In particular—and not exclusively for poor communities such as Robert Taylor Homes that possess little political or economic capital—both conflictual and contradictory relations can form between gang and community. In such situations, the youth gang itself becomes a locally recognized community institution, decried yet supported, excluded yet relied on, loathed yet embraced. I explicate how this has occurred in the Robert Taylor community and address the implications for public policy concerning intervention in gang activity at the neighborhood or community level. I begin with a historical description of the role that youth gangs have played in the social life of Taylor Homes since its construction in 1962 and then address the contemporary status of gang-community relations.

From Gang War to Drug War

The Robert Taylor Homes were built in the early 1960s to alleviate the tremendous shortage of housing in the South Side ghettos of Chicago. Its 28 buildings, each with 16 floors and approximately 1,000 persons, occupy a 2-mile stretch of land between the city's downtown industrial corridor and the heart of an all-black ghetto, 2 miles away. Today, the housing development contains more than 20,000 persons, 96% of whom report public assistance as their sole form of income. Although the majority of households are classified as "single parent" and "female headed," a significant proportion have other elders in residence—grandparents, husband, and so forth. Nearly 70% of the population is under 18 years of age. The census tracts that make up the community are among the poorest in the United States. Youth gang activity, specifically violent crime and drug distribution, is popularly understood as the signature social phenomenon of the community. In 1994, gang activity in Taylor Homes reached such "intolerable" proportions that the CHA (and the Clinton administration) fought to suspend the constitutional rights of the population and institute novel law enforcement strategies.

Contrary to popular wisdom and 30 years of news reporting,[4] however, gangs did not always have such an imposing presence in the housing development. Their organization and practices have changed over the years, not only as a response to many of the social-structural shifts outlined by the "underclass" researchers, but also as a consequence of shifting relationships with other actors in the community. As one resident stated,

> Back then, things was different, gangs was fighting with their fists or zip guns and we could control 'em. You know! If you was fighting, your momma would take you inside and whup you, and sometimes other folks' mommas would whup you too!

Many residents argue that in the 1960s and early 1970s, youth gang activity was violent at times, but there were social controls in place that limited the deleterious effects of gang activity, drug dealing, and street fighting. Although these control mechanisms were not in existence specifically to limit the consequences of youth gang activity on the broader community, indirectly they helped to minimize both gang recruitment and the use of public spaces for intergang altercations. Two of the most important means by which the residential population mitigated the hazards associated with gang activity were to be found in local tenant networks.

The most visible formal tenant network was formed by the councils. Each building in the community had a president and floor captains who were responsible for disseminating information (e.g., job opportunities, shifts in CHA policies), reporting maintenance problems, and searching for violations of the housing authority lease by other tenants. Representatives from each building were appointed to the local advisory council (LAC), the primary organization that represented Taylor Homes in CHA decision making. The LAC representatives wielded significant power in affecting the social life in the community: They could help ensure that a tenant's apartment received prompt attention and maintenance; they were often given part-time jobs and asked to find prospective employees; and over time, they began to control the types of informal economic activities that took place in the community.[5] To varying degrees, building presidents were successful in preventing youth gangs from recruiting other members, selling drugs, fighting, or stockpiling weapons in their building.

Alongside the LACs were more informal networks of (predominantly) female heads of households, that is, "Mamas' Mafias." Groups of mothers and grandmothers (and occasionally, elder male kin) formed close-knit social groups in buildings, sometimes on adjacent floors. For example, the top four floors might have a group of adults who helped each other by watching over the behavior of their children in stairwells, hallways, and the public spaces outside of the buildings. Or if a parent needed to run an errand or go to work, another household might provide day care. Of course, with such exchange came reciprocity and people called on one another in times of need for day care, cooking, food sharing, and so on (Stack, 1974). Ms. Jackson, a 63-year-old woman who has been living in Taylor Homes continuously for three decades, argues that such informal networks helped residents fulfill a variety of functions (all names of persons are pseudonyms):

> Ms. Louis, Ms. Watkins, myself, Louise on the third floor . . . we all were friends when we moved in 'cause we didn't have nobody else to turn to. We had just moved in. . . . If I needed to go to the store, or go get my [public assistance] check, I knew someone would watch my kid. Or, late at night, I just told my son to play between the tenth and fourteenth floor and I knew he'd be safe and not get into trouble. Sometimes, we had problems 'cause the gangs was recruiting, but mostly we was able to keep them away from our kids. We just told Ms. Lincoln and she called CHA or told the police. We was friends! We did all sorts a' things with each other.

The 1970s ushered in a series of changes that affected the capacities of both informal and formal tenant networks to respond to local youth gang activity. On the one hand, the LAC became involved in bitter struggles against the CHA and local law enforcement agencies over police protection, elevator safety, and apartment conditions. In-fighting within the organization increased during this time and residents began to complain that some LAC representatives were being bribed by the CHA for their cooperation. This dissension carried over to less formal, everyday social life: Resident relations grew strained and networks of peers found themselves choosing sides as different candidates sought an elected position on the councils. On the other hand, broader shifts were occurring that were impacting the community. For example, from 1966 to 1974, the proportion of residents in Taylor Homes who received welfare doubled, although the overall number of tenants declined; in the 1960s, the community had many "normal" two-parent, employed families,[6] but this number decreased dramatically in the 1970s and continued to remain low in the 1980s. Problems in tenant screening also contributed to shifting household organization: CHA staff did not actively incorporate tenants' desires to mix working and low-income families, or integrate single- and two-parent families in the development.

On a broader scale, the large-scale out-migration of industries to suburbs and overseas furthered the jobless rate in Taylor Homes and the surrounding community. Coupled with the tremendous decline in the support by the government for the inner city (e.g., decreased low-income housing allocations, relative declines in transportation and community block grants, etc.), the 1970s witnessed the decimation of community-based institutions such as schools, legal and medical clinics, job training centers, libraries, and so on (Wacquant, 1992).

At the same time, another important development was taking place: the emergence of a lucrative informal economy anchored in the distribution of illicit goods and services. Although in the 1960s and early 1970s there were some households in Taylor Homes that supplemented their income with part-time unreported earnings for baby-sitting, car repair, or the sale of home-cooked meals, toward the mid-1970s these informal economic activities became subordinate to illicit and more dangerous activities such as drug sales, prostitution, weapons trafficking, and the sale of stolen car parts and accessories. Licit, unreported activities continued to be important, but the money that could be earned through home-cooked meals began to pale in comparison to drug selling and car theft. This relative difference proved deeply attractive, especially to the young unemployed population in the housing development who had no other meaningful employment prospects. As Johnny, a janitor who works at a youth center in Taylor Homes, recalls,

You know, when I was getting out the army—after Vietnam—we had a lotta people 'round here that was outta work. They needed jobs, man, they needed to support their families. And, all the steel and good-paying jobs was leaving. That's when me and a lotta people started getting involved in illegal shit. Me and my brother Tee started stealing cars, and the Disciples up north started selling smack (heroin). Hell, it seemed that everyone was getting a piece! But, you know, we didn't want to be doing that stuff really. . . . It's just that there was no other work 'round here.

The absence of employment in "good-paying jobs" is particularly important in understanding the attractiveness of illicit income-generation opportunities. Many such opportunities existed in the urban poor areas of Chicago for several decades (Drake & Cayton, 1945/1993), but in the mid-century postwar era, there were still sufficient employment prospects in manufacturing industries and the municipal sector. Only after the 1960s, when legal, nonmenial employment grew sparse, did drug selling take on a dominant role in ghetto economies. And in the 1970s, income from the informal economy became a *primary* form of income, not simply an activity on the side that could supplement government income maintenance programs.

In Taylor Homes, as illicit economic activity escalated toward the end of the 1970s, the local youth gangs began to exert greater control and to affect other residents' opportunities for income generation. Gangs such as the (Conservative) Vice Lords, the Disciples, and other smaller "sets" controlled one or more buildings in the development. Not only did they dominate drug distribution within their territory, but they also facilitated the resale of stolen car parts for tenants in their area and they provided protection for women who were using their apartments as brothels. In one parking lot, several unemployed males worked as car mechanics and the local gang helped them through direct patronization as well as by advertising their services in surrounding neighborhoods.

As youth gangs' stature in the community shifted from "delinquent" to "economic," so too did their relations with the broader residential population. Perhaps the most important factor affecting this change was the increase in the number of residents involved with youth gangs in informal economic activities. In some cases, residents became reliant on such income for their livelihood. Equally as important was the aging taking place within the gang. Toward the end of the 1970s, gang members in Taylor Homes were not exiting the gang into legal employment as they entered their mid-20s, a pattern that had previously been the norm (according to many older gang members who were interviewed). Instead, many older members chose to remain within the gang to continue earning money for their children and families—arguing that the lack of well-paying jobs in the city forced them to continue selling drugs. Thus, in marked contrast to the 1960s when tenant organizations, police officers, and social workers were responding to the delinquency of juveniles, after the early 1980s these actors were facing gang members who were young adults and less responsive to classical intervention efforts that stressed the value of education, hard work, and so forth. J. T., a high-ranking gang leader in Taylor Homes in his mid-30s, supports three children and gives money to two "girlfriends." He is deeply skeptical of many gang-intervention strategies:

> What are they gonna give me? Teach me how to work a minimum-wage job?! Shit, I got a family, I got investments. At least we take care of the people in our nation [gang]. Shit, even in all our buildings, if people support us then we make sure they ain't starvin, you know? They got food to eat and clothes for their kids. You got something better than that? Bring it on! But, don't bring that "go to school" shit when education don't guarantee you a good job.

Such economic and demographic shifts had a powerful effect on gang-community interactions in the housing development. The LAC, for example, had been historically antagonistic toward youth gangs and had worked effectively to curb gang recruitment and intergang violence *within* the buildings. They did so by garnering the support of residents and engaging the latter in protests or community-watch patrols. And in many cases, as gang members and leaders were the children or kin of Taylor Homes residents, the LAC appealed to residents' roles as parent, grandfather, aunt, and so on to exert pressure on the gangs. With more sympathetic relations emerging between gangs and residents, the LAC could no longer rely on these mechanisms to combat gang activity. Gang members were now household providers as well as kin; they were friends but also employers; their use of violence and intimidation was feared, but at the same time such force was useful in helping to settle disputes that arose in economic transactions. The LAC realized that their base of support was withering: "Who could blame 'em?" asks Ms. Jefferson, a LAC building president in the 1970s:

> We had tenants that was so poor that they couldn't feed their kids. How could they say no to all that drug money that was coming 'round. It wasn't that bad back then [in the 1970s] as it was now [in the 1990s], but some people was still starvin, umm-umm. And, they didn't have no jobs: so they started to steal or do whatever to make money, and I mean *whatever!*

The shifting economic base in Taylor Homes from the 1960s to the 1980s—from working families and public assistance recipients to primarily public assistance recipients and informal economic entrepreneurs—also correlated with a change in the type, level, and effects of gang-related violence in the housing development. Tiffany is a social worker who grew up in Taylor Homes in the 1960s and who now works with its residents. She sums up the shift in the stature of gang violence during this time period:

> It used to be *gang* wars that went on 'round [Taylor]. Now it's *drug* wars! And, there's a difference, 'cause gang wars didn't make everyone worried to death. They was bad, but you know, we didn't all hide inside the buildings, afraid to go outside. [Today] I make sure when [the Disciples] start shooting, my auntie and my grandma stay inside the building. These gangs'll do anything for the rock [crack]. It's drug wars, now, it's a business and they killin' [people] in that business.

To be sure, the period of gang wars (in the 1960s and early 1970s), in which different gangs fought over "pride" or "turf," for example, presented numerous difficulties for the resident population and for social service agencies attempting gang intervention. But as I have tried to indicate, many community leaders felt that they could exert sufficient influence over the gangs and engage in successful conflict resolution. With the shift to drug wars, even such minimal comforts were threatened. In the 1980s, especially, once crack cocaine was introduced into the community, a noticeable escalation in the level of gang violence took place. Zip guns and hand-to-hand conflicts gave way to the use of powerful handguns and assault weapons in practices such as "drive-bys." Gang-related violence in Taylor Homes in the 1960s and 1970s generally did not threaten the lives of innocent bystanders, but after the mid-1980s residents in open public spaces as well as private apartments were in danger of being caught in gang-related cross fire.[7]

One of the most pronounced incidents of the changing nature of gang violence in Taylor Homes occurred in 1992. Amid a drug war that involved Taylor Homes youth gangs, several children were shot and killed, one while playing in the hallway, another while looking out of her apartment window, and another while playing in front of a housing development building. Events such as these made many residents hesitant to confront gang leaders directly. As one tenant argued, "Hell, the police don't even wanta arrest 'em. If *they* so scared, how you expect *us* to tell [the Disciples and Vice Lord gangs] to stop shooting?! We could get killed just for lookin' at 'em funny!" Even tenant leaders who had worked in conflict resolution for three decades agreed that greater caution had to be exercised in working with the local gangs.

Contradiction and Cooperation

The response of community leaders and tenants in Taylor Homes to the increased gang-related violence in the early 1990s did not evidence a complete hatred for the local youth gangs. Instead, the reactions were mixed and suggested the complex relationships that the gangs had formed with other tenants in the community over the past three decades. For example, the deaths of the three children who were caught in the middle of gang-related conflicts received tremendous media attention and helped to mobilize resident protests against "gang violence." Marches by tenant leaders and other community activists took place within the community, and the leaders of the LAC met with local and citywide gang leaders to help form a truce. Local youth center staff also protested by holding "take back the night" demonstrations and by revoking membership privileges from local gangs that did not publicly denounce their role in the violence that took place. But the most vocal publicly held rallies were not targeted against the gangs themselves. Instead, tenants of Taylor Homes and some sympathetic social service providers demonstrated at the local police station and at CHA sponsored "town hall" meetings. Although residents were upset at the increased gang activity, they blamed the CHA and the local police equally for the deaths of the children and the rising tide of violence in the community. At the heart of their criticisms was the perceived lack of police protection and inadequate security provisions by the CHA. Ms. Jefferson explains:

> You gotta understand. We always had some sorta gang problem. But, today, we need police to walk up in these buildings and catch the gang members [who have] got all these guns with 'em in stairwells, when they in the elevator. You know who does the [body] searches when you come in the building? The gang! The security guards don't do nothing for us! That's why we are complainin' to the police. The gangs is outta control. We really can't do nothing to stop them, 'cause it's a business and all these people [in Taylor] are making money too [from selling drugs]. But, it's the police's responsibility to come up in these buildings.

Ms. Lincoln is not atypical of many residents when she argues that the CHA's inadequate maintenance is partially to blame for the disastrous effects of gang violence on the broader community:

> Keep our apartments clean. Make sure that [the] security [guards] leave the lobby and walk through the hallways and stairwells. Don't let weapons come in the buildings when the metal detector goes off! We ain't asking for much [from CHA]. These gang members is our kids. We'll take care of 'em. But, they need work, and we need to have CHA take care of our homes.

The primary response by law enforcement after a barrage of gang-related violence was the "sweep," the controversial warrantless search of domestic spaces by the CHA security force. Ms. Lincoln, Ms. Jefferson, and other community activists decried the use of sweeps and other "emergency procedures" because these were ex post facto strategies that neither provided protection for residents nor acted as effective deterrents. Moreover, these efforts generally took place days after the fighting had escalated, at which point the tenant groups had themselves reestablished a truce among the rival gangs.

The reluctance on the part of tenants to blame only the gangs was also partly a consequence of the numerous services that the local gangs provided in the community. Tenant leaders historically have had great difficulty obtaining money from the CHA or other agencies for social and recreational programming. They have also struggled with the local alderman for timely street repairs and prompt sanitation provision. The gangs helped them address these and other concerns. Ms. Lincoln and the youth gang in her building worked together in the summers to pick up trash in and around her buildings. The gangs also gave back-to-school parties for the children at the eastern end of Taylor Homes, distributing shoes, pens and paper, clothing, and food. The gangs channeled money from drug sales into a quasi-community fund with which groceries could be purchased for residents or emergency loans made. And as noted above, many tenants relied on the informal economic income of household members to supplement public assistance money.

In the context of diminished public and private services, negligent civic institutions and political leaders, and few monetary sources of support, tenants find themselves facing a difficult dilemma: accept the gangs' money and manpower or fight against them and receive little support from other organizations in the city. The choice is not easy and is not always consistently made. Ms. Lincoln, for example, refused to cooperate with the gangs in her building until the late 1980s. She had always provided the police and the CHA with information concerning drug distribution that occurred in her building. She worked diligently to keep her stairwells clean and her elevators in working condition, and she helped drug addicts and households experiencing financial difficulties by locating city services and emergency resources. Toward the end of the decade, she became frustrated with the CHA's use of sweeps and failure to provide daily enforcement or proper maintenance. Most important, however, she argues that the inadequate police response to increased violence occurring in her building forced her to accept the assistance of the youth gang in her building. This "vigilante peer group," as Suttles (1968) affectionately deems the *protective* neighborhood youth gang, enabled Ms. Lincoln to address her concerns:

Little girls was getting raped by that storeowner and the police did nothin'! In that one store, they'd sell themselves for diapers. Can you believe that?! In the buildings, it wasn't any better, 'cause the [CHA] security guards was assaulting women comin' in the building or harass them all the time. There was nothing I could do. I knew Toto [the gang leader in her building] was pissed off at this, 'cause his lil sister got raped. His boys help us by escorting young women at night. You know, back and forth from the store, or around to other buildings. I ain't proud of this! But, our young women ain't been hurt in a long time, so I just work with it for now.

There are hundreds of stories that articulate a dilemma similar to Ms. Lincoln's.[8] The gang's active involvement in crack-cocaine economies is perceived by many residents to be at the heart of the community's social problems. But at the same time that residents speak out against the gang's distribution of drugs and its use of violence, they also find that gang leaders are the only local individuals willing and (financially) able to meet community needs. There are numerous resolutions to this contradiction. Ms. Lincoln works with the gangs for security and nightly escort but refuses to allow them to sell drugs openly in the building. Other tenant leaders are "on the gang's payroll" and willingly accept money from gang leaders in exchange for noncooperation in police investigations. Others such as Johnny and his brother loathe the gang-related violence but need the gangs' support for their own illicit income. In such cases, the gangs are used only for economic assistance (e.g., contract disputes, security, loans): Johnny states, "They help us find customers, but we don't go drinking with 'em or nothin' like that. Strictly business, you dig?!" The majority of residents do not participate in economic activities directly (or do not admit to doing so) and are extremely vocal in their criticisms of gang-related violence. But within their households, there may be someone who receives money from the local gangs—gangs allow non-gang members to sell drugs and they employ residents at dances or parties. Or, because the gangs are fairly large in number and because a single apartment may contain two or three families, there may be a gang member living in the household itself. In such cases, the extraeconomic resources are welcomed, but not publicly disclosed.

Conclusion

The complex relationships between gangs and residents in the Robert Taylor housing development make problematic some popular contemporary portrayals of urban gang-community relations as "the enemy within." I have argued that in Taylor Homes both macrolevel social forces and local developments (e.g., demographic changes in the number of public assistance recipients in the development, the changing age structure of Taylor Homes gangs) affect the interactions between local youth gangs and other actors in the community. And I have suggested that gang-community relations in Taylor Homes are fluid, taking on a different character at different time periods (cf. Sanchez-Jankowski, 1991). In the last decade, the high rates of joblessness, the marked evisceration of public and private institutions in the surrounding ghetto neighborhoods, and the money gained by youth gangs from illicit economic activities have combined to transform the youth gang into an "economic" as well as a "delinquent" social group (Padilla, 1992; Spergel, 1995; Taylor, 1990a). Although the majority of residents do not welcome the heightened social instabilities that accompany drug dealing and "corporate" youth gang violence, they nonetheless are forced to accept the manpower, resources, and services that the youth gangs offer.

When one considers that the gangs in Taylor Homes are 30 years old and that many tenants were gang members themselves at an earlier age, one can understand the ways in which the local gang has become a recognized and dominant institution in the housing development. This shift in the status and community-based power of the gang has occurred not only in Taylor Homes but in other urban poor minority communities in the United States, and it forces us to rethink our extant prevention and intervention efforts. In severely distressed communities, one-dimensional policing strategies such as "Hammer and the Rock" in Los Angeles (Davis, 1990) or the sweeps in Chicago, have proven ineffective as methods for combating gang violence or providing law enforcement for community residents. Similarly, social work efforts that treat such urban-based gangs as "juvenile delinquent" peer groups that can be "the vehicle of its own transformation" (Spergel, 1995, p. 174) will also be of limited value in the present era. Both strategies, ultimately, do not adequately consider the ways in which gangs have become novel *community* actors, locally recognized social groups with power not only to determine social interaction and garner collective support from the residential population but also to acquire and distribute monetary resources. In this sense, their role in urban poor communities differs from previous time periods in which they protected community members from strangers (Suttles, 1968) or engaged primarily in "petty misdemeanors" (Drake & Cayton, 1945/1993). In communities such as Robert Taylor Homes, the gang has an economic dimension that is historically unprecedented. With this role, there emerge contradictions and conflicts such as those described above, in which residents simultaneously support, yet loathe, their local youth gang. These contradictions must be taken into account to devise social policies responsive to the deleterious effects of contemporary gang activity on the broader community.

Notes

1. For an interesting typology of urban gangs, see Fagan (1989).

2. Researchers have argued that understanding the organization and behavior of youth gangs may differ according to community context; they have not often devoted extensive analytic attention to explicating these relations, however. Instead, the link is made assertively and quite generally. For example, see Moore (1990a).

3. "These well organized groups have a very strong leader or manager. The main focus of their organization is participation in illegal money-making ventures. Membership is based on the worth of the individual to the organization. Each member understands his or her role and works as a team member. Criminal actions are motivated by profit. Unlike scavenger gangs, crimes are committed for purpose, not for fun." (Taylor, 1990a).

4. Lemann (1991) is perhaps the best example of the limited value of journalistic reportage in understanding youth gang activity. Lemann erroneously singles out the youth gang as the agent responsible for the impoverished living conditions of Robert Taylor Homes in the 1960s.

5. In using the term "informal economy," I reference the variety of activities that escape governmental or other organizational regulation. These include both licit activities in which earned income is not reported (e.g., baby-sitting, car repair) and illicit activities such as drug distribution that transgress formal legal codes of conduct.

6. In the 1960s and early 1970s, the CHA defined a "normal" family as a household with two parents, at least one of whom was employed. See *Chicago Housing Authority Statistical Reports* for this time period.

7. Moore's work provides an interesting contrast. She argues that in Los Angeles neighborhoods, violence actually decreased in the 1980s when drug selling accelerated.

8. Sanchez-Jankowski (1991) argues with respect to this phenomenon that, "Unlike the police, [gangs] are not restrained from taking immediate action against anyone considered a community threat. . . . Unlike the police, the gang can administer physical injury without regard to laws designed to restrain such action. The vast majority of the residents in many of the gang communities that I studied saw this procedure as effective in controlling crime" (p. 184).

13

The Community
Response to Gangs

Section A: Organizing the
Community Response in Aurora, Colorado

WILLIAM K. ATKINSON, II

Aurora, Colorado, was unlikely to be pegged a hotbed of gang activity in 1986. Located on the eastern edge of Denver, predominantly white collar, well educated, and affluent, Colorado's third-largest city had earned the title of one of the nation's fastest growing cities in the late 1970s and was positioning itself for more economic prosperity. Yet, signs of a growing gang presence were already evident. In the northwest area of the city, police began to identify individuals with links to Los Angeles gangs expanding their narcotics distribution network. These same gangsters had begun recruiting new gang members from local middle schools and high schools.

By 1988, the Aurora Police Department was tracking almost 50 gang members in the city. A year later the number had swelled to 200 to 250 active members with coinciding increases in gang graffiti, crack houses, drug sales, recruitment at schools, and the public flaunting of gang colors and dress. The growth was so swift and alarming, that in a memo to then-Police Chief Gerald Williams, Division Chiefs Verne Saint Vincent and J. Michael Stiers proposed the 12-member Gang Intervention Unit to provide street coverage, ties to police narcotics and intelligence units, and a presence in middle and high schools. The division chiefs contended that gang activity would continue to increase without police intervention and that recognizing and addressing gang problems in their formative stages would probably have the most positive and long-lasting impact on gang activity. In keeping with Aurora's long-standing commitment to community policing, they also noted that the police department would need community input and support to address the root causes of gangs.

The catalyst for community support was Mayor Paul Tauer, who initiated a 9-month citizen study of what should be done to counteract gang activity in Aurora. More than 50 citizens representing many community organizations, worked in three groups—Alternatives and Activities, Education and Prevention, and Enforcement and Consequences—to develop a strategy to more effectively coordinate existing community resources and identify and obtain additional resources to combat the gang problem.

Sandwiched between the debut of the Aurora Police Department Gang Intervention Unit in May 1989 and the publication of the citizens' Aurora Community Gang Task Force report in August, was Aurora's first gang-related drive-by shooting.

The Aurora Gang Task Force

In September 1989, the all-volunteer Aurora Gang Task Force (AGTF) was formed to carry out the recommendations of the original Aurora Community Gang Task Force. Numerous organizations, citizens, and elected officials joined AGTF's volunteer ranks. Columbia/HCA's Aurora

Regional Medical Center took a central role, providing leadership, meeting space, staff time, and in-kind donations. By recognizing gangs as a public health hazard, the hospital deliberately expanded its role beyond traditional hospital-based health care to caring for the health of the community. As an independent, corporate-owned organization, it also shrugged off political concerns and dealt frankly with those who were less inclined to accept the presence of gangs or to acknowledge their ability to metastasize throughout schools and neighborhoods.

With the hospital leading the effort, the AGTF obtained 98% of its funding from private sector donations and drew its membership from a broad base of community volunteers and organizations including law enforcement, schools, civic organizations, churches, social services, government agencies, military, media, and business. The group organized into a steering committee and five subcommittees including: Alternative Activities, to identify, promote, and enhance after-school activities and programs for at-risk youth; Education, to sponsor numerous programs for schools, neighborhoods, and other organizations; Legislation, Enforcement, and Prosecution, to implement tougher prosecution and sentencing of gang-motivated crime and to lobby for legislation to better control gang-related behavior; Recruitment and Orientation, to reach new members and educate them about AGTF goals; and Public Affairs, to disseminate consistent and responsible information about gangs to the public, media, and other interested agencies and community groups in and outside Colorado.

AGTF initiatives enjoyed several early successes. In May 1990, the Aurora City Council approved a controversial law holding parents responsible if they showed "reckless disregard" for the gang activities of their children. A local Rotary group donated video surveillance equipment and portable cellular phones to the Gang Intervention Unit and a nearby military installation provided night vision equipment. Through the distribution of *Aurora Colors,* a videotape produced and financed by Aurora Regional Medical Center, the AGTF began to earn widespread recognition and garner interest beyond the city's boundaries. Responding to requests from across the nation, *Aurora Colors* and a growing packet of timely gang-related information has been distributed free of charge to over 3,000 agencies or communities.

AGTF Activities and Accomplishments

During its next 2 years, the AGTF expanded its focus beyond traditional drug entrepreneurial street gangs to motorcycle gangs, Hispanic and Asian gangs, skinheads, white supremacists, and hate groups.

Through the Legislation, Enforcement, and Prosecution Committee, the AGTF attempted to have statewide impact by seeking sponsorship and passage by the state legislature of several bills to curb firearm use and persistent juvenile delinquency. The committee even went a step further, soliciting community support for its proposed legislation through the creation of Safekids, a grassroots organization attracting 800 members. One successful bill made it a felony to discharge a firearm into a structure or vehicle. Amid much controversy, the legislature also passed a state statute restricting juvenile firearms possession.

Education Committee members addressed over 5,000 individuals, some at large community forums, most at small gatherings of PTAs or interested neighbors. AGTF representatives also traveled to several surrounding states, sharing the successes and pitfalls of this innovative organization.

The AGTF also continued to assert its influence elsewhere, establishing a youth advisory committee to solicit input from high school students; serving as a model for an antigang effort in Colorado's Jefferson County; urging the city council to beef up police staffing; and supporting passage of a city ordinance holding parents responsible for their gun-toting children. The AGTF also supported the efforts of city government's Aurora Youth Initiative to provide activities and intervention programs for at-risk youth.

Despite all the AGTF's efforts, gang ranks continued to swell. By 1992, Aurora's gangsters numbered approximately 1,200 and accounted for 24% of the Denver metro area gang population. The police reacted with strong enforcement to demonstrate Aurora's continued determination to curb gangs and their activities. For example, in April they launched Project HICOP (High Intensity Community Oriented Policing). The project involved sweeping through drug-ridden areas, making mass arrests in an attempt to control gang-related drug trafficking, and assigning PAR (police area representative) officers to assist citizens in keeping crime out of their neighborhoods. That June, Aurora was honored for outstanding achievement by the National Conference of Mayors' 1992 City Livability Awards program because of its efforts to mobilize an effective response to gangs.

Public Health and Safety

In 1993, more affluent, suburban "yuppie" gangs made a brief appearance in Aurora and were swiftly addressed by school and police officials. Even so, their appearance confirmed for Aurora residents that gangs cross all social, economic, and ethnic backgrounds and indiscriminately wreck havoc.

Once again acknowledging the health hazards posed by gangs, the AGTF formed the Injury Control Committee to explore the public health and cost implications of gang and youth violence. It also invited Dr. Kenneth Powell, of the Center for Injury Prevention and Control at the Centers for Disease Control, to discuss gang-related youth violence with AGTF members.

An updated version of *Aurora Colors*, *Aurora Colors II*, emphasizing the growing problem of youth violence, was produced by Aurora Regional Medical Center in 1994. Also, the AGTF continued to garner recognition, receiving first place from the Denver Regional Council of Government Innovations Award Program. The group was named a finalist in the Innovations in State and Local Government Awards Program sponsored by the Ford Foundation and the John F. Kennedy School of Government at Harvard University. Perhaps as a result, numerous communities from across the United States, as well as international teams, have made site visits to Aurora to examine firsthand the AGTF public-private approach to gangs.

The Future

Despite recognition, it was difficult to maintain interest and momentum in the AGTF as it matured and a conclusive solution to the gang problem remained frustratingly elusive. In 1995, the AGTF was restructured to strengthen and broaden active participation; reduce time demands on many of the original, high-level, core volunteers; and acknowledge the difficulty of weaving together the ideas of many different individuals from different backgrounds. Six committees now handle resource procurement, membership, and grant administration; education and training; communications; legislation; preventative and alternative activities; and data collection and emerging issues.

Additionally, despite 6 years of AGTF efforts, gang-related statistics from the Aurora Police Department portray mixed results. Community policing efforts and gang prevention activities have presumably helped decrease the number of gang-related homicides or attempted homicides from 16 in 1993 to 6 in 1994. They may have also helped influence a drop in gang members listing Aurora addresses by more than 200 between 1993 and 1994. But although the Gang Intervention Unit made 53 fewer arrests in 1994 than in 1993, drug trafficking involving gangs is increasing. Even so, just as the Aurora Police Department continues its gang offensive with enforcement, prosecution, and intervention efforts, the AGTF will continue to be a vehicle through which citizens can make an investment in their neighborhoods and their city—a city that does not tolerate gangs.

Section B:
Gang Reduction Efforts by the Task Force on Violent Crime in Cleveland, Ohio

MICHAEL L. WALKER
LINDA M. SCHMIDT

The Cleveland Task Force on Violent Crime began in 1981 as a one-year project of the Cleveland Bar Association, but due to interest in its crime reduction mission and successes with its projects, the task force continues today. The task force mission has always been to act as a catalyst to bring people together to solve shared crime reduction problems.

By 1987, changes in local gang activity were becoming apparent. The neighborhood street gangs were becoming more violent. The favorite weapon of the day was a baseball bat—a bat with nails inserted all around the head was brought in to the task force by a concerned citizen who had found it jutting out of a pond on his property.

Like most U.S. cities, Cleveland had to go through the process of coming to terms with street gangs. By 1989, The Task Force on Violent Crime was in a position to act upon findings from Huff's (1989) gang research findings. Cleveland was just beginning to come out of denial. The power brokers were ready and willing to sit down and talk about the problem. In one way, Cleveland was aided by the three high-profile gang incidents that occurred in Columbus, Ohio (the children of the governor and the mayor were assaulted by gang members, and a gang member who went on local television threatening to shoot rivals who

---

EDITOR'S NOTE: As this book goes to press, the name of the task force has been officially changed to Partnership for a Safer Cleveland.

came into his neighborhood was killed the next day) (Huff, 1990). Those incidents became the catalyst that prompted Columbus authorities to take a serious look at gangs and also gave Cleveland the opportunity to recognize and to begin efforts toward managing its own gang problems. Cleveland had to work its way through the three stages of the gang awareness process that Huff (1990) discusses: denial, overreaction, and misidentification. First, we denied it as long as we could; second, we overreacted with suppression efforts and sensational media stories of gang violence; and third, we misidentified both gang members and the causes of gangs. It was easy to stay in denial as long as (a) we lacked accurate information about gangs on which to base anything, (b) we had not determined what constituted a gang (there was no consensus on a definition in 1989), and (c) we didn't know who joined gangs or why.

With the completion of Huff's gang study in May 1988, it became apparent that Cleveland could no longer deny it had an emerging gang problem. The task force, in conjunction with Maureen Floyd of the Federation for Community Planning and Ken Trump of the Cleveland Public Schools, set about interviewing key individuals from the police, schools, court, probation, social services, and youth and community organizations. The purpose of this survey was to determine how large the perception of the problem was and to formulate recommendations for the task force's Youth Violence Committee.

While the survey was under way, task force staff interviewed youth in the streets and at the juvenile court. Through information gathered from these youth, a gang profile sheet was developed for juvenile court intake and probation staffs in the hope of better tracking youth gang members for court action and diversion programs. Huff's (1989) study had determined that Cleveland had between 15 and 20 viable street gangs by 1988. The late Alice Palmer, who was assigned by Juvenile Court in July 1990 as the gang liaison for the task force, began keeping a list of all gangs that came to her attention through the court intake process. They are listed by name, neighborhood, and school where they are active. Cleveland currently has 140 street gangs. This number fluctuates because some gangs only last a few weeks, and others form coalitions with some of the larger sets.

Huff's (1989) study also showed that Ohio gangs grew from three main origins: dancing (stepping), skating, or rap groups; street corner groups; and individuals from outside Ohio bringing out-of-state gang information and membership in. We saw the progression from these

origins to groups calling themselves social clubs, fraternities, and sorori-
ties to the bolder Crips, Folks, People, and Blood sets. The skinhead
movement came in little by little until 1993, when it became very apparent on the streets. With the exception of the white supremacy movement,
Cleveland gangs have remained (or, in some instances, such as the Vice
Lords have become) multiracial. Currently, Cleveland is seeing a growth
in Hispanic-only gangs, which follows what is occurring in California,
as well.

In 1987-1989, the task force began noting an increase in gang graffiti
occurring at about the same time crack cocaine was arriving on the scene
in Cleveland. The graffiti denoted drug sale turf, and with them came a
new level of violence and more organized gangs coming in from out of
state—Detroit, Michigan, drug gangs; Jamaican posses; and Long Beach,
California, Crips. Weapons of choice evolved from baseball bats, knives,
and chains to .22s, .25s, Tech 9s, Mac 10s, ouzis, and 9mm weapons.

Because the graffiti were visible and the drug arrests and usage
measurable, the popular view was that all gangs were drug gangs. But
this was not (and is not) the case in Cleveland. As gangs grew around
this new level of violence, other groups also grew out of the perceived
need for protection and the notion that there is safety in numbers. By July
1990, we had documented 98 street gangs in the Greater Cleveland area.
Gangs grew up around schools, neighborhood centers, and neighborhoods. In the early days, if you didn't live in a neighborhood, you
couldn't come into it without paying a fee. Today, one can't come into
the neighborhood, period. Kids began riding buses with clothes-filled
book bags 12 months of the year so that they could change their clothes
between gang turfs to travel safely through other neighborhoods. Fear
fueled new growth in gangs. The task force countered by developing a
training program for any organization impacted by youth gangs. That
training included everyone from bus drivers and shopping mall security
staff to teachers, physicians, law enforcement, and youth service providers. The training program included gang recognition and containment, as well as how to manage fear.

In July 1990, the task force conducted a second series of interviews of
several key individuals in Cleveland—the police chief, safety director,
school superintendent, administrative judge of juvenile court, and the
director of the city Community Relations Board (one of the problems
Cleveland had throughout this survey process was the frequent changes
in key leadership positions within city government and the school system).

Now, the Task Force on Violent Crime's Youth Violence Committee had several recommendations resulting from the two surveys as well as intelligence information gathered from the streets. Among the recommendations were the development of a unit in the Cleveland Police Department to focus only on youth gangs (completed); the development of a division of the Cleveland Public Schools' Department of Safety and Security to focus strictly on youth gangs (completed); more responsible reporting of gang incidents by the media (completed); support of political leaders by acknowledging the gang problem (completed); expansion of the Community Relations Board's Youth Services Program to coordinate with the schools and community for gang intervention programs (ongoing); the strengthening of penalties for gang related crimes (ongoing); the development of alternative education programs in place of suspension and expulsion (ongoing); the development of a gang liaison person within Cuyahoga County Juvenile Court to work closely with the police and schools (completed); the development of educational programs for all youth-serving agencies (completed and frequently updated); the development of diversionary programs (some completed, others still in development); enhancement and support of the Drug Abuse Resistance Education (DARE) program (ongoing); the development of after-school programs (a few have been developed by community agencies, but many more are still needed); the removal of gang graffiti through the Anti-Graffiti and Beautification project (ongoing); development of a parent's guide to gang awareness (completed, but update in progress); and gaining the support and cooperation of the business community for our gang reduction efforts (some partnerships developed, but others still needed). The task force continues to work on these recommendations and others.

In October 1990, the Cleveland Police Department developed a youth gang unit, which is still in existence today. The task force works closely with this unit, nonarrest incidents are referred to the task force and the task force refers arrest incidents to the unit. The groups cotrain at conferences and both are members of the Midwest Gang Investigators Association (MGIA), Ohio Chapter. Our collaborative efforts have been successful. On one occasion, the task force staff was called to a downtown hospital to conduct a mediation between two rival gang members and their parents. A nurse had overheard a hospitalized youth say to a friend that as soon as he got out of the hospital, he was going to kill the kid who owned the gun he was shot with. The nurse immediately told the pediatrician in charge of the youth's care, and he called the task force. The gangs involved were two of the largest and most violent in Cleveland. We realized that because of the status of these two young men that it was possible that large numbers of their respective gangs might show up. A hospital emergency room is not the place to take that kind of risk, so backup was requested from the Cleveland Police Department Youth Gang Unit.

The mediation and the intervention were successful. That success was a direct result of a nurse and a doctor getting involved and a city having the resources available to provide the necessary services. The task force has since provided youth gang recognition seminars for hospital emergency room staffs, trauma unit staffs, as well as physician and nursing staffs. In this way, youth are referred to medical and psychological services they might not otherwise receive. Often, youth are brought into the emergency room by their gang friends after an initiation that got out of hand (broken hand, fingers, ribs, jaw, cuts requiring stitches, etc.). When a medical staff member can recognize the signs of gang initiation at the time of hospital admittance, intervention and diversion programming can begin early.

The education subcommittee of the task force's Youth Violence Committee was very successful in reducing youth violence through staff and teacher gang education training and through the introduction of uniforms into several schools in Cleveland and surrounding communities. The most memorable meeting we conducted was held at Harry E. Davis Intermediate School. On this day, the subcommittee invited several Harry E. Davis students to join the committee to discuss school uniforms as a method of reducing gang violence in their building. The students led us immediately into a debate about rights and we led them toward compromise. After much discussion, we came to a consensus: We would hold a meeting and vote on the use of uniforms at their school. Two students modeled the uniforms at the meeting. One of the models had been the most outspoken opponent of uniforms, but she became its strongest proponent when she saw how nice the uniforms were. Parents liked the idea because the cost was reasonable and they realized that uniforms brought a larger degree of safety to their children. Uniforms were adopted in January 1991 at the school. Prior to the introduction of uniforms, the school had 144 A-7 (unruly) filings in juvenile court. By the end of the first year with uniforms, there were only 28 filings, and the count has continued to go down each year.

In the late 1980s, the task force began two projects in the Cleveland Public Schools: the Youth Resource Centers (intermediate schools) and Young Gentlemen/Young Ladies Clubs (elementary). Efforts are currently being made to expand these two successful projects into more schools. The Young Gentlemen/Young Ladies Clubs have become a national model. Also of note is the WriteWay project, which is a writing project beginning its second year as a component of the Youth Resource Centers. This component was well received by the students and the community.

The Anti-Graffiti and Beautification pilot project was begun by the task force in 1987 and turned over to the Cleveland City Council in 1990. This pilot project took a several-block area of Cedar Avenue and routinely removed graffiti from buildings and cleaned vacant lots. In the 3 years the task force ran the program, graffiti only reappeared once on a cleaned building. Municipal court judges sentenced local misdemeanants to work on the project, removing the graffiti in their own neighborhoods.

The Media subcommittee of the Youth Violence Committee worked to educate the print and broadcast sectors concerning why they should not name gangs in their news programs or articles. It was easy to cite examples where they had named a gang and within days a rival gang did something to get equal time. The media quickly became supportive of telling the story without naming the specific gang. The media has come a long way in Cleveland. Recently, a youth was killed by a group of other youth. The story was tucked away in the last pages of the metro section, with just a 5-inch column, no photos, and no mention of "gang." Chances are good that it won't be seen by too many people. In the beginning of our efforts, that story would have been headline news, with explicit photos of the scene. Tension and violence would have followed on the streets.

The task force staff continues with efforts at youth violence reduction. New projects and programs are being developed to keep current with gang growth and development. Among those are the West Side Market project employing young people from the housing estates to carry bags of groceries to shoppers' cars; the Tabula Rasa project focused on working with females at risk of gang involvement; and the daytime curfew project to pick up truants from the street and deposit them at one of two specified school sites for program and resource management.

The task force is able to continue its youth violence reduction mission because of support and assistance from city government, the school system, the courts, local and state law enforcement agencies, social and youth-serving agencies, and the community at large. Collaboration is key to managing gangs and youth violence. The road from 1987 until today has been long and arduous, but our efforts have been rewarded by those who have been inspired to develop and run their own programs in the schools or neighborhood and community centers.

The task force has been fortunate to have hundreds of volunteers who give of their time and talents willingly. We know we will never eradicate gangs, but we do know now that we can manage gangs and limit their influence over our children and our communities.

Section C:
Gang Development and Strategies
in Schools and Suburban Communities

KENNETH S. TRUMP

Gang growth and development is not limited to inner-city neighborhoods, nor is it confined to only certain segments of the overall community. Limited attention has been given to the role of gang development and gang member behavior in schools and to the relationship of this process in schools to gang growth and activity in the broader community. Likewise, the development of gangs in suburban communities has only recently gained increased attention from researchers and practitioners around the country.

In this section, I highlight specific examples of gang development and responses in schools and in three suburban communities in the Cleveland, Ohio, area. Lessons learned from these experiences have been strikingly similar to those in comparable schools or communities across the United States. Recognition of these processes and understanding the successes and obstacles encountered in these specific cases may save valuable months and even years for those about to encounter gangs in their community.

Gang Evolution in the Cleveland Public Schools

The gang presence in the Cleveland Public Schools was first detected in late 1985 and early 1986 in a relatively small number of high schools and junior high schools across the city. School-based crimes and disruptions by gang members generally involved assaults, fighting (including riots), threats and intimidation, and trespassing. Incidences of possession and use of weapons, as well as possession of smaller amounts of drugs, were also attributable to gang members, but these offenses occurred less frequently in schools than the public perceived them to occur.

Candy Rodriguez, a former juvenile gang-drug probation officer and lifelong westside Cleveland resident, attributes the emergence of the two original westside gangs, the Folks (originally the Falcons, then later spelled Folkz) and the Wu Shu Kings, to an evolution from the break-dancing groups and party crews formed in 1984 and 1985. Conflicts from dance competitions, "battles of the DJs," neighborhood rivalries, boy-friend and girlfriend relationships, and "he said, she said" teen rumors exacerbated the natural rivalries created by the original purpose of these competitors. During the same time period, adversarial relationships among youth from several eastside communities, most notably the Hough, Cedar, and John Adams High School neighborhoods, intensified for similar reasons.

Schools were not immune to the gang emergence in the community. The altercations originating at dances, parties, community festivals, athletic events, and similar sites of youth interaction on weekday eve-nings and weekends quickly found their way to the educational facilities the next school day. These conflicts were intensified by citywide court-ordered busing, which unintentionally mixed rival groups and neigh-borhoods in the same school. "Friday Fight" days (from weekday school conflict buildup) were suddenly replaced with weekend community spillover in the form of Monday morning riots, fights, assaults, and so forth upon the opening of school doors.

Gang activity from 1986 to 1988 was characterized by frequent retali-atory offenses between gang members that progressively increased in intensity and severity. The gang structure remained generally disorga-nized and fluid in nature, although increased structure and organization emerged as youth became influenced by the knowledge of gang names, signs, symbols, structure, and activity from other major U.S. cities, most notably Chicago and Los Angeles. Females, initially involved as coun-terparts to the male-dominated gangs, began to increase their involve-ment in gang-related conflicts. Gang presence, first recognized at the high school level, started to appear at the junior high schools, especially in younger relatives and associates of the high school gang members.

School and city officials consistently denied the presence of gangs from 1985 through 1988. One school superintendent told a staff member that there were no gangs in the schools, but there were occurrences of "organized youth student group conflict" at isolated times. City officials held the position that Cleveland did not have any gangs, with the qualifying comment, "like Los Angeles or Chicago." This perception of gangs as drug-selling organized criminal enterprises was fueled by the influx of crack cocaine in Cleveland from 1987 to 1990 and also furthered the gang denial by equating the disorganized, but growing, youth gangs with the more organized crack distribution networks. Meanwhile, frontline youth-service providers struggled daily with the increasing gang violence and the political pressures of denial.

As the official denial continued, Michael Walker of the Task Force on Violent Crime formed the Youth Violence Committee, cochaired by Cleveland Municipal Judge C. Ellen Connally, in late 1987. Representatives working with the committee included, but were not limited to, Cleveland Police Officers William Gant and Janice Abernathy, City Community Relations Representative Carrie Thomas, and myself and J. Patrick Hyland, one of the first and strongest supporters to pursue the issue of gangs in schools, representing Cleveland Public Schools Security. These and other mid-level and frontline officials tactfully rebutted the official denial positions by their respective agencies and assertively pursued proactive strategies to deal with the gang growth.

Numerous reports by police, school, and Task Force on Violent Crime staff were generated from 1987 to 1989, documenting specific gang activity that had now spread throughout Cleveland, as well as extensive recommendations for a coordinated response to the problem. As these efforts occurred behind the scenes and in addition to the regular duties of the professionals involved in the process, the local media began providing increased coverage of gang incidents. Pressure from the media, parents, teachers, youth, residents, and others eventually reached a level that could no longer be officially denied.

In late 1989, the federal Caribbean Task Force operated by the U.S. Attorney's Office in Cleveland expanded its focus to street gangs and was renamed the Caribbean/Street Gang Task Force. This entity focused on organized criminal drug distribution networks in the Greater Cleveland area but, although successful in dealing with these organized enterprises, was not designed to address juvenile youth gang crime.

Although the presence of gangs was documented by Huff (1989) and in a report by current Cleveland Police Lieutenant Tom Campbell in 1988, it was not until fall 1990 that the city formed a centralized Youth Gang Unit in the police department to address street-level youth gangs, combining previously decentralized juvenile detectives with a new squad of detectives specifically assigned to work on gangs. At the same time, city officials formed the Youth Gang Unit, they announced other social programs and coordinating initiatives to address the gang problem that now officially existed in the city.

By 1990, Cleveland had completed at least 5 years of the official denial stage. Gangs were now significantly more structured, better organized, and more entrenched in the communities and schools than in the mid-1980s. Gang offenses had shifted from assaults and threats to murder, drive-by shootings, felonious assaults, possession and use of weapons, increased drug trafficking, and regular threats and actual occurrences of gang-related crimes in and around schools. In my role as the Cleveland Public Schools' "unofficial" gang investigator, I provided in-service training to the city police upon formation of its unit in 1990, but the school district, although not openly contradicting city officials by denying that there were gangs in the community, remained silent and made no significant movement toward addressing gangs in schools. Finally, in spring 1991, confronted with an overwhelming gang problem, the Cleveland Public Schools applied for and received a grant for over $135,000 to create the Youth Gang Unit in its security division. Plans were developed for implementing this program in fall 1991.

Meanwhile, I joined with Robert Kumazec, then a detective and now a sergeant in the Cleveland Police Youth Gang Unit, to form the Ohio Chapter of the Midwest Gang Investigators Association (MGIA) in July 1991. The MGIA is a seven-state nonprofit organization designed to coordinate the dissemination and utilization of information about gang-related, cult, and extremist group activity; support new techniques for the identification and apprehension of gang members; and garner legislative and public support for reducing and preventing gang activity. MGIA membership includes criminal justice, judicial, school security, and other youth-service professionals with an interest in MGIA goals. The Ohio chapter, with regions established in Columbus and Cincinnati, has grown to include more than 800 members statewide, representing over 400 different agencies, making it the largest of the seven state chapters and illustrating the need to better organize Ohio's network in response to gang activity.

In fall 1991, the partially grant-funded five-officer Youth Gang Unit was formed within the Division of Safety and Security of the Cleveland Public Schools. The unit—a supervisor and four officers—served as a specialized resource team to address gang-related concerns impacting 127 schools with over 73,000 students. Unit officers, consisting of two veteran school security officers and two experienced professionals with gang knowledge and experience newly hired for the project, performed consistent and prioritized enforcement, investigations, and intervention with school gang-related incidents citywide. They conducted staff, parent, and student antigang education, while also working with broader communitywide initiatives, agencies, and officials to reduce gang activity and to identify youth alternatives to gangs.

School Youth Gang Unit officers did not inherit an easy situation. The gang problem had become so severe by 1991 that the officers spent a large portion of their first school year in a reactive posture. Once established, the team was able to be more proactive in preventing incidents through early intervention and education programs during its second year. Although effective in managing the school aspect of gang development, unit officers continued to see the overall gang problem worsen, with more structure, increased initiations, older gang members progressing to more intense criminal activity (primarily drugs), both older and younger gang members being killed, and the knowledge and acceptance of gang life seeping into the elementary schools.

During its first 2 years of operation, school Youth Gang Unit officers worked diligently to gain control over this increasing school gang presence. Efforts paid off with a 39% reduction in school gang incidents, from 381 in 1991-1992 to 232 in 1992-1993. In addition to handling all investigations and interventions, unit staff provided training for over 15,000 people during the 2-year period, including students, school staff, parents, and other youth service providers. The program eventually received extensive attention in national journals and at professional conferences.

Three distinct factors were critical to the success of the school Youth Gang Unit. First was the dedication and commitment of the officers, Rickey Darden, Eugene Goddard, Khalid Samad, and James Zielinski. Their willingness and ability to work under diverse and adverse conditions was clearly illustrated in the 39% gang incident reduction and reflected their uniqueness in being able to perform suppression, intervention, and prevention functions at an equally competent level at any time.

Second, the cooperation and support of the Cleveland Police Department Youth Gang Unit was essential to the school unit's success in managing the school gang activity. Lieutenant Wayne Torok, Officer-In-Charge of the Cleveland Police Youth Gang Unit, and then-Sergeant (now Commander) David Swan took a unique and exceptionally progressive position in working with the school Youth Gang Unit staff. They set aside traditional barriers common to police systems and aggressively pursued and maintained communications, shared intelligence, cooperated on enforcement, and collaborated on projects that reinforced the mission of the school unit. Their position received the critical support of then-Police Chief Edward Kovacic. The absence of such consistent support would have meant failure for the school Youth Gang Unit.

Finally, the importance of the interest and support of service recipients—principals, teachers, parents, and youth—as well as the ongoing relationships developed with probation officers, law enforcement entities, social service providers, city officials, and the media, cannot be overstated. These individuals recognized the need for the services; adapted their operational procedures and systems; and maintained an ongoing, consistent relationship that provided school Youth Gang Unit staff with the necessary tools and processes to make a difference in the schools. Their programs and efforts in the community also provided the necessary counterpart to the school-based strategies.

Gangs in Suburban Communities

As people in Cleveland increasingly addressed the problems in the city, others in suburban communities started to detect the impact of emerging gang problems within their cities. This emergence developed as suburban youth mirrored the inner-city youth gang development process, interacted with gang-affiliated and delinquent youth from both the inner city and other suburban communities, and relocated from chronic gang areas to communities with emerging or no actual gang problem. Like most of Cleveland's neighboring suburbs, the three southwest cities of

Parma, Parma Heights, and Seven Hills, Ohio, were not immune to these trends. These three communities, here referred to as the tri-city area, cover a combined area of approximately 30 square miles with over 122,000 residents. Each city is governmentally, legally, and operationally separate from the others, but their proximity and similarities have united them in addressing many common concerns and issues of community growth and development. This relationship is further enhanced by their sharing of the Parma City School District, which provides public educational services to over 13,000 students from the three cities.

Tri-city officials began noticing an increase in juvenile crime and gang activity in 1990, with an increased presence of delinquent youth groups, gang names and known members, gang graffiti, vandalism, juvenile drug activity, and other indicators similar to those identified earlier by Cleveland gang authorities. The Tri-City Task Force on Juvenile Behavior was officially formed in 1992 to enhance communications between the three city police departments, the public school system, the shared Metropark system, and other city and community officials. As the task force improved communications and information sharing, gang crimes in Cleveland and clearer identification of an emerging gang problem and juvenile drug activity in the tri-city area caused task force officials to seek funding in 1993 for full-time dedicated personnel to design, implement, and evaluate specific programs and strategies and to coordinate the task force as a formal entity.

The task force received funding support in late 1993 from the Bureau of Justice Assistance (BJA) of the U.S. Department of Justice and from the Ohio Office of Criminal Justices via the Cuyahoga County Criminal Justice Services Agency. The grants provided resources to hire two full-time juvenile gang, drug, and school security specialists, both of whom were founding members of the Cleveland Public Schools' Youth Gang Unit. The grants also provided funds for targeted police suppression details, training, intervention services, and other program start-up needs, all beginning in January 1994. The BJA award also included technical assistance services from the Police Executive Research Forum (PERF), which, combined with other initiatives, enhanced the task force's prevention and intervention efforts.

Once the task force program received funding, it was clear that a structure was needed to ensure a political and administrative dichotomy in the overall program. The task force was subsequently organized into two operational bodies and one advisory body:

1. *Council of Governments (COG):* The COG is the legal entity responsible for overall policy direction of the task force. The COG is constituted of key officials, including the mayor, law director, and police chief of each city, as well as the superintendent of public schools. COG membership also includes the commanding officers of the three police departments or their juvenile detectives. The COG met monthly during the first few months of the program and then on an average of every 2 months once the program was operational.

2. *Core Group:* The Core Group is responsible for program development and implementation. This group meets monthly, using the Police Executive Research Forum's SARA (scan, analyze, respond, and assess) problem-solving model to formulate gang and juvenile crime prevention, intervention, and suppression strategies. Efforts of the Core Group focus on both short- and long-term issues and programs. Members include representatives from the three city police departments (commanding officers and juvenile detectives); the Metropark Ranger Department; and the public school offices of intervention services, pupil services, and safety and security.

3. *Advisory Committee:* The Advisory Committee serves as a broad-based representation of the three communities to provide periodic input into problem identification and resolution related to gangs and youth violence. The committee includes representatives from the public and private schools, adult and juvenile courts, youth-service providers, elected officials, churches, business community, residents, and youth.

This structure provides the opportunity for oversight and direction from the key agency heads via the COG and the opportunity for program development and implementation by key personnel directing field operations for the involved agencies. The Advisory Committee affords periodic input from perspectives that differ from those involved in the task force operation. The two full-time school-based staff report to the Seven Hills Police Chief, John R. Fechko, who serves as the project director.

During its first 18 months of full operation, the Tri-City Task Force focused on addressing short- and long-term needs with a balance of suppression, intervention, and prevention strategies. Program accomplishments during this time period included 60 targeted police suppression details, 88 school-based investigations, 55 school-based student interventions, and 115 educational presentations to over 9,460 attendees. The task force initiated new prevention, intervention, and diversion programs, including expansion of the DARE program to four additional schools by using Metropark Rangers to conduct classes, piloting of the federal Alcohol, Tobacco, and Firearms (ATF) Gang Resistance Education and Training (GREAT) program in one junior high, and creation of a teen court program in cooperation with the YMCA to serve as a juvenile court diversion program for first offenders.

School-based task force personnel performed a districtwide school security assessment and began implementing a comprehensive school safety and security program to minimize the potential for expansion of gang, drug, and other juvenile crime in schools. A 24-hour hotline was established to receive anonymous reports on gang, drug, weapon, and school safety concerns. A $65,000 state grant was secured to improve school physical security, and teams were established and training conducted to develop incident tracking systems, crisis preparedness plans, and staff development on school security issues. One of the most effective aspects of the task force has been the linkages between the police and full-time school-based project staff for the timely investigation, intervention in, and prevention of potential problems and gang growth.

Tri-City Task Force officials agree that the program has neutralized the trend of continued gang emergence by targeting specific behaviors, crimes, and attitudes associated with gangs. Although gangs have unquestionably not been eliminated in the three-city area, officials believe that they have successfully managed the issue to the point of slowing the emergence of gang-specific activity. A 51-question youth safety survey was administered in 1994 and again in 1995 to public school students Grades 7 to 11. Preliminary analysis of the 1995 survey data indicates that although gangs continue to grow in many communities across the country, gang emergence in the tri-city communities has been neutralized and in some areas reduced (Huff, 1995).

Lessons Learned

The key to successfully organizing the community response to gangs unquestionably rests with timely recognition of gang emergence and quickly overcoming the denial process. Effective responses strike a balance in addressing short- and long-term needs by balancing suppression, intervention, and prevention strategies. Programs should be targeted to include a variety of coordinated services to youth, parents, schools, criminal justice personnel, residents, businesses, and community members. In summary, communities should strive to provide services including

1. School-based intervention and investigation services for gang, drug, and other security incidents, concerns, and issues

2. Technical assistance in designing, refining, and implementing a comprehensive school safety and security program

3. Targeted police suppression details and prosecution focused on problem areas and behaviors associated with gangs, drugs, and other juvenile crime collectively identified by a multiagency group focused on these issues

4. Training and education programs on gang, drug, juvenile crime, school safety, and related issues for youth, school employees, criminal justice personnel, parents, community groups, youth service professionals, etc.

5. Intelligence gathering, data collection and analysis, information sharing, and ongoing assessment of gang, drug, and juvenile crime trends, with accompanying response strategies, policies, programs, and procedures to minimize the growth and impact of these negative behaviors in their early stages

6. Facilitation of regular communication, information sharing, training, and joint cooperative efforts with neighboring communities, law enforcement agencies, and professional organizations to further networking, consistent programming, and information and resource sharing

7. Service as initiators or facilitators of new prevention and intervention programs by agencies and community organizations that further goals and objectives associated with gang and juvenile crime reduction

8. Service as a catalyst for the creation, modification, and implementation of legislation, strategies, programs, policies, and procedures to minimize the growth and impact of gangs, drugs, juvenile crime, and school safety threats

9. Service as a resource for technical assistance and current information for public officials, youth service providers, and others interested in gangs, drugs, juvenile crime, and school safety

10. Collaborative efforts with local media to accurately inform the community about gang and juvenile crime problems and community responses without creating panic or overreaction

Careful analysis of the process of gang growth and community response described in earlier sections of this chapter by Atkinson, Walker, and Schmidt provides insight into the similarities and common threats experienced in cities across the nation. Combined with an understanding of the role of schools and the recognition that gangs are not limited in their areas of impact, individuals experiencing or about to experience gangs in their community should be equipped to better recognize gang emergence processes and to respond in a more timely, effective manner.

References

Adler, F. (1975). *Sisters in crime.* New York: McGraw-Hill.

Aguayo, S. (1986). Salvadoreans in Mexico. *Refugees, 34,* 30-31.

Anderson, E. (1990). *Streetwise: Race, class, and change in an urban community.* Chicago: University of Chicago Press.

Anderson, E. (1994, May). The code of the streets. *Atlantic Monthly,* pp. 81-94.

Asbury, H. (1927). *The gangs of New York.* New York: Paragon.

Badey, J. (1988). *Dragons and tigers.* Loomis, CA: Palmer.

Ball, R. A., & Curry, G. D. (1995). The logic of definition in criminology: Purposes and methods for defining "gangs." *Criminology, 33*(2), 225-245.

Beard, L. H. (1986). Prison gangs: Texas. *Corrections Today, 18,* 12, 18, 22.

Biernacki, D., & Waldorf, P. (1981). Snowball sampling: Problems and techniques of chain referral sampling. *Sociological Methods and Research, 10,* 141-163.

Black, D. (1992). *Triad takeover: A terrifying account of the spread of triad crime in the West.* London: Sidgwick & Jackson.

Block, C. R. (1991). *Early warning system for street gang violence crisis areas.* Chicago: Illinois Criminal Justice Information Authority.

Block, C. R., & Block, R. (1994). Street gang crime in Chicago. *Research in Brief.* Washington, DC: U.S. Department of Justice, Office of Justice Programs, National Institute of Justice.

Block, R., & Block, C. R. (1992). *Lethal and non-lethal street gang crime in Chicago.* Washington, DC: National Institute of Justice.

Blumenthal, R. (1982, December 24). Gunmen firing wildly kill 3 in Chinatown bar. *New York Times,* p. A1.

Bobrowski, L. J. (1988). *Collecting, organizing and reporting street gang crime.* Chicago: Chicago Police Department, Special Functions Group.

Bogardus, E. (1943). Gangs of Mexican-American youth. *Sociology and Social Research, 28,* 55-66.

Booth, M. (1991). *The triads.* New York: St. Martin's.

Bourgois, P. (1989). In search of Horatio Alger: Culture and ideology in the crack economy. *Contemporary Drug Problems, 16*(4), 619-650.

Bourgois, P. (1995). *In search of respect: Selling crack in El Barrio.* New York: Cambridge University Press.

Bowker, L. (1978). *Women, crime and the criminal justice system.* Lexington, MA: Lexington.

Bowker, L., & Klein, M. (1983). The etiology of female juvenile delinquency and gang membership: A test of psychological and social structural explanations. *Adolescence, 13,* 739-751.

Boyle, G. J. (1995, September 29). Victimizers call us to compassion, too. *Los Angeles Times,* p. B5.

Bresler, F. (1981). *The Chinese mafia.* New York: Stein & Day.

Brown, C. (1985). *With friends like these: The Americas watch report on human rights and US policy in Latin America.* New York.

Brown, W. (1983). *The other side of delinquency.* New Brunswick, NJ: Rutgers University Press.

Brown, W. K. (1977). Black female gangs in Philadelphia. *International Journal of Offender Therapy and Comparative Criminology, 21,* 221-228.

Bryant, R. (1990). Chinese organized crime making major inroads in smuggling heroin to U.S. *Organized Crime Digest, 11*(17), 1-6.

Buford, B. (1991). *Among the thugs: The experience, and the seduction of, crowd violence.* New York: Norton.

Bureau of Justice Statistics. (1993). *Performance measures for the criminal justice system* (Discussion papers from the BJS-Princeton Project). Washington, DC: U.S. Department of Justice, Office of Justice Programs.

Burns, T. F. (1980). Getting rowdy with the boys. *Journal of Drug Issues, 10,* 273-286.

Bursik, R. J., Jr., & Grasmick, H. G. (1993). *Neighborhoods and crime.* New York: Lexington.

Butterfield, F. (1991, January 15). Killing of 5 in Boston's Chinatown raises fears of Asian gang wars. *New York Times.*

Cain, M. (Ed.). (1989). *Growing up good: Policing the behavior of girls in Europe.* London: Sage.

California Basic Educational Data System. (1989). *Three year summary: Number of dropouts in California Public High School Instruction.* Sacramento: Author.

Camp, G., & Camp, C. (1987). *Prison gangs: Their extent, nature, and impact on prisons.* Washington, DC: Government Printing Office.

Campbell, A. (1984). *The girls in the gang.* New York: Basil Blackwell.

Campbell, A. (1987). Self-definition by rejection: The case of gang girls. In *Social Problems, 34,* 451-466.

Campbell, A. (1990a). Female participation in gangs. In C. R. Huff (Ed.), *Gangs in America* (1st ed.). Newbury Park, CA: Sage.

Campbell, A. (1990b). *The girls in the gang* (2nd ed.). New Brunswick: Rutgers University Press.

Canada, G. (1995). *Fist, stick, knife, gun.* Boston: Beacon.

Center for Successful Child Development. (1993). *Beethoven's fifth: The first five years of the Center for Successful Child Development: Executive summary.* Chicago: Ounce of Prevention Fund.

Center for Successful Child Development. (n.d.). [Unpublished project report].

Chang, M. (1991, May). Facts about Hong Kong triad societies. *Wide Angle Magazine,* pp. 30-39. (In Chinese)

Chesneaux, J. (1972). *Popular movements and secret societies in China, 1840-1950.* Stanford, CA: Stanford University Press.

Chesney-Lind, M. (1986). Women and crime: The female offender. *Signs, 12,* 78-96.

Chesney-Lind, M. (1993). Girls, gangs and violence: Anatomy of a backlash. *Humanity and Society, 7,* 321-344.

Chesney-Lind, M., Rockhill, A., Marker, N., & Reyes, H. (1994). Gangs and delinquency: Exploring police estimates of gang membership. *Crime, Law and Social Change, 21,* 201-228.

Chi, Z. X. (1985). *Gangs, election, and violence.* Taipei: Jiao Dian. (In Chinese)

Chin, K. (1990). *Chinese subculture and criminality: Non-traditional crime groups in America.* Westport, CT: Greenwood.

Chin, K. (1995a). *Chinatown gangs.* New York: Oxford University Press.

Chin, K. (1995b, Spring). Triad societies in Hong Kong. *Transnational Organized Crime, 1,* 47-64.

Chin, K., & Fagan, J. (1994). Social order and the formation of Chinese youth gangs. *Advances in Criminological Theory, 6,* 149-162.

Chin, K., Fagan, F., & Kelly, R. (1994). *Gangs and social order in Chinatown.* Final report submitted to the National Institute of Justice. Washington, DC.

Cloward, R. A., & Ohlin, L. E. (1960). *Delinquency and opportunity: A theory of delinquent gangs.* Glencoe, IL: Free Press.

Cohen, A. K. (1955). *Delinquent boys: The culture of the gang.* Glencoe, IL: Free Press.

Cohen, A. K. (1990). Foreword and overview. In C. R. Huff (Ed.), *Gangs in America* (1st ed.). Newbury Park, CA: Sage.

Cohen, S. (1980). *Folk devils and moral panics: The creation of the Mods and Rockers.* New York: St. Martin's.

Cohen, S. (1985). *Visions of social control: Crime, punishment and classification.* Cambridge: Polity.

Coleman, J. S. (1961). *The adolescent society.* New York: Free Press.

Coleman, J. S. (1971). *Youth: Transition to adulthood.* Chicago: University of Chicago Press.

Coleman, J. S. (1988). Social capital in the creation of human capital. *American Journal of Sociology, 94*(Suppl.), S95-S120.

Coleman, J. S. (1990). *Foundations of social theory.* Cambridge, MA: Harvard University Press.

Coleman, J. S., Bremner, R. H., Clark, B. R., Davis, J. B., Eichorn, D. H., Griliches, Z., Kett, J. F., Ryder, N. B., Doering, Z. B., & Mays, J. M. (1974). *Youth: Transition to adulthood* (Report of the Panel of the President's Science Advisory Committee). Chicago: University of Chicago Press.

Coleman, J. S., & Hoffer, T. (1987). *Public and private high schools: The impact of communities.* New York: Basic Books.

Connell, R. W. (1987). *Gender and power.* Stanford, CA: Stanford University Press.

Cook, P. J., & Moore, M. H. (1995). Gun control. In J. Q. Wilson & J. Petersilia (Eds.), *Crime* (pp. 267-294). San Francisco: ICS.

Cooper. B. M. (1987, December 1). Motor city breakdown. *Village Voice,* pp. 23-35.

Covey, H. C., Menard, S., & Franzese, R. J. (1992). *Juvenile gangs.* Springfield, IL: Charles C Thomas.

Cox, V. (1986). Prison gangs: Inmates battle for control. *Corrections Compendium, 10,* 1,6-9.

Crist, R. W. (1986). Prison gangs in Arizona. *Corrections Today, 18,* 13, 25-17.

Crittenden, D. (1990, January 25). You've come a long way, moll. *Wall Street Journal,* p. A14.

Crouch, B., & Marquart, J. (1989). *An appeal to justice: Litigated reform of Texas prisons.* Austin: University of Texas Press.

Cummings, S. (1993). Anatomy of a Wilding gang. In S. Cummings & D. Monti (Eds.), *Gangs: The origins and impact of contemporary youth gangs in the United States.* Albany: State University of New York Press.

Currie, E. (1993). *Reckoning: Drugs, the cities, and the American future.* New York: Hill & Wang.

Curry, G. D. (1991, November). *Measuring street gang-related homicide.* Paper presented at the American Society of Criminology annual meetings, San Francisco.

Curry, G. D. (1994). *Gang research in two cities* (Final Technical Report Grant No. 90CL1095). Washington, DC: U.S. Department of Health & Human Services, Family Youth Services Bureau.

Curry, G. D. (1995, August). *Automated gang data bases.* Presentation at National Gang Enforcement and Prevention Training Conference, Denver, CO.

Curry, G. D., Ball, R. A., & Decker, S. H. (1995). *An update on gang crime and law enforcement recordkeeping.* St. Louis: University of Missouri, Department of Criminology and Criminal Justice.

Curry, G. D., Ball, R. A., & Fox, R. J. (1994). Gang crime and law enforcement recordkeeping. *Research in brief.* Washington, DC: U.S. Department of Justice, National Institute of Justice, Office of Justice Programs.

Curry, G. D., Box, R. J., Ball, R. A., & Stone, D. (1992). *National assessment of law enforcement anti-gang information resources* (Draft 1992 Final Report). West Virginia University, National Assessment Survey.

Curry, G. D., & Spergel, I. A. (1988). Gang homicide, delinquency, and community. *Criminology, 26,* 381-405.

Curtis, L. C. (Ed.). (1987, November). Policies to prevent crime: Neighborhood, family, and employment strategies. *Annals of the American Academy of Political and Social Science, 494.*

Curtis, R. A. (1992). Highly structured crack markets in the southside of Williamsburg, Brooklyn. In J. Fagan (Ed.), *The ecology of crime and drug use in inner cities.* New York: Social Science Research Council.

Daly, K., & Chesney-Lind, M. (1988). Feminism and criminology. *Justice Quarterly, 5,* 497-538.

Daly, M. (1983, February). The war for Chinatown. *New York Magazine,* pp. 31-38.

Dannen, F. (1992, November). Revenge of the Green Dragons. *New Yorker,* pp. 76-99.

Davidson, T. (1974). *Chicano prisoners.* New York: Holt, Rinehart & Winston.

Davis, M. (1990). *City of quartz: Excavating the future in Los Angeles.* London: Verso.

Dawley, D. (1973). *A nation of lords: The autobiography of the Vice Lords.* New York: Anchor.

Decker, S. (1995). *Gangs, gang members and drug sales.* St. Louis: University of Missouri, Department of Criminology and Criminal Justice.

Decker, S., & Kempf, K. (1991). Constructing gangs: The social construction of youth activities. *Criminal Justice Policy Review, 5,* 271-291.

Decker, S., & Van Winkle, B. (1994). Slinging dope: The role of gangs and gang members in drug sales. *Justice Quarterly, 11,* 583-604.

Decker, S., & Van Winkle, B. (1996). *Life in the gang: Family, friends and violence.* New York: Cambridge University Press.

Diana Koricke in East Los Angeles. (1993, March 29). *World news tonight.* New York: NBC.

Dillon, R. (1962). *The hatchet men: The story of the tong wars in San Francisco's Chinatown.* New York: Coward-McCann.

Dombrink, J., & Song, J. (1992). *Asian racketeering in America: Emerging groups, organized crime, and legal control.* Final report submitted to the National Institute of Justice.

Dolan, E. F., & Finney, S. (1984). *Youth gangs.* New York: Julian Messner.

Doyle, D., & Luckenbill, D. (1991). Mobilizing law in response to collective problems: A test of Black's theory of law. *Law & Society Review, 25,* 103-116.

Drake, S. C., & Cayton, H. (1993). *The black metropolis: A study of Negro life in a northern city* (Rev. & enlarged ed.). Chicago: University of Chicago Press. (Original work published 1945)

Dubro, J. (1992). *Dragons of crime: Inside the Asian underworld.* Markham, Ontario: Octopus.

Edgerton, R. B. (1978). *Deviant behavior and cultural theory* (Module in Anthropology, No. 37). Reading, MA: Addison-Wesley.

Ehrensaft, K., & Spergel, I. (1991). *Police technical assistance manual* (Youth Gang Suppression and Intervention Program). Chicago: University of Chicago, School of Social Service Administration.

Elliott, D., Wilson, W. J., Huizinga, D., Sampson, R. J., Elliott, A., & Rankin, B. (in press). The effects of neighborhood disadvantage on adolescent development. *Journal of Research in Crime and Delinquency.*

Emery, J. (1990, October 28). Wah Mee sentence to be appealed. *Seattle Times*, p. B2.

English, T. J. (1995). *Born to kill.* New York: William Morrow.

Esbensen, F. A., & Huizinga, D. (1993). Gangs, drugs, and delinquency in a survey of urban youth. *Criminology, 31*, 565-589.

Fagan, J. (1989). The social organization of drug use and drug dealing among urban gangs. *Criminology, 27*(4), 633-669.

Fagan, J. (1990). Social processes of delinquency and drug use among urban gangs. In C. R. Huff (Ed.), *Gangs in America* (1st ed.). Newbury Park, CA: Sage.

Fagan, J. (1992a). Drug selling and licit income in distressed neighborhoods: The economic lives of drug users and dealers. In G. Peterson & A. Harrell (Eds.), *Drugs, crime and social isolation.* Washington DC: Urban Institute Press.

Fagan, J. (1992b). The dynamics of crime and neighborhood change. In J. Fagan (Ed.), *The ecology of crime and drug use in inner cities.* New York: Social Science Research Council.

Fagan, J. (1993). The political economy of drug dealing among urban gangs. In R. Davis, A. Lurigio, & D. P. Rosenbaum (Eds.), *Drugs and community* (pp. 19-54). Springfield, IL: Charles C Thomas.

Fagan, J. (1996). Legal and illegal work: Crime, work, and unemployment. In B. Weisbrod & J. Worthy (Eds.), *Dealing with urban crisis: Linking research to action.* Evanston IL: Northwestern University Press.

Fagan, J. (in press). The dynamics of crime and neighborhood change. In J. Fagan (Ed.), *The ecology of crime and drug use in inner cities.* New York: Social Science Research Council.

Fagan, J., & Chin, K. (1990). Violence as regulation and social control in the distribution of crack. In M. de la Rosa, E. Lambert, & B. Gropper (Eds.), *Drugs and violence* (Research Monograph No. 103). Rockville, MD: U.S. Public Health Service, National Institute on Drug Abuse.

Fagan, J., & Freeman, R. (in press). Crime, work, and unemployment. In M. Tonry (Ed.), *Crime and justice: A review of research.* Chicago: University of Chicago Press.

Fagan, J., & Wilkinson, D. L. (in press-a). Firearms and youth violence. In D. Stoff, J. Breiling, & J. Maser (Eds.), *Handbook of antisocial behavior.* New York: Wiley.

Fagan, J., & Wilkinson, D. L. (in press-b). The role of scripts in understanding gun violence among adolescents. *Law and Contemporary Problems.*

Fagan, J., Piper, E., & Moore, M. (1986). Violent delinquents and urban youths. *Criminology, 24*, 439-471.

Fainstein, N. (1986). The underclass/mismatch hypothesis as an explanation for black economic deprivation. *Politics & Society, 15*, 403-452.

Farley, J. E. (1987). Disproportionate black and Hispanic unemployment in U.S. metropolitan areas. *American Journal of Economics and Sociology, 46*(2), 129-150.

Farley, R., & Allen, W. R. (1987). *The color line and the quality of life in America.* New York: Russell Sage.

Farrington, D. (1991). Childhood aggression and adult violence. In D. Pepler & K. H. Rubin (Eds.), *The development and treatment of childhood aggression* (p. 9). Hillsdale, NJ: Lawrence Erlbaum.

Farrington, D. P. (1985). Age and crime. In M. Tonry & N. Morris (Eds.), *Crime and justice: An annual review of research* (Vol. 7, pp. 189-250). Chicago: University of Chicago Press.

Federal Bureau of Investigation. (1978). *Crime in the United States, 1977.* Washington, DC: Government Printing Office.

Federal Bureau of Investigation. (1994). *Crime in the United States—1993.* Washington, DC: U.S. Department of Justice.

Feldman, H. W., Mandel, J., & Fields, A. (1985). In the neighborhood: A strategy for delivering early intervention services to young drug users in their natural environments. In A. S. Friedman & G. M. Beschner (Eds.), *Treatment services for adolescent substance abusers.* Rockville MD: National Institute on Drug Abuse.

Fight Crime Committee. (1986). *A discussion document on options for changes in the law and in the administration of the law to counter the triad problem.* Hong Kong: Fight Crime Committee, Security Branch.

Finestone, H. (1976). *Victims of change: Juvenile delinquents in American society.* Westport, CT: Greenwood.

Fishman, L. T. (1995). The Vice Queens: an ethnographic study of black female gang behavior. In M. Klein, C. Maxson, & J. Miller (Eds.), *The modern gang reader.* Los Angeles: Roxbury.

Fleisher, M. S. (1995). *Beggars and thieves: Lives of urban street criminals.* Madison: University of Wisconsin Press.

Flowers, R. B. (1987). *Women and criminality.* New York: Greenwood.

Fong, R. (1987). *A comparative study of the organizational aspects of two Texas prison gangs: Texas Syndicate and Mexican Mafia.* Unpublished doctoral dissertation, Sam Houston State University, Huntsville, TX.

Fong, R. (1990, March). The organizational structure of prison gangs: A Texas case study. *Federal Probation,* pp. 36-43.

Fong, R., Vogel, R., & Buentello, S. (1995). Blood-in, blood-out: The rationale behind defecting from prison gangs. *Gang Journal, 2,* 45-51.

Freeman, R. B. (1991). Employment and earnings of disadvantaged young men in a labor shortage economy. In C. Jencks & P. E. Peterson (Eds.), *The urban underclass.* Washington DC: Brookings Institution.

Freeman, R. B. (1992). Crime and the economic status of disadvantaged young men. In G. Peterson & A. Harrell (Eds.), *Drugs, crime and social isolation.* Washington DC: Urban Institute Press.

Fry, J. (1973). *Fire and blackstone.* Philadelphia: J. B. Lippincott.

Fullerton, H. N. (1987, September). Labor force projections: 1986-2000. *Monthly Labor Review,* pp. 16-29.

Giordano, P., Cernkovich, S., & Pugh, M. (1978). Girls, guys and gangs: The changing social context of female delinquency. *Journal of Criminal Law and Criminology, 69*(1), 126-132.

Girls in the hood. (1992, August 6). *Street stories.* New York: CBS.

Glaser, D. (1971). *Social deviance.* Chicago: Markham.

Glick, C. (1941). *Shake hands with the dragon.* New York: McGraw-Hill.

Glick, C., & Hong, S. (1947). *Swords of silence: Chinese secret societies, past and present.* New York: Whittlesey.

Gold, A. (1991, March 21). Leader of Chinatown group slain. *New York Times,* p. B2.

Gold, M. (1970). *Delinquent behavior in an American city.* Belmont, CA: Brooks/Cole.

Goldstein, A. P., & Huff, C. R. (1993). *The gang intervention handbook.* Champaign, IL: Research Press.

Goldstein, H. (1990). *Problem-oriented policing.* New York: McGraw-Hill.

Goldstein, P. J. (1989). Drugs and violent crime. In N. A. Weiner & M. E. Wolfgang (Eds.), *Pathways to violent crime.* Newbury Park, CA: Sage.

Goldstein, P. J., Brownstein, H. H., Ryan, P., & Belluci, P. A. (1989). Crack and homicide in New York City, 1989: A conceptually-based event analysis. *Contemporary Drug Problems 16*, 651-687.

Gong, Y. E., & Grant, B. (1930). *Tong war!* New York: N. L. Brown.

Gora, J. (1982). *The new female criminal: Empirical reality or social myth.* New York: Praeger.

Gordon, R. A., Short, J. F., Jr., Cartwright, D. S., & Strodtbeck, F. L. (1963). Values and gang delinquency: A study of street-corner groups. *American Journal of Sociology, 69*, 109-128. (Reprinted in Short & Strodtbeck, 1965)

Gould, T. (1988, May). Who killed Bob Moeini? *Vancouver Sun Magazine*, pp. 49-56.

Grace, M., & Guido, J. (1988). *Hong Kong 1997: Its impact on Chinese organized crime in the United States.* Washington, DC: Foreign Service Institute, U.S. Department of State.

Grant, B. (1979). *The boat people.* Sydney, Australia: Penguin.

Hagan, J. (1993). The social embeddedness of crime and unemployment. *Criminology, 31*, 465-492.

Hagedorn, J. M. (1994a). Homeboys, Dope Fiends, Legits, and New Jacks. *Criminology, 32*, 197-219.

Hagedorn, J. M. (1994b). Neighborhoods, markets, and gang drug organization. *Journal of Research in Crime and Delinquency, 32*, 197-219.

Hagedorn, J. M. (1995). *Forsaking our children.* Chicago: Lake View Press.

Hagedorn, J. M. (with Macon, P.). (1988). *People and folks: gangs, crime, and the underclass in a rustbelt city.* Chicago: Lake View Press.

Hamid, A. (1990). The political economy of crack-related violence. *Contemporary Drug Problems, 17*(1), 31-78.

Hamid, A. (1992). Flatbush: A freelance nickels market. In J. Fagan (Ed.), *The ecology of crime and drug use in inner cities.* New York: Social Science Research Council.

Hanson, K. (1964). *Rebels in the streets: The story of New York's girl gangs.* Englewood Cliffs, NJ: Prentice Hall.

Harris, M. G. (1988). *Cholas: Latino girls and gangs.* New York: AMS.

Haviland, W. A. (1988). *Cultural anthropology.* New York: Holt, Rinehart & Winston.

Hawkins, J. D., & Catalano, R. F., Jr. (1992). *Communities that care.* San Francisco: Jossey-Bass.

Hawkins, J. D., Lishner, D. M., Jenson, J. M., & Catalano, R. F., Jr. (1987). Delinquents and drugs: What the evidence suggests about prevention and treatment programming. In B. S. Brown & A. R. Mills (Eds.), *Youth at high risk for substance abuse* (pp. 81-131). Rockville, MD: U.S. Department of Health and Human Services.

Hechtman, M. (1977, July 11). Chinatown gang foe knifed, ex-"mayor" stabbed 3 times. *New York Daily News*, p. 4.

Hirschi, T. (1969). *Causes of delinquency.* Berkeley: University of California Press.

Hoaglin, D. C., Mosteller, F., & Tukey, J. W. (1983). *Understanding robust and exploratory data analysis.* New York: John Wiley.

Hochschild, J. L. (1989). Equal opportunity and the estranged poor. *Annals of the American Academy of Political and Social Science, 501*, 143-155.

Horowitz, R. (1983). *Honor and the American dream: Culture and identity in a Chicano community.* New Brunswick, NJ: Rutgers University Press.

Horowitz, R. (1990). Sociological perspectives on gangs. In C. R. Huff (Ed.), *Gangs in America* (1st ed.). Newbury Park, CA: Sage.

Howell, J. C. (1994). Recent gang research: Program and policy implications. *Crime & Delinquency, 40*, 495-515.

Howell, J. C., Krisberg, B., Hawkins, J. D., & Wilson, J. J. (Eds.). (1995). *A sourcebook: Serious, violent, and chronic juvenile offenders.* Thousand Oaks, CA: Sage.

Huff, C. R. (1989). Youth gangs and public policy. *Crime & Delinquency, 35*, 524-537.

Huff, C. R. (Ed.). (1990). *Gangs in America* (1st ed.). Newbury Park, CA: Sage.

Huff, C. R. (1994). Gangs in the United States. In A. Goldstein & C. R. Huff (Eds.), *The gang intervention handbook* (pp. 3-20). Champaign, IL: Research Press.

Huff, C. R. (1995). *Evaluation of the Tri-City Task Force Project: Preliminary Report.*

Hunt, D. (1990). Drugs and consensual crimes: Drug dealing and prostitution. In J. Q. Wilson & M. Tonry (Eds.), *Crime and justice: An annual review of research. Vol. 13: Drugs and crime.* Chicago: University of Chicago Press.

Hutchison, R. (1993). Blazon nouveau: Gang graffiti in the barrios of Los Angeles and Chicago. In S. Cummings & D. Monti (Eds.), *Gangs: The origins and impact of contemporary youth gangs in the United States.* Albany: State University of New York Press.

Institute for Intergovernmental Research. (1995). *National youth gang center* [pamphlet]. Tallahassee, FL: Office of Juvenile Justice and Delinquency Prevention Pamphlet.

Institute for Law and Justice. (1994). *Gang prosecution in the United States* (Final report prepared for the National Institute of Justice). Alexandria, VA: Author.

Irwin, J. (1970). *The felon.* Englewood Cliffs, NJ: Prentice Hall.

Jackson, P. I. (1991). Crime, youth gangs, and urban transition: The social dislocations of postindustrial economic development. *Justice Quarterly, 8,* 379-397.

Jacobs, J. (1977). *Stateville: The penitentiary in mass society.* Chicago: University of Chicago Press.

James, G. (1991, November 18). Man dies in 5th Ave. restaurant shootout. *New York Times,* p. B3.

Jarrett, R. (1994). Living poor: Family life among single parent, African-American women. *Social Problems, 41,* 30-49.

Jencks, C. (1991). Is the American underclass growing? In C. Jencks & P. E. Peterson (Eds.), *The urban underclass.* Washington DC: Brookings Institute.

Jiminez, J. B. (1989). Cocaine, informality, and the urban economy in La Paz, Bolivia. In A. Portes, M. Castells, & L. Benton (Eds.), *The informal economy.* Baltimore: Johns Hopkins University Press.

Joe, K. A., & Chesney-Lind, M. (1995). Just every mother's angel: An analysis of gender and ethnic variations in youth gang membership. *Gender & Society, 9*(4), 408-430.

Johnson, B. D., Goldstein, P. J., Preble, E., Schmeidler, J. Lipton, D., Spunt, B., & Miller, T. (1985). *Taking care of business: The economics of crime by heroin abusers.* Lexington, MA: Lexington.

Johnson, B. D., Hamid, A., & Sanabria, H. (1990). Emerging models of crack distribution. In T. Mieczkowski (Ed.), *Drugs and crime: A reader.* Boston: Allyn-Bacon.

Johnson, B. D., Williams, T., Dei, K., & Sanabria, H. (1990. Drug abuse and the inner city: Impacts of hard drug use and sales on low income communities. In J. Q. Wilson & M. Tonry (Eds.), *Drugs and crime.* Chicago: University of Chicago Press.

Johnson, J. H.; & Oliver, M. L. (1991). Economic restructuring and black male joblessness in US metropolitan areas. *Urban Geography, 12,* 542-562.

Johnston, W. (1991, March/April). Global work force 2000: The new world labor market. *Harvard Business Review, 69,* 115-127.

Kachigan, S. (1986). *Statistical analysis.* New York: Radius.

Kaplan, D., Goldberg, D., & Jue, L. (1986, December). Enter the dragon: How Hong Kong's notorious underworld syndicates are becoming the number one organized crime problem in California. *San Francisco Focus,* pp. 68-84.

Kasarda, J. D. (1988). Jobs, migration and emerging urban mismatches. In M. G. H. McGeary & L. E. Lynn (Eds.), *Urban change and poverty* (pp. 148-198). Washington DC: National Academy Press.

Kasarda, J. D. (1989). Urban industrial transition and the underclass. *Annals of the American Academy of Political and Social Science, 501,* 26-47.

Kasarda, J. D. (1992). The severely distressed in economically transforming cities. In G. Peterson & A. Harrell (Eds.), *Drugs, crime and social isolation.* Washington DC: Urban Institute Press.

Keiser, R. L. (1969). *The Vice Lords: Warriors of the street.* New York: Holt, Rinehart & Winston.

Kelly, G. (1977). *From Vietnam to America: A chronicle of the Vietnamese immigration to the United States.* Boulder, CO: Westview.

Kerr, P. (1987, August 9). Chinese now dominate New York heroin trade. *New York Times,* p. A1.

Kessel, J., & Hum, P. (1991, March 16). Crime in Chinatown: Wave of killings hits Toronto as rival gangs battle for lucrative market. *Ottawa Citizen,* p. B5.

Kifner, J. (1991, January 8). Abducted Chinese illegal aliens rescued. *New York Times,* p. B3.

Kinkead, G. (1992). *Chinatown.* New York: HarperCollins.

Klein, M. (1968). Impressions of juvenile gang members. *Adolescence, 3,* 53-77.

Klein, M. (1971). *Street gangs and street workers.* Englewood Cliffs, NJ: Prentice Hall.

Klein, M. W. (1995a). *The American street gang: Its nature, prevalence, and control.* New York: Oxford University Press.

Klein, M. W. (1995b, September 19). Deference to gangs makes them kings of the roost. *Los Angeles Times.*

Klein, M. W. (1995c). Street gang cycles. In J. Q. Wilson & J. Petersilia (Eds.), *Crime* (pp. 217-236). San Francisco: Institute for Contemporary Studies.

Klein, M. W., Gordon, M. A., & Maxson, C. L. (1986). The impact of police investigations on police-reported rates of gang and nongang homicides. *Criminology, 24,* 489-512.

Klein, M., Maxson, C., & Cunningham, L. (1988). *Gang involvement in cocaine "rock" trafficking.* Los Angeles: University of Southern California, Center for Research on Crime and Social Control, SSRI.

Klein, M. W., & Maxson, C. L. (1989). Street gang violence. In N. Wiener & M. Wolfgang (Eds.), *Violent crime, violent criminals* (pp. 198-234). Newbury Park, CA: Sage.

Klein, M. W., & Maxson, C. L. (1994). Gangs and cocaine trafficking. In D. MacKenzie & C. Uchida (Eds.), *Drugs and the criminal justice system: Evaluating public policy initiatives.* Newbury Park, CA: Sage.

Klein, M. W., Maxson, C. L., & Cunningham, L. C. (1991). "Crack," street gangs, and violence. *Criminology, 29*(4), 623-650.

Knox, G. (1992). *Gangs and related problems among Asian students: Preliminary findings from the first national Asian gang survey.* Unpublished manuscript.

Kozel, N. J., & Adams, E. H. (Eds.). (1985. *Cocaine use in America: Epidemiological and clinical perspectives* (National Institute of Drug Abuse Research Monograph No. 61). Rockville MD: U.S. Department of Health and Human Services.

Lanzetta, M. de P., Castano, G. M., & Soto, A. T. (1989). The articulation of formal and informal sectors in the economy of Bogota, Colombia. In A. Portes, M. Castells, & L. Benton (Eds.), *The informal economy.* Baltimore: Johns Hopkins University Press.

Lauderback, D., Hansen, J., & Waldorf, D. (1992). Sisters are doin' it for themselves: A black female gang in San Francisco. *Gang Journal, 1*(1), 57-72.

Lavigne, Y. (1991). *Good guy, bad guy: Drugs and the changing face of organized crime.* Toronto: Random House.

Lay, R., & Dobson. C. (1993, March 14). Rise and fall of Machine Gun Johnny. *South China Morning Post Spectrum,* p.4.

Lee, C. Y. (1974). *Days of the tong wars.* New York: Ballantine.

Lee, F. R. (1991, November 25). For gold earrings and protection, more girls take the road to violence. *New York Times,* pp. A1, B7.

Lee, H. (1989, February 5). Blood of the flower. *New York Daily News Magazine,* pp. 8-9.

LeFeber, W. (1984). *Inevitable revolutions: The United States in Central America.* New York.

Leibow, E. (1967). *Talley's corner.* Boston: Little, Brown.

Lemann, N. (1991). *The promised land: The great black migration and how it changed America.* New York: Knopf.

Leslie, C., Biddle, N., Rosenberg, D., & Wayne, J. (1993, August 2). Girls will be girls. *Newsweek,* p. 44.

Levy, F. (1987). *Dollars and dreams: The changing American income distribution.* New York: Russell Sage.

Lewis, N. (1992, December 23). Delinquent girls achieving a violent equality in DC. *Washington Post,* pp. A1, A14.

Lieberson, S. (1980). *A piece of the pie: Black and white immigrants since 1880.* Berkeley: University of California Press.

Liu, P.-c. (1981). *A history of the Chinese in the United States of America, II.* Taipei: Li Min. (In Chinese)

Liu, W. T. (1979). *Transition to nowhere: Vietnamese refugees in America.* Nashville, TN: Charter House.

Loper, A. B., & Cornell, D.G. (1995, October). *Homicide by girls.* Paper presented at the Annual Meeting of the National Girls Caucus, Orlando, FL.

Lorch, D. (1990, July 30). Mourners returned fire, police say: Retaliation is expected over cemetery shootout. *New York Times,* p. B1.

Lorch, D. (1991, January 3). Immigrants from China pay dearly to be slaves. *New York Times,* p. B1.

Los Angeles County District Attorney. (1992). *Gangs, crime and violence in Los Angeles.* Los Angeles: Author.

Lubasch, A. (1992, October 3). 7 sentenced to life terms in a gang case. *New York Times,* p. L26.

Ludlow, L. (1987, May 10). Golden Dragon massacre: Pain still felt a decade later. *San Francisco Examiner,* p. B1.

Lynn, L. E., Jr., & McGeary, M. (Eds.). (1990). *Inner-city poverty in the United States.* Washington, DC: National Academy Press.

Ma, L. E. A. (1990). *Revolutionaries, monarchists, and Chinatowns.* Honolulu: University of Hawaii Press.

MacCoun, R., & Reuter, P. (1992). Are the wages of sin $30 an hour? Economic aspects of street-level drug dealing. *Crime & Delinquency, 38,* 477-491.

MacLeod, J. (1987). *Aint no makin it: Leveled aspirations in a low-income neighborhood.* Boulder, CO: Westview.

Majors, R., & Billson, J. M. (1992). *Cool pose: The dilemmas of black manhood in America.* New York: Touchstone.

Mann, C. (1984). *Female crime and delinquency.* University: University of Alabama Press.

Marinucci, C., Winokur, S., & Lewis, G. (1994, December 12). Ruthless girlz. *San Francisco Examiner,* pp. A-1.

Marsh, R. E. (1980). Socioeconomic status of Indochinese refugees in the United States: Progress and problems. *Social Security Bulletin, 43,* 11-12.

Massey, D. S. (1990). American apartheid. *American Journal of Sociology, 96,* 329-357.

Massey, D. S., & Eggers, M. L. (1990). The ecology of inequality: Minorities and the concentration of poverty, 1970-80. *American Journal of Sociology, 95,* 1153-1188.

Maxson, C. L. (1995). Street gangs and drug sales in two suburban cities. *Research in Brief.* Washington, DC: National Institute of Justice, Office of Justice Programs, U.S. Department of Justice.

Maxson, C. L., Gordon, M. A., & Klein, M. W. (1985). Differences between gang and nongang homicides. *Criminology, 23*(2), 209-222.

Maxson, C. L., & Klein, M. W. (1989). Street gang violence. In N. A. Weiner & M. E. Wolfgang (Eds.), *Pathways to criminal violence.* Newbury Park, CA: Sage.

Maxson, C. L., & Klein, M. W. (1990). Street gang violence: Twice as great, or half as great? In C. R. Huff (Ed.), *Gangs in America* (1st ed., pp. 71-102). Newbury Park, CA: Sage.

Maxson, C. L., Klein, M. W., & Gordon, M. A. (1990). *Street gang violence as a generalizable pattern.* Los Angeles: University of Southern California, Social Science Research Institute.

Mayer, J. (1989, September 8). In the war on drugs, toughest foe may be that alienated youth. *Wall Street Journal,* p. 1.

McGahey, R. (1986). Economic conditions, neighborhood organization and urban crime. In A. J. Reiss, Jr., & M. Tonry (Eds.), *Communities and crime* (pp. 231-270). Chicago: University of Chicago Press.

McRobbie, A., & Garber, J. (1975). Girls and subcultures. In S. Hall & T. Jefferson (Eds.), *Resistance through rituals: Youth subculture in post-war Britain.* New York: Holmes & Meier.

Meehan, P. J., & O'Carroll, P. (1992). Gangs, drugs, and homicide in Los Angeles. *American Journal of Diseases of Children, 146,* 683-687.

Merton, R. (1949). *Social theory and social structure.* Glencoe, IL: Free Press.

Meskil, P. (1989, February 5). In the eye of the storm. *New York Daily News Magazine,* pp. 10-16.

Mieczkowski, T. (1986). Geeking up and throwing down: Heroin street life in Detroit. *Criminology, 24,* 645-666.

Miller, W. B. (1973). Race, sex and gangs: The Molls. *Society, 11,* 32-35.

Miller, W. B. (1975). *Violence by youth gangs and youth groups as a crime problem in major American cities.* Washington, DC: Government Printing Office.

Miller, W. B. (1980). The molls. In S. K. Datesman & F. R. Scarpitti (Eds.), *Women, Crime, and Justice.* New York: Oxford University Press.

Miller, W. B. (1982). *Crime by youth gangs and groups in the United States.* Washington, DC: Office of Juvenile Justice and Delinquency Prevention, U.S. Department of Justice.

Minke, P. (1974). *Chinese in the mother lode (1850-1870).* Saratoga, CA: R & E Research Associates. (Originally published in 1960)

Moloney, P. (1991, March 4). Bloodbath in Chinatown: More police urged for Chinatown. *Toronto Star,* p. A3.

Moore, J. W. (1978). *Homeboys: Gangs, drugs and prison in the barrios of Los Angeles.* Philadelphia: Temple University Press.

Moore, J. W. (1990a). Gangs, drugs, and violence. In M. De La Rosa, E. Lambert, & B. Gropper (Eds.), *Drugs and violence: Causes, correlates, and consequences* (NIDA Research Monograph 103, pp. 160-176). Rockville, MD: National Institute of Drug Abuse.

Moore, J. W. (1990b). Mexican-American women addicts: The influence of family background. In R. Glick & J. Moore (Ed.), *Drugs in Hispanic communities.* New Brunswick, NJ: Rutgers University Press.

Moore, J. W. (1991). *Going down to the barrio: Homeboys and homegirls in change.* Philadelphia: Temple University Press.

Moore, J. W. (1992). Institutionalized youth gangs: Why white fence and El Hoyo Maravilla change so slowly. In J. Fagan (Ed.), *The ecology of crime and drug use in inner cities.* New York: Social Science Research Council.

Moore, J. W. (1994). *The chola life course: Chicana heroin users and the barrio gang. International Journal of the Addictions, 29*(9), 1115-1126.

Moore, J., & Devitt, M. (1989). Addicted Mexican-American mothers. *Gender & Society, 3,* 53-78.

Moore, J., & Mata, A. (1981). *Women and heroin in Chicano communities* (Final Report for NIDA). Los Angeles: Chicano Pinto Research Project.

Moore, J., & Vigil, J. D. (1993). Barrios in transition. In J. Moore & R. Pinderhughes (Eds.), *In the barrios: Latinos and the underclass debate.* New York: Russell Sage.

Moore, J., Vigil, J. D., & Levy, J. (1995). Huisas of the street: Chicana gang members. *Latino Studies Journal, 6*(1), 27-48.

Morgan, W. P. (1960). *Triad societies in Hong Kong.* Hong Kong: Government Press.

Moss, P., & Tilly, C. (1991). *Why black men are doing worse in the labor market: A review of supply-side and demand-side explanations* (Paper prepared for the Social Science Research Council, Committee on Research on the Urban Underclass, Subcommittee on Joblessness and the Underclass). New York: Social Science Research Council.

Muehlbauer, G., & Dodder, L. (1983). The losers. *Gang delinquency in an American suburb.* New York: Praeger.

Naffine, N. (1987). *Female crime: The construction of women in criminology.* Sydney, Australia: Allen & Unwin.

National Drug Intelligence Center (NDIC). (1995). *NDIC Street Gang Symposium: Selected findings.* Jonestown, PA: Author.

National Research Council. (1993). *Losing generations: Adolescents in high-risk settings.* Washington, DC: National Academy Press.

Needle, J., & Stapleton, W. V. (1983). *Reports of the national juvenile justice assessment centers, police handling of youth gangs.* Washington, DC: U.S. Department of Justice, Office of Juvenile Justice and Delinquency Prevention.

New Mexico analyzes prison gang problem, conducts threat assessment. (1990). *Corrections Digest, 21*(26), 1-7.

Nguyen, L. T., & Henkin, A. B. (1982). Vietnamese refugees in the United States: Adaptation and transitional status. *Journal of Ethnic Studies, 9*(4), 101-116.

O'Callaghan, S. (1978). *The triads: The mafia of the Far East.* London: W. H. Allen.

Office of Juvenile Justice and Delinquency Prevention (OJJDP). (1994). *FY 1994 discretionary competitive program announcements and application kit.* Washington, DC: U.S. Department of Justice.

Ogbu, J. (1978). *Minority education and caste: The American system in cross-cultural perspective.* New York: Academic Press.

Ogbu, J. (1987). Variability in minority school performance: A problem in search of an explanation. *Anthropology and Education Quarterly, 18*(4), 312-334.

Oliver, M. L., Johnson, J. H., & Farrell, W. C. (1993). Anatomy of a rebellion: A political-economic analysis. In R. Gooding-Williams (Ed.), *Reading Rodney King, Reading urban uprising.* New York: Routledge.

Oliver, W. (1994). *The violent social world of black men.* New York: Lexington Books.

Orfield, G. (1988). Exclusion of the majority: Shrinking college access and public policy in metropolitan Los Angeles. *Urban Review, 20,* 147-163.

Ostner, I. (1986). Die Entdeckung der Madchen. Neue Perspecktiven fur die. *Kolner-Zeitschrift-fur Soziologie und Sozialpsychologie, 38,* 352-371.

Ounce of Prevention Fund (1994). A head start on Head Start: Effective birth-to-3 strategies. Chicago: Author.

Padilla, F. (1992). *The gang as an American enterprise.* New Brunswick, NJ: Rutgers University Press.

Padilla, F. (1993). The working gang. In S. Cummings & D. J. Monti (Eds.), *Gangs* (pp. 173-192). Albany: State University of New York Press.

Pelz, M. E. (1988). *The Aryan Brotherhood of Texas: An analysis of right-wing extremism in the Texas prisons*. Unpublished doctoral dissertation, Sam Houston State University, Huntsville, TX.

Police chief urges Fujianese immigrants not to be afraid of reporting crime to authorities. (1992, May 7). *Sing Tao Jih Pao*, p. 28. (In Chinese)

Porter, B. (1982). California prison gangs: The price of control. *Corrections Magazine, 8*, 6-19.

Posner, G. (1988). *Warlords of crimes*. New York: McGraw-Hill.

President's Commission on Organized Crime. (1984). *Organized crime of Asian origin* (Record of hearing III—October 23-25, 1984, New York, New York). Washington, DC: Government Printing Office.

Price, K. (1975). *The Black Muslims in Texas prisons*. Master's thesis, Sam Houston State University.

Quicker, J. (with Galeai, Y. N., & Batani-Khalfani, A.). (1992). Bootstrap or noose? Drugs, gangs, and violence in South Central Los Angeles. In J. Fagan (Ed.), *The ecology of crime and drug use in inner cities*. New York: Social Science Research Council.

Quicker, J. C. (1983). *Homegirls: Characterizing Chicano gangs*. San Pedro, CA: International University Press.

Rand, A. (1987). Transitional life events and desistance from delinquency and crime. In M. Wolfgang, T. Thornberry, & R. Figlio (Eds.), *From boy to man, from delinquency to crime* (pp. 134-162). Chicago: University of Chicago Press.

Reinarman, C., Waldorf, D., & Murphy, S. (1989, November). *The call of the pipe: Freebasing and crack use as norm-bound episodic compulsion*. Paper presented at the Annual Meeting of the American Society of Criminology, Reno, NV.

Reiner, I. (1992). *Gangs, crime, and violence in Los Angeles. Findings and proposals from the district attorney's office. Executive summary*. Los Angeles: District Attorney, County of Los Angeles.

Reiss, A. J., Jr. (1986a). Co-offender influences on criminal careers. In A. Blumstein, J. Cohen, J. Roth, & C. Visher (Eds.), *Criminal careers and "career criminals"* (Vol. 2). Washington, DC: National Academy Press.

Reiss, A. J., Jr. (1986b). Why are communities important in understanding crime? In A. J. Reiss, Jr., & M. Tonry (Eds.), *Communities and crime* (pp. 1-33). Chicago: University of Chicago Press.

Reiss, A. J., Jr., & Roth, J. (Eds.). (1993). *Understanding and preventing violence*. Washington, DC: National Academy Press.

Reiss, A. J., Jr., & Tonry, M. (Eds.). (1986). *Communities and crime*. Chicago: University of Chicago Press.

Report from the field on an endless war. (1989, March 12). *New York Times*, Sec. 4, p. 1.

Reuter, P., MacCoun, R., & Murphy, P. (1990). *Money from crime* (Report R-3894). Santa Monica, CA: RAND.

Rice, R. (1963, October 19). A reporter at large: The Persian queens. *New Yorker*, pp. 153-187.

Roberts, S. (1971, June 13). Crime rate of women up sharply over men's. *New York Times*, pp. 1, 72.

Rodgers, B. W. (1969). Developmental exposure and changing vocational preferences in the Out-Island Bahamas. *Human Organization, 28*, 270-278.

Rosenbaum, M. (1988). *Women on heroin*. New Brunswick, NJ: Rutgers University Press.

Rothman, D. J. (1980). *Conscience and convenience: The asylum and its alternatives in progressive America*. Boston: Little, Brown.

Ruiz v. Estelle, 503 F. Supp. 1265 (S.D. Tex. 1980).

Sampson, R. J. (1987). Urban black violence: The effect of male joblessness and family disruption. *American Journal of Sociology, 93*(2), 348-382.

Sampson, R. J. (1992). Family management and child development: Insights from social disorganization theory. In J. McCord (Ed.), *Facts, forecasts, and frameworks* (pp. 63-92). New Brunswick, NJ: Transaction.

Sampson, R. J. (1993). The community context of violent crime. In W. J. Wilson (Ed.), *Sociology and the public agenda* (pp. 259-286). Newbury Park, CA: Sage.

Sampson, R. J. (1994). *Community-level factors in the development of violent behavior: Implications for social policy.* Unpublished manuscript.

Sampson, R. J., & Groves, W. B. (1989). Community structure and crime: Testing social disorganization theory. *American Journal of Sociology, 94,* 774-802.

Sampson, R. J., & Laub, J. H. (1993). *Crime in the making: Pathways and turning points through life.* Cambridge, MA: Harvard University Press.

Sampson, R. J., & Lauritsen, J. (1993). Violent victimization and offending: Individual, situational, and community-level risk factors. In A. J. Reiss, Jr., & J. A. Roth (Eds.), *Understanding and preventing violence. Vol. 3: Social influences* (pp. 1-114). Washington, DC: National Academy Press.

Sanchez-Jankowski, M. (1991). *Islands in the street: Gangs and American urban society.* Berkeley: University of California Press.

Sanders, W. G. (1994). *Gangbangs and drive-bys: Grounded culture and juvenile gang violence.* New York: Aldine de Gruyter.

Sante, L. (1991). *Low life: Lures and snares of old New York.* New York: Farrar, Giroux and Straus.

Santiago, D. (1992, February 23). Random victims of vengeance show teen crime. *Philadelphia Inquirer,* p. A1.

Sarnecki, J. (1986). *Delinquent networks.* Stockholm: National Council for Crime Prevention.

Sassen, S. (1991). The informal economy. In J. H. Mollenkopf & M. Castells (Eds.), *Dual city: Restructuring New York.* New York: Russell Sage.

Sassen-Koob, S. (1989). New York City's informal economy. In A. Portes, M. Castells, & L. A. Benton (Eds.), *The informal economy: Studies in advanced and less developed countries* (pp. 60-77). Baltimore: Johns Hopkins University Press.

Scheer, R. (1995, August 27). New national monument: The jailhouse. *Los Angeles Times,* p. B4.

Schwartz, G. (1987). *Beyond conformity or rebellion: Youth and authority in America.* Chicago: University of Chicago Press.

Shacklady-Smith, L. (1978). Sexist assumptions and female delinquency. In C. Smart & B. Smart (Eds.), *Women and social control.* London: Routledge Kegan Paul.

Shannon, L. W. (1986). Ecological effects of the hardening of the inner city. In R. M. Figlio, S. Hakim, & G. F. Rengert (Eds.), *Metropolitan crime patterns* (pp. 27-54). Monsey NY: Criminal Justice Press.

Shaw, C. R. (1930). *The Jack-Roller: A delinquent boy's own story.* Chicago: University of Chicago Press.

Shaw, C. R., & McKay, H. D. (1931). *Social factors in juvenile delinquency* (Vol. 2, no. 13). Washington, DC: Government Printing Office.

Shaw, C. R., & McKay, H. D. (1942). *Juvenile delinquency and urban areas.* Chicago: University of Chicago Press.

Shaw, C. R., & McKay, H. D. (1969). *Juvenile delinquency and urban areas* (Rev. ed.). Chicago: University of Chicago Press.

Shelden, R. G., Snodgrass, T., & Snodgrass, P. (1993). Comparing gang and non-gang offenders: Some tentative findings. *Gang Journal, 1,* 73-85.

Sheley, J., Wright, J., & Smith, M. D. (1993, November-December). Kids, guns and killing fields. *Society,* pp. 84-87.

Sherman, L. (1970). *Youth workers, police, and the gangs*. Unpublished master's thesis, University of Chicago.

Short, J. F., Jr. (1976). Gangs, politics, and the social order. In J. F. Short, Jr. (Ed.), *Delinquency, crime, and society*. Chicago: University of Chicago Press.

Short, J. F., Jr. (1990a). Gangs, neighborhoods, and youth crime. *Criminal Justice Research Bulletin, 5*(4), 1-11.

Short, J. F., Jr. (1990b). New wine in old bottles? Change and continuity in American gangs. In C. R. Huff (Ed.), *Gangs in America* (1st ed.). Newbury Park, CA: Sage.

Short, J. F., Jr., & Moland, J., Jr. (1976). Politics and youth gangs: A follow-up study. *Sociological Quarterly, 17*, 162-179.

Short, J. F., Jr., & Strodtbeck, F. L. (1965/1974). *Group process and gang delinquency*. Chicago: University of Chicago Press.

Simon, R. (1975). *Women and crime*. Lexington, MA: Lexington.

Skogan, W. (1990). *Disorder and decline*. New York: Free Press.

Skolnick, J. (1988). *The social structure of street drug dealing* (BCS Forum). Sacramento: State of California.

Skolnick, J. H., Correl, T., Navarro, E., & Rabb, R. (1988). *The social structure of street drug dealing* (monograph). Sacramento: Office of the Attorney General, State of California.

Snodgrass, J. (1982). *The Jack-Roller at seventy: A fifty year follow-up*. Lexington, MA: Lexington.

Soja, E., Morales, R., & Wolff, G. (1983). Urban restructuring: An analysis of social and spatial change in Los Angeles. *Economic Geography, 58*, 221-235.

Spergel, I. A. (1988). *Report of the Law Enforcement Youth Gang Symposium*. Chicago: School of Social Service Administration, University of Chicago.

Spergel, I. A. (1989). Youth gangs: Continuity and change. In N. Morris & M. Tonry (Eds.), *Crime and justice: An annual review of research* (Vol. 12). Chicago: University of Chicago Press.

Spergel, I. A. (1995). *The youth gang problem: A community approach*. New York: Oxford University Press.

Spergel, I. A., & Curry, G. D. (1990). Strategies and perceived agency effectiveness in dealing with the youth gang problem. In C. R. Huff (Ed.), *Gangs in America* (1st ed., pp. 288-309). Newbury Park, CA: Sage.

Spergel, I. A., & Curry, G. D. (1993). The national youth gang survey: A research and development process. In A. Goldstein & C. R. Huff (Eds.), *Gang intervention handbook* (pp. 359-400). Champaign-Urbana, IL: Research Press.

Stack, C. (1974). *All our kin: Strategies for survival in a black community*. New York: Harper & Row.

Steffensmeier, D. (1983). Organization properties and sex-segregation in the underworld, *Social Forces, 61*, 1010-1032.

Steffensmeier, D. J., & Steffensmeier, R. H. (1980). Trends in female delinquency: An examination of arrest, juvenile court, self-report, and field data. *Criminology, 18*, 62-85.

Steinberg, J. (1991, July 6). Tourist in car killed as she chances upon Chinatown gunfight. *New York Times*, p. L23.

Stepick, A. (1989). Miami's two informal sectors. In A. Portes, M. Castells, & L. Benton (Eds.), *The informal economy*. Baltimore: Johns Hopkins University Press.

Strom, S. (1991, January 2). 13 held in kidnapping of illegal alien. *New York Times*, p. B3.

Stumphauzer, J. S., Veloz, E. V., & Aiken, T. W. (1981). Violence by street gangs: East Side story? In R. B. Stuart (Ed.), *Violent behavior: Social learning approaches to prediction, management, and treatment* (pp. 68-82). New York: Brunner-Mazel.

Sullivan, M. (1989). *Getting paid: Youth crime and unemployment in three urban neighborhoods.* New York: Cornell University Press.

Sullivan, M. (1991). Crime and the social fabric. In J. Mollenkopf & M. Castells (Eds.), *The dual city.* New York: Russell Sage.

Sutherland, E. S. (1947). *Criminology* (4th ed.). Philadelphia: J. B. Lippincott.

Suttles, G. D. (1968). *The social order of the slum: Ethnicity and territory in the inner city.* Chicago: University of Chicago Press.

Takagi, P., & Platt, T. (1978). Behind the gilded ghetto: An analysis of race, class and crime in Chinatown. *Crime and Social Justice, 9,* 2-25.

Taylor, C. S. (1990a). *Dangerous society.* East Lansing: Michigan State University Press.

Taylor, C. S. (1990b). Gang imperialism. In C. R. Huff (Ed.), *Gangs in America* (1st ed.). Newbury Park, CA: Sage.

Taylor, C. S. (1993). *Girls, gangs, women, and drugs.* East Lansing: Michigan State University Press.

Taylor, D. G., Taub, R. P., & Peterson, B. L. (1986). Crime, community organization, and causes of neighborhood decline. In R. M. Figlio, S. Hakim, & G. F. Rengert (Eds.), *Metropolitan crime patterns.* Monsey NY: Willow Tree Press.

Taylor, I. (1971). "Football mad": A speculative sociology of soccer hooliganism. In E. Dunning (Ed.), *The sociology of sport.* London: Cass.

Taylor, R., & Covington, J. (1988). Neighborhood changes in ecology and violence. *Criminology, 26,* 553-590.

Texas Department of Corrections (TDC). (n.d.). *TDC prison gangs.* [Confidential interoffice communication].

Thomas, W. I., Park, R. E., & Miller, H. A. (1921). *Old world traits transplanted.* New York: Harper & Brothers.

Thompson, J. (1976, February). Are Chinatown gang wars a cover-up? *San Francisco Magazine,* pp. 20-21.

Thomsen, G. (1996). Perceptions of school and the future: A case study of 12th grade Latino students' perceptions of their adult opportunities and their current school experiences. Unpublished doctoral dissertation, University of Wisconsin–Milwaukee.

Thornberry, T., Krohn, M., Lizotte, A., & Chard-Wierschem, D. (1993). The role of juvenile gangs in facilitating delinquent behavior. *Journal of Research in Crime and Delinquency, 30*(1), 55-87.

Thornberry, T., Smith, C., Loeber, R., Van Kammen, W. B., Huizinga, D., & Weiher, A. W. (n.d.). *Resilient youth.* Unpublished manuscript.

Thrasher, F. M. (1963). *The gang: A study of 1313 gangs in Chicago.* Chicago: University of Chicago Press. (Abridged ed.; Original work published 1927; Rev. ed., 1936)

Tienda, M. (1989). Puerto Ricans and the underclass debate. *Annals of the American Academy of Political and Social Science, 501,* 105-119.

Tienda, M. (1991). Poor people and poor places: Deciphering neighborhood effects on poverty outcomes. In J. Huber (Ed.), *Macro-micro linkages in sociology* (pp. 244-262). Newbury Park, CA: Sage.

Tonry, M. (1995). *Malign neglect: Race, crime and punishment in America.* New York: Oxford University Press.

Toobin, J. (1994, May 23). Capone's revenge. *New Yorker,* pp. 46-59.

Toy, C. (1992a). Coming out to play: Reasons to join and participate in Asian gangs. *Gang Journal, 1*(1), 13-29.

Toy, C. (1992b). A short history of Asian gangs in San Francisco. *Justice Quarterly, 9*(4), 601-619.

Treaster, J. (1993, June 9). Behind immigrants' voyage, long reach of Chinese gang. *New York Times*, p. A1.

U.S. Department of Justice. (1985). *Oriental organized crime: A report of a research project conducted by the Organized Crime Section, Federal Bureau of Investigation, Criminal Investigative Division.* Washington, DC: Government Printing Office.

U.S. Department of Justice. (1988). *Report on Asian organized crime.* Criminal Division, Washington, DC.

U.S. Senate. (1992). *Asian organized crime* (Hearing before the Permanent Subcommittee on Investigations). Washington, DC: Government Printing Office.

U.S. v. Chen I. Chung a/k/a "Tony Chan" et al. Indictment No. 90 CR 1019(S-2)(RR). (E.D. N.Y. May 17, 1991).

U.S. v. Yin Poy Louie et al. Indictment. (S.D. N.Y. 1985).

Valentine, B. (1978). *Hustling and other hard work: Life styles in the ghetto.* New York: Free Press.

Vicusi, W. K. (1986a). Market incentives for criminal behavior. In R. B. Freeman & H. J. Holzer (Eds.), *The black youth unemployment crisis* (pp. 301-346). Chicago: University of Chicago Press.

Vicusi, W. K. (1986b). The risks and rewards of criminal activity: A comprehensive test of criminal deterrence. *Journal of Labor Economics, 4,* 317-340.

Vigil, J. D. (1988a). *Barrio gangs: Street life and identity in Southern California.* Austin: University of Texas Press.

Vigil, J. D. (1988b). Group processes and street identity: Adolescent Chicano gang members. *Ethos, 16,* 421-445.

Vigil, J. D. (1993). Gangs, social control, and ethnicity: Ways to redirect. In S. B. Heath & M. W. McLaughlin (Eds.), *Identity and inner-city youth: Beyond ethnicity and gender.* New York: Teachers College Press.

Vigil, J. D., & Yun, S. C. (1990). Vietnamese youth gangs in southern California. In C. R. Huff (Ed.), *Gangs in America* (1st ed., pp. 146-162). Newbury Park, CA: Sage.

Vigil, J. D., & Yun, S. C. (in press). Lives in the wind: The story of Vietnamese youth gangs. In K. Hazlehurst (Ed.), *Justice and reform.* Queensbrook, Australia: Pavelar.

Vigil, J. D., Yun, S., & Long, J. M. (1992). Youth gangs, crime, and the Vietnamese in Orange County, California. In J. Fagan (Ed.), *The ecology of crime and drug use in inner cities.* New York: Social Science Research Council.

Wacquant, L. D. (1992). Redrawing the urban color line: The state of the ghetto in the 1980s. In C. Calhoun & G. Ritzer (Eds.), *Social problems.* New York: McGraw-Hill.

Wacquant, L. D., & Wilson, W. J. (1989). The costs of racial and class exclusion in the inner city. *Annals of the American Academy of Political and Social Science, 501,* 8-25.

Waldorf, D. (1992). *When the Crips invaded San Francisco: Gang migration.* (Technical Report, Grant 5 R01 DA06486, National Institute on Drug Abuse). San Francisco: Institute for Scientific Analysis.

Waldorf, D., & Lauderback, D. (1993). *Gang drug sales in San Francisco: Organized or freelance?* Alameda, CA: Institute for Scientific Analysis.

Warr, M. (1996). Organization and instigation in delinquent groups. *Criminology, 34*(1), 11-37.

Washton, A., & Gold, M. (1987). Recent trends in cocaine abuse as seen from the "800-cocaine hotline." In A. M. Washton & M. Gold (Eds.), *Cocaine: A clinician's handbook.* New York: Guilford Press.

Wiatrowski, M. D., Griswold, D. B., & Roberts, M. K. (1981). Social control theory and delinquency. *American Sociological Review, 46,* 525-541.

Williams, T. (1989). *The cocaine kids: The inside story of a teenage drug ring.* Redding, MA: Addison-Wesley.

Wilson, J. Q., & Kelling, G. (1982, February). Broken windows. *Atlantic Monthly,* pp. 46-52.

Wilson, W. J. (1987). *The truly disadvantaged: The inner city, the underclass, and public policy.* Chicago: University of Chicago Press.

Wilson, W. J. (1991). Studying inner-city social dislocations: The challenge of public agenda research. *American Sociological Review, 56,* 1-14.

Wilson, W. J. (1996). *When work disappears: The world of the new urban poor.* New York: Knopf.

Woodson, R. L. (1981). *Youth crime and urban policy: A view from the inner city.* Washington, DC: American Enterprise Institute for Public Policy Research.

Wright, R., Decker, S., Redfern, A., & Smith, D. (1992). A snowball's chance in hell: Doing fieldwork with active residential burglars. *Journal of Research in Crime and Delinquency, 29,* 148-161.

Yablonsky, L. (1973). *The violent gang.* New York: Penguin.

Zatz, M. (1985). Los Cholos: Legal processing of Chicano gang members. *Social Problems, 33,* 13-30.

Zhang, S. (1984). *The activities of Hong Kong organized crime groups.* Hong Kong: Tien Ti. (In Chinese)

Zimring, F. E., & Hawkins, G. (in press). *American violence.* New York: Oxford.

Index

About the Editor

C. Ronald Huff is Director and Professor in the School of Public Policy and Management and Director of the Criminal Justice Research Center at The Ohio State University. He has also held faculty positions at the University of California–Irvine and Purdue University and served as a visiting professor at the University of Hawaii. Prior to his academic career, he held professional positions in mental health, children's services, and in a maximum security institution for mentally disordered offenders. His publications include more than 50 journal articles and book chapters and 10 books. He recently completed a major NIJ-funded study of the criminal behavior of gangs and non-gang, at-risk youth in Colorado and Florida and a companion study of gangs in Ohio. He has served as a consultant on gangs to the U.S. Senate Judiciary Committee, the FBI National Academy at Quantico, the U.S. Department of Justice, numerous other federal agencies, and five states. His recent honors include the Donald Cressey Award from the National Council on Crime and Delinquency, the Paul Tappan Award from the Western Society of Criminology, and the Herbert Bloch Award from the American Society of Criminology.

About the Contributors

William K. Atkinson, II, is President and CEO of St. Luke's Medical Center in Denver, Colorado, and formerly held that same position with the Aurora Regional Medical Center (formerly Humana Hospital) in Aurora, Colorado, from 1987-1995. He holds a doctorate in public policy and public affairs from the University of Colorado at Denver, as well as master's degrees in both public health and public administration. He has chaired the Aurora Gang Task Force for many years and has received numerous honors for his extensive community service.

Richard A. Ball is Professor of Sociology at West Virginia University. He holds a Ph.D. in sociology from The Ohio State University, and since 1966, he has conducted basic and applied research in criminal justice. He recently served as coprincipal investigator of OJJDP's national juvenile hate crime study and is currently a senior research associate of the National White Collar Crime Center. He is coauthor of *House Arrest and Correctional Policy: Doing Time at Home* (Sage, 1988) and *Criminological Theory: Context and Consequences* (Sage, 2nd ed., 1995). His recent work has appeared in *Criminology* and *Crime & Delinquency.*

Meda Chesney-Lind is Professor of Women's Studies at the University of Hawaii at Manoa. She has served as Vice President of the American Society of Criminology and President of the Western Society of Criminology. The author of more than 50 papers and monographs on the subject of women and crime, she has recently coauthored the first comprehensive book on female delinquency to be published in the United States since the 1950s. That book, *Girls, Delinquency, and Juvenile Justice* (Brooks/Cole, 1992) received the Michael J. Hindelang Award from the American Society of Criminology. Her other awards include the Distinguished Scholar Award from the Women and Crime Division of the American Society of Criminology, and the University of Hawaii Board of Regents' Medal for Excellence in Research.

Ko-lin Chin is Associate Professor in the School of Criminal Justice at Rutgers University. He received his Ph.D. in sociology from the University of Pennsylvania. He is the author of *Chinese Subculture and Criminality* (Greenwood Press, 1990) and *Chinatown Gangs* (Oxford University Press, 1996) and coeditor of the *Handbook of Organized Crime in the United States* (Greenwood Press, 1994). He is currently conducting a study on illegal Chinese immigrants.

G. David Curry is Associate Professor of Criminology and Criminal Justice at the University of Missouri—St. Louis. He earned his Ph.D. in Sociology and completed an NIMH postdoctoral fellowship in evaluation research at the University of Chicago. His research focuses on organized violence. He recently served as coprincipal investigator of OJJDP's national juvenile hate crime study and is currently conducting research on gang involvement, with funding from NIJ, OJJDP, and DHHS. He is author of *Sunshine Patriots: Punishment and the Vietnam Offender* (Notre Dame University Press, 1985). His recent work has appeared in the *Journal of Research in Crime and Delinquency, Crime & Delinquency,* and *Criminology.*

Steven Jay Cuvelier is Associate Professor of Criminal Justice at Sam Houston State University and Senior Associate at the Center for Correctional Policy Studies. He holds a Ph.D. in sociology from The Ohio State University. His principal interests lie in the quantitative analysis of nonlinear systems, computer simulation, and computer-aided decision support systems.

Scott H. Decker is Professor and Chair in the Department of Criminology and Criminal Justice at the University of Missouri—St. Louis. He earned his Ph.D. in criminology from Florida State University. His primary research interests are in violence, the link between drug abuse and crime, and crime control policy. He is coauthor of *Life in the Gang: Family, Friends and Violence* (Cambridge University Press, 1996) and *Burglars on the Job* (Northeastern University Press), which won the 1994-1995 Outstanding Scholarship Award from the Crime and Delinquency Division of the Society for the Study of Social Problems. His recent work appears in *Criminology, Justice Quarterly,* and the *Journal of Research in Crime and Delinquency.*

Jeffrey Fagan is a Professor in the School of Criminal Justice at Rutgers University and Director of the Center for Violence Research and Prevention at the School of Public Health at Columbia University. He has researched violence among youth gangs, within families, in drug markets, and among adolescent males. He has studied legal and illegal "work" careers; the situational contexts of gun use by adolescents; the jurisprudence of adolescent violence; racial disparities in juvenile justice; treatment interventions for violent adolescents; intoxications and aggression; women's involvement in drug use and selling; and the effectiveness of criminal sanctions in deterring drug selling and drug use. His publications have appeared in *Criminology, Crime and Justice, Advances in Criminological Theory,* and the *Journal of Criminal Law and Criminology.* He is past editor of the *Journal of Research in Crime and Delinquency.*

John M. Hagedorn is Assistant Professor, Department of Criminal Justice, University of Illinois–Chicago. He has been researching Milwaukee gangs and drugs since 1984. He also has long been active in the reform of public welfare bureaucracies. He is the author of *People and Folks: Gangs, Crime, and the Underclass in a Rustbelt City* (Lake View Press, 1988). In his most recent book, *Forsaking Our Children: Bureaucracy and Reform in the Child Welfare System* (Lake View Press, 1995), he argues for neighborhood-based and family-centered reforms.

Robert J. Hunter is currently Assistant Professor of Criminology at The University of Northern Iowa. His research interests include shock incarceration, adult sentencing patterns, the death penalty, and media-influenced juror bias. His publications have appeared in *Federal Proba-tion, Journal of Contemporary Criminal Justice, American Journal of Criminal Law, American Jails,* and other journals.

Karen A. Joe is Assistant Professor of Sociology at the University of Hawaii at Manoa. She has been involved in juvenile and criminal justice research for 14 years. Her current research interests include the study of missing and runaway youth, youth gangs, and drug use among hidden populations.

Malcolm W. Klein is Professor of Sociology and Director of the Social Science Research Institute at the University of Southern California. He earned his Ph.D. in social psychology at Boston University. He served as Chairman of the USC Department of Sociology for 13 years, founded USC's Social Science Research Institute, and has received the Univer-sity's Raubenheimer Award. He has served on the boards of the Ameri-can Society of Criminology, American Sociological Association, and Society for the Study of Social Problems and on numerous national advisory panels and committees. He is author or editor of numerous articles and chapters in a broad range of areas, including street gangs, diversion, deinstitutionalization, criminal justice planning, police han-dling of juvenile offenders, and comparative justice systems. His most recent research, sponsored by DHHS, NIJ, OJJDP, and the California Wellness Foundation, involves gang migration, juvenile violence, inves-tigating gang structure and crime relationships, and gang resistance. His latest book is *The American Street Gang* (Oxford University Press, 1995), and he is coeditor of *The Modern Gang Reader* (Roxbury Press, 1995).

Janet L. Lauritsen is Assistant Professor in the Department of Criminol-ogy and Criminal Justice at the University of Missouri—St. Louis. She completed both a Ph.D. in sociology and a postdoctoral fellowship at the University of Illinois. Her research interests include victimization risk, the social context of crime, and adolescent sexual behavior and child-bearing. Her most recent work appears in the *Journal of Quantitative Criminology, Social Forces, Criminology,* and the National Academy of Sciences's *Understanding and Preventing Violence, Volume 3.*

James W. Marquart is Professor of Criminal Justice in the College of Criminal Justice at Sam Houston State University. He received his Ph.D. in sociology from Texas A&M University. His research interests include organizational change within correctional agencies, capital punishment, and prisoner health care. He is author or coauthor of numerous books, book chapters, and journal articles.

Cheryl L. Maxson is Associate Research Professor in the Sociology Department and Director of the Center for Research on Crime and Social Control in the Social Science Research Institute at the University of Southern California, where she received her Ph.D. Her research interests are in criminology, juvenile justice, and law and society, and she has directed research studies on national, state, and local issues. She is author or coauthor of numerous articles on street gangs, status offenders, police response to juveniles, juvenile justice legislation, drug sales, and community treatment of juvenile offenders. She is coeditor of *The Modern Gang Reader* (Roxbury Press, 1995) and coauthor of *Responding to Troubled Youth* (Oxford University Press, in press). Her current research, sponsored by the California Wellness Foundation, DHHS, NIJ, and OJJDP, concerns juvenile violence, developing resistance to gang membership, investigating gang structure and crime relationships, and gang migration.

Dorothy Merianos is completing her master's degree at Sam Houston State University in the College of Criminal Justice. In her thesis she explores the use of public health data to infer medical condition and health care needs of elderly inmates. Her research interests include geriatric inmates, public health issues, and sex offenders and their treatment.

Joan W. Moore is Distinguished Professor Emerita at the University of Wisconsin–Milwaukee. She has been conducting research with Chicano gangs in Los Angeles since the mid-1970s. She is the author of *Homeboys: Gangs, Drugs, and Prison in the Barrios of Los Angeles* (Temple University Press, 1978) and *Going Down to the Barrio* (Temple University Press, 1991) and is coeditor of *Drugs in Hispanic Communities* (Rutgers University Press, 1991).

Paige H. Ralph is Associate Professor at Lake Superior State University. She received a Ph.D. in criminal justice from Sam Houston State University in 1992. Her research interests include violent inmate behavior, inmate gangs, community corrections, and sentencing disparity.

Linda M. Schmidt is Project Director for the Youth Gang Diversion Project of the Task Force on Violent Crime in Cleveland, Ohio. Her expertise focuses on youth violence and youth gangs. She has provided extensive technical assistance and training on the prevention, containment, and control of youth gangs to the FBI, the Midwest Gang Investigators' Association, the Cleveland Police Department's Youth Gang Unit, and numerous other law enforcement agencies; more than 100 schools; juvenile detention facilities; the Ohio Department of Youth Services; social service agencies; prison; businesses; churches; physicians; and community and parent organizations. She also coauthored *Youth Gangs: A Parents' Guide for the '90s* and *Criminal Street Gangs in Greater Cleveland*.

Randall G. Shelden is Professor and Chair of the Department of Criminal Justice at the University of Nevada–Las Vegas. He received his Ph.D. in sociology from Southern Illinois University in 1976. He is coauthor of *Girls, Delinquency and Juvenile Justice* (Brooks/Cole, 1992) the recipient of the Michael Hindelang Award from the American Society of Criminology, and author of *Criminal Justice in America: A Sociological Approach* (Little, Brown, 1982). He is also the senior coauthor of *Youth Gangs in American Society* (Wadsworth, in press).

James F. Short Jr. is Professor Emeritus of Sociology at Washington State University, where he has served in various capacities since receiving his Ph.D. (University of Chicago, 1951). He has written widely in areas of sociology, criminology, and risk analysis. His books include *Suicide and Homicide* (with A.F. Henry, 1954), *Group Process and Gang Delinquency* (with F.L. Strodtbeck, 1965), *The Social Fabric: Dimensions and Issues* (editor and contributor, 1986), *Delinquency and Society* (1990), and *Organizations, Uncertainties, and Risk* (editor and contributor, with Lee Clarke, 1993). A former editor of the *American Sociological Review*, and associate editor of the *Annual Review of Sociology*, he has served as president of the

Pacific and American Sociological Associations. He is a Fellow and current president-elect of the American Society of Criminology and a recipient of the Edwin H. Sutherland Award for that society. He has been a Fellow at the Center for Advanced Study in the Behavioral Sciences, the Institute of Criminology at Cambridge University, the Rockefeller Center in Bellagio, and the Centre for Socio-Legal Studies at Oxford University. His honors include a NIMH and a Guggenheim Fellowship, the Bruce Smith Award from the Academy of Criminal Justice Sciences, and the Paul W. Tappan Award from the Western Society of Criminology. He was the 1990 Beto Chair Professor of Criminal Justice at Sam Houston State University.

Kenneth S. Trump is Director of Safety and Security for the Parma City School District (Ohio's ninth largest school system) and Assistant Director of the federally funded Tri-City Task Force Comprehensive Gang Initiative for Parma, Parma Heights, and Seven Hills, Ohio (metropolitan Cleveland area). He is also Adjunct Assistant Professor of Criminal Justice at Ashland University. Prior to his current positions, he served more than 7 years with the Division of Safety and Security of the Cleveland Public Schools, where he designed and supervised the division's Youth Gang Unit. Since 1989, he has provided extensive consultation and training throughout the state and the nation (including the FBI National Academy, U.S. Attorneys' National Conference, DHHS's Youth Gang Drug Prevention Program, and the California Gang Investigators'/ATF National Gang Conference) on youth violence, gangs, and school safety and security issues. He holds a master of public administration degree from Cleveland State University and is cofounder and vice president of the Ohio Chapter of the Midwest Gang Investigators' Association.

Sudhir Alladi Venkatesh is a Ph.D. candidate in the Department of Sociology at the University of Chicago. He is completing a dissertation entitled, *Public Housing, Private Lives: A Historical Ethnography of Chicago's Robert Taylor Homes, 1962-1995*. In his research, he examines the relations between residents, youth gangs, and the state in the Robert Taylor Homes public housing development. He is a Junior Fellow at the Society of Fellows, Harvard University.

James Diego Vigil is Professor of Anthropology at the University of California, Los Angeles. He received his Ph.D. in anthropology from UCLA and has held various teaching and administrative positions. As an urban anthropologist focusing on Mexican Americans and other ethnic minorities, he has conducted research on ethnohistory; education; culture change and acculturation; and adolescent and youth issues, especially street gangs. This work has resulted in several books and dozens of articles in journals and chapters in edited books. Particularly noteworthy are his early experiences in public school, teaching youth in elementary school, junior high school, and high school. He has continued to conduct research and evaluate programs on these age groups, including southeast Asian populations, and is currently completing a study on the family dynamics of residents in a public housing project.

Michael L. Walker is the Executive Director of the Task Force on Violent Crime, a nonprofit organization that develops innovative programs to reduce violent crime in Cleveland by utilizing the human and financial resources of the justice system, schools, businesses, public housing, and the larger community. He has provided specialized training and consultation on the prevention, containment, and control of youth gangs to the FBI, the Cleveland Police Department's Youth Gang Unit, and numerous other law enforcement agencies; hundreds of schools; juvenile and adult correctional facilities; the Ohio Department of Youth Services; businesses; churches; physicians; and community and parent organizations. He is a graduate of The Ohio State University, where he had a dual major in political science and communication.

Steve C. Yun is completing his medical studies at the University of Southern California. He first met James Diego Vigil as an undergraduate student at the University of Wisconsin–Madison, and has continued to work with Vigil in Los Angeles. He has lectured at numerous conferences on the cross-cultural and public health aspects of urban street gangs. His work has been supported by the University of Wisconsin Foundation and the Social Science Research Council.